MUSICAL LISTENING IN THE AGE OF TECHNOLOGICAL REPRODUCTION

Musical Cultures of the Twentieth Century

Volume 1

www.ashgate.com/musicalcultures

Other titles in the series:

Composing for the State
Music in Twentieth-Century Dictatorships
Edited by Esteban Buch, Igor Contreras Zubillaga and
Manuel Deniz Silva

Musical Listening in the Age of Technological Reproduction

Edited by

GIANMARIO BORIO
University of Pavia and Giorgio Cini Foundation, Italy

ASHGATE

Published by
Ashgate Publishing Limited
Wey Court East
Union Road
Farnham
Surrey, GU9 7PT
England

Ashgate Publishing Company
110 Cherry Street
Suite 3-1
Burlington, VT 05401-3818
USA

www.ashgate.com

British Library Cataloguing in Publication Data
A catalogue record for this book is available from the British Library.

The Library of Congress has cataloged the printed edition as follows:
Musical listening in the age of technological reproduction / edited by Gianmario Borio.
pages cm. – (Musical cultures of the twentieth century)
Includes bibliographical references and index.
ISBN 978-1-4724-4216-1 (hardcover : alk. paper) – ISBN 978-1-4724-4217-8 (ebook) – ISBN 978-1-4724-4218-5 (epub)
1. Music appreciation. 2. Music and technology. 3. Music – Philosophy and aesthetics. I. Borio, Gianmario, editor.

MT90.M888 2015
781.1'7 – dc23

2015021667

ISBN 9781472442161 (hbk)
ISBN 9781472442178 (ebk – PDF)
ISBN 9781472442185 (ebk – ePUB)

Bach musicological font developed by © Yo Tomita

MIX
Paper from responsible sources
FSC® C013985
FSC www.fsc.org

Printed in the United Kingdom by Henry Ling Limited,
at the Dorset Press, Dorchester, DT1 1HD

In memory of Giovanni Morelli

Contents

List of Figures, Tables and Music Examples

Figures

Tables

Music Examples

List of Contributors

Maurizio Agamennone is Associate Professor of Ethnomusicology at the University of Florence. His writings deal with improvisational practices and other forms of sung poetry, performative procedures in living polyphonies, production of 'migrant musicians' within globa(gloca)lization, performing structures and practices in the European musical avant-garde, and intercultural comparison in today's music. He founded and is the editor of *Per Archi – Rivista di storia e cultura degli strumenti ad arco*. His recent books include *Musiche tradizionali del Salento* (2005), *Varco le soglie e vedo. Canto e devozioni confraternali nel Cilento Antico* (2008) and *Su Daniele Paris. Storie e memorie di un direttore d'orchestra* (2009).

Alessandro Arbo is Associate Professor in the Music Department of the University of Strasbourg and co-founder of the Labex Groupe de Recherches Expérimentales sur l'Acte Musical. The author of numerous essays and books on the philosophy of music, he also edited *Le corps électrique: voyage dans le son de Fausto Romitelli* (2005), *Perspectives de l'esthétique musicale: entre théorie et histoire* (2007), *Wittgenstein and Aesthetics: Perspectives and Debates* (with M. Le Du and S. Plaud, 2012), *Ontologie musicale. Perspectives et débats* (with M. Ruta, 2014). His books include *Archéologie de l'écoute. Essais d'esthétique musicale* (2010) and *Entendre comme. Wittgenstein et l'esthétique musicale* (2013).

Gianmario Borio is Professor of Musicology at the University of Pavia and Director of the Institute of Music at the Fondazione Giorgio Cini, Venice. In 1999 he was awarded the Dent Medal by the Royal Musical Association. In 2013 he was Distinguished Visiting Professor at the Italian Academy for Advanced Studies in the USA. His publications deal with several aspects of the music of the twentieth century (theory and aesthetics, political background, audiovisual experience), as well as the history of musical concepts and the theory of musical form. He is a fellow of the Academia Europaea.

Esteban Buch is Directeur d'Etudes at the Ecole des Hautes Etudes en Sciences Sociales in Paris, and a member of the Centre de Recherches sur les Arts et le Langage. A specialist in relations between music and politics in the twentieth century, his books include *Beethoven's Ninth. A Political History* (2003), *Le cas Schönberg* (2006), *L'affaire Bomarzo. Opéra, perversion et dictature* (2011), and he edited *Tangos cultos: Kagel, J.J. Castro, Mastropiero y otros cruces musicales* (2012) and co-edited *Du politique en analyse musicale* (with N. Donin and L. Feneyrou, 2013).

Roberto Calabretto is Associate Professor in Musicology and Film Studies at the University of Udine. His research deals with the role of music in the audiovisual context, with particular emphasis on Italian cinema. He is the author of *Pasolini e la musica* (1999), *Lo schermo sonoro* (2010) and *Antonioni e la musica* (2012).

Vincenzo Caporaletti, musicologist, musician and composer, teaches Transcultural Musicology at the University of Macerata, and Jazz Analysis in the Santa Cecilia Conservatory in Rome. He was multi-instrumentalist and composer in the Italian progressive rock group Pierrot Lunaire as well as a session musician; in the jazz scene, among others, he worked as guitarist for several years with American clarinettist Tony Scott. His books include *I processi improvvisativi nella musica. Un approccio globale* (2005), *Esperienze di analisi del jazz* (2007), *Jelly Roll Morton, the 'Old Quadrille' and 'Tiger Rag': An Historiographic Revision* (2011) and *Swing e Groove. Sui fondamenti estetici delle musiche audiotattili* (2014).

Eric Clarke is Heather Professor of Music at Oxford University. He was an Associate Director of the Arts and Humanities Research Council Research Centre for the History and Analysis of Recorded Music (2004–2009), and of the Arts and Humanities Research Council Research Centre for Musical Performance as Creative Practice (2009–14). His research embraces a number of areas within the psychology of music, music theory and musical aesthetics/semiotics. His books include *Ways of Listening: An Ecological Approach to the Perception of Musical Meaning* (2005), *Music and Mind in Everyday Life* (2010) and *Music and Consciousness* (2011). He is a Fellow of the British Academy and of Academia Europaea.

Nicolas Collins studied composition with Alvin Lucier at Wesleyan University, worked for many years with David Tudor, and has collaborated with numerous soloists and ensembles around the world. He has been Visiting Artistic Director of Stichting Studio for Electro-Instrumental Music (Amsterdam), and a Deutscher Akademischer Austausch Dienst composer-in-residence in Berlin. He is editor-in-chief of the *Leonardo Music Journal*, and a Professor in the Department of Sound at the School of the Art Institute of Chicago. His book *Handmade Electronic Music: The Art of Hardware Hacking* (2nd edn, 2009) has influenced emerging electronic music worldwide.

Nicholas Cook is 1684 Professor of Music at the University of Cambridge. His books range from *Music: A Very Short Introduction* (2000), which has appeared in 15 different languages, to *The Schenker Project: Culture, Race, and Music Theory in Fin-de-siècle Vienna* (2007), which won the Society for Music Theory's Wallace Berry Award in 2010. His latest book is *Beyond the Score: Music as Performance* (2013). He is serving as a British Academy Wolfson Research Professor from 2014 to 2017, working on a project entitled 'Musical Encounters: Studies in Relational Musicology'. He is a Fellow of the British Academy and of Academia Europaea.

Angela Ida De Benedictis is Scientific Curator of more than 20 musical Collections at the Paul Sacher Foundation in Basle. PhD in Musicology from the University of Pavia, and post-doc. in Berlin with a grant from the Alexander von Humboldt Stiftung on music and technology. Director of the Scientific Board of the Centro Studi Luciano Berio and member of the Scientific Committee of Archivio Luigi Nono. She has taught at the Universities of Pavia, Padua, Salerno and Bern. She has edited the writings of Luigi Nono (2000) and Luciano Berio (2013), and published books and essays of theory and analysis featuring twentieth-century music.

Nicolas Donin is head of the Analysis of Musical Practices team, a joint research group of the Institut de Recherche et de Coordination Acoustique/Musique, Université Pierre et Marie Curie and Centre National de la Recherche Scientifique in Paris. His work focuses on contemporary musical practices, particularly composition and performance, using both a musicological and a cognitive approach. He co-edited *Théories de la composition musicale au XXe siècle* (with L. Feneyrou, 2013).

Steven Feld is Distinguished Professor of Anthropology at the University of New Mexico. He has been active in New Mexico music scenes since the 1970s, when he was a founder of the New Mexico Jazz Workshop. From 1975 to 2000 he studied the sound world of the Bosavi rainforest region in Papua New Guinea. He has more recently researched the sound world of Greek Macedonia and Romany ('Gypsy') instrumentalists, and produced a multi-CD project on the worldwide culture of bells. His current research is on jazz in the West African city of Accra, Ghana, where he also performs and records with Accra Trane Station.

Michele Girardi is Associate Professor of Musical Dramaturgy at Pavia University. He is a specialist in opera and in nineteenth- and twentieth-century music. He is the author of *Puccini: His International Art* (2000) and, since 2002, the editor of *La Fenice prima dell'opera*.

Giovanni Giuriati is Professor in Ethnomusicology at the Università di Roma 'La Sapienza' and Director of the Intercultural Institute for Comparative Music Studies, Fondazione Giorgio Cini, Venice. He was member of the Scientific Committee of the Archivi di Etnomusicologia of the Accademia Nazionale di Santa Cecilia and President of the European Seminar in Ethnomusicology (2005–8). He has carried out research in Cambodia, Bali, Indonesia and on Italian folk music with special reference to the region around Naples. He is member of the International Advisory Board of the Ashgate–SOAS Series in Ethnomusicology and of the Ethnomusicology Forum.

Dietrich Helms is Professor of Music History at the University of Osnabrück. He studied Musicology, Sociology and English at the Universities of Münster,

Oxford and East Anglia. Since 2005 he has been Co-chair of the German Society for Popular Music Studies (formerly ASPM), and since 2001 editor of *Beiträge zur Popularmusikforschung*. His research interests include music as a communication system, (English) Renaissance music, popular music and musical theatre (especially for children and adolescents).

Mark Katz is the Ruel W. Tyson, Jr. Distinguished Professor of the Humanities at the University of North Carolina at Chapel Hill, and Director of the University of North Carolina's Institute for the Arts and Humanities. He is the author of *Capturing Sound: How Technology has Changed Music* (2004; rev. edn, 2010) and *Groove Music: The Art and Culture of the Hip-hop DJ* (2012) and co-editor of *Music, Sound, and Technology in America* (with T.D. Taylor and T. Grajeda, 2012). He is the creator and director of Next Level, an international hip-hop diplomacy programme sponsored by the US Department of State.

Sebastian Klotz, Professor of Systematic Musicology at the University of Leipzig, received his PhD and habilitation from Humboldt University, Berlin. He was a researcher at the German Historical Institute in Rome, Bosch Fellow and Visiting Associate Professor of Music at the University of Chicago. He is the leader of the TransCoop project 'Music as a Medium of Urban Transformation: Berlin, Chicago, Kolkata', supported by the Alexander von Humboldt Stiftung, and a member of the panel of experts in musicology at the European Science Foundation. His recent interests include music as 'knowledge system', theories of musical action and the transformation of music studies from a text-based to a sound-based philology.

Martin Laliberté, composer and researcher, trained as a musician, composer and musicologist in Canada, the USA and Paris, where he completed a PhD at the Institut de Recherche et Coordination Acoustique/Musique and Ecole des Hautes Etudes en Sciences Sociales in 1994 and an HDR at the University of Paris 8 in 2005. He is currently Tenured Professor and Chair of Music and Technology at the University of Paris-Est, where he co-founded the Arts Faculty. He is an active composer of vocal, instrumental and electroacoustic music, and has published many works on contemporary music and its concepts and tools.

Emilio Sala is Associate Professor of Musical Dramaturgy at the University of Milan. His research focuses on the musical dramaturgy of opera, melodrama and film music, and his books include *L'opera senza canto: Il mélo romantico e l'invenzione della colonna sonora* (1995) and *The Sounds of Paris in Verdi's 'La traviata'* (2013). He has published articles and reviews in *Cambridge Opera Journal*, *Musica e storia*, *Musica/Realtà*, *Musicalia*, *Opera Quarterly*, *Orages*, *Revue de musicologie*, *Revue d'histoire littéraire de France*, *Il Saggiatore musicale*, *Studi verdiani* and elsewhere.

Nicola Scaldaferri is Associate Professor of Ethnomusicology at the University of Milan, where he is the Director of the Laboratory of Ethnomusicology and Visual Anthropology. He received his PhD in Musicology at the University of Bologna, was a Fulbright Scholar at Harvard University, and Visiting Professor at St Petersburg State University. His interests include twentieth-century music, sound technologies, Balkan epics, Italian folk music and instruments from Western Africa.

Gianfranco Vinay is Maître de Conférences at the Music Department of the University of Paris 8. He is the author of *Stravinsky Neoclassico. L'invenzione della memoria nel '900 musicale* (1987), and the editor of the contributed volumes *Stravinsky* (1992) and *Gershwin* (1992). His recent books include *Charles Ives et l'utopie sonore américaine* (2001), *Quaderno di Strada de Salvatore Sciarrino* (2007) and *Immagini gesti parole suoni silenzi. Drammaturgia delle opere vocali e teatrali di Salvatore Sciarrino* (2010). He recently co-edited *I Balletti Russi di Diaghilev. Tra mito e storia* (with P. Veroli, 2013).

Preface

This volume inaugurates the series *Musical Cultures of the Twentieth Century*, which stems from the scholarly activities promoted by the Istituto per la Musica of the Fondazione Giorgio Cini, in Venice, with the occasional collaboration with other research institutions. The relationship between technological transformations and ways of listening is a particularly suitable topic to launch a series that aims to present a forum on issues that have emerged during the last century, considered in all their complexity and variety, and investigated from a multi-disciplinary perspective with the contribution of different methodologies.

The volume is dedicated to Giovanni Morelli, who directed the Istituto per la Musica from 1985 – the year of its foundation – until 2011, when the eminent musicologist prematurely passed away. Morelli carried out his research and didactic activity in many areas, such as the reproduction of music and the repercussions of technological innovations on composition and its reception. He founded the international journal *Acoustical Arts and Artifacts – Technology, Aesthetics, Communication* (*AAA TAC*) (2004), which was anchored in the scientific programme of the Istituto per la Musica, and published the book *Prima la musica, poi il cinema. Quasi una sonata: Bresson, Kubrick, Fellini, Gaál* (2011): these are eloquent testimony to his interests. The publication of the present volume coincides with the thirtieth anniversary of the foundation of the Istituto per la Musica, thus adding symbolic importance and being promising for future work.

Musical Listening in the Age of Technological Reproduction is the result of a group effort. Interwining a broad range of expertise, it takes advantage of the open and dynamic dialogue that took place among the authors over several months. The combination of scholars of different traditions and backgrounds has given rise to a pluralism of research methods and a multiplicity of writing styles. The variety of perspectives from chapter to chapter would hardly be reflected by a conventional preface aiming to present the thematic organization and scientific objectives of the book. For this reason, the editor has chosen to offer his own perspective in Chapter 1, conceived as a first look at the multifarious facets of the theme designated in the book title. It is, in fact, only through the cross-fertilization of the different positions and investigations that the volume will realize its potential.

The editor would like to express his gratitude to all who have made this book possible: first and foremost, the authors, who contributed their experience and shared their considerable knowledge before, during and after the conference 'Musical Listening in the Age of Technological Reproducibility. Giovanni Morelli in Memoriam' which took place in Venice on 22–24 March 2013. Warm thanks go to the collaborators at the Istituto per la Musica, particularly Alessandro Cecchi, who dedicated invaluable energy to the revision of the drafts, the retrieval of biographical data and editing. The translators – Laurie Schwartz, Mark Weir, Jane North, John O'Donnell and Brent Waterhouse – and Lisa Navach, who patiently and meticulously re-read the final version, deserve a special mention.

Gianmario Borio

PART I
Facets of a Theoretical Question

Chapter 1
Aesthetic Experience Under the Aegis of Technology

Gianmario Borio

Benjamin's Seminal Essay and Adorno's Responses

There is something 'auratic' about Walter Benjamin's 'The Work of Art in the Age of its Technological Reproducibility', first published as a shortened French translation in 1936. The fragmentary discourse, the peremptory nature of some of his assertions and the character of 'work in progress' drew criticism even among its first readers; and yet the fascination this text has continued to exert demonstrates that it represents a historical watershed. It gave rise to a wide-ranging debate concerning the repercussions of new media on the reception of artistic products whose scope has gradually altered, according to the technological innovations and changes in social structures. The issues he raised, even though often only hinted at or ambivalently formulated, have established a conceptual framework in which commentators have taken a variety of positions and come up with diverging explanations.

Benjamin started from some observations concerning the reception of visual arts, and focused on the perceptive and cultural changes introduced by two new artistic genres: photography and cinema. Three passages deserve mention for their relevance to the domain of music: the 'aura', the prevalence of the 'exhibition value' and the 'reception in distraction'. For Benjamin, the first consequence of technical reproducibility is the dissolution of a work's *hic et nunc*, that direct and immediate presence which clearly figures in the appreciation of paintings and sculptures. In the so-called 'modern' Western culture, which has seen the origins of criticism and aesthetics, a full experience of the work of art derives from a direct encounter with the object itself. To define this distinctive experience, Benjamin used the term 'aura', current in theosophy and esoteric thought:

> what withers in the age of the technological reproducibility of the work of art is the latter's aura. This process is symptomatic; its significance extends far beyond the realm of art. *It might be stated as a general formula that the technology of reproduction detaches the reproduced object from the sphere of tradition. By replicating the work many times over, it substitutes a mass existence for a unique existence. And in permitting the reproduction to reach the recipient in his or her own situation, it actualizes that which is reproduced.* These two processes lead

> to a massive upheaval in the domain of objects handed down from the past – shattering of tradition which is the reverse side of the present crisis and renewal of humanity. (Benjamin 2002a: 104; 2003: 254)

In Benjamin's approach, the concept of aura embraces the essential elements of the experience of beauty in the modern era. The outcome of an artistic work is a creation which has no correspondence in any other object, past or present, with an exceptional and unrepeatable structure. The work of art is metaphorically surrounded by an aura which captures the observer's attention and remains a permanent stimulus to reception. Thus, first the aura testifies the artist's imaginative achievement and visionary capacity; secondly it represents the driving force of the historic process, the tradition consolidated in the work and prolonged in its reception. This dual character led Benjamin to describe it as 'the unique apparition of a distance, however near it may be' (2002a: 104–5; 2003: 255). The aura is the symbol of something far off that becomes present and bursts into the observer's consciousness, situated in a certain space and time, with all its potential for meaning. The multiplication of specimens, the potential ubiquity of the work and its universal availability – phenomena presupposing means of technical reproduction – lead to the dissolution of the aura; this is the final stage in a social process closely linked to the affirmation of democracy, the free market and mass culture.

Spiritualist philosophies, influenced by Eastern religions, consider the aura as an energy field releasing radiations; perceived only by the initiated, it transmits information on the profound nature of a person, natural phenomenon or object; the information cannot be mediated by other signs. By applying this concept to the sphere of aesthetic reception, Benjamin promoted the *Bildung* to a requisite for an adequate and exhaustive interpretation of artworks. Reception goes beyond perception, being something for which the observer is prepared thanks to previous aesthetic experiences and the exercise of critical reason. However, rather than being limited to the moment of illumination that characterizes the reception of masterpieces, the link with the religious sphere evoked by the term 'aura' also refers to the historical evolution of the arts. In fact, the reception of autonomous art preserves a trace of the ritual within which the ancient people perceived statues and paintings, thus the identification of their meaning also took place. This is why Benjamin calls the reception of art works a 'secularized ritual' (2002a: 105; 2003: 256). The approach to them differs from the practices associated with the use of manufactured objects or the attitude towards nature. It implies concentration, reverence, absorption:

> The reception of works of art varies in character, but in general two polar types stand out: one accentuates the artwork's cult value; the other, its exhibition value. (Benjamin 2003: 257)

> The scope for exhibiting the work of art has increased so enormously with the various methods of technologically reproducing it that, as happened in

> pre-historic times, a quantitative shift between two poles of the artwork has led to a qualitative transformation in its nature. Just as the work of art in pre-historic times, through the absolute emphasis placed on its cult value, became first and foremost an instrument of magic which only later came to be recognized as a work of art, so today, through the absolute emphasis placed on its exhibition value, the work of art becomes a construct [*Gebilde*] with quite new functions. Among those, the one we are conscious of – the artistic function – may subsequently be seen as incidental. This much is certain: today, photography and film are the most serviceable vehicles of this new understanding. (Benjamin 2002a: 106–7; 2003: 257)

The 'cult value' is linked to contemplation, an attitude that characterizes the reception of the art work starting from the emancipation of the subject and the affirmation of the principle of autonomy. Contemplation is not only the most appropriate conduct *vis-à-vis* a work of art, but also the distinguishing mark for those who possess the means to understand it. In the history of the cultural exercise of the perceptive apparatus, it highlights the primacy attributed to sight, with its capacity to analyse and classify information. At the same time, this aspect of Benjamin's essay goes beyond the boundaries of visual arts and can be considered the key to aesthetic reception *tout court*. In art music, for example, it emerges in the superiority of the score *vis-à-vis* every performance, being the evidence of the author's will and *conditio sine qua non* for the work's survival. The affirmation of the 'exhibition value' goes hand in hand with the crisis of the contemplative model of reception, replaced by a model no longer dependent on attention. Benjamin associated it with the sense of touch, which suggests a large, sensitive surface and a permanent, non-oriented availability. The closing section of the third version of the essay (Benjamin 2003) is devoted to mass art, the reactions of the public and its 'participation' in performances and events. These new dynamics unfold in the framework of 'reception in distraction' (Benjamin 2002b).

'The Work of Art in the Age of its Technological Reproducibility' had a considerable influence on Theodor Adorno's aesthetics (1997: 310–11; 1975; Levin 1990). His first response, the essay 'On the Fetish-character in Music and the Regression of Listening' (2002), is of particular significance in our context because it transfers Benjamin's interrogative to the musical domain. Adorno dismisses the potential that Benjamin had glimpsed in 'reception in distraction' as illusory: 'Deconcentrated listening makes the perception of the whole impossible' (Adorno 2002: 305). He is convinced that the means of reproduction are subjected to the ideology of advanced capitalism, which, after giving the rules for the production and exchange of goods, extended its influence to the behaviour of the individual and even to his perceptive system. The reception model inaugurated by mass music also had an effect on art music, which now is listened to in an 'atomized' manner and thus deprived of its true sense. At the heart of Adorno's essay there is the concept of fetish, previously discussed by both Marx and Freud. First, music is invested by the character of fetish which the Marxian theory sees as a distinctive feature of consumption: the person playing a disc worships the cultural commodity because it reflects the effort invested and money necessary to purchase it. Secondly, listening to reproduced music implies a fetishistic relationship with the object: the listener regresses to a primitive phase of psychological development; the way in which music is experienced takes on the features of the masochist pathology, in which the subject enjoys sacrificing him/herself and being subjected to an external power.

This ruthless diagnosis of the ideological features of music in the era of technical reproducibility remained a constant in Adorno. However, in his writings one can also recognize a domain more closely linked to the artistic procedures and functions of the media. In an article that was part of the project 'Current of Music', Adorno argues, for example, that there is a peculiar relationship between original and reproduction in music because reproduction, understood as performance of a score, is an immanent property of music:

> It is true that we cannot say that in music the 'original' is more authentic than its reproduction because it actually exists only in being reproduced. … The authenticity which Benjamin attributes in the visual arts to the original must be attributed to live reproduction in music. This live reproduction has its 'here' – either the concert room or the opera – and its 'now' – the very moment it is executed. And what Benjamin calls the 'aura' of the original certainly constitutes an essential part of the live reproduction. It is exactly this aura which leads people to be eager to attend live performance even if they cannot follow the music as well from their cheap seats as they could have followed in front of their radio sets. It is this aura which is reflected in all the talk about the fascinating conductor, the cult of the virtuoso, and all the well known 'irrational' features of people's reactions to live music. (Adorno 2009: 89)

For Adorno it is not possible to establish a precise link between an 'auratic' and a 'technological' work. In fact, the aura can be at the service of the artistic reification, becoming an instrument of its commercial diffusion. Authenticity is transformed into the authority of a ubiquitous presence which the user regards with an attitude of glorification:

> The phonograph record destroys the 'now' of the live performance and, in a way, its 'here' as well. … Now, when they are played again and again, they can no longer uphold the dignity of the occasion. They are losing their aura because they no longer keep their distance from the listeners. They show, instead, a tendency to mingle in his every day life because they can appear at practically every moment …. If this means a loss of authenticity in our sense of the term, this can also mean an increase of authenticity in another sense, just as the authority of an advertisement increases when it is repeated again and again. The more often you hear the Seventh Symphony, the less, probably, will you cease to discuss it. The exposition value which Benjamin sees increasing against the cult value of a particular work, and which is closely akin to the fatality of

> plugged music, appears to us to be even more authoritarian than the former. Here the theory of the aura becomes involved in difficulties which cannot be hidden for the very simple reason that they are not difficulties of an antagonistic theory, but are created by contradictions in reality. Although a symphony loses the authority of its uniqueness, it accumulates new authority by ubiquity and its faculty of appearing at any time. (Adorno 2009: 90–92)

Far from making things clearer, the shift in approach creates new problems. First, Adorno was able to define the interpretation of music as reproduction because he adopted Schoenberg's theoretical framework, so that performance is essentially the 'reproduction' of a meaning fully enshrined in the score (Schoenberg 1984; Adorno 2006). This position had a certain legitimacy as a reaction to the abuses of interpretational subjectivity that characterized musical performance in the late nineteenth and early twentieth century. However, it reveals all its shortcomings as soon as it is adopted as a general principle. In fact, the performing arts differ from their visual counterparts inasmuch as the identity of the work is not contained in a specific object, but is created and renewed in the continuous articulation of the relationship between written medium and performance. Secondly, even if one accepts the equivalence of the 'reproduction' and performance of a musical text, this has little to do with the dynamics discussed by Benjamin, which specifically concern the relationship between art and media. His initial hypothesis – that the use of mechanical and electrical media exerted a considerable influence on the experience of arts – can be perfectly transferred to music. In fact, new technologies have an impact on all three spheres of its experience: production, performance and reception. Thirdly, music has achieved a second form of aural existence thanks to electronic means: listening to a recorded performance is now an additional alternative to listening to a live performance, and this twofold possibility has consequences both for listening modalities and for the definition of the aesthetic experience. An important aspect, which undoubtedly contributes to reconfiguring the relationship between original and reproduced, is that the technological reproduction of a performance (*not* of a work) is also production. In spite of the myth of absolute fidelity, the performance is not simply replicated on a medium that is transportable, transmissible and further multipliable; rather, a new product is created ad hoc, starting from the score and from a performance of this score. Thus, the heart of the issue does not consist in originality or uniqueness, but in the differentiation of the modality of reception.

'Reception in Distraction' and 'Tactility': Further Developments

The considerations offered so far concerning Benjamin's theory of technical reproducibility help us to identify its point of contact with the domain of music. The question whether 'reception in distraction' applies only to music for a mass audience or can be considered a legitimate form of reaction also in art music is secondary; it is the reiteration and sharing of social practices that bestow legitimacy on a behaviour.

On the other hand, it is important to ask whether 'reception in distraction' can be reconciled with the aesthetic experience. Technical reproducibility has given rise to a specific type of music; on account of its mass diffusion, linked to the primary form of production on a disc, it has been called 'popular music' – a term Adorno used to express the German *leichte Musik*. Thanks in part to the impulse of the 1968 political movements, popular music became a specific sector of musicological study, broadening its field of research and improving its methodology. However, as research progressed, people became increasingly aware of the instability of this concept. Alf Björnberg made the following observations:

> Technological and social developments in the course of the 20th century have resulted in several musical genres, from the point of view of production, distribution, function and use, having increasingly assumed popular-musical characteristics, for instance, the overwhelming part of historical art music or forms of non-western music previously not included in the circulation processes of the transnational music industry (cf. 'world music'). Rather than designating a particular genre or group of genres, the concept of 'popular music' could thus to an increasing extent be said to define the general conditions of music in contemporary information society. (Björnberg 2007: 136)

When the field of enquiry is extended to popular music, the issue of the repercussions of electronic media sets in motion a whole series of questions: In how many and in which ways is 'reception in distraction' manifested? Does this behaviour exclude the aesthetic experience? Can the traditional musical work lend (or bend) itself to this type of reception? What changes may this lead to in the history of art music? Does it denote the peculiar form of reception of popular music? And if so, is there no place for the aesthetic experience in popular music? Or, on the contrary, has popular music revealed a dimension for listening to art music which can be added to the previous modalities? The tangled skein of these problems has become all the more difficult to unravel because mediatized reception has ended up by conditioning the theory of the aesthetic experience too. That is to say, the awareness of the scope of action of the media has required the very concept of aesthetic experience to be enlarged to include sensorial experiences (erotic, culinary, springing from design, and so on) connected with the enjoyment of the beautiful even if extraneous to the artwork (Shusterman 1997). In this context, too, cinema has represented a watershed. The theorists of cinema have introduced categories like identification, immersion, use and manipulation: such categories were not envisaged in Idealist-Romantic aesthetics, grounded in the free creativity of a single author, in the autonomy of the product and the model of contemplative reception.

'Reception in distraction' is not an original formulation of Benjamin's: it occurs in an article by Siegfried Kracauer, published a decade before the essay on 'mechanical reproduction'. This article, which overviews the architecture of the new cinema halls in Berlin, anticipates in a few insights Benjamin's future ideas. Kracauer notes that the recent evolution of the ways in which film products are presented increasingly resembles a 'total art work of the effects' which 'assaults every one of the senses using every possible means' (1987: 92). In fact, the new reception is largely determined by the incorporation of technological innovations and, in sociological terms, it is becoming independent of the class and instruction level of the individual. The total of cinema-goers is no longer the sum of individualities, but a 'homogeneous cosmopolitan audience' (Kracauer 1987: 93). The form of entertainment described by Kracauer is made up of a multitude of fragments which maintain a direct relationship with the external world and which, in the momentum of performance, make for a unity quite different from the one postulated by traditional aesthetics. At the same time, there is a change in the perceptive processes by which this unity is grasped, or more precisely, *posed*. The event 'exposes disintegration instead of masking it' (Kracauer 1987: 96), and the reception is configured as a chain of associations and attributions which allows the active participation of the audio spectator in the creation of meaning.

Among the philosophers of the Frankfurt School, the proclivity to identify an ideological element that often reveals the underlying falsity in harmonic and plain situations is compensated by the aspiration to discover instances of emancipation in oppressed situations. This also happens to the term 'distraction', with which Kracauer alludes to a latent dimension of a phenomenon standardized in the form of *divertissement*. The mirroring of the external world – immediate, anarchic, dazzling and not subject to predetermined schemes – supersedes the illusory character of art and creates the conditions for a higher recognition: 'Here, in pure externality, the audience encounters itself; its own reality is revealed in the fragmented sequence of splendid sense impressions; were this reality to remain hidden from the audience, they could neither attack nor change it; its disclosure in distraction is therefore of *moral* significance' (Kracauer 1987: 94). The specific attention to cinema is motivated by the fact that the reproduction is seen not as a procedure applied to the work *a posteriori* (as in the case of copies of a painting), but as an integral part of the creative process. Kracauer, Benjamin and Adorno are all recognizing that the use of mechanical and electronic media in the domain of art represents a true watershed with repercussions in both social and aesthetic terms; moreover cinema – the new art form of the technological era – gives the most authentic picture of the aesthetic issues facing the modern world. The introduction to *Composing for the Films* by Adorno and Eisler actually begins with a reference to this priority: 'The motion picture cannot be understood in isolation, as a specific form of art; it is understandable only as the most characteristic medium of contemporary cultural industry, which uses the techniques of mechanical reproduction' (Adorno and Eisler 1994: xxxv). However, this conjunction of technical means and social form also has positive implications for the development of artistic creativity. In one of the dialectical shifts that are so characteristic of Adorno's philosophy, he observed in 1963:

> Film is, despite the backwardness in its substantive and aesthetic aspects dictated by the profit motive, the most technologically progressive process because

> it is most free of a dependence upon a material that is handed to it already finished, merely to be transmitted and depicted. Production and reproduction collapse [in cinema]; what is produced is only that which is seen on the screen. (Adorno 1976c: 396, in Levin 1990: 46)

As Miriam Hansen has remarked, cinema offers a privileged access to our existence and our understanding of the environment: it paves the way for a different vision of the world, confronting us with experiences that have no equivalent in everyday life and forcing us to review them in a collective dimension (1987: 221; 2012). The notion of 'reception in distraction', associated by Hansen with that of the 'optical unconscious', is a tool to outline the receptive processes *vis-à-vis* an art that is no longer auratic. Thus, the 'distraction' can free itself from its passivity and reconfigure itself as a type of perception linked to the need to dominate the multiple stimuli provided by the environment (Eiland 2005). Unlike what Benjamin imagined, there is contemplation also in music. However, in the mean time this receptive attitude – analytical and introspective – has lost its normative force, becoming one particular case alongside the other attitudes that have developed under the dual influence of mass communication and sound technology. In the first phase of modernity, one of the features of the listening mode that prevailed might be defined as the 'suppression of images'. Such a utopian character – a music without images – has been a driving force in traditional aesthetics; the technologies of musical reproduction in the twentieth century restored the image to the perceptive process.

In Marshall McLuhan's writings the concept of tactility plays an important role, setting up a link with 'The Work of Art in the Age of its Technological Reproducibility' (Carey 2005). Benjamin (2002a: 119; 2003: 267) speaks of a 'tactile quality', exemplified in the ways in which the Dadaists present their works, which are no longer works. They have the effect of a slap in the face of the receiver, striking him/her almost physically and directing his/her attention towards something beyond the object. This tendency has been consolidated in the reception of film products: the peremptory nature of their images and their abrupt cuts bursting into the receiver's perceptive apparatus allowed him/her no time to reflect. Just as the concept of contemplation, directly connected to the visual field, can be extended to various areas of reception, here tactility is interpreted in a broad sense as an index of a disquieting and ungovernable proximity, but also as a key to shape the experience: 'the tactically dominant element that rules over the regrouping of apperception' (Benjamin 2010: 34).

This dual interpretation of the concept of tactility also characterizes McLuhan's use of the term. And it is precisely phonography which suggests the paradigm for the sense of proximity evoked by the new media:

> For the sensation of having the performing instruments 'right in the room with you' is a striving toward the union of the audile and tactile in a finesse of fiddles that is in large degree the sculptural experience. To be in the presence of

> performing musicians is to experience their touch and handling of instruments as tactile and kinetic, not just as resonant. (McLuhan 1964: 282)

At the same time McLuhan considers tactility a distinguishing feature of the electronic era as a whole, which thus became antithetical to the culture of visibility of 'typographic man'. The experiential quality linked to the whole surface of the human body takes on the traits of a cultural marker: 'It begins to be evident that "touch" is not skin but the interplay of senses, and "keeping in touch" or "getting in touch" is a matter of a fruitful meeting of the senses, of sight translated into sound and sound into movement, and taste, and smell' (McLuhan 1996: 60). Benjamin's 're-grouping of apperception' is translated here into a multi-polar device which intercepts the objects, and reorganizes their meaning through constantly shifting interactions of the perceptive organs. In fact, the dislodging of visual culture does not mean that vision is sidelined; rather, it is recollocated in a dialectic in which the mental schemes that can be linked to the various senses are activated and combined. Another aspect of the prevalence of tactility, viewed as both a perceptive and a cognitive model, emerges when McLuhan refers to it as the 'world of the interval' (McLuhan and Pakey 1968: 264). Here, too, as in Kracauer and Benjamin, the emphasis lies on the discontinuity of the experience, which derives in part from the media themselves but is also a cognitive potential proper to humankind.

Discontinuity, a salient feature of creativity in the electronic age, is also the element which characterizes what McLuhan calls the 'acoustic space'. In its original form it designates the space of pre-literate communication in tribal societies, in which the word was amalgamated with the emotion, but it can also be applied to the space of the present, which transpires in the functioning of electronic media: a non-centric, non-directional space, fluid and unlimited, characterized by the simultaneous presence of diverse entities. Given its affinity with the new forms of communication, the notion of 'acoustic space' is closer to that of 'tactility': 'Hearing is structured by the experience of picking up information from all directions at once' (McLuhan, in Schafer 2005: 67). A further element to be taken into consideration is the special position occupied by art – and in particular experimental art – in McLuhan's approach: the artist is able to put him/herself in a different and more productive relationship with the environment, to seize the thought forms implicit in the media, to anticipate the changes and set up 'counter-environments'. The artist's experience is situated in a circuit of perception–comprehension–transformation; his/her research involves exploration of the environment, identifying the network of relationships in which the detail is inscribed and capturing the effects of the outside world on the sensorial apparatus (McLuhan 1966).

Associative versus Structural Listening: A False Opposition

The considerations on tactility encountered in both Benjamin and McLuhan provide insights that can help us to tackle some of the questions concerning musical listening in the era of technical reproducibility. For example, developing them in combination can provide elements to appraise the debate concerning 'structural listening', sparked off by Rose Rosengard Subotnik's article in 1985. Its starting point is a notion that Adorno introduced in describing the behaviour of the 'expert', a figure who stands at the apex of his typology of listeners:

> The fully adequate mode of conduct might be called 'structural hearing'. Its horizon is a concrete musical logic: the listener understands what he perceives as necessary, although the necessity is never literally causal. The location of this logic is technique; to one whose ear thinks along with what he hears, its several elements are promptly present as technical, and it is in technical categories that the context of meaning is essentially revealed. (Adorno 1976b: 5)

Subotnik believes that this attitude is emblematic of the musical culture prevailing in music colleges and in the scientific milieu. It is linked to the foundations of modern aesthetics: the creative subject, the autonomy of its action and the immanence of musical meaning. Subotnik argues that this receptive scheme excludes significant aspects of the musical experience such as the chains of association produced by the stylistic components and corporeal-affective elements of sound. The debate that followed consisted, with few exceptions, in the reinforcement and expansion of this critique. What has been lacking, however, is a precise physiognomy for 'postmodern listening' or the emergence of an alternative theory of listening (Dell'Antonio 2004). Adorno's 'structural listening' has the same premises as those underlying Felix Salzer's 'structural hearing'. It is a procedure whereby the acoustic data are ordered according to coherence and logic, aim to perfect the musical appreciation, and thus also have a social purpose: 'to develop the innate, although unconscious tendency of many musical people to follow the music's motion and direction' (Salzer 1952: 257). Finally, for both Adorno and Salzer, 'structural listening' has a dialectic relationship with musical analysis. On one hand, listening cannot possibly be equated with analysis because it is an activity concerning the music in its aural phenomenicity; on the other hand, through analysis the listener can achieve a greater awareness of relations that are not immediately tangible, thus recuperating a spontaneous attitude in live performance and reception.

In an essay on listening problems posed by post-tonal compositions, Adorno described 'structural listening' as a procedure in which the listener seizes the 'multidimensionality' of the musical construct, a quality that can be modified in the course of history according to the change in the aesthetic and technical paradigms. The examples of *neue Musik* cited by the philosopher to illustrate this dynamic show that the sensible aspect of sound ('das sinnlich Wohlgefällige', Adorno 1976a: 246–7) cannot be separated from the auditory process as a whole: as well as conveying an appeal or 'shock', in Benjamin's sense, it is also invariably the 'bearer of a musical relation' ('Träger eines musikalischen Sinnzusammenhangs', Adorno 1976a: 247). This functional aspect of the acoustic elements in the context of musical communication makes any clear separation between perception and comprehension artificial. Pierre Boulez had in mind the same association between sound object and linguistic system when he affirmed, in his *Leçons de musique*, that 'listening is totally dominated by the codes of the language' (2005: 422).

The changes Adorno believed to be necessary in order to relaunch 'structural listening' in the new context of the avant-garde languages suggest that his concept of 'musical logic' can be extended in principle. McLuhan insisted on the tactile component and experience of discontinuity, but was careful not to entirely rule out rationality, preferring to advocate forms of 'non-linear logic'. In a discussion of the new customs inaugurated by television, he remarked that 'the tactual mode of perceiving is sudden but not specialist. It is total, synesthetic, involving all senses' (McLuhan 1964: 334). This implies that 'reception in distraction' also does not reject the idea of unity, but rather transfers it to a new semantic field. Examples of this new unity are provided by analyses of popular music which reconstruct listening experiences different to those of notated composition, but still bound up with the pursuit of meaning. Thus, it is possible to take Adorno's 'structural listening' one step further: not as a single act of perception, but as a 'situated' listening, a parallel form of what Habermas (1987a: 306) calls 'situated reason', viewing communicative processes as social practices that reflect rational forms.

A crux in this matter is the matching of structural listening to the figure of the expert, which Adorno takes for granted in his listening typology. In this connection, too, we can see a different approach with respect to Benjamin. In his essay on 'mechanical reproduction', Benjamin makes an interesting point about the vanishing role of the expert as repository of a know-how elaborated in the solitude of academia. The modes of behaviour and expectations developed in the forms of entertainment of late-industrial society provide the key to such a change: 'It is inherent in the technology of film, as of sports, that everyone who witnesses these performances does so as a quasi-expert' (Benjamin 2002a: 114; 2003: 262). Several decades later, Habermas – attempting a synthesis between the analytical and critical inclination, inherent in every cultural discourse, and the need for the circulation of knowledge of democratic societies – highlighted the gap between the 'culture of the experts' and the 'broader public' (1987b: 276, 326–7). The growing professionalization of scientists and critics, deriving from the Enlightenment impulse to examine and explain the structural relations of things and events, has contributed to the 'impoverishing of the lifeworld [*Lebenswelt*]'. To believe in the possibility of releasing from esoteric forms the cognitive potentials accumulated in the exercise of science and criticism and placing them at the service of the rational configuration of existence has been truly frustrated. However, precisely the electronic technologies and the communication circuits provide opportunities for a correction of the trajectory; in fact, the multiplication of listening practices has not ruled out the pursuit of a meaning of the aesthetic experience which can (or must) have repercussions in the whole gamut of everyday life.

McLuhan viewed the media as 'extensions' of the human organs, and conversely interpreted the functioning of the senses as an indicator of socio-cultural forms. For example, one of the salient features of the 'electric age', following the model of tactility, consists in the fact that its communication circuits provide evidence of the substantial interdependence of the senses. Furthermore, the means of communication, like the senses, are devices for perfecting perception and organizing experience. There is a close relationship between perceiving, understanding and acting: this conviction combines with the thesis of a continuous impact of technology on the environment and that of a 'contra-environmental' function of art (McLuhan 1966). We find a similar nexus of ideas in Benjamin: '*Just as the entire mode of existence of human collectives changes over long historical periods, so too does their mode of perception*' (2002a: 104; 2003: 255). Therefore, it is misleading to postulate a dimension of immediate experience opposed to the rational aspects of the artefact and which, in terms of reception, would take the place of the process of comprehension. Put in this framework, 'structural listening' appears as a form of reception of musical works which is contextually determined and strategically orientated. Here we have one of the possible forms of the network of perceptive dimensions, underpinned by a continuous interchange between intuition and rationality.

Any separation between a pre-rational, intuitive sphere of listening and the analytical activity is also ruled out by the four-part listening scheme discussed by Pierre Schaeffer in *Traité des objets musicaux*: *écouter*, an orientated and intentional activity; *ouïr*, simple hearing, with no intention or interpretation; *entendre*, listening to particular qualities, and *comprendre*, receiving the sound as the sign of something other than itself – they are all presented as 'acts of consciousness' (1966: 675) which can happen simultaneously or follow on from one another in any order. There is a range of possibilities, differing in degrees of subjectivity or objectivity, from hearing the raw sound, without any selection or 'listening intention', to comprehending the sound as the sign of something that lies outside it. In particular, Schaeffer linked the listening activity to the phenomenological concept of intentionality, freeing it from the physicalist prejudice in which it is viewed as an accumulation of sensations. The premises for his theory are found in Maurice Merleau-Ponty's *Phenomenology of Perception* (1962), in which perception is seen as the crux of the relationship between consciousness and the world: 'any perception of a thing, a shape or a size as real, any perceptual constancy refers back to the positing of a world and of a system of experience in which my body is inescapably linked with phenomena' (1962: 303–4). Thus, perception always means something more than experiencing a set of sensations, and implies the identification of an immanent sense in a field of phenomenic data.

Differentiation of Aesthetic Experience

The approaches to musical listening we have outlined (from Adorno and Salzer to Schaeffer and Boulez) have as a premise that one can distinguish between listening as an everyday exercise of the auditory sense, and musical listening within the context of the aesthetic experience. However, in recent decades the specificity and autonomy of the aesthetic experience have been called into question, not least by the mutations in the media landscape and the artistic communication. The Idealistic-Romantic theory of art, which remains fundamental to the above-mentioned authors, posits a double movement between the aesthetic and extra-aesthetic spheres. On one hand, the aesthetic experience is accomplished starting from the perception of an individual work; on the other, the feelings and attributions of sense deriving from such a perception do not belong 'ontologically' to the work; rather, they are processes taking place in the consciousness of the receiving subject. The aesthetic experience, while being unique and irreducible, is embedded in the stream of consciousness which includes previous experiences, accumulated knowledge and the social attributes of the artistic object. The philosophers thinking in terms of Utopia give a particular emphasis to this, arguing that it is the spur to reorganize the lifeworld and 'prefiguring' experiences at every level. Conversely, a theory starting from artistic practices in their physical aspect excludes this dialectic; from this perspective, the aesthetic experience is seen as an ecstatic event which manifests itself primarily in affective, energetic and motor reactions.

Kleine Apologie der ästhetischen Erfahrung, the small book Hans Robert Jauss published in 1972 as the first step in a systematic critique of Adorno's *Aesthetic Theory*, can be considered the first sign of this reappraisal. The crucial issue is the 'distance' between the artistic object and its receiver, which for Adorno makes it possible to distinguish the aesthetic experience from the 'pre-artistic experience' (Jauss 1982: 13–37; Adorno 1997: 345–7). Jauss interprets this distance as a symptom of the exclusion of those moments of identification – enjoyment, taste, catharsis – which instead are fundamental for the communicative process in the arts. Here the rehabilitation of the affective components has the function of an embankment against those who view the aesthetic experience as the confrontation of an isolated subject and the work's spiritual content, which stands out in its otherness, enigmatic quality and elusiveness. Subsequently, the contrast with Adorno has taken on the features of a critique of the aesthetics of modernity as a whole. Various factors have contributed to the accentuation of the sensorial and corporeal moments: a renewed interest among philosophers in 'intuitive knowledge', the impact of the media and mass culture, a new evaluation of performance combined with a critique of the concepts of work and text, and also that combination of phenomena in contemporary society attributed to the 'aestheticization of the lifeworld' (Bubner 1989: 143–56). I shall deal only with those aspects of this change in perspective which can help us to understand the nature of musical listening under the aegis of technology.

After making a study of performances of avant-garde theatre in the second half of the twentieth century, Erika Fischer-Lichte (2008) recast the aesthetic experience as a 'liminal experience' which destabilizes the spectator's system of meanings and the affective and energetic transformations. Hans Ulrich Gumbrecht paved the way for an 'aesthetics of presence' which pays particular attention to 'moments of intensity' (2004: 97–8) produced by an unmediated encounter between our senses and the pleasure object; his theory reinstates the notion of *Erlebnis* and gives less importance to the pursuit of meaning. Martin Seel distinguished between the aesthetic experience, within the context of the arts, and experiences of the beautiful acquired in other contexts. In the first case, the key elements are 'presentation events' (*Darbietungsreignisse*, Seel 2008); *Darbietung* (presentation) marks a distance with respect to *Darstellung* (representation), highlighting the event character of the experience and, once again, diminishing the weight of the hermeneutic process.[1] The theories of the three authors, standing as a paradigm for the current discourse of aesthetics, consider performance its prime reference; for each of them the nature of the artistic representation changes and becomes an event with the features of a collective ritual. Fischer-Lichte's aesthetic of the performative act and Gumbrecht's aesthetic of presence are in fact theories of live performance, and exclude technical reproduction and media communication; in the same way, Gumbrecht's concept of *Erlebnis* brings out the vital dimension also present in the definition of a 'live concert'.

Such conceptions have contributed to another fundamental change of direction of the discourse in the musical domain: the key moment in the communication process now seems to be the performative act with its social conventions and emotional implications, while the text is relegated to a document of cultural history which has little to do with the genuine aesthetic experience. Calling for a 'drastic' (as opposed to 'gnostic') attitude towards music, Carolyn Abbate states that:

> Listening as phenomenon takes place under music's thumb, and acoustic presence may transfix or bewilder; it frees the listener from the sanctioned neatness of the hermeneutic. In more practical terms, the experience of listening to a live performance solicits attention more for the performers and the event and far less for the work than is perhaps generally admitted. (Abbate 2004: 512)

This point of view shifts the attention to the performative act and the emotions provoked in the listener; the historical and hermeneutic procedures give way to an ethnology of modern rituals far removed from the questions concerning technologies, medial diffusion and popular music. In reality, there is a close kinship because, as Philip Auslander (2008; 2012) has shown, the emphasis on 'live' is only possible in the context of a mass culture subject to 'reception in distraction'.

In tackling the issues posed by such theories, it may be helpful to reconsider Benjamin's distinction between *Erlebnis* and *Erfahrung* in light of the processes introduced by electronic technologies (Jay 2005: 312–60; Hansen 1987; Elsaesser 2009). *Erlebnis* is an event, *Erfahrung* a process. The former is a single, immediate occurrence which primarily involves the senses; the latter implies a mental elaboration of the sensations, their conversion into linguistic forms and their relocation in a

---

1 'By "presentation" I mean not primarily representation, whereby *something as something* is presented, but a demonstration in which a *presentation* is performed' (Seel 2008: 101).

framework of meanings. *Erlebnis* can also be seen as the event giving rise to the process which is consolidated in *Erfahrung*. However, on closer inspection there is a circular movement, because *Erfahrung* can exist only when it can have an effect on the lifeworld, thereby completing a trajectory which begins and ends in the vital flow. The practices of the artistic avant-gardes can be interpreted in the light of a growing awareness of the limits of *Erfahrung*, a repository of notions and rules which can crystallize into a coercive system. The fact that they highlight the moment of performance, with its undeniable challenge to the receiver, can be interpreted as an alarm signal concerning the failed transition to the lifeworld. In this sense, the aesthetics of presence got it exactly right. However, the theoretical framework can be repristinated if we reject the primacy of one of the two terms (in this case, *Erlebnis*) and consider the hypothesis that the reproduction technologies can create a connection between *Erlebnis* and *Erfahrung*.

Let us go back to the aura. The reception of art music is not characterized by a direct, frontal relationship with the artistic object, as is the case in the visual arts. Such a singular object does not exist in music, because music has two forms of existence: as text and as performance. Here the aura is manifested in the interplay between the normative reference – the text without which there can be no performance – and the emotions aroused by an impeccable, enthralling performance. In popular music this tension is radicalized in the relationship between the cold electronic medium and the hot atmosphere of the concert. Neither of these two poles has the upper hand, and not unlike in art music, one refers to the other. However, their content has changed: the disc presents a version of the work that has been technologically perfected and aesthetically approved, and as such, is the condition for its large-scale diffusion; the performance invests the text as codified in the disc with new energy, by means of accentuations and expressions which vary according to spatial and temporal contingencies. Here the performance is characterized by a degree of extemporary creativity, spontaneity and reactive capacity unimaginable in art music. The interactions between musicians and public show just how extraordinary the situation is, and seen from the perspective of the aesthetic experience, denote a prevalence of the *Erlebnis* component. A rock concert strikes the observer as an incantatory ritual characterized by a high degree of emotion; the intensity of the amplified sound, which symbolically embraces the listener, triggers a totalizing sensorial experience. For its part, the disc also has an auratic dimension, although one with a different modality: its sonic information gives tangible form to a nexus of meanings emanating from a specific place and time, and irradiating in any number of different places and times. It is important to distinguish this dimension from Adorno's 'restored aura': this phenomenon goes hand in hand with the character of fetish which the disc, as a commodity, takes on in place and time thanks to its collocation in the circuit of economic valorization. The disc can also be a vehicle of authentication and thus bridge the gap between *Erlebnis* and *Erfahrung*. The moment of mediation, which is fundamental for the media not only in terms of etymology, occurs here between the two poles of the aesthetic experience, and does not in the least rule it out.

Live Performance and Multiple Mediations

Once the theory of the aesthetic experience concentrates on the context of 'liveness', two orders of problems come to the fore: (1) Can the type of aesthetic experience proposed by this new theoretical approach be produced in a reception context highly characterized by the use of technologies? (2) Can the same weight be attributed to performances and to the emotional response they possess in an aesthetic of presence, even when the performance data are stored in a medium and accessed by electronic means? Auslander's main thesis is that once live performance has been projected onto a cultural field dominated by the media, it undergoes a chameleon-like change in character and procedures attempting to resemble the media (Auslander 2008; 2012). Taken together, his arguments show that reciprocal implication governs the relationship between 'live' and mediatized: the term 'live' enters the cultural discourse only when technical reproducibility and the electronic media have reached a level of diffusion with consequences for everyday life. Reproducibility, as seen in Benjamin, may achieve a theoretical definition only when the detachment of what is reproduced from the original in its vital presence and emanations becomes tangible.

Auslander has shown how the symbiosis of 'live' and mediatized assumes different configurations according to historical period, artistic genre and socio-cultural context. He cites examples above all from two domains: images from video clips shown in rock concerts, and video recordings used in performing art. However, the field of reciprocal relations could be extended to the recent issues in *Regietheater*, which often draws on cinematographic procedures or uses video projections, or again the live broadcasts of orchestral concerts and operas on specialized television networks or in large venues not designed for this type of reception. These, too, are mixed forms of 'live' and mediatized: with the latter, they share the spatial separation of performers and receivers, reproduction on screen and loudspeakers, and the unconventional venue (with all the consequent acoustic differences and social implications), while they are linked to the 'live' by the temporal unity of performance and reception and the receiver's sense of emotional participation (often shared by a circle of *aficionados*).

If these complex issues are given due consideration, the theoretical potential of the aesthetics of presence appears as quite limited. One of the problems consists in the fact that while the aesthetics of performance and *Erlebnis* claim a re-appropriation of the body, emotion and collective experience, the most widespread form of musical reception takes place in a cold and sterilized sphere. One could say that in technological reproduction, the presence of the performer is replaced by a new proximity – the source of the sound signal; the sound as such, in its physical quality and micrological life, is the new body which becomes present to the ears of the listener in 'splendid isolation'. Observation of these environmental conditions and perceptive attitudes throws new light on the problem, removing us from 'reception in distraction' and bringing us once again into the realm of 'structural listening'. The decision of Glenn Gould, taken in 1964 at the height of his career, to abandon public concerts and dedicate himself entirely to studio recordings is paradigmatic. It reflects not only ethical and political considerations, but also his interest in a musical experience characterized by 'analytic clarity, immediacy, and indeed almost tactile proximity' (Gould 1966: 48). Thus, the means of reproduction, which gave impetus to 'reception in distraction', reveal a second facet which has a greater affinity with concentration: they provide the ideal conditions for structural listening. The meticulous work of dissection and editing which a conscientious performer such as Gould (similarly to Karajan and Celibidache) put into the preparation of his recordings responds to the need to achieve clarity in both structure and sound articulation. The performative project, which every performer elaborates in studying the score, has more chances in the context of discographic production – that is ideologically suspect and emotionally neutral – than in the traditional and ritual context of live performance. The means of reproduction free the performer from the acoustic limits imposed by the concert hall and the contingencies of public performance; in fact, they benefit, rather than hamper, the transmission of musical sense. Moreover, the diffusion of discographic products has had a positive effect on the formation of the performer: he/she can draw on whole segments of the history of musical interpretation in recordings that have to be considered not merely as the acoustic documentation of a performance, but as the final outcome of the interpretative process. There can be room for the exercise of both criticism and free creativity in a highly regulated production system. In the sphere of art music, technical reproducibility also has considerable consequences in terms of the dissemination of knowledge. The production of discs has made available to a circle of musicians and listeners samples of the musical culture of several centuries, creating an unprecedented reference repertory. Lastly, the diffusion and ready accessibility of recordings paved the way for a new type of teaching which can go into aesthetic questions in detail, directly comparing different interpretative styles and verifying the outcomes of musical analysis.

If the means of technical reproduction are subjected to historical developments largely independent of artistic genres and production sectors, it is not surprising that The Beatles' *Sgt. Pepper's Lonely Hearts Club Band*, *Anthem of the Sun* by The Grateful Dead, *Uncle Meat* by The Mothers of Invention and Miles Davis's *Bitches Brew* all appeared in the space of only three years (1967–9). These discs are milestones in rock, not least because they feature a musical content that cannot be replicated live and whose presentation in concert would necessitate major changes. Giving the 'work concept' a concrete configuration and establishing a stylistic model, they assume a function in rock history comparable to that fulfilled by Gould's Goldberg Variations or Karajan's Ninth Symphony in the interpretative history of art music. Microphone placing, mixing of tracks, control of reverberation and montage of fragments recorded at different times have become prime compositional instruments. In line with Benjamin's pioneering approach, the discourse on technical reproduction has concentrated almost exclusively on the phenomena of reception and the way these have transformed listening habits; the multiple mediations introduced by electronic devices call our attention to their role in production. This is a further aspect showing how the aesthetic experience does not have the performance and reception as its sole showcase, but is also enacted in the creative process. The composer who writes scores and the one who is also active as a performer, especially in the context of popular music, are both also listeners. One of the decisive factors in their production is precisely listening to the music of others and his/her own (whether recorded or live). From the point of view of production, the aesthetic experience is characterized by the same circuit of perception and comprehension observed in the field of reception. However, musical listening as the trigger for the creative engine has its own dynamic and certain specific features: here electronic technologies live in greater promiscuity with previous practices. Right from the first compositions using electronic apparatus, the writing-based competences were combined with performing practice and the elaboration of the sound in the studio. This promiscuity has become the benchmark for music making in the era of digital technologies. In its current development, technology is giving new impetus to the aesthetic experience and posing the question of new modes of listening transversally within all the musical genres.

Translated by Mark Weir

References

Abbate, Carolyn (2004) 'Music – Drastic or Gnostic?', *Critical Inquiry*, 30/3, pp. 505–53.

Adorno, Theodor W. (1975) 'Culture Industry Reconsidered', trans. Anson G. Rabinbach, *New German Critique*, 6, Autumn, pp. 12–19.

——— (1976a) 'Anweisungen zum Hören neuer Musik', in *Der getreue Korrepetitor. Lehrschriften zur musikalischen Praxis* [1963], *Gesammelte Schriften 15*, Frankfurt am Main: Suhrkamp, pp. 188–248.

——— (1976b) *Introduction to the Sociology of Music*, trans. E.B. Ashton, New York: Seabury Press.

——— (1976c) 'Über die musikalische Verwendung des Radios', in *Der getreue Korrepetitor. Lehrschriften zur musikalischen Praxis* [1963], *Gesammelte Schriften 15*, Frankfurt am Main: Suhrkamp, pp. 369–401.

——— (1997) *Aesthetic Theory*, ed. Gretel Adorno and Rolf Tiedemann, trans. Robert Hullot-Kentor, London and New York: Continuum.

——— (2002) 'On the Fetish-character in Music and the Regression of Listening', in *Essays on Music*, ed. Richard Leppert, trans. Susan H. Gillespie, Los Angeles, CA: University of California Press, pp. 288–317.

——— (2006) *Towards a Theory of Musical Reproduction: Notes, a Draft and Two Schemata*, ed. Henri Lonitz, Cambridge: Polity Press.

——— (2009) *Current of Music: Elements of a Radio Theory*, ed. Robert Hullot-Kentor, Cambridge: Polity Press.

——— and Eisler, Hanns (1994) *Composing for the Films*, London: Athlone Press.

Auslander, Philip (2008) *Liveness: Performance in a Mediatized Culture*, London: Routledge.

——— (2012) 'Digital Liveness: A Historico-philosophical Perspective', *Journal of Performance and Art*, 34/3, pp. 3–11.

Benjamin, Andrew (ed.) (2005) *Walter Benjamin and Art*, New York: Continuum.

Benjamin, Walter (2002a) 'The Work of Art in the Age of its Technological Reproducibility: Second Version', in *Selected Writings*, vol. 3: *1935–1938*, ed. Michael W. Jennings and Howard Eiland, Cambridge, MA: Harvard University Press, pp. 101–33.

——— (2002b) 'Theory of Distraction', in *Selected Writings*, vol. 3: *1935–1938*, ed. Michael W. Jennings and Howard Eiland, Cambridge, MA: Harvard University Press, pp. 141–2.

——— (2003) 'The Work of Art in the Age of its Technological Reproducibility: Third Version', in *Selected Writings*, vol. 4: *1938–1940*, ed. Michael W. Jennings and Howard Eiland, Cambridge, MA: Harvard University Press, pp. 251–83.

——— (2010) 'The Work of Art in the Age of its Technological Reproducibility (First Version)', trans. Michael W. Jennings, *Grey Room*, 39, pp. 11–37.

Björnberg, Alf (2007) 'On Aeolian Harmony in Contemporary Popular Music', in *Critical Essays in Popular Musicology*, ed. Allan Moore, Aldershot: Ashgate, pp. 275–82.

Boulez, Pierre (2005) *Points de repère*, vol. 3: *Leçons de musique. Deux décennies d'enseignement au Collège de France*, ed. Jean-Jacques Nattiez, Paris: Bourgois.

Bubner, Rüdiger (1989) Ästhetische Erfahrung, Frankfurt am Main: Suhrkamp.

Carey, James W. (2005) 'Walter Benjamin, Marshall McLuhan, and the Emergence of Visual Society', in Genosko (2005), pp. 273–81.

Dell'Antonio, Andrew (ed.) (2004) *Beyond Structural Listening? Postmodern Modes of Hearing*, Berkeley, CA: University of California Press.

Eiland, Howard (2005) 'Reception in Distraction', in Benjamin (2005), pp. 3–13.

Elsaesser, Thomas (2009) 'Between Erlebnis and Erfahrung: Cinema Experience with Benjamin', *Paragraph*, 32/3, pp. 292–312.

Fischer-Lichte, Erika (2008) *The Transformative Power of Performance: A New Aesthetics*, London: Routledge.

Genosko, Gary (2005) *Marshal McLuhan: Critical Evaluations in Cultural Theory*, vol. 2: *Theoretical Elaborations*, New York: Routledge.

Gould, Glenn (1966) 'The Prospects of Recording', *High Fidelity Magazine*, 16, pp. 43–63.

Gumbrecht, Hans Ulrich (2004) *The Production of Presence: What Meaning Cannot Convey*, Stanford, CA: Stanford University Press.

——— and Marrinan, Michael (eds) (2003) *Mapping Benjamin. The Work of Art in the Digital Age*, Stanford, CA: Stanford University Press.

Habermas, Jürgen (1987a) *The Philosophical Discourse of Modernity: Twelve Lectures*, trans. Frederick Lawrence, Cambridge: Polity Press.

——— (1987b) *The Theory of Communicative Action*, vol. 2: *Lifeworld and System: A Critique of Functionalist Reason*, trans. Thomas McCarthy, Boston, MA: Beacon Press.

Hansen, Miriam Bratu (1987) 'Benjamin, Cinema and Experience: "The Blue Flower in the Land of Technology"', *New German Critique*, 40, pp. 179–224.
——— (2012) *Cinema and Experience: Siegfried Kracauer, Walter Benjamin and Theodor W. Adorno*, Berkeley, CA: University of California Press.
Jauss, Hans Robert (1972) *Kleine Apologie der ästhetischen Erfahrung*, Konstanz: Universitätsverlag.
——— (1982) *Aesthetic Experience and Literary Hermeneutics*, Minneapolis, MN: University of Minnesota Press.
Jay, Martin (2005) *Songs of Experience: Modern American and European Variations on a Universal Theme*, Berkeley, CA: University of California Press.
Kracauer, Siegfried (1987) 'Cult of Distraction: On Berlin's Picture Palaces', *New German Critique*, 40, pp. 91–6.
Levin, Thomas Y. (1990) 'For the Record: Adorno on Music in the Age of Its Technological Reproducibility', *October*, 55, pp. 23–47.
McLuhan, Marshall (1964) *Understanding Media: The Extensions of Man*, New York: McGraw-Hill.
——— (1966) 'Art as Anti-environment', *Art News Annual*, 31, pp. 55–8.
——— and Pakey, Harley (1968) *Through the Vanishing Point: Space in Poetry and Painting,* New York: Harper and Row.
Merleau-Ponty, Maurice (1962) *Phenomenology of Perception*, trans. Colin Smith, London: Routledge and Kegan Paul.
Riesman, David (1957) 'Listening to Popular Music', in Rosenberg and White (1957), pp. 408–17.
Rosenberg, Bernard and White, David Manning (1957) *Mass Culture: The Popular Arts in America*, Glencoe, IL: The Free Press.
Salzer, Felix (1952) *Structural Hearing: Tonal Coherence in Music*, 2 vols, New York: Charles Boni.
Schaeffer, Pierre (1966) *Traité des objets musicaux*, Paris: Seuil.
Schafer, Murray R. (2005) 'McLuhan and Acoustic Space', in Genosko (2005), pp. 66–73.
Schoenberg, Arnold (1984) 'For a Treatise on Performance' [1923–24], in *Style and Idea*, ed. Leonard Stein, London: Faber and Faber, pp. 319–20.
Seel, Martin (2008) 'On the Scope of Aesthetic Experience', in Shusterman and Tomlin (2008), pp. 98–105.
Shusterman, Richard (1997) 'The End of Aesthetic Experience', *Journal of Aesthetics and Art Criticism*, 55/1, pp. 29–41.
——— and Tomlin, Adele (2008) *Aesthetic Experience*, New York: Routledge.
Subotnik, Rose Rosengard (1988) 'Towards a Deconstruction of Structural Listening: A Critique of Schoenberg, Adorno, and Stravinsky', in *Explorations in Music, the Arts, and Ideas: Essays in Honor of Leonard B. Meyer*, ed. Eugene Narmour and Ruth A. Solie, Hillsdale, NY: Pendragon Press, pp. 87–122.
Théberge, Paul (2005) 'Counterpoint: Glenn Gould and Marshall McLuhan', in Genosko (2005), pp. 48–65.

Chapter 2
Ideological, Social and Perceptual Factors in Live and Recorded Music

Eric Clarke

The condition of music in its post-recording age has provoked assessments that range from euphoria at the dawn of a new age to despair at the erosion of what are seen as 'core values'. Among musical traditions, Western art music (WAM) has been one of the more reluctant to embrace recording and its consequences as affording genuinely new opportunities, rather than simply new channels for old attitudes – with the exception of a few 'maverick' performers and producers such as Glenn Gould and John Culshaw.

In this chapter I consider the intertwining of perceptual, social and ideological factors in live and recorded music, and although my principal focus is on the WAM tradition, I am going to start with the American National Anthem, and the controversy over Beyoncé's performance of the anthem at President Obama's second inauguration ceremony on 21 January 2013. On the day after the ceremony, and following on from a clip of the rousing end to Beyoncé's performance, *The Wall Street Journal*'s Digital Network presenter, Simon Constable, comments 'That was Beyoncé apparently *not* singing the national anthem at yesterday's inauguration,' and hands over to a reporter (John Jurgensen), who explains:

> We are hearing Beyoncé's voice there, but apparently what we're hearing is a vocal recorded previously to the inauguration. Reports are saying – and this is confirmed by the US Marine Corps Band – that her vocals were not live. So she was either lip-syncing or singing along to a pre-recorded vocal track. Now this really isn't that uncommon – this happens pretty frequently, but what it brings into question are all these ideas about authenticity and what we expect from a live performance.[1]

And an extract from the British *Daily Telegraph* similarly picks up on anxieties about authenticity and 'fakery' that revolve around the distinction between live and recorded performance:

> For millions watching on television, Beyoncé's soaring rendition of America's national anthem was the highlight of Monday's presidential inauguration ceremony.

---

[1] See 'Report: Beyonce Lip-synced Inaugural Performance', *Wall Street Journal*, http://www.youtube.com/watch?v=DTuGXoJGH5g, 22 January 2013 (accessed 30 June 2015).

> But admiration turned to disappointment on Tuesday after it was reported that the performance was mimed, not live. … The story exploded onto social media networks, including Facebook and Twitter, with some fans expressing dismay that the performance was pre-recorded. Many observed that at one point during the performance Beyoncé had dramatically pulled out her earpiece, sparking a debate over whether this was part of the charade or – for the faithful – evidence that she had indeed decided to sing live after all.[2]

Anxieties over music's 'falsification' at the hands of the recording industry and the fraudulence of apparently live performances that turn out to have been pre-recorded are clearly heightened when the music is a country's national anthem and the event is the inauguration of a president. The totemic function of a national anthem sung by a black woman at the second inauguration of the USA's first black president, and in this case its ceremonial role in setting the seal on a national electoral process, clearly raises the stakes particularly high. But this is only a more pronounced version of a cultural concern that lies deeply embedded in attitudes to musical truth. As the *Wall Street Journal* reporter John Jurgensen notes, lip-syncing or more general miming are common for a pop musician like Beyoncé: the British charts programme *Top of the Pops*, which ran from 1964 to 2006, *required* its performers to mime to their own commercial recordings for the first two years of broadcasts, after which a variety of mixed regimes were employed – ranging from pre-recorded backing tracks with live vocal performances to entirely live performances. On a number of celebrated occasions musicians either deliberately or accidentally ruptured any sense of the 'truth' of what was going on – either as the result of technical failures, or in order to ridicule or play games with the mimed format. Since *Top of the Pops* was an (apparently) live performance programme that was nonetheless explicitly designed to rank the sales of *recordings*,[3] it is perhaps no surprise that live performance became curiously and confusingly entangled with recordings.

The blurring of the 'live' and 'mediatized' categories in examples like this, and the controversies surrounding the valorization of live and mediatized performance, have led some authors to argue for the unsustainability of the live/mediatized distinction, in part because various 'boundary conditions' seem to make it untenable. Consider a music event where some members of the audience are in the 'live' auditorium, and others are outside watching and hearing the same performance on screens and over loudspeakers in the same 'real time' as those in the auditorium.[4] Are these outdoor

---

2 *The Daily Telegraph*, 22 January 2013.

3 By contrast, the BBC's *Juke Box Jury*, which ran from 1959, adopted a format which explicitly foregrounded the recorded nature of the music (from records played very visibly on a jukebox in the studio) that constituted its musical material.

4 The free, live relays of opera productions from The Royal Opera House Covent Garden to audiences in open-air venues around the UK are one such example: see 'BP Big Screens', *Royal Opera House*, http://www.roh.org.uk/about/bp-big-screens (accessed 30 June 2015).

audiences experiencing the performance as live or mediatized – or both? What is changed if there is a one-second delay in the digital relay? Or a 30-second delay? Or a one-day delay? Live radio broadcasts – despite their acousmatic character – share a great deal with live performances, and distinguish themselves from recordings: they offer a programme of music and start and finish at times that are not under the control of the listener; they are subject to interruptions, delays, 'deficiencies' (poor performances, audience or environmental noise) or 'excesses' (extraordinary and compelling performances, exceptional responses by audiences) that cannot be foreseen; and they are unique – broadcast on a single occasion, perhaps never to be repeated (unless a recording of the live broadcast is relayed at a later date).[5] Or this was true until recently, when the advent of various 'play it again'[6] and hard disc or flash memory recording technologies built into radio receivers have had the consequence that there is no longer that sense of 'once missed, gone forever' – one of the defining qualities of liveness. And yet there is still something very particular about watching/listening to music at the time it is originally broadcast, attributable perhaps to the community of participants (real or imaginary) of which the listeners feel themselves to be members – a feeling that is palpably absent when watching or listening later.[7] Experiencing 'liveness' seems to depend as much on the sense of being part of a particular imagined community – an audience – as it does on either ontological considerations or perceptual criteria.

A second kind of argument against the idea of any tenable distinction between live and mediatized is that live performance is increasingly influenced by the conditions of mediatized performance. As Nicholas Cook puts it: 'Recordings imitate the concert hall, while concerts imitate recordings, and it is at this ideological level that we might speak most convincingly of a convergence between them and a homogeneity of practice across the larger field of classical performance' (2013: 376).

Indeed, for Georgina Born the radical consequences of recording penetrate even further and are 'constitutive of all musical experience – art and popular, past and present – over the last century. Against this background … any *non*-recording-based musical experience has to be understood in a post-mediated light: as the negation, supplement or mimesis of recording' (2010: 236).

It is hard not to recognize that the live and the mediatized have become increasingly mutually dependent and mutually influential – and we may need to draw the distinction according to criteria and in conceptual 'places' that are not what or where we thought they would be: not, for instance, on the basis of being in the same physical space, nor in any detailed sense even at the same chronological

---

5 The musician and writer Hans Keller, a fierce critic of recordings, was a devotee, defender and prodigious contributor to radio broadcasting for similar reasons.

6 Such as the BBC's iPlayer service.

7 The term 'appointment television' is used to denote those television shows that attract, or are intended to attract, the equivalent of a live audience: a virtual community of viewers all watching at the same time.

time, but perhaps according to social constructions that depend on real and imagined communities. If a socially constructed understanding of 'liveness' is to replace a narrowly empirical outlook, then it is important also to question the explicit or implicit value judgements that cling to these two conditions of music – particularly the tendency to view liveness as somehow intrinsically more significant or authentic. But it is also important not to turn that into the claim that there are no experiential distinctions, and I will use the remainder of the chapter to consider some of the broad perception–action consequences – in other words the affordances – of different live and mediatized conditions of musical engagement.

When Thomas Edison made his famous tin-foil recording in 1877, he could have had little idea how far-reaching – literally and metaphorically – the consequences of his invention would be. Little more than a century ago all music was necessarily heard live, while today vastly more music is heard around the globe in mediatized form. The technological and cultural history of this revolution in music has been the subject of a significant amount of writing; but there has been rather less discussion of the consequences of recording for listening.[8] From a psychological perspective, recordings have many of the same paradoxical perceptual characteristics as films and photographs. Overwhelmingly – though of course not exclusively – they are presented and consumed within the illusory-realist perspective that what you hear or see is what happened in reality: in other words, that there is something close to a transparency between real-world events that took place and the sights or sounds that are presented.

In this sense, recordings constitute paradoxical perceptual sources: on the one hand they are real or digital objects made of shellac, vinyl, magnetic tape, silvered plastic, or coded on a hard drive or flash memory somewhere, from which sounds can be made by an appropriate technology; and on the other hand they are 'portals' into a virtual world of instruments and voices – and what we then imagine that we hear are the sounds of those instruments and voices, rather than the sounds of the record, disc or file. Pictures and photographs have the same paradoxical perceptual quality, as the psychologist James Gibson – discussing pictures from the perspective of ecological perception – points out:

> A picture, photographic or chirographic, is always a treated surface, and it is always seen in the context of other nonpictorial surfaces. Along with the invariants for the depicted layout of surfaces, there are invariants for the surface as such. It is a plaster wall, or a sheet of canvas, a panel, a screen, or a piece of paper. ... The information displayed is dual. The picture is always both a scene and a surface, and the scene is paradoxically *behind* the surface. This duality of the information is the reason the observer is never quite sure how to answer the question, 'What do you see?' (Gibson 1986: 281)

[8] Though see Sterne (2003), Clarke (2007) and Katz (2010).

Trompe l'oeil paintings play with this latent awareness of the duality of 'scene and surface' – as well as with the presence of more or less likely objects. The door of the State Music Room in Chatsworth House in Derbyshire, England has a painting by the eighteenth-century Dutch artist Jan van der Vaart that is inserted into it. The painting is clearly intended to deceive the viewer about the presence of the violin, but it also involves an equal deception about the surfaces that are involved – whether the viewer is looking at a violin, or a piece of painted canvas, or the surface of a door ….

In a similar manner, recordings that, either through age or deliberate processing, make audible their real or apparent recording medium problematize how listeners might respond to the question 'What do you hear?' – perhaps in response to a playback of the 1911 78 r.p.m. recording of Elena Gerhardt and Artur Nikisch performing Schubert's 'An die Musik'. Depending on expertise and specific focus, a listener might reasonably answer: 'the past', 'an old recording of singing', 'a 78 r.p.m. recording', 'Elena Gerhardt' or 'Schubert's "An die Musik"'. Until relatively recently it might have been unlikely for listeners to respond that they heard the sound of shellac, or a 78 r.p.m. recording, but in an era of sampling and re-mastering and the transfer of recordings from one medium to another, the sound of the *medium* as well as the sound of the *music* has taken on increased significance – certainly for transfer engineers or historians and analysts of recordings. And even for less specialized listeners, the sound of the medium can be a powerful perceptual characteristic, exploiting the sense of historical distance that accompanies the characteristically thin and crackly sound of older recording technologies (see Link 2001; Reynolds 2011). There is something about the sound quality of the Gerhardt recording that makes us pay special attention to it, and to attribute a kind of integrity and authenticity to it that is based on assumptions about an earlier and less 'managed' era of music making – however unwarranted those assumptions might be.

So what are the attributes of recordings that have an impact on the ways people listen, and what is different about recordings as perceptual sources compared with live performance? Most obviously there is the acousmatic character of recordings: music heard over loudspeakers or headphones is heard out of sight of the performers and instruments that made those sounds, and yet with acoustical properties that seem to specify the direct presence of instruments and performers. This is quite different from hearing music coming from another room or from around the corner since it affords quite different responses for a listener, and in that sense *sounds* quite different. If music from around the corner is intriguing, a listener can move towards it – changing the acoustic signal that is available and usually bringing its source into sight. No such exploration and consequent perceptual discovery is possible with acousmatically presented music: the music is already as present as it can be, and its source is never going to become visible however much you peer into your smartphone or hi-fi system.

One of the consequences of acousmatic presentation is the heightening of a particular kind of 'impoverishment of information' that is a characteristic of aesthetic objects in a 'high art' context. Our usual relationship with the environment involves a thorough interdependence of perception and action: we notice something and act in relation to it, and in doing so find out more about it in a continuous and reciprocal process. But in many 'art' traditions of music, painting, sculpture, dance and drama, aesthetic objects and their circumstances of engagement hold perception and action apart – sculptures you cannot touch, painted scenes you cannot enter, music and drama you cannot join in with – and in doing so they limit the information that is available to the perceiver. When I hear a sound that I don't quite understand coming from my printer, I can fiddle about with it and see whether the paper tray is perhaps not properly engaged, and in doing so I discover something about the possible source of the sound that has significant consequences for how I *hear* the sound. By contrast, when I hear a sound that I can't make sense of in a live performance of Helmut Lachenmann's Tuba Concerto, I can do nothing about it and have no way to try to make additional perceptual information available – other than looking around the orchestra from my fixed seat in the hope of seeing what it is that is making the sound. I am simply subject to the flow of perceptual information, powerless to intervene, and as a result forced to adopt what might be called a contemplative perceptual attitude. Acousmatic presentation of music takes this rupture between perception and action one step further: when I listen to a *recording* of Lachenmann's Tuba Concerto, I can't even look around the orchestra. The music now occupies a virtual space that is paradoxically superimposed on, or piped into, the real space of the bedroom, living room, studio or lecture hall in which I encounter it. The emphasis on abstraction and ineffability, which are powerfully associated with the ideology of WAM's autonomy and absolutism, is given extra impetus when the sounds of music are abstracted from the physical and visual circumstances of their production, and when all possibility of engagement between musicians and listener is eliminated. This loss is undeniably an impoverishment, but it also affords a particularly intense kind of auditory attention and involvement, and perhaps particularly in headphone listening, when the music conjures up a virtual musical space that is primarily located inside the listener's head – an extreme of individual, autonomous listening. In an autobiographical account of his own teenage engagement with music entitled *Lost in Music*, Giles Smith reflects on his preference for 'listening through headphones, which is even now my favourite way to hear things, to sink into them, sealed off, so that there's no distraction. At which point, pop was not the soundtrack to your life, it *was* your life' (1995: 40). The same attitude is reflected in a magazine advertisement from 2005, which shows the tear-streaked face of a woman in profile wearing Sennheiser headphones, under the banner 'Resistance is useless'. Mixed up with the offensive implication of sexual violence, the advertisement also tells us that listening with these headphones will be overwhelmingly immersive, will break down the listener's own subjectivity, and take her over.

Recordings afford not only this powerfully solitary communion with the virtual performers, but also a particular kind of intimacy and familiarity with a specific performance that was unimaginable in pre-recording listening. We have become so accustomed to this that it now seems almost too obvious to mention, but before the widespread availability of recordings, the breadth and depth of listeners' musical experiences were determined by their local circumstances. If you got to a performance of the Beethoven Violin Concerto, for example, you heard it in whatever version and with whatever merits or failings the local performance offered – and you might never hear it again. And if you wanted to hear Joseph Joachim play, and were lucky enough to do so, you simply heard him play whatever happened to be programmed, and probably never again. By comparison, recordings afford listeners unprecedented control over musical content and – through repetition – unprecedented familiarity with a specific performance: Gerhardt singing Schubert, Gould playing Bach – you can now listen to them again and again, get to know every detail of their performance, analyse them in minute detail.[9]

This access to music, and the democratizing, intensifying and analytical possibilities of recordings, seem obviously positive virtues, but there are those who would disagree. The Austrian-born English musicologist Hans Keller, for example, argued that it is repeatability more than any other single factor that renders recording 'anti-musical', and that the predictability of a recording is antithetical to the fundamentally creative nature of performance. 'Performance … is the improvisatory tail-end of composition, and improvisation can't be repeated …', he claimed:

> The central truth about *all* creativity is the meaningful contradiction of the recipient's expectations, which the creator arouses before he contradicts them. The gramophone record's repeatability has had a disastrous and well-definable effect not only on the sheer act of listening, but also on musical education and, thence, on performance itself. (Keller 1990: 22)

The homogenization of performance style was one such 'disastrous effect', with Keller claiming – along with many others who have voiced the same view – that modern performance has become safer, more bland, less distinguishable than it was before recording took such a grip on musical culture. By contrast, broadcast music – of which Keller was a staunch and robust defender – although acousmatically presented, dislocated from 'the event', portable and installable – does not afford either the repetition or the control of content that domestic listeners with their own collection of recordings can enjoy, and in this respect it retains the attributes of unpredictability and uniqueness that are characteristic of live performance – or at least it did so at the time when Keller was writing.[10]

Repeatability allows interruptibility, since without the uniqueness of the live event, and the social constraints that go with it, listeners can decide whether their priorities lie with the continuity of whatever it is that they are listening to, or with responding to the unpredictable flow of daily life: a phone call, a knock at the

---

[9] For instance, using audio analysis packages such as *Sonic Visualiser*: see http://www.sonicvisualiser.org/ (accessed 30 June 2015).

[10] The advent of 'play it again' technologies and services, as noted above, has subsequently changed all that.

door or a distracting train of thought. The permanence of a recording ironically threatens to diminish its significance, since if it is always available, then it can be indefinitely deferred. If recorded music can be interrupted and resumed, can make way for the practical demands of everyday reality, then there is less reason for listeners to commit their undivided and constant attention to it. Keller, again, asserts that another of the 'disasters' of recording is 'the constant assault on our ears, whether in the form of background or foreground music, which gramophone record and tape have made possible, and which has had a devastating effect on both the quality of our listening and our powers of musical concentration' (1990: 24–5). Keller was of a generation that – arguably – lived through a significant transition from an age of widespread *musica practica* (at least among the European Jewish middle class of which Keller was a member) to a recording age in which, for a while, recordings became 'reference points'. It is perhaps not surprising that this change seemed to him simply to be a loss. But with the vastly greater access to recordings of all ages and types that we now have, and the influence of downloading and streaming practices which mean that people increasingly do not own recordings in the same way at all, the reifying effect of a single, repeated version against which Keller railed is arguably much less of a consideration.

Sound, Space and Listening Position

Having considered some of the broader perceptual and social consequences of the distinction – contested or otherwise – between live performance and recording, I now turn to a more narrowly focused consideration of the 'listening position' that is characteristic of the dominant ideology of classical record production. The history of recording is dominated by a search for 'fidelity' – the ideal of a completely transparent medium that presents the music 'exactly as it is', without transformation or loss of presence.[11] The impossibility, or paradox, of this fantasy is obvious: just as a camera captures an image from a particular point of view, so too the microphone records sound from a particular 'point of hearing'. In the era of acoustical recording, when performers had to arrange themselves around a large recording horn, there was essentially no room for manoeuvre – literally for the performers, as well metaphorically for the recording engineer who had to make the most of whatever physical arrangement of instruments and voices could be managed. But with the development of electrical recording, magnetic tape and stereo, producers and engineers found themselves in a position similar to that of film directors and camera operators: the microphone allowed them to make choices about the perspective from which sounds were recorded, and thus the overall auditory scene (see Bregman 1990) that they were trying to create –

[11] Arguably, in the MP3 era 'fidelity' has been at least partially displaced by portability, since the MP3 protocol is manifestly lower in audio quality than other digital formats, but far more convenient for a whole range of mobile and interchangeable technologies.

largely in terms of the size and character of the acoustical space. The creation of a recording is the creation of a virtual world, and what kind of virtual world you want to end up with then becomes a question of musical aesthetics as much as technological possibilities.

Just as it is a film director's decisions about lighting, camera angle, editing style and so on that establish a subject-position in film, so the classical record producer inevitably establishes what might be called a 'listener-position' by means of microphone placement, sound treatment, spatial positioning and pacing. Two people who quite early on recognized the radical and creative possibilities of this opportunity in classical music were the performer and producer Glenn Gould, and the producer John Culshaw (see Patmore and Clarke 2007). At the time when they started their production careers – the 1950s and 1960s – the dominant paradigm within classical recording was, and arguably still is, to achieve a listener-position which places the listener in 'the finest seat in the house' – to quote an advertisement for Pye sound equipment from 1957 (see Symes 2004). Culshaw's outlook was directly opposed to this view. His aim was to employ technology to create an aural experience that was fundamentally different from what could be heard in the opera house or concert hall. Writing in 1966, in response to indignation at Glenn Gould's proposal that future technological developments might allow listeners to manipulate recordings during playback, he observed:

> Most of this indignation derives from the fact that such things *can* be done – the suspicion that technology, as a science, is interfering with music which, as an art, since the middle of the 19th century has been taking on some of the trappings of religion. Howls of protest go up every time that technology comes to the assistance of music, despite the fact that without technology there would be no music at all …. (Culshaw 1966: 28)

Just as cartoon characters occupy a virtual reality in which they are endowed with skills and capacities that exceed or defy everyday reality without departing from it altogether, so Culshaw was interested in using studio technology to create a listener-position, and perhaps a performance, that was unattainable in the reality of the concert hall or the opera house.

While there has been increasing interest in a whole range of perspectives on music and space (for example, Born 2013; Dibben 2013; Doyle 2005; Moore et al. 2009; Thompson 2002), and on what might be described as the spatial component of the listener position, there has been little empirical investigation of listeners' capacities to detect and occupy these different listener-positions – and particularly little in relation to the WAM tradition. This is not too surprising, since pop music has been considerably more interested in exploring the spatial possibilities of recording. But while the spatial conditions of the recorded WAM tradition are less dramatically evident, there are nonetheless significant issues at stake. The spatial presentation of WAM is often strongly conditioned by assumptions about the kind of space (and by implication the type of building) in which the music should ideally be performed and heard: Tallis's *Spem in alium* or the Bach B minor Mass in a chapel or cathedral with all the space and resonance that suggests (as well as the religious context, of course); the Brahms Clarinet Quintet in a (secular) domestic setting or small concert hall; Stravinsky's *Rite of Spring* in a theatre or large concert hall. Behind these apparently practical or 'straightforwardly normative' decisions lie more interestingly complex cultural assumptions and attitudes, but little is known even about listeners' sensitivities to the virtual spaces and apparent performer positions that a recording can convey. In a preliminary study, I have therefore collected some listening data on precisely this issue, focusing on a number of recordings of one piece of classical music.

Bach BWV 1001: A Listening Study

With such a wide-open field, an enormous range of music might present itself as an appropriate place to start, but Bach's unaccompanied violin music has certain advantages. First, as music for a solo instrument, it presents a focal source on which the sound is centred (the position of the performer) – arguably more distinctly focused than for solo piano music, where the source of the sound is not so clearly identified with the performer, but with the instrument, and moreover an instrument whose sounding surface is significantly extended in space.[12] Secondly, the unaccompanied violin music is commonly played in a variety of locations, including chapels and churches, chamber music venues and concert halls, and therefore provides the opportunity for performers, producers and engineers to present or portray the music in a variety of virtual spaces on a recording. And thirdly, the prominent status of this music in the violin canon means that a large number of readily available commercial recordings exist. Although almost any extract of this music could act as suitable material for a listening study, the opening of the first movement of the first unaccompanied sonata in G minor (BWV 1001) was selected on the basis of a number of advantageous characteristics. It presents in its first two bars a relatively self-contained phrase of varied music (long and short note values, double-stopped chords and running melodies, loud and soft sounds), ending with a short rest before proceeding to the next phrase. This short period of silence (during the rest) is potentially an important source of spatial information, since it allows a listener to get some sense of the resonance of the acoustic space, so the extract used in the study included the rest and the short run of notes (G–E♭) that starts the next phrase, ending on the E♭ quaver towards the end of bar 2. This relatively self-contained opening phrase (together with the first few notes of the succeeding phrase) also constitutes a sufficiently brief, but musically reasonable, unit to be used in a study that requires participants to listen to it repeatedly: while it varies according to the speed of the performance, the mean duration of the 15

[12] The surface area of a concert grand piano is of the order of $1.8m^2$, compared to less than $0.1m^2$ for a violin.

extracts used in the study (see below) was 24.7 seconds, with a range from the shortest at 20 seconds to the longest at 31 seconds.

From more than 30 readily available modern recordings, 15 were selected that represented a range of approaches (see Table 2.1).[13]

Table 2.1 Recordings of the G minor unaccompanied violin sonata by J.S. Bach (BWV 1001) used in the listening study, listed in alphabetical order by surname

1. Arzewski, Cecylia	6. Fischer, Julia	11. Mullova, Viktoria
2. Cole, Nathan	7. Homburger, Maya	12. Papavrami, Tedi
3. Edinger, Christiane	8. Huggett, Monica	13. Schröder, Jaap
4. Ehnes, James	9. Ibragimova, Alina	14. Steinhardt, Arnold
5. Faust, Isabelle	10. Jansen, Janine	15. Szeryng, Henrik

Using the digital audio editor *Audacity*, each of these 15 recordings was edited so as to finish on the E♭ quaver in bar 2, with a slight fade through the final four notes of the phrase (A–E♭) so as not to end too abruptly, and saved (in WAV format) in two iTunes playlists, organized into two different random orders. Twenty postgraduate and postdoctoral members of the Faculty of Music at the University of Oxford were recruited as volunteer participants for the study, all with normal hearing. Each participant took part individually in the study, which consisted of two parts. In the first part each participant was asked to listen to the 15 extracts and, using a seven-point scale, to 'indicate how large the performance space seems to be in each recorded extract by circling the appropriate number' – from 'small' (1) through 'medium' (4) to 'large' (7). After a short pause, each participant was asked in the second part to 'indicate how close or distant the performer seems to be in each recorded extract by circling the appropriate number', using a seven-point scale ranging from 'very close' (1) to 'very distant' (7). The extracts were presented in two different random orders (one for size, the other for distance) counterbalanced across participants, and were played direct from iTunes on a Macbook laptop computer, using studio-quality headphones (Sennheiser HD 25-SP II). In order to familiarize the participants with the materials and response categories, and to check that the volume was set to a comfortable level, the run of 15 experimental trials for each part of the study was preceded by two practice trials, consisting of the same extract of music played from two recordings that were not used in the experimental trials. Each participant carried out the two parts of the study in the same order (size judgements first, distance judgements second), was fully debriefed about the aims of the study at the end, and was asked if there was any difference in the overall difficulty of the two judgement tasks (size or distance).

[13] Only recordings from the stereo LP era onwards were considered, to avoid the problems of using recordings made with radically different audio technologies.

Results

A primary aim of the study was simply to assess whether these listeners were able to make consistent judgements about size and distance in these extracts – irrespective of the particular judgements that they might make about individual recordings. This can be reduced to a simple question about the correlation between different participants' responses to each of the extracts: a high correlation between the participants' judgements would indicate strong agreement and a degree of certainty about the two spatial attributes (size and distance) of the recordings, while little or no correlation between the responses would indicate either uncertainty and an inability to make a reliable judgement – or strong individual differences between the participants.

A standard way to assess the reliability of a set of judgements is to use a statistic known as Cronbach's Alpha, which can take a value between 0 (a random relationship between responses) and 1 (complete consistency between responses). The Alpha value for the size judgements in this study is 0.615, and for distance is 0.461, both of which are statistically significant ($p = 0.000$ for size; $p = 0.018$ for distance), though rather more weakly so for the distance judgements. What this means is that these 20 participants were able to make quite strongly reliable and consistent judgements of the perceived size of the space in these 15 recording extracts, and while showing statistically significant consistency, were somewhat less sure/reliable in their distance judgements. This corresponds with the participants' own judgements of the difficulty of the two tasks: of those who expressed any opinion (13 of the 20), nine found the distance judgements harder, compared with four who found the size judgements harder.

Having established that the participants could make more or less reliable judgements, the next step was to assess whether there were significant differences in perceived size and distance between the 15 extracts, and what any such differences might demonstrate. A direct way to establish whether there are statistically significant differences is to perform two separate Analyses of Variance (ANOVAs) on the ratings of size and distance. Both ANOVAs show strongly significant results – $F\,(14{,}266) = 16.26$ for size ($p = 0.000$) and $F\,(14{,}266) = 14.24$ for distance ($p = 0.000$) – indicating that there are significant differences between the extracts in terms of both of the perceptual variables. Figures 2.1 and 2.2 show the average (mean) values for the two sets of judgements across the 15 extracts arranged in alphabetical order of surname (Arzewski to Szeryng), corresponding to the ordering in Table 2.1. Both figures show sizeable differences between the extracts, with a range from 2.50 (no. 8 – Monica Huggett) to 6.35 (no. 7 – Maya Homburger) for the size judgements, and a slightly narrower range from 2.10 (nos 10 and 13 – Janine Jansen and Jaap Schröder) to 5.45 (no. 3 – Christiane Edinger) for the distance judgements.[14] There seems at first sight to be little relationship

[14] There may be little significance in this small difference in the range for size and distance, since there is no way of knowing whether the participants understood the two scales (size and distance) as covering the same potential range of values.

between the two patterns of judgements, but there is a weak positive correlation between the two sets of figures ($r = 0.55$; $p = 0.02$), indicating (not surprisingly, perhaps) that large size is associated with distance, and small size with closeness. So Maya Homburger's recording (no. 7) is rated as the largest space and the fourth most distant position in relation to the listener, while Monica Huggett's (no. 8) is the smallest space and the third closest position. Notice, however, that recording no. 11 (Viktoria Mullova) is rated as the second largest space, and equal to recording no. 3 (Christiane Edinger), but while Edinger is rated as most distant, Mullova is in the middle of the distribution. Or compare recordings 5 (Faust) and 6 (Fischer), which are very similar in terms of size, but rather distinct in terms of position.

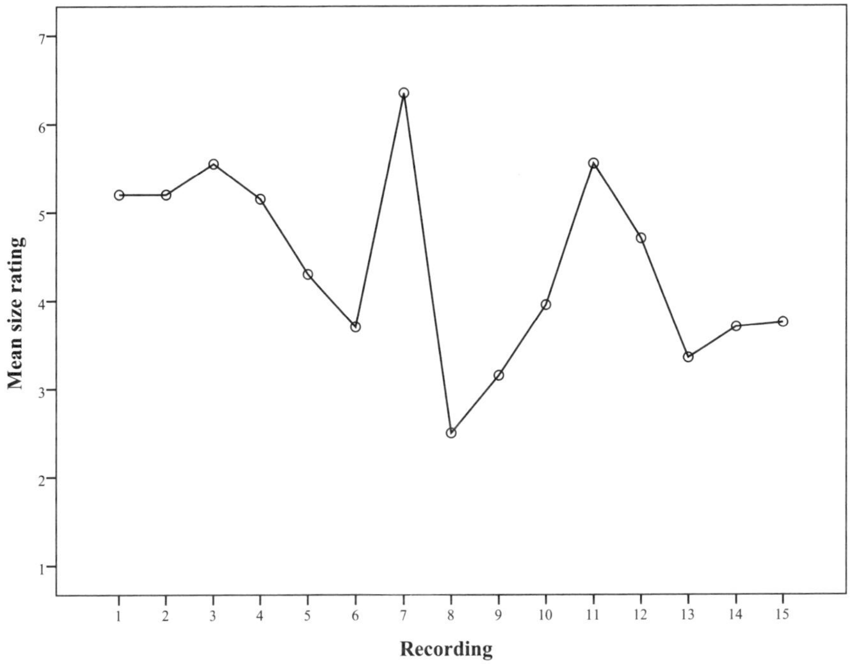

Figure 2.1 Mean ratings of the size of the space (from 1 = small to 7 = large) in the listening study, arranged in alphabetical order of surname (Arzewski–Szeryng) as shown in Table 2.1

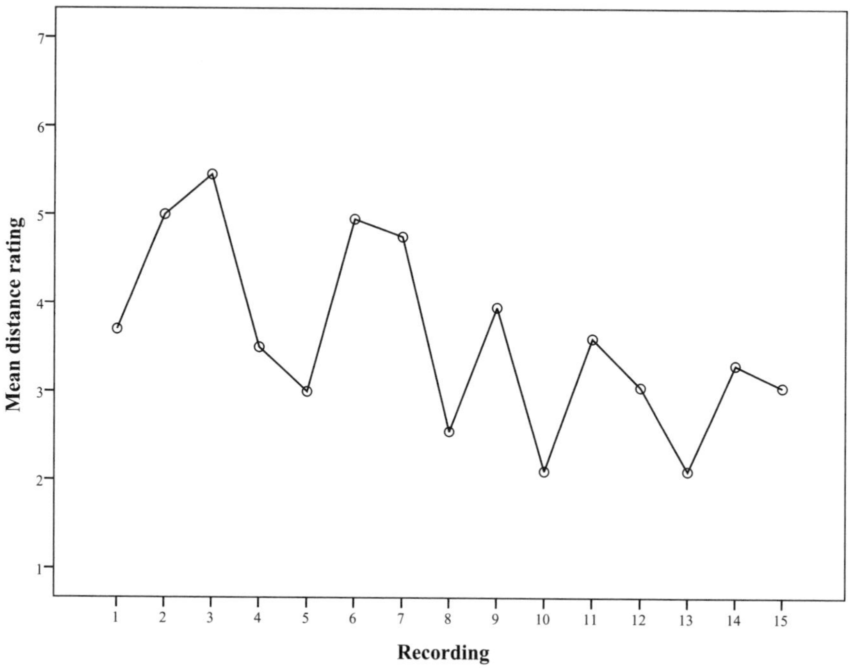

Figure 2.2 Mean ratings of the distance of the performer (from 1 = close to 7 = distant) in the listening study, arranged in alphabetical order of surname (Arzewski–Szeryng) as shown in Table 2.1

To summarize, the listeners who participated in this study were clearly able to make reliable judgements about two aspects of the virtual space of the recording (size and distance). While there was a weakly positive correlation between the two judgements (large size being associated with distance, small size with proximity), there was also evidence of independence between the two sets of responses, suggesting that the two perceptual dimensions cannot be collapsed together. There was some evidence that listeners found it harder to make the distance judgements, and some listeners reported that they found themselves wrestling with apparently contradictory cues: a large space (indicated by considerable resonance) and a performer who seemed both distant (quite a lot of ambient sound in relation to the direct sound of the instrument) and close (the audible sound of breathing, or of bow on string). What this demonstrates, of course, is that the virtual spaces specified in studio recordings can defy everyday ecological realities in intriguing or perhaps unsettling and unconvincing ways – as has been widely exploited in pop music (see Clarke 2013). More generally, however, it acts as another reminder of how powerful the spatial dimension of recorded music can be in terms of the virtual worlds that it can specify and, perhaps, the values with which those worlds engage. The listening study reported here is only a modest empirical step, showing at least that there is an identifiable and reasonably stable phenomenon to be investigated.

But it opens up a potentially fascinating domain for more sophisticated empirical enquiry: an ecological acoustics of mediatized listening.

Conclusion

To summarize and conclude, recordings have profoundly affected the way we listen: they have expanded our musical horizons by making a previously unimaginable diversity of music available to an unprecedented number of people; they have dramatically changed the ways in which we encounter music; they have allowed new kinds of music to be created; they have made it possible to become familiar with a specific performance as never before; they have enabled the separation of the purely auditory component of music from all the other circumstances of live musical events; and they have fundamentally changed the ecology of music. Confined for a time to the 'special place' of the concert hall, opera house and bourgeois salon, Western art music can now be heard almost anywhere and at any time. This ubiquity has been both welcomed as democratization, and regretted as a flattening of culture and a homogenization of performance; but whatever else it means, it has certainly thrown into doubt the already dubious distinction between 'musical listening' and 'everyday listening'.

There are, of course, circumstances in which listeners engage with music in that concentrated manner that the term 'musical listening' has been taken to imply,[15] and recordings play a significant role here too. The particular focus on sound that the acousmatic character of recordings affords, as well as its abstraction from the circumstances of live performance, makes possible the most intensely solitary listening. By contrast with people's pragmatic and fluctuating engagement with music embedded in everyday reality, the abstracted solitariness of acousmatic listening can engage a reflective or contemplative kind of consciousness, rather than the instrumental consciousness of the everyday perception–action cycle. Contrary to gloomy pronouncements on the destructive effects of recordings on both listening capacities and creative practices, recordings – understood as a resource rather than a prescription or dogma – have provided people with an unparalleled opportunity to enter into, and learn from, musical cultures from every part of the world. This access is of a particular kind, of course – acousmatic, de-contextualized, disengaged from the specificity of time and place, and affording no real social interaction between the listener and the virtually present musicians (even if it may sometimes conjure up the impression of it). The rapidly increasing interpenetration of music in various kinds of mediatized conditions (in recordings; on films, videos and games; streamed and broadcast) with 'live' reality (in homes, shops, cars, places of entertainment and the streets of our cities) has resulted in

---

[15] It is questionable whether only this kind of focused and 'undistracted' listening should be regarded as 'musical listening', as Anthony Gritten (2011) has argued – pointing out the musical (and other) virtues of so-called 'distracted listening'.

an astonishingly increasing familiarity with – and skill in – moving seamlessly between real and virtual spaces: therefore, the distinction between live and not-live has become increasingly blurred and blended, with fascinating, disturbing and sometimes controversial consequences. But there is no doubt that we are living through an unprecedented change in music's 'being in the world', and one which continues to transform the way we listen.

References

Born, Georgina (2010) 'For a Relational Musicology: Music and Interdisciplinarity, beyond the Practice Turn', *Journal of the Royal Musical Association*, 135, pp. 205–43.

——— (ed.) (2013) *Music, Sound and Space: Transformations of Public and Private Experience*, Cambridge: Cambridge University Press.

Bregman, Albert S. (1990) *Auditory Scene Analysis: The Perceptual Organization of Sound*, Cambridge, MA: MIT Press.

Clarke, Eric F. (2007) 'The Impact of Recording on Listening', *Twentieth-century Music*, 4, pp. 47–70.

——— (2013) 'Music, Space and Subjectivity', in Born (2013), pp. 90–110.

Cook, Nicholas (2013) *Beyond the Score: Music as Performance*, New York: Oxford University Press.

Culshaw, John (1966) 'The Mellow Knob, or the Rise of Record and the Decline of the Concert Hall as Foreseen by Glenn Gould', *Record and Recording*, 10, pp. 26–8.

Dibben, Nicola (2013) 'The Intimate Singing Voice: Auditory Spatial Perception and Emotion in Pop Recordings', in *Electrified Voices: Medial, Socio-historical and Cultural Aspects of Voice Transfer*, ed. Dmitri Zakharine and Nils Meise, Göttingen: V&R Unipress, pp. 107–22.

Doyle, Peter (2005) *Echo and Reverb: Fabricating Space in Popular Music Recording 1900–1960*, Middletown, CT: Wesleyan University Press.

Gibson, James J. (1986) *The Ecological Approach to Visual Perception* [1979], Hillsdale, NJ: Lawrence Erlbaum.

Gritten, Anthony (2011) 'Distraction in Polyphonic Gesture', in *New Perspectives on Music and Gesture*, ed. Anthony Gritten and Elaine King, Farnham: Ashgate, pp. 99–122.

Katz, M. (2010) *Capturing Sound: How Technology Has Changed Music*, rev. edn, Berkeley, CA: University of California Press.

Keller, Hans (1990) 'The Gramophone Record', in *The Keller Column*, ed. Robert Matthew-Walker, London: Alfred Lengnick, pp. 22–5.

Link, Stan (2001) 'The Work of Reproduction in the Mechanical Aging of an Art: Listening to Noise', *Computer Music Journal*, 25, pp. 34–47.

Moore, Allan F., Schmidt, Patricia and Dockwray, Ruth (2009) 'A Hermeneutics of Spatialization for Recorded Song', *Twentieth-century Music*, 6, pp. 81–112.

Patmore, David and Clarke, Eric F. (2007) 'Making and Hearing Virtual Worlds: John Culshaw and the Art of Record Production', *Musicae Scientiae*, 11, pp. 269–93.
Reynolds, Simon (2011) *Retromania: Pop Culture's Addiction to Its Own Past*, London: Faber and Faber.
Smith, Giles (1995) *Lost in Music*, London: Picador.
Sterne, Jonathan (2003) *The Audible Past: Cultural Origins of Sound Reproduction*, Durham, NC: Duke University Press.
Symes, Colin (2004) *Setting the Record Straight: A Material History of Classical Recording*, Middletown, CT: Wesleyan University Press
Thompson, Emily (2002) *The Soundscape of Modernity: Architectural Acoustics and the Culture of Listening in America, 1900–1933*, Cambridge, MA: MIT Press.

Chapter 3
On the Evolution of Private Record Collections: A Short Story

Esteban Buch

> Several times in my inner life, I had already experienced the process of inoculation as something salutary. In this situation, too, I resolved to follow suit, and I deliberately called to mind those images which, in exile, are most apt to waken homesickness: images of childhood. My assumption was that the feeling of longing would no more gain mastery over my spirit than a vaccine does over a healthy body. I sought to limit its effect through insight into the irretrievability – not the contingent biographical but the necessary social irretrievability – of the past.
>
> (Benjamin 2006)

She told me the story in her Parisian apartment, with a sad touch on her voice. More than 20 years after leaving her country of birth, she's still waiting for the occasion to bring to Europe her old collection of LPs. These LPs were just too many, too heavy and too old to travel, to say nothing of the present lack of a turntable to play them. Besides, there were few rarities among them, few things you couldn't replace by new records, so why bother? Yet she couldn't stop considering these records as one of her most private properties, as something that defined the very notion of what it meant to own things. She had collected them during her teens, beginning with the day she asked her father for money to buy Pink Floyd's *Atom Heart Mother*, and they have remained at her parents' home as a material souvenir without anyone to recall its meaning, or at least the meaning it had for her. The reason for leaving behind her precious collection was sound. Yet the sadness of the loss remained alive in my friend's memory, colouring her voice with a domestic, special kind of technological mourning.

Now, she said, her first personal choices and passions from the late 1970s and 1980s appear to her like a distinct region of her musical past. There were Pink Floyd, Led Zeppelin, The Doors, Frank Zappa, Yes, Queen, later Talking Heads and The Police, not to mention The Beatles and, last but not least, the rock bands from her own country, Serú Girán, Invisible, Los Redondos. All that rock was like a major island in her archipelago of tastes (Glevarec and Pinet 2009), an island still displayed separately in her parents' house, like a discrete monument to her own absence.

At least, she continued, this lasting temporary situation allows for a pleasure she indulges in once a couple of years or so: that of rediscovering those albums of her teens, with their colourful covers, every time she visits her old home sweet home across the ocean. That music is like an echo of the joys and pains of becoming somebody else than just the daughter of mom and dad. And the scratches and scars of these old vinyl plates are like the marks of time in an estranged part of her body. She can still remember the unfortunate day when the pickup of the turntable felt brusquely on 'Moonchild', the beautiful song from the double album *A Young Person's Guide to King Crimson*. That late-night catastrophe had permanent physical consequences, which, so sadly deplored back then in the 1980s, now appear like a proof that she had truly been alive, after all, when she was 17.

Her records were very different from her parents' own collection of LPs, one they had built up in the 1960s, providing her childhood with a multi-style soundtrack. Music, she told me with the kind of voice you usually address to the ear of a shrink, never counted among the reasons to quarrel with them. They really liked music, different kinds of music, thanks to a then not-so-frequent omnivorous taste (Peterson 1992).

Her parents' collection included classical music, beginning with the whole German canon, from Bach's *Art of the Fugue* up to Mahler's *Lied von der Erde*. They believed in Bach, as the saying goes, but they did not really try to convert her to the religion of music. That prevented fugues from turning into songs for runaway girls, my friend added, borrowing from a young writer born in the same town as she, and who had stayed there, at least so far. Lying on the floor beside the turntable, listening to the music in the dark without moving, she would slowly learn to love her own favourites among the classics, Schumann's Piano Concerto, Brahms' Fourth, Mozart's *Magic Flute*, Schubert's String Quintet, a few others. At some point in our conversation she recalled her father giving her for her tenth birthday a double album with Beethoven's Eighth and Ninth Symphonies, played by a Berlin Philharmonic oddly named after the city of his own birth, that of his own *Berliner Kindheit*.

Besides classical music, nearly every Sunday morning, Thelonious Monk would play with Sonny Rollins in the living room. For some reason, that was the only jazz record in the collection, but it was one of the most regularly played of all. She learnt most of the solos by heart, and she sung them while the record played, mimicking the instruments. For some other reason, she continued, rock music was totally absent, except for The Beatles' *Abbey Road*, allowing the teenager she was to build on that very lack a sound space of her own. On the other hand, the collection of these Romantic left-wingers included Pete Seeger and Joan Baez and Violeta Parra and Mercedes Sosa and a whole bunch of protest songs from all over the world, as well as many hours of *chanson française* and its international allies, Georges Brassens and Paco Ibañez and Fabrizio de André.

All these records, rock and classic and folk, had a material life of their own. Now she can listen to 'Moonchild' in the Internet, but the scratch isn't there any more, and she misses it. And now that she can easily retrieve the Monk-Rollins sessions on her computer, she is always disappointed not to hear that weird arrhythmia in Rollins's second chorus of 'The Way You Look Tonight'. She could also make sense of that other scratch in the Andante of Beethoven's third

Razumovsky Quartet, the cello pizzicato sounding for her like a jazz walking bass that would hit a stone rolling across the sidewalk. Now all she can do is to listen to the absence of the scratch.

When I was eight or nine years old, my friend went on while opening a bottle of cognac, my father bought a Grundig magnetic tape recorder. The same as for scratches on vinyl LPs, I like to remember distorted tapes, she said. This fancy machine inaugurated a new way of having music at home, namely copying LPs in big, open magnetic tapes. With a microphone, her father would add a spoken introduction in a neutral, radio-like voice, involuntary merged with the sound of everyday life. Put together in these three-hour tapes, Brassens' songs became a fluid, almost endless experience.

The open tapes, with their quasi-professional aura, were an alternative to the LPs, and also a monumental precursor to the cassette, my friend said. But while the tapes were her father's thing, the cassettes were her own. She would start recording them in high school by borrowing her friends' LPs. This allowed for an experience that was shorter than listening to open tapes, but one that opened up time in its own way: namely, the freedom to spend the night in her bedroom, alone or not, listening to the music without going to bed at all, or doing in bed other things than sleeping. Yes, she insisted with a smile, tapes were crucial in her early sex life. Eventually some of these cassettes did manage to cross the ocean. They are still in her Parisian apartment, like relics, or archaeological vestiges. I still like to play these cassettes, my friend went on, in my old Sony Professional Walkman – the best recording device ever made, she added, mimicking an imaginary ad. At that point, she read from a paper by Tim Anderson she had to hand:

> Th[e] fetishisation of a recording as a 'time container' is not contingent on whether or not the technology is state-of-the-art. In fact, it is often the case that the most valued recordings are also the most anachronistic. The force of these older recording technologies rests in their perceived abilities to best re-present sensations of times past. (Anderson 2008: 65)

That powerful recording machine, which she showed me right away, had been another turning point in her sonic experience. Walking around while listening to the LPs reproduced in cassettes was an extraordinary experience. Soon she started to make her itineraries coincide with the length and mood of this or that piece, and even to select her destinations according to the music she felt like listening to. The music in her ears would give colour and form to all things real, including the voices she would allow, or not, to get through the curtain of her earphones. Now we're used to that, my friend told me with a smile, but back then it was pretty strange. Time became space, and vice versa.

Even if the country of her birth remained associated for her with the sound of LPs and magnetic tapes, analogue technologies had actually started to fade out some years before she left. To a certain extent, she said, her trip to Europe had begun to take shape in her mind the first time she listened to a CD. In 1984 or 1985, a rich friend who had just brought this new thing from Italy introduced her to the future. She can't remember today what music it was, but she was astonished by its aural perfection, and also by the promise of eternity that this digital, yet hands-off, technology brought along (Straebel 2009). No scratches, no distortions – only fingerprints. It would take her many disenchanting years to realize that the CD, for all its aural fidelity and optical prestige, was in fact the less reliable, most fragile of all recorded music. And of course, she added while showing to me an old Xerox of a *New Yorker* article by David Denby, with CDs you have to deal with 'a slightly unpleasant surprise: the image of your own face staring back from the mirrorlike surface' (Straebel 2009: 24). In any case, for several years the CD was for her no more than a curiosity while visiting the two or three friends who could afford a CD player.

She arrived in Europe a few months after the fall of the Berlin Wall, just in time to see Pink Floyd's *The Wall* performed by Roger Waters at Potsdamer Platz. It was the very first time one of her favourite LPs materialized in music played live by people of flesh and blood not born in her own country. A few weeks later, in Paris, she started, out of nothing, a new collection of records. A collection of CDs, it goes without saying.

Yet, now that she was a graduate student, it was too late for the new CDs to replace the old LPs as a tool for working out her personal identity. Being herself had become something pretty independent of purchasing, possessing and listening to music of her own. On a practical level, rather than replacing her old rock and classical LPs, many of which were never reissued as CDs (Imre and Cox 2009), she looked for more recent discoveries, like Björk and Massive Attack, and for various trends in contemporary music, ranging from Scelsi to Steve Reich to the spectralists to the young French composers trained at Boulez's Institut de Recherche et Coordination Acoustique/Musique. She also remained faithful to classical music, especially when sung by female voices. But her life as a foreign student in Paris didn't allow for much spending on music, let alone the difficulty of storing the CDs in her tiny *chambre de bonne*. So for several years she didn't buy much music at all, and certainly not in the way she used to, namely by asking in a record store for novelties and rarities. Instead, she felt happy just with listening to it, thanks to what she already had, but also to the radio, to public libraries and to some concerts, those she was able to pay for. And she also became very found of silence, she added calmly.

Things changed again for her around 2005, with the stabilization of peer-to-peer technology (Granjon and Combes 2007; Chaney 2008). The emotion of seeing the first MP3 file turn green on her computer screen, to signify that the download was complete, was as strong as the pleasure of listening again to 'D'yer Mak'er', the funny, frenzied Led Zeppelin song she had so often danced to, alone or with friends. Downloading music through eMule, far from making her feeling guilty, gave way to an euphoria of collecting she hadn't experienced since her teens. Without much thought, she started to get MP3 files of all those LPs she had left behind. This even allowed her to complete that period collection with albums she had never owned, or with this or that live recording recently found in some radio station. The pleasure of discovering new old things was not as strong as that of hearing again the actual old material she had at home, but it still added to her feeling of getting back something she had lost. It was as if full regions of her past came back to her. And all for free. For it was both illegal and free, of a kind of freedom that went beyond the issue of money and the lack of it, as well as beyond the issue of the law itself.

She also downloaded hours and hours of music she didn't know: obscure works from famous composers, rare versions of standard works, experimental recordings from this or that experimental artist, like the fabulous, bizarre tango by Vito Acconci she loved so much. It was a wholly chaotic world of music, a world without outer borders or inner logic, except curiosity, routine and chance. For weeks and weeks, night and day, she'd let the downloading go on, on an old computer connected to a big external hard drive. All she had to do was to wait for riches to flood overnight into her ever-growing digital archive. Every morning she would discover the harvest of the night, and with that music in her ears she would work all day on her other, new computer. Technical happiness was in the air.

Within a few months she had more music than she had ever owned, or even dreamed of owning. Some of these pieces would become favourites, while others she would only listen to once or twice. Or never at all, so quickly would her attention focus on something else. Doing several things while listening to the music became a habit. And each day there was so much new stuff on her hard drive that she soon gave up the idea of putting some order to it. After all, she could search any time for whatever she wanted to listen to. As for those pieces she didn't know how to search for, many of them were simply forgotten after the first listening, while others would reappear once in a while, at random. Her hard drive became host to a quite baroque potpourri of genres, periods and people from different places and times. In a certain way, I thought while listening to my friend, the real time of downloading had come to organize the time of her music hearing (Grandjon and Combes 2007).

Lack of time for ordering things was a problem with works in several movements, like classical music or concept rock albums. She never got used to listening randomly or incompletely to *Dichterliebe* or Mahler's Fifth or The Beatles' *Sgt. Pepper* or Gainsbourg's *L'homme à tête de chou*. But her memory was still good enough to replace mentally each number – that is, each MP3 file, in the frame of the complete, original work. LPs' and CDs' track orders had always remained faithful to the composer's intentions, to the score, and to instrumental practice. Not so MP3 files, and that was also true of the ripping of these old CDs, which now looked obsolete without redemption, too ugly and damaged ever to become vintage – but you never know, she whispered.

Even without reading Lydia Goehr, she realized that the very idea of what a music work is was definitely changing, and perhaps fading away (Goehr 1992; Beuscart 2007; Buch 2012). And it must be said, she admitted, that sometimes she would feel strangely satisfied with it. It is weird to listen to Tchaikovsky's *Pathétique* in reverse order. But why, after all, should this beautiful music always finish with the saddest moment?

This euphoria came to a brutal end the day when, without a warning, the external hard drive refused to respond. The computer's error message hit her like the betrayal of a lover. The crash, in fact, affected both her old computer and the hard drive where the files were stored. The storage device wouldn't react either when plugged into the new computer, the one she wanted to spare from the dubious, potentially dangerous business of illegal downloading. So the party was over. She cried, or thought she might want to. Of course, she had known all the time that such a thing might happen. Yet for reasons that were both practical and metaphysical she had decided to leave it up to fate, like people who live on a seismic zone but don't care to reinforce their houses. And fate, or divine punishment, did come one day.

In fact, my friend never knew for sure whether the files were indeed destroyed. Maybe a specialist might still be able to extract them from her damaged hard drive, she added while showing me the big, heavy, obsolete storage device. I don't know what I have and what I lost. What is the ontology of a damaged MP3 file? What would Roger say of *that*? She smiled, alluding to philosopher Roger Pouivet's (2010) case for seeing rock albums as works in themselves, rather than as recordings of these same works, as in the classical music paradigm. Whatever the case, the technical fragility of peer-to-peer exchanges, together with the increasing legal pressure on free downloading, reminded her that the perfect collection had never been anything but a dream.

Before this incident, though, she had started to copy her favourite pieces onto an iPod, a device that, like her old Walkman, allowed her to make space and time to match, while adding new ways of planning her itineraries – namely playlists. So some of the files did survive the crash. Back up, back up, back up everything once and again – the lesson holds for music and desires and memories, she would say to herself. Yet every day she would leave it for some other time. Besides, iPods didn't allow files to be copied back, so the whole business of saving things became uncertain. When in turn the iPod crashed a few months later, she took it stoically, almost fatalistically, as just a confirmation that everything solid melts in the air, as Marx once said. Yet the subjective consequences were more serious than the first time, for after the second crash my friend gave up for good the very idea of possessing music.

She was right, for at that very moment – I'm talking about two or three years ago – streaming services became massive. With Deezer and Spotify, with music records systematically embedded in YouTube clips, there was no point in storing music at home. Streaming, my friend realized, had made the very notion of collection unstable and perhaps obsolete, at least as a way to relate to individual pieces of music as discrete entities. And that was true of the huge collection of records you could find on YouTube, all those pure and poor sounds embedded in faked videos. Obviously, she thought as an echo of her readings of Adorno, the cultural industry had given up making money by pushing people to cumulate physical objects in their domestic environment.

Yet life goes on, and so does business. The shaping of personal identity through recorded music, she explained in a professorial tone, it's all now in the way you surf across the universe. In that digital universe of recorded music, the keyword is: playlist. Play your list, list and play, listen to your play. Playlists, that's where subjectivity is supposed to lie, that's common knowledge now, even if playlists are also provided by streaming services. So now that everything is out there for everybody – I mean, she said, everybody who has access to it – the issue is how to find a personal way to relate to and interact with everything. If you care at all for a personal way of doing things, of course, she added.

As for herself, my friend quickly saw in streaming a new way to reconstruct her old collection of LPs. This time it would be really virtual, because nothing would be actually there in her house, not even in the 'spiritualized' form – she air-quoted – of a computer file. A pure shape. A shape no flood nor fire nor crash nor virus would damage, for it would be only in her head, as pure information.

But was it the third time she would rebuild it? Or the fourth? She could not tell any more. For this time, she said with anxiety in her eyes, the trouble was elsewhere than in the machines. The trouble was with her, with her embodied memory, that of a middle-aged person with, perhaps, too many things accumulated in her mind and cells. Coming after all these technical issues, this was a problem she had never encountered before. The fact is that soon after paying for her first Deezer Premium service, and soon after realizing that YouTube had largely turned that very gesture into a waste of money, her memory had begun to go away. She had more and more trouble remembering the things she once liked to listen to, she was more and more unable to tell whether this or that record did actually belong in her collection. Almost mechanically, her fingers and her mind would search for the old stuff on her computer. But what *was* that old stuff? Frank Zappa's *Joe's Garage* was definitely part of it, she was still able to sing most of the songs: 'Catholic Girls' …. The Beatles' 'Yellow Submarine' was also there, with its quotation of Brahms' Fourth Symphony. And so was Toscanini's Fourth, of course.

But what about Zappa's *Sheik Yerbouti*? What about Beethoven's Seventh by Furtwängler? Were they really in her personal, private, unique, once-in-a-lifetime collection, or were they just reckless leases from some friend too shy to ask for them back? Barenboim and Klemperer's First Beethoven Concerto was surely in it – or was it not? And what about these other songs she once knew by heart? 'Brain Damage': she could still remember, with some blanks, the old Pink Floyd song she had so often tripped to while looking into the ceiling. But for how long would she still remember it without searching for the lyrics in the Internet? And why try to remember lyrics in the first place, since it was so easy to find them on the Internet? Her playlist, rather than reflecting her conscious choices, was becoming like a negative print of her amnesia.

Her memory troubles developed into a new, radical kind of technological disenchantment. Why have a personal playlist? What's the purpose of a collection made, not of objects, but of vanishing memories? And still more radically: Why care about things past? Wouldn't it be better to listen only to new things, or to listen to old ones as if they were new? Why store sounds at home in the first place, whether as scores, plates, tapes, files, playlists or memories? If collections of music are so permanently unstable, why should we recollect music at all? Why do we keep trying to reconstruct old listening experiences? Wouldn't it be better to become deaf to the past? Move away from the recorded past! Move into the unheard-of future of the past!

That was her state of mind, my friend told me, after a sleepless summer night of listening randomly, in a Cagean way, to the murmur of the street below her open windows. At dawn she was in her way to the kitchen when she saw on a shelf Walter Benjamin's *La obra de arte en la edad de su reproductibilidad técnica* (1989), the old volume of collected papers translated into her mother tongue she had brought along on that first trip to Europe. Sitting on her balcony with a big cup of coffee, she skimmed through the pages at random, her eyes attracted by the underlined excerpts she had so often commented on in her classes. Then she started reading it anew from the beginning, without caring for the marks of her former readings, nor for the arrows she had drawn to show the differences between Benjamin's successive versions.

She realized, as if for the first time, how sublimely ambivalent Benjamin was about the past. He had seen better than anyone that mechanical reproducibility was changing the history of culture, without really making up his mind about the value of what had been lost with it. Of course, the principle of mechanical reproduction was not born out of a moral concern, but it had nevertheless triggered an endless moral controversy, with Benjamin as a major actor. Was the vanishing of the aura to be deplored, or was it to be celebrated? Did the distinction between deploring and celebrating make sense at all as far as auras are concerned? The commentators in this famous text had very different views on that, and they were too many to all be remembered and commented on. Even if we should try to make things clear for our dear students, she mumbled with a smile that was both tender and ironic.

Since the start, my friend thought of saying to her students that Adorno's famous letter of March 1936 to Benjamin had put forward a complex field of interpretations. His call to stay away from Brecht could be heard as the pure voice of nostalgia, and not only that of jealousy. Yet 'Schoenberg's music is emphatically *not* auratic,' says Adorno, as if to neutralize the affiliation of avant-garde to Romanticism, and to underline instead its contemporaneity with mechanical reproduction (Adorno and Benjamin 2001: 131). Following him, we can say, she went on, that the ambivalence revolves around the notion of 'technique', which designates things so hopelessly dissimilar as turntables and tonal harmony.

And from then on there had always been some people to read Benjamin's essay as a manifesto for a new politics of art, and some others to read it as an obituary for an old apolitical culture. To see Benjamin as a mere guardian of tradition was ludicrous, she thought, remembering the insolent paper Antoine Hennion and Bruno Latour had dedicated to the essay some years ago: 'L'art, l'aura et la distance selon Benjamin ou comment devenir célèbre en faisant tant d'erreurs à la fois …' (1996). But so was the idea of opposing squarely, as Noël Carroll (1998) and others do, Benjamin's fascination with mass art and Adorno's nostalgia for grand art. In other words, if it is impossible to reach an agreement on the axiological sign of Benjamin's diagnosis, the reason is nowhere to be found but in Benjamin's text.

That day, my friend closed the book before the end. For one thing, she could recall this end, the call to politicize art as a response to fascism's aestheticization of politics. But this *is* the end, all the children are insane, she whispered, with The Doors in her head. She asked herself if it was possible to reflect on the becoming of culture without indulging in some kind of schizoid behaviour, the mind split between past and future, between estrangement and Utopia. She thought yes; then she thought no. She asked herself if it was possible to study the technological mutations of sound recording without indulging in some kind of nostalgia. She answered no, no, no.

My friend meditated for hours, until the sun started to creep down. At dusk, her beautiful head shining like the Virgin Mary's in Fra Angelico's *Annunciazione*, she took her iPhone and recorded an improvised monologue on nostalgia, coloured with echoes of Benjamin, Adorno, Borges, maybe Bareskin, maybe Rupert. Then, without listening to the recording she had just made, she erased it on the spot. From now on she would envision a life saturated with the sound of silence and the silence of theory – including her own theory of cultural silence.

It was precisely at this point that I called her. I'm going to a conference in Venice about listening, I said on the phone, and I need some help. Could I come along? Yes, yes, yes, she answered, but I'm not sure I can help. I'm sure you can. I'm coming. All right. We talked all night. Or rather, she did. She evoked her successive collections of music, her experiences of technological mourning, and her efforts to rationalize nostalgia by reading again and again Walter Benjamin.

A structural condition, that's what the jargon calls it, she said near the end of our conversation. Nostalgia is a structural condition, and also a consequence, of every technique aimed at capturing time as time goes by. And that is particularly true of music, the art of time, right? And if it is true of music, it is also true of most scholarly work about it, even seemingly neutral descriptions of state-of-the-art recording practices. For *nostalgia* designated originally the homesickness, the *Heimweh* of those Swiss mercenaries who, in the eighteenth century, could not hear the national song 'Ranz-des-Vaches' without feeling a furious desire to desert and to return to their country. That's why there is no essential difference between Jean-Jacques Rousseau transcribing in his *Dictionnaire de musique* a live performance of the 'Ranz-des-Vaches' by some alpine actor network, and the first authors who, around the turn of the new millennium, ten years ago, turned the dematerialization of music into a subject of scholarly research. Home is not something you can hear in a record, she said.

In other words – my friend added in a quieter voice, to show that she knew the point was controversial – music is a technique for mechanically reproducing identities by putting a person in contact with her past imagination. If collecting music can become a 'pathology of nostalgia' (Anderson 2008), it is because music is already a remembrance of things past, and for that very reason, a synonym for nostalgia. It is nostalgia itself. By the way, do you remember that scene in *Nostalghia*, Tarkovsky's movie, with the 'Ode to Joy' sounding across a beautiful Italian *piazza*? Do you remember the sound of the tape of Beethoven's Ninth, and the body of that man burning alive while crawling over its distorted recording?

'Now tell me what *you* think,' my friend said.

I didn't really answer. I started mumbling that a case could also be made for recorded music as an experience of the future, or at least as the experience of yearning for the future. Since our childhood, I thought, for myself rather than for her, we have been waiting all the time for a new technology to come. Waiting for the miracle to come, like Leonard Cohen in 'The Future'. The promise of a new listening machine has been a constant in our lives, as well as the promise of a change in the ways of listening and, of course, in the music itself – I mean the music we learned to hear with older machines. But I didn't find the words to make my point. Desire and reproducibility definitely play a part in that story, they are tied together as by some kind of tape. Yes, well, maybe, but how?

I also thought, even if I didn't say it either, that my friend was too busy with the silence of the past not to become deaf to the present – our present, this time in which I kept looking and listening to her without speaking, fascinated by her beautiful mouth and voice, intimidated by her intellectual authority, grateful for her warmth and generosity. I left her house at dawn, and I went directly to the airport, just in time to catch my flight to Venice. I didn't record our talk. I didn't take notes. I told my colleagues all she said exactly as I remembered it. That is, badly.

References

Adorno, Theodor W. and Benjamin, Walter (2001) *The Complete Correspondence, 1928–1940*, ed. Henri Lonitz, trans. N. Walker, Cambridge, MA: Harvard University Press.

Anderson, Tim J. (2008) 'As if History was Merely a Record: The Pathology of Nostalgia and the Figure of the Recording in Contemporary Popular Cinema', *Music, Sound, and the Moving Image*, 2/1, pp. 51–76.

Benjamin, Walter (1989) *Discursos interrumpidos I: Filosofía del arte y de la historia*, trans. J. Aguirre, Buenos Aires: Taurus.

——— (2006) *Berlin Childhood around 1900*, trans. H. Eiland, Cambridge, MA: Harvard University Press.

Beuscart, Jean-Samuel (2007) 'Les transformations de l'intermédiation musicale', *Réseaux*, 141–2/2, pp. 43176.

Buch, Esteban (2012) 'Relire Ingarden: l'ontologie des oeuvres musicales, entre fictions et montagnes', *Intersections: Canadian Journal of Music*, 32/61, pp. 61–81.

Carroll, Noël (1998) *A Philosophy of Mass Art*, New York: Oxford University Press.

Chaney, Damien (2008) 'Pourquoi acheter un CD quand on peut le télécharger?', *Management & Avenir*, 20/6, pp. 30–48.

Glevarec, Hervé and Pinet, Michel (2009) 'La "tablature" des goûts musicaux: un modèle de structuration des préférences et des jugements', *Revue française de sociologie*, 50/3, pp. 599–640.

Goehr, Lydia (1992) *The Imaginary Museum of Musical Works: An Essay in the Philosophy of Music*, Oxford: Clarendon Press.

Granjon, Fabien and Combes, Clément (2007) 'La numérimorphose des pratiques de consommation musicale. Le cas de jeunes amateurs', *Réseaux*, 25/145, pp. 291–334.

Hennion, Antoine and Latour, Bruno (1996) 'L'art, l'aura et la distance selon Benjamin, ou comment devenir célèbre en faisant tant d'erreurs à la fois …', *Cahiers de médiologie*, 1, pp. 234–41.

Imre, Andrea and Cox, Elizabeth J. (2009) 'Are We on the Right Track? Issues with LP Record Collections in U.S. Academic Libraries', *Notes*, 65/3, pp. 475–86.

Peterson, Richard A. (1992) 'Understanding Audience Segmentation: From Elite and Mass to Omnivore and Univore', *Poetics*, 21, pp. 243–58.

Pouivet, Roger (2010) *Philosophie du rock*, Paris: PUF.

Straebel, Volker (2009) 'From Reproduction to Performance: Media-specific Music for Compact Disc', *Leonardo Music Journal*, 19/1, pp. 23–30.

Chapter 4
Music and Technical Reproducibility: A Paradigm Shift

Alessandro Arbo

Technologically Mediated Listening

No one is likely to argue with the contention that musical listening today is above all a technologically mediated phenomenon. It is increasingly rare for listening to involve actual musicians in flesh and blood; we are much more likely to be in the presence of loudspeakers, headphones, screens and all kinds of interfaces. This goes for all genres of music: many are unthinkable without reproduction and recording technology, such as jazz, rock, pop and music made for mass consumption in general, but also traditional forms of music, right down to the galaxy (minor, perhaps, but still a galaxy) of notated music in a European tradition stretching from the Middle Ages to contemporary production. Furthermore, technological mediation is not restricted to recorded music: it also plays a large part in live music, so that the distinction between these two ways of cultivating the musical experience can easily become blurred. One only has to think of major concerts broadcast via livestreaming, corresponding to a reproduction of the event with a varying time lapse, or the operas shown in cinemas worldwide in which, thanks to quite standard electronic equipment, much of the audience is watching a performance that has been filmed and to some extent also 'edited'.

This phenomenon has characterized music reception for over a century. Its origins can be traced back to the second half of the nineteenth century and the invention of the first mechanical systems for recording music (the phonograph and gramophone), but also its diffusion using first electrical then electromagnetic networks (from the Théâtrophone to the radio). Since the early twentieth century – in particular following the celebrated essays published by Benjamin and Adorno in the 1930s (see Benjamin 2008; Adorno 2002) – scholars have been in two minds concerning these innovations. Have we lost or gained by being able to listen to music using radio, records, television, cassettes, and more recently computers, telephones and tablets? In the short term, the answer is surely that we have both lost and gained. The experience of listening to music produced by musicians has become much more limited and informed, but also, more often than not, more exclusive; whereas the experience of music which is broadcast, reproduced or recorded is more common and immediate, but often involves little or no attention paid to the phenomenon. In the long term, the evolution of recording technology has gone hand in hand with a progressive improvement in production standards: this has led to a different balance between the aesthetics of perfection and imperfection (see Hamilton 2003), producing a substantial impact on the procedures of improvised music. There is no doubt that, before attempting any value judgements, we should try to understand properly the changes which, whether we like it or not, have affected the listening experience, resetting the worldwide musical culture.

Let us begin by reviewing the main aspects of the problem researchers have been involved in. Technical reproduction of music has enabled listeners to:

1. approach works, improvisations and music making in general wherever the listeners find themselves, reducing the centrality of reception in standard venues (churches, concert halls, during ceremonies and so on);
2. repeat the listening process at will (leading to new phenomena of inattention and even 'saturation');
3. increase their abilities to analyse the performance (even to the extent of listening 'under the microscope');
4. make compilations of works or excerpts according to personal choice (in playlists that amplify and render more proactive a phenomenon introduced by tape recording).

We have become so used to these possibilities (or to considering these possibilities as implicit in the listening experience) that the technological means have come to be a sort of prosthesis: an instrument we use every day, without being aware of it, to create our preferred soundworld, but also to hear many more things than we could ever hear without it. Now, in the case of notated music (art music or *musique savante*), there does seem to be considerable justification for such transparency. However effective the means prove to be in enhancing listeners' power of analysis (or, we could say, in setting them free from the passive role they have apparently been relegated to in the concert hall), they are obliged to remain 'invisible', just like the spectacles we end up by forgetting we have perched on our nose. We might say that this forms part of the rules of the game when listening to Bach, Beethoven or Brahms (to limit ourselves to the canonical three Bs). But surely this is no longer so true if we extend the series to Boulez, for example. And it becomes even less true (not to say completely untrue) if we go on to evoke Bayle. Why is this? Because in this latter case the technology comes into play right from the outset: it is impossible to conceive of acousmatic music without implying the possibility of duplicating, manipulating and recording sounds or noises, even when they are produced acoustically. However, a more considered answer to this question involves investigating the different possible ways of being of the musical work – examining its ontological status. More specifically, in what follows I shall attempt to present a broad outline of the 'works' which currently constitute the objects of our listening experiences.

Oral, Notated, Phonographic

Our experience of music today can take on a broad range of forms, depending on the amount of attention we are willing to give to the music to which we happen to be listening. On a very basic level, musical objects act as a simple, sonorous backdrop destined to provide, more or less discreetly, furnishings for the moments and/or actions that make up our daily lives (from going shopping in a supermarket to waiting in a subway station and so on). However, if our attention increases, we are soon faced with more complex objects such as works, performances or improvisations, whose reception implicitly leads the listener to adopt one specific attitude or another. For example, when listening to improvised music – whether live or recorded – our expectancies will be concentrated on features such as inventiveness, self-assurance or originality as they emerge during the improvisation, in line with a given performance practice. Among the various ways music presents itself within one area or another of our experience, one in particular should be considered quite closely, given the importance that it has taken on worldwide: the idea of the work.

As is well known, this notion began to assume central importance in the time of Beethoven, with the rise of the concert hall. In such contexts it acts as an ideal, capable of regulating prevailing musical practices.[1] It would, however, be an error to consider it solely in this light, excluding the fact that it corresponds to a certain kind of entity or again restricting its application to a historically and geographically limited repertory such as 'art' music from the classical period to our day. In reality, a recording by U2 or a popular villotta from the Friuli region of Italy are also generally identified as musical works. Broadly speaking, when we talk about a musical work, we refer to a socially constructed artefact (see Davies 2003: 40–46) whose nature implies an intentional origin and an aesthetic function.[2] Unlike natural objects, by definition a work has an author (maybe more than one person, and possibly anonymous). To attest the author's existence implies the presence not only of human beings endowed with the sense of hearing, but also of listeners possessing certain cultural, or more generally cognitive, dispositions. Moreover, the constitution of the work depends on fixing a trace or an inscription (without which it is difficult to explain the functioning of the social object) (see Ferraris 2009: 176–9).

In a more specific sense, the reception of a 'work' of music implies that the sounds are not grasped generically – that is, considering only general aesthetic or expressive qualities that may emerge such as softness, drive, ruggedness and so on – but of qualities perceived as the result of an intentional activity rooted in a given context of artistic production. As complex as this way of listening may seem cognitively speaking, it is actually one of the most common, at least in cases in which the music in question is the object of a non-distracted act of listening: that

---

1 See the well-known analysis of Goehr (1992), esp. pp. 89–119.

2 See the definition of the work of art proposed in Pouivet (2007): 7–66. For a discussion of a number of more specific definitions of the musical work of art, see Garda (2007): 310–12.

which we are listening to, when we put a CD in the stereo or click on a YouTube link, is not simply generically music, but, let's say, a traditional Calabrian song, the album *The Six Wives of Henri VIII* (1973) by Rick Wakeman or Bach's *Cello Suite No. 2* played by Mario Brunello.

In principle, human memory can cope with the transmission of a piece of music, as is evident in oral cultures. Even though it may seem inappropriate to speak of 'works',[3] it is possible to recognize the transmission of pieces or repertories associated with practices that may be highly specialized. The introduction of notation marked a turning point in guaranteeing the identity and stability of repertories, with the transmission of the fundamental parameters of pitch, duration and, to a certain extent, the timbre of the sounds involved in the piece. The advent of reproduction and recording technologies constituted a further step forward in the evolution of the art, transmitting the specific sound qualities.[4] This process has transformed the whole status of the 'audio' dimension: when emancipated from the parameters that serve to describe it and inscribe it on the stave, sound takes on the value of an 'authentic "object" produced by a machine and wholly submitted to the expertise and discretion of a musician who is at one and the same time a technician and a sound engineer' (Molino 2008: 74).

When examining how musical cultures organize themselves, it is appropriate to highlight the diversity of the means used to conserve the trace: in oral cultures the memory of musicians and listeners; in written cultures the score; in phonographic cultures the technological data storage devices – discs, tapes and memories, whether magnetic or based on semiconductors. In the first case, the (psychological) memory transmits a performance scheme based on sensorimotor skills, which are often 'audio-tactile' (Caporaletti 2005: 74–5): they correspond to the chief structural features of the musical object, identifiable in morphologies of intervals, intensity, rhythms and vocal or gestural inflections which can be very subtle. In the second, a graphic or notational trace represents the instruction required to produce the desired musical object. The identification of the work, or of one instance of it, becomes independent from the history of its production, tending towards the status of the allographic arts (see Goodman 1968: 117–22). In the third case, a specimen of the work is generated from a trace fixed on an external support thanks to adequate decodification of the data provided by a mechanical, electrical or electronic device. As has often been observed, this third stage, by doing without the mediation of the musician-performer implied in the second stage, makes the relationship between the listener and the work more direct, thus appearing to return somehow to the first case (some analysts speak of 'secondary orality', starting from Ong 2002). Actually, as we shall see in what follows, it is important to maintain a clear distinction between the two cases, and to speak of 'phonography' in the latter case.

---

3 I have already argued in favour of this hypothesis in Arbo (2014b).

4 These changes have been succinctly summarized by Jacques Haïns (2001: 817): the recording contains the potential for 'a new musical aesthetic' able to integrate not only the traditional parameters but also control over intensity, spatiality and timbre.

Taking into account its essential features, a work in the oral tradition relies on a scheme that can be memorized and adapted to a whole range of situations: variations, modifications and adaptations are all part of its nature (see Molino 2007: 488). Using the terminology introduced by Roman Ingarden and adapted by Stephen Davies to show the differences between the main types of oral production, we can say that here the work is ontologically 'thin': the distance between the given scheme and its realization is significant (the performance features more attributes than are contained in the trace) (see Ingarden 1986: 9–14; Davies 2001: 20). However, this should not lead to the conclusion that this type of artefact has no real prescriptive value: a deviation from the scheme can be considered erroneous or excessive by an audience of competent musicians and listeners, demonstrating that it can be inadequate to be reproduced or varied in terms of performing practices.

In notated music, which has the specific attribute of a trace fixed thanks to some notational criteria, a 'thinner' structure (a type) continues to give rise to a 'thicker' entity (its occurrence). In this kind of music, however, the correspondence of the latter to the former is established in a more binding manner. The notation ensures a prescription when it occurs in what Nelson Goodman (1968: 134) has called a 'notational system' based on a syntactic requirement of 'disjointness'. In reality, every musical notation demonstrates that this principle applies only to part of the instructions given to the performer, who has available many possibilities. Lastly, the phonographic work, in its identification with an audio (or audiovisual) trace fixed on an external support, cancels every difference between performing scheme, score and performance, thereby manifesting the greatest degree of ontological thickness (and for this reason is sometimes defined as 'saturated') (see Pouivet 2010: 63). This is the case for much electronic music and rock music, and perhaps even more obviously for some of their specific derivations, such as techno, noise, dubstep and so on.

As media studies have suggested, the dynamics of composition go hand in hand with the way in which the technologies of memorization and transmission of the traces are developed. This is certainly true also in our case (see Tiffon 2005): the way in which the trace is fixed is important in understanding how musical works function, and consequently the criteria for appreciating and organizing the perceivable data that we count on when listening. To go back to our example, our awareness in front of a notated artefact, based on a score, means that, for the canonical three Bs, we tend to think of the work as a specific relationship of one particular entity (the performance) to another (the score). We can insist on one or the other, but without necessarily implying the presence of a means of reproduction, which we expect to document as faithfully as possible the specific realization of this process (for years the obsession with hi-fi has been going in this direction: even today, anyone who purchases the extraordinary Bose loudspeakers generally expects such transparency).[5]

[5] For an interesting enquiry into the socio-technical aspects of hi-fi and their fundamental contrast with those of digital music, see Magaudda (2008): 259–63.

Let us take, instead, the case of electroacoustic music, acousmatic music or a disc by Pink Floyd. Here, right from the beginning, the work depends on technological manipulation, and in particular on the editing of a master. In other terms, we are no longer in the presence of the – more or less successful or sophisticated – recording of a work; we are now facing a new reality which, according to Theodore Gracyk's thesis on rock music, philosophers tend nowadays to label the 'recording artefact' or 'work-recording' (see Gracyk 1996; Edidin 1999; Pouivet 2010; Darsel 2009: 178–82). In particular, it has been argued that a work of rock coincides not with the audio structure constituted by the recorded song, but with the studio-constructed track (see Kania 2006; Kania and Gracyk 2011: 86). In this case, recording has introduced a radical change, modifying all the levels of attention we implement in the act of listening: the work involves not only pitches, rhythms and degrees of intensity conceived by the composer, but a whole 'sound' audible in all its irreducible uniqueness.

If the passage from oral to notated to phonographic can be seen as a historical development, there must be no misconceptions about this progression. In particular, the advent of an operational mode based on a new support or a new memorization technique does not imply a sudden change in the status quo, and nor is it necessarily exclusive: far from replacing what came before, the two overlap, and the previous mode goes on working in a more limited way. This has meant, for example, not only that oral works have continued to exist following the advent of writing and recording, but that certain aspects of a notated or phonographic work can still be linked to an oral form of transmission. A Chopin mazurka not only tolerates, but actually demands a large number of deviations from the notation: to a great extent, these depend on performing conventions passed down by example (and that can be attributed in part to schools of interpretation characterized by particular features sometimes identified across several generations). To go back to the example of rock music, it comes as no surprise that a work fixed once and for all in an album can be re-created in a concert, where it behaves according to the modalities of oral music (with variations, solos, new arrangements and improvisations all being part of the re-creation); it can even be the subject of a transcription, down to the slightest details.

Recording, Works, Performances

Fundamentally, one can say that with the development of phonography, musical recording has revealed its two-faced character. It presents itself on the one hand as the document or 'mere' record of a musical event (where the quotation marks highlight the difficulty of the concept of total neutrality: it is no secret that simply positioning the microphones differently can modify the perspective in an auditory scene), and on the other as a laboratory for the construction of the musical object.

Record ← Musical recording → Construction

This conceptual tension highlights the fact that the means of reproduction/recording no longer appear as the *vehicle* of an autonomous musical reality: in many cases they are a *catalyst* determining its essential aspects. As we have seen, in the first place this paradigm shift concerns the musical genres created in the wake of technical reproducibility, like jazz, rock and pop, but also many other 'contaminations' that flourished in close symbiosis with the record trade. However, it has had a different effect on a much broader perspective. If we go back to the three Bs, can we still say that, when we listen to a Beethoven symphony by the Berliner Philharmoniker under Herbert von Karajan, or to Glenn Gould playing a piece by Bach, we are hearing the document of a performance? Practically never: in both cases, the disc is the outcome of the ingenious editing of a series of original sound takes. The technological means has enabled us to listen to a version that not only has never been played, but in some cases could never have been: one only has to think of certain *p* or *pp*, simply unattainable on brass instruments, or the sound of a piano that seems to become suddenly darker or to move away from the listener.[6]

These objects, too, appear as new artefacts populating our musical world. However extreme the case of Gould may have been with respect to his era, nowadays it is a commonplace: the work of performers is hardly over once they have played the last note in the work (assuming that they have in fact played it through from beginning to end). In a certain sense, the interpretation is prolonged in the recording studio: mixing, balancing the volumes, choosing the right takes deeply influences the outcome. When we are dealing with notated works, what we hear on disc or online should coincide with the document of a work's performance. But our attention is actually focused on a result that we can only presume coincides with a musical event situated in a specific time and space: more often it is the synthesis of a number of events selected and edited in a certain manner. This leads to the problem of the authenticity of the recording *vis-à-vis* its source, which in some famous cases has verged on counterfeiting (like the one, recounted by producer John Culshaw, of the high Cs sung by Elisabeth Schwarzkopf to help out Kirsten Flagstad: see Haïns 2001: 808). As Evan Eisenberg has pointed out, the evolution of the modalities of discographic production documents the passage – involving three generations of producers represented by Fred Gaisberg, Walter Legge and John Culshaw (see Eisenberg 1987: ch. 8) – to a stage where the recording is appraised not according to its ability to reconstruct an original soundscape, but rather as an independent and original artefact.

This change is generally clear to performers of and listeners to many musical genres, who recognize the difference between a recorded and live version of the same piece. However, the tendency to ask the former to reflect the latter has taken on new forms which generally reveal a greater awareness of the impossibility of

6 These aspects, which have often been remarked on, have been examined by Pierre Emmanuel Lephay (2014).

bridging the gap.[7] In a situation characterized by an extreme variety of tastes and criteria, this consciousness goes hand in hand with the need to go back to sound recordings that are as direct and natural as possible (a need asserted by many producers of the baroque and classical-romantic repertory).

In any reflection on the role played by recording and technical reproduction in the creation of artefacts presupposing new forms of listening, it is important to distinguish between two basic situations: (1) the *construction* of a work and (2) the preparation of a definitive version of the *interpretation* of a work, involving editing and fine-tuning in the post-production phase. For this second outcome, the term 'recordings of compositions' is sometimes used (see Edidin 1999). This expression highlights two significant aspects: first, the composition exists prior to the recording; secondly, through the work carried out in the studio, the performer seeks to highlight all its distinctive features, in particular the ones which are difficult (if not impossible) to perform, although indicated in the score: for example, a sudden *pianissimo* by a wind section which could never be attained at that pitch, or a sound marked 'at a distance' which is literally projected to the rear of the hall. Another solution consists in speaking of 'works of phonography'.[8] However, I prefer to consider all these artefacts as 'works of performance'[9] because it seems to me that when the musician-performer (or the musician directing the performance) highlights certain aspects of the work or the improvisation, she/he actually intends to call attention to the specific performance she/he has sought to achieve. The idea of 'construction of a work' can account for most of the electronic or electroacoustic music produced in the studio, but also for much of the discographic production of rock and pop music; while that of 'construction of a work of performance' covers the recordings of most of the Western musical repertory in the notated tradition, from the Middle Ages to the present, and to a certain extent also the recordings of much improvised music.

This demarcation is very rough and ready. It becomes indispensable, however, when we think of the way in which the listener's attention and judgement are oriented (granting the listener a degree of competence with respect to the genre in question). Let us again consider rock music. The idea of identifying the work with a master disc that can be duplicated in its entirety and which is not susceptible to modification seems valid if we consider how it is treated in certain networks of evaluation and appreciation: for a specialist of this genre, no re-make or re-mix – still less a cover – could ever replace the original version of *The Dark Side of the Moon*. But in a concert situation we do not expect the work to function like this. We know perfectly well that we are not there to listen to a disc: variations and differences in instrumentation are part of the live experience, and indeed constitute much of the anticipated pleasure.

---

7 See Nicholas Cook's (1998: 9–11) observations concerning the inability of the Pet Shop Boys, as they themselves candidly acknowledged, to recreate on stage the sound obtained in the recording studio.

8 As proposed by Lee B. Brown (2000).

9 I first introduced this notion in Arbo (2014a), see esp. pp. 182–5.

This means that even if the piece itself (the structure or a certain melodic or harmonic scheme) does not *constitute* the work as a whole, it plays a primary part in its nature. In other words, in the live version, rock is listened to as 'oral music' or, if we prefer to avoid this rather ambiguous label, as music based on an 'audio-tactile' principle.[10] The same cannot be said about much electronic or acousmatic music (typically the works produced during the 1950s in the Cologne and Paris studios, but also the experimental electronics generated in rock and pop music). In this case, it surely responds to the maximum ontological density of the recording artefact. Here the ideal of transparency loses much of its *raison d'être*: what can we imagine 'transmitting' the recording of a piece like *Le tièdre* by Pierre Schaeffer? Its soundscape does not have the substance of an event or a performance act recorded in the real world. Works of mixed music, or live electronics, represent a different case, occupying a no man's land – even though the fact that the listener's attention is clearly focused on the ability of the performer suggests a considerable diminution in the ontological thickness. Closer inspection reveals important differences in the functioning of artefacts: while implying the process of construction in the studio, some have their origin in a performance, and others seem to have definitively done away with such an origin. However, I am convinced that we need to come up with a fundamental demarcation in order to avoid confusing musical objects that have different forms of reception and evaluation. Once again, the difference may seem banal in the case of written cultures, but surely less banal in examples that lie in the no man's land between one context and another – in pieces which combine real-time electronics, recorded electronics and instrumental performance, or again pieces with notated sections alternating with improvised parts. In fact, our ability to evaluate and react correctly depends on our knowledge of the artefact.

What we have called 'works of performance' normally bear the signature of a performer or the main performers, who are responsible for the final product. This element has taken on such importance on disc covers, and in the tags which accompany MP3 and MP4 files, as to almost entirely eclipse the other protagonists in the production process, from the producer him/herself to the sound engineers and technicians. This is evident in the record business: customers do not actually want to hear the Saint-Saëns Violin Concerto in itself, but how Renaud Capuçon interprets this work – the product is a 'work of performance', in fact, awaited for its novelty and artistic interest.

Beyond the Work

I have insisted on speaking of 'works' because in practice this notion still plays a central role in most of today's musical cultures. However, this should not conceal another vast sphere influenced by technical reproducibility: improvisation. This term is used for a whole galaxy of practices which in fact differ greatly: they may

[10] I refer to the sense of this term in Caporaletti (2005): 74–82.

be applied to a given material (either melodic or rhythmic), but also its absence. We speak of improvisation referring both to oral transmission in folk traditions before the advent of technical reproducibility (such as the *katajjaq* competitions among Inuit women, traditional Indian music, a lot of Asiatic and African music, and so on) and to jazz, whose origins and development are bound up with the advent of phonography (see Eisenberg 1987: 143). Moreover, there are many other musical practices that are strictly dependent on electronic equipment for the amplification and manipulation of sound (the wide spectrum of what is called experimental music, often based on the combination of acoustic and electronic instruments, and in which the sound may be processed in real time).

As soon as we venture into this vast phenomenology, the boundaries between improvisation and work cannot be established clearly and coherently. There are works that contain improvised parts, just as there are improvisations based on very detailed instructions and with a specific prescriptive value. Nonetheless, it is less plausible to speak of a work in cases where the performance is extemporized without any specific normative intention. It would be improper to consider as a work a performance of *katajjaq* filmed and reproduced on YouTube, or the recording of an improvisation of Indian music.

It would undoubtedly be more difficult to decide to which category the recordings of Keith Jarrett's improvisations should be assigned as constituting documents of an improvisation bearing its author's signature. The hypothesis that we are dealing with a work seems to be borne out when we consider how the artefact is considered in many reception contexts;[11] however, we cannot do away with every ambiguity, not least because a jazz improvisation does not start life as an object intended to be re-performed, but as a unique event situated in space and time.[12] This calls into question an essential requisite for the idea of a musical work: the intention of creating an artefact that can be re-identified. Many improvisations have been the subject of meticulous transcriptions, often being the basis for further performances; but in these cases it is difficult to bridge the gap separating the descriptive value of the transcription from the normative value of the score.[13] The latter case, in fact, seems to edge us towards a different criterion of appreciation: in listening to a good performance of such a score, we would consider aesthetic properties that are very different than those applied to the original (the correctness and at the same time 'lifelike' character of certain dynamics or phrasing, for example, rather than the melodic or harmonic inventiveness). It seems more correct in this case to speak of a work derived from (or based on) an improvisation, not of the improvisation as a work.

---

[11] As Eisenberg (1987: 150) suggests, 'in jazz the record is the work'. This is also the position of Caporaletti (2005): 80.

[12] It is no coincidence that many of Jarrett's improvisations are referred to by the venue in which they took place, starting with the celebrated *The Köln Concert*.

[13] The debate has been well summarized in Davies (2001): 11–19.

Lastly, the sphere of improvised musical practices also includes the various experiences of the 'happening', first introduced during the 1960s, or the musical installations which, in view of their extemporaneous character, can be associated with experiences of environmental art. Here the idea of work seems to be definitively undermined, or indeed excluded, by the aim of inducing a certain attitude in the 'artist-listener' or the 'artist-spectator'. Technical reproducibility has had only a limited impact on this brand of practice: perhaps, in view of the enormous diffusion of recorded music, such experiences have taken on an even more particular and exclusive significance than they could originally claim.

In a different direction, it would seem that the new forms of data transmission that have appeared in recent years – from peer-to-peer networks to webcasting – have put the work's centrality to the test, challenging its role as the prevailing model for the conception and reception of music. Owing to the more differentiated and decontextualized forms of listening it has produced, the Internet seems to have brought about a fragmentation of the units of meaning (in one way or another favoured by audio formats such as LPs, CDs or DVDs) that had characterized the production of both popular and art music until the early twenty-first century. Music production has in fact witnessed a tendency towards easily convertible tracks that can furthermore be decomposed and recomposed at will, often intended for tablet apps and provided with interactive content including texts, images and videos (such as Björk's 2011 app album *Biophilia*) (see Ghosn 2013: 29–34). It is too soon to say whether this type of production will in the medium term mark the end of the idea of the work, or will relaunch it in different forms. It is perhaps meaningful to note that, above and beyond the proliferation of formats, the most technologically advanced productions continue, at least in the majority of cases, to be associated with a relatively simple and well-defined intentional origin. This origin is in turn associated with a specific individuality that is either creative (the artist who wrote the music, even though, often, nothing was actually written) or performative (the talented musician thanks to whom the aesthetic qualities of the music produced become palpable) – in spite of the fact that the productions in question often result from a complex and well-organized exercise in teamwork.

Item: Music

As Eisenberg remarked, the term 'recording' seems inadequate when we talk about the result of work in the studio: these recordings no longer 'record' anything whatsoever. They are a phono-montage or, in his words, the 'composite photograph of a minotaur' (Eisenberg 1987: 89). We are so used to this phenomenon that we do not even realize that the natural order of things has been completely subverted: a live performance in which we fail to perceive the dynamic contrasts we are familiar with from a disc can strike us as ineffective, unmusical or even unnatural (for example, a guitar will always be too weak compared to the orchestra, the sheer volume of sound will never be sufficient in a large hall, and so on). Acting on

Andy Hamilton's idea of applying to musical recording what Benjamin wrote about photography, it is surely not far-fetched to say: 'Much futile thought had been devoted to the question of whether recording is an art. The primary question – whether the very invention of recording had not transformed the entire nature of music as an art – was not rad' (Hamilton 2003: 354).

What makes this problem particularly insidious is the fact that, with the passage to technical reproducibility, music has not undergone a change of name. In my opinion, this detail is highly significant: when discussing photography or cinema, we implicitly recognize that these are new arts, distinct from what preceded them (painting and theatre, respectively), whereas we continue to use the same term for music that has been constructed and edited in the studio: what should strictly perhaps be called 'phonography' – when we refer, for example, to *Urania* by Pan Sonic – is still presented in the same category as a Palestrina motet (see Figure 4.1).

	Technical reproduction ↓	
Painting	→	Engraving, lithography, photography
Theatre	→	Cinema, video art
Music	→	Music

Figure 4.1 Generation of new arts by virtue of mechanical reproduction

To consider the problem from a different point of view, we can say that the advent of technical reproducibility has brought about a further semantic broadening: in practice, nowadays 'music' denotes a vast and very heterogeneous quantity of objects, processes, practices and artefacts. To adopt Goodman's distinction, technical reproducibility has fostered a change from the status of a prevalently *allographic* art (as in written cultures) to that of a prevalently *autographic* art *with multiple specimens*. This change has to be borne in mind when we consider the experience of listening to musical artefacts in the iPad era. If an audio or video track recorded by Gould can be seen (and evaluated) as an interpretation of a work by Bach, it is at the same time an original 'performance work': an artefact, bearing a signature, that can be 're-created' as often as you like. It is unique and remarkable, for all its distance (at times measured in light years!) from anything Bach himself could ever have imagined. Indeed, one could say, using Goodman's terms once again, that such an artefact is no longer a specimen of the work by Bach, but a new work that alludes to that of Bach.

More generally, according to the organization of phonographic cultures today, for the listener a recording can stand as: (1) the document of a performance of a musical work or of an improvisation, (2) a performance work realized using studio technology (and impossible without it) or (3) the musical work itself (the recording artefact, from Stockhausen to pop). We can note that while listeners can occasionally distinguish (or believe they can) between the document of a performance and the construction of a performance work, in most cases we cannot expect the ear to register significant differences.[14] This is because the criterion is epistemic, not phenomenological: the classification depends on what we know with respect to the genesis of the artefact (acquired from the documents that accompany it: labels, texts or information provided with its circulation). In order to grasp the sense of this difference, we can observe that the document of a single performance can present itself – without there having to be any studio manipulation – as a performance work, on condition that the performer recognizes it as such, whereas a performance work does not necessarily correspond to the document of a performance (at most, it can be seen as creating the illusion of an actual performance). In listening with a proper awareness, what enables us to choose is to bear in mind the intentions – if not declared, at least conjectural – of the musician who produced the artefact.

Conclusion

We might conclude by emphasizing that, if our way of listening has undergone such profound changes, this is not only because technology has enhanced our hearing, but because it has deeply modified the identity of the object of this listening: that extraordinary confluence of sounds, meanings and values which, in spite of everything, we continue to call music. In particular, this convergence has influenced the way in which music is presented as a work or an artefact tied to a given context of production. Technical reproducibility has multiplied the types of works in our musical universe, and has at the same time weakened the meaning of the notion of the work and made its confines more unstable. We now find ourselves confronted not only with the document of the performance of a work or an improvisation, but very often also with recording-constructed works or performance works. The complexity of the ensuing phenomenology represents a challenge for musicological research today, taking into account an ever broader typology of artefacts seen in the light of the contexts in which they are produced and received.

Translated by Mark Weir

References

Adorno, Theodor W. (2002) *On the Fetish-character in Music and the Regression of Listening*, in *Essays on Music*, ed. Richard Leppert, trans. Susan Gillespie, Berkeley, CA: University of California Press, pp. 288–317.

[14] The problem has been pointed out, with reference to the categories of Edidin, by Kania and Gracyk (2011): 85–6.

Arbo, Alessandro (2014a) 'Qu'est-ce qu'un enregistrement musical(ement) véridique?', in *Musique et enregistrement*, ed. Pierre-Henry Frangne and Hervé Lacombe, Rennes: PUR, pp. 173–92.

——— (2014b) 'Qu'est-ce qu'une œuvre musicale orale?', in *Les corpus de l'oralité*, ed. Mondher Ayari and Antonio Lai, Vallier: Delatour France, pp. 25–45.

Benjamin, Walter (2008) *The Work of Art in the Age of its Technological Reproducibility, Second Version*, in *The Work of Art in the Age of its Technological Reproducibility, and Other Writings on Media*, ed. Michael W. Jennings, Brigid Doherty and Thomas Y. Levin, trans. Edmund Jephcott, Rodney Livingstone, Howard Eiland et al., Cambridge, MA: Harvard University Press, pp. 19–55.

Brown, Lee B. (2000) 'Phonography, Rock Records, and the Ontology of Recorded Music', *Journal of Aesthetics and Art Criticism*, 58/4, pp. 361–72.

Caporaletti, Vincenzo (2005) *I processi improvvisativi nella musica. Un approccio globale*, Lucca: LIM.

Cook, Nicholas (1998) *Music: A Very Short Introduction*, New York: Oxford University Press.

Darsel, Sandrine (2009) 'Qu'est-ce qu'une œuvre musicale?', *Klesis – Revue philosophique*, 13, pp. 178–82.

Davies, Stephen (2001) *Musical Works and Performances: A Philosophical Exploration*, Oxford: Oxford University Press.

——— (2003) *Themes in the Philosophy of Music*, Oxford: Oxford University Press.

Edidin, Aaron (1999) 'Three Kinds of Recordings and the Metaphysics of Music', *British Journal of Aesthetics*, 30/1, pp. 24–39.

Eisenberg, Evan (1987) *The Recording Angel: Explorations in Phonography*, New York: McGraw-Hill.

Ferraris, Maurizio (2009) *Documentalità. Perché è necessario lasciare tracce*, Rome: Laterza.

Garda, Michela (2007) 'Le teorie dell'opera d'arte musicale nel Novecento', in *Storia dei concetti musicali*, vol. 2: *Espressione, forma, opera*, ed. Gianmario Borio and Carlo Gentili, Rome: Carocci, pp. 295–316.

Ghosn, Joseph (2013) *Musiques numériques. Essai sur la vie nomade de la musique*, Paris: Seuil.

Goehr, Lydia (1992) *The Imaginary Museum of Musical Works*, Oxford: Oxford University Press.

Goodman, Nelson (1968) *Languages of Art: An Approach to a Theory of Symbols*, Indianapolis, IN: Bobbs-Merrill.

Gracyk, Theodore (1996) *Rhythm and Noise: An Aesthetics of Rock*, Durham, NC: Duke University Press.

Haïns, Jacques (2001) 'Dal rullo di cera al CD', in *Enciclopedia della musica*, vol. 4: *Piaceri e seduzioni della musica del XX secolo*, ed. Jean-Jacques Nattiez, Turin: Einaudi, pp. 783–819.

Hamilton, Andy (2003) 'The Art of Recording and the Aesthetics of Perfection', *British Journal of Aesthetics*, 43/4, pp. 345–62.

Ingarden, Roman (1986) *The Work of Music and the Problem of its Identity*, trans. Adam Czerniawski, Berkeley, CA: University of California Press.

Kania, Andrew (2006) 'Making Tracks: The Ontology of Rock Music', *Journal of Aesthetics and Art Criticism*, 64/4, pp. 401–14.

——— and Gracyk, Theodore (2011) 'Performances and Recordings', in *The Routledge Companion to Philosophy and Music*, ed. Andrew Kania and Theodore Gracyk, London: Routledge, pp. 80–90.

Lephay, Pierre Emmanuel (2014) 'La prise de son et le mixage, éléments de l'interprétation. Les exemples de Herbert von Karajan et Glenn Gould', in *Musique et enregistrement*, ed. Pierre-Henry Frangne and Hervé Lacombe, Rennes: PUR, pp. 113–22.

Magaudda, Paolo (2008) 'Tecnologie musicali e pratiche di ascolto: i quadri socio-tecnici dell'alta fedeltà e dell'mp3', in *L'ascolto musicale. Condotte, pratiche, grammatiche*, ed. Daniele Barbieri, Luca Marconi and Francesco Spampinato, Lucca: LIM, pp. 257–66.

Molino, Jean (2007) 'Qu'est-ce que l'oralité musicale?', in *Musiques. Une encyclopédie pour le XXIe siècle, vol. 5: L'Unité de la musique*, ed. Jean-Jacques Nattiez, Paris and Arles: Cité de la Musique and Actes Sud, pp. 477–527.

——— (2008) 'Musique, Technique, Innovation', in *Il nuovo in musica. Estetiche, technologie, linguaggi*, ed. Rossana Dalmonte and Francesco Spampinato, Lucca: LIM, pp. 57–83.

Ong, Walter (2002) *Orality and Literacy: The Technologizing of the Word*, New York: Routledge.

Pouivet, Roger (2007) *Qu'est-ce qu'une œuvre d'art*, Paris: Vrin.

——— (2010) *Philosophie du rock. Une ontologie des artefacts et des enregistrements*, Paris: PUF.

Tiffon, Vincent (2005) 'Pour une médiologie musicale comme mode original de connaissance', *Filigrane*, 1, pp. 115–39.

Chapter 5

Algorithmic and Nostalgic Listening: Post-subjective Implications of Computational and Empirical Research

Sebastian Klotz

Music perception is one of the most dynamic fields in music cognition studies, in music psychology and in empirical and systematic musicology. It is rarely considered, though, how perception becomes visible and how it is being prepared for scientific treatment. It clearly organizes in complex ways cultural and social dispositions, knowledge forms and communicative expectations. These implications become evident once one abandons a positivistic stance towards empirical findings so that the conceptual framings, the motivation of research procedures and the cultural assumptions about listening become manifest. I propose to use the culturally informed term 'listening' in order to capture the full complexity of human auditory appropriation which cannot be addressed from the more narrow perspective of perception. To clarify my approach, some key questions are addressed: How can functional and contextual methodologies be combined in order to achieve a richer understanding of music perception? How do culturalistic and empirical paradigms of listening interact? To what extent do media technologies steer research paradigms concerning auditory perception in cognitive and computational musicology? How is the relation to cultural meanings and to biographical and cultural learning processes addressed, if at all? Which paradigms observe the technological mediatedness of auditory objects?

This project is nurtured by the fact that musicology in general finds itself at a critical juncture that deeply affects its research agenda, habits of co-operation and its place within the humanities and empirical sciences.[1]

I will pay particular attention to the conceptualization and situatedness of listening in different research scenarios. This serves to underline the many approaches to human – and technologically informed – listening. I will focus on the following four research arenas spanning the last 15 years, listed with key questions and typical research procedures:

1. Culturalistic musicology/musical semantics; non-experimental – How and what do sounds signify in the listening process?

[1] See European Science Foundation (2012), co-edited by the author.

2. Corpus-based musical feature extraction; coupling psychological tests with the computational modelling ('algorithmic listening') of human listening – What is the implicit knowledge of listeners *vis-à-vis* popular music?
3. Studies of autobiographical memories in music cognition ('nostalgic listening'); elaborate time-dependent localization procedure; hypotheses of cortical networks evoked by music – Do autobiographically familiar tracks show a different cognitive representation?
4. The social systems theory of musical cognition – If experimental music resists pure referentiality and causality, what do the sounds evoke if not their own operativity, which in turn is directed towards (and indeed mirrors) the dynamics of human consciousness?

Musical Semiosis: The Model of the Sonic Saddle

In 1997 John Shepherd and Peter Wicke proposed a performative semiological model of the perception of sounds and the auditory construction of meaning (see Figure 5.1). The auditory objects of (popular) music, with a critical sound dimension, pose an analytical challenge to traditionally text-oriented musicology. The authors draw on post-structuralist literary theory, on the functional semantics of language and music, and on the works of Victor Zuckerkandl, a key source on the phenomenology of sounds and their existential relationship with human beings. Furthermore, materialist music sociologies are relevant to the appropriation of sounds as a social practice able to generate social configurations.

The model assumes a dynamic plateau of acoustic perception to which we project our hearing capacities and which organizes the elements, leading to a construction of meaning on the listeners' side. Syntactic processes tied to the dimension of metre, timbre, inflection, pitch and duration are elements of immediate material relevance. The sonic saddle arises out of the medium, as a dynamic sound-image belonging to the world of inner and constructed experience. In the saddle, the elements that feed into music's semanticity are co-extensive with the dynamic states of human consciousness. The saddle enables a music-based construction of meaning that works distinct from language-based processing of meaning. The saddle replaces the signifier and allows a simultaneous articulation of inner and outer, social and discursive worlds. The authors focus on the modalities of the musical construction of meaning, as proved by the model of the sonic saddle emerging as a technology of articulation (see Shepherd and Wicke 1997: 164).

Despite the absence of empirical modelling, it represents a bold and thought-provoking theoretical proposal. The saddle appears to be less a model of the listening process than of the agencies implicated in the construction of meaning.

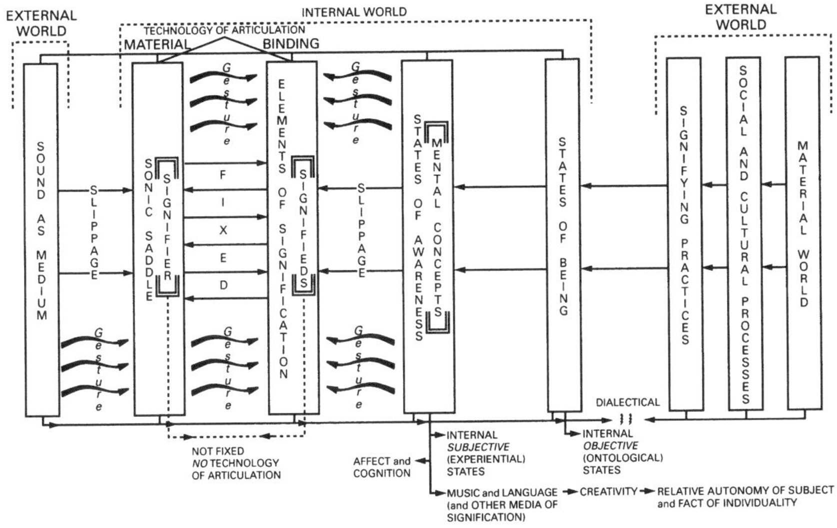

Figure 5.1 In this semiological model, the sonic saddle (second box from the left) mediates between the external and internal world

Source: Shepherd and Wicke (1997): 173. Reprinted by kind permission of Polity Press.

It is situated in a psychological presence whose interconnection to empirical cognitive research remains unclear. On the other hand, it evidences the difficulties that music cognition studies suffer in addressing the creation of meaning as soon as it cannot be empirically modelled. New musicology rarely puts forward workable theoretical models that could serve as a basis for a cross-disciplinary dialogue with experimental studies. The sonic saddle fulfils the role of a model within a competitive academic environment, in which it should stimulate discussion and a critical testing of the hypotheses. The point is that this critical dialogue with cognition studies rarely takes place. The sonic saddle addresses fundamental concerns and offers a complex theory which is condensed into a model that carries well-argued assumptions and a refined thesis; however, the project has been completely ignored by the neighbouring research communities. To the empirical community, the lack of references to this field and to applied research in general did not arouse any interest. This should not hamper the future development of alternative models aiming at a sound-based understanding of music. The poor reception of the sonic saddle is evidence of the proliferation of research arenas and of the scarce interaction between culturalistic and naturalistic communities in the field of cultural listening and auditory perception. While Shepherd and Wicke's (1997: 164) statement on the 'impossibility of creating levels of analysis whose status matches that of moments of musical articulation in reality' held true in the 1990s, cognitive modelling and functional imaging have advanced to a point which almost resolves this questions, but provokes many others.

Towards the Simulation of Human Listening

Ten years on from the model of the sonic saddle, parallel initiatives in the realm of music psychology, computational modelling and corpus-based musicology have turned their attention to the same content features that Wicke and Shepherd focused on, yet within a different conceptual frame.

According to the proponents of musical feature extraction (MFE), human auditory capacities scan and extract certain features from auditory objects that become a substantial portion of the listening process. Computational MFE aims at the possibility to model the ways human subjects listen using algorithms based on a large sample of musical data which have been double-checked by way of psychological experiments with human subjects; thus it helps to apply the computational modelling to human auditory capacities and to their implicit knowledge about musical structures. Daniel Müllensiefen, Geraint Wiggins and David Lewis have singled out the following high-level features of musical auditory objects, arising from low-level features, that were helpful in designing a computational modelling: melodic contour, phrase segmentation, harmonic labelling, rhythm classification, instrumentation/arrangement (Müllensiefen et al. 2008: 141f.). In the computational approximation and modelling of human listening, it is crucial to know which features to select, and with what calibration, before an algorithm detects these features in symbolically coded music. Müllensiefen et al. discuss the various psychological and technical options concerning the feature of melodic contour. What singles out this project is the interaction of empirical evaluation, achieved on the basis of psychological experiments, with statistical and probabilistic modelling. Unless researchers know precisely how human subjects confront a feature – such as melodic contour – and to what extent it influences their implicit knowledge and anticipatory behaviour, it is impossible to start running computational procedures on the symbolically coded data. In scanning the large database for generic patterns such as tonality sequences of melodies, Bayesian inference and chord-labelling algorithms built on the Dirichlet distribution have been applied (Müllensiefen et al. 2008: 150; Rhodes et al. 2009).

At the stage of MFE research portrayed here, the pragmatic impulse to achieve reliable modelling of key dimensions of auditory material clearly eclipses the follow-up question of the construction of cultural meanings. Computerized modelling seems to fall short of the complexity of musical interaction by defining music as consisting of various content dimensions. It relies on a quasi-essentialist strategy of content modelling as a prerequisite for computation and for acquiring ground-truth data for advanced statistical processing. Paradoxically, critical musicology has abandoned such essentialist attributions. 'Sense' is no longer identified with structural musical features. Rather, it emerges out of a multi-faceted auditory appropriation. This appropriation implies gestural and mimetic learning procedures in which some of Wicke and Shepherd's assumptions ring true and maintain their urgency.

On the other hand, MFE shows a consequentiality which may open up new vistas working towards the technical anticipation and simulation of the human auditory capacity. It is not clear whether researchers within MFE and beyond are aware of this fundamental shift from the lexical and syntactic use of databases towards a new processuality which, although context-based, works towards a dynamic modelling in which algorithmic and human judgments become inseparable. Listening should now be regarded as a phenomenon distributed among human and technical actors. Statistics and technologies acquire listening agency:

> The idea is to model the implicit knowledge of western pop music listeners by the proxy of a statistical description of the music corpus that the listeners build their listening experience on. The assumption is that using information about the prevalence of musical features in real music within the modeling framework is substantially better than merely applying musical features to relate music data to behavioural data as if a long enculturation in a musical culture had never happened or was irrelevant. (Müllensiefen et al. 2008: 152)

Samples from popular music repertory were turned into MIDI files that would allow various computational coding procedures of the symbolically coded material. Symbolic coding, and not the audio files, presented the basis of the MFE:

> The music corpus used for M4S is a collection of 14,067 transcriptions of pop songs from the 1950s to 2006 in the MIDI file format. These files were commercially acquired and were produced, to a high standard, by musicians for a distributing company (Geerdes MIDI Music; http://www.midimusic.de) which normally sells its MIDI files to studio musicians, entertainers or karaoke enterprises where they are used as backing tracks. (Müllensiefen et al. 2008: 134)

In a complex preparatory experiment, Müllensiefen and Klaus Frieler developed criteria for an important high-level feature, melodic similarity, to be judged by human subjects and by computational modelling. During this experimental set-up, subjects were confronted with auditory discrimination tasks that involved erroneous or manipulated stimuli in order to test the range of stability of the judgments on melodic similarity from previous hearings:

> Materials. To obtain ecologically valid results 14 existing melodies from western popular songs were chosen as stimulus material. Among these melodies were songs like 'As long as you love me' by the Back Street Boys, 'Summer is Calling' by Aquagen, and 'From Me to You' by the Beatles. All melodies were between seven and ten bars long (15–20 sec.). The melodies were selected according to several criteria: They should contain at least three different phrases and two thematically distinct motives. They should have a radio-like, popular character and they should be unknown to the subjects to precluded effects from previous knowledge. … For each melody six comparison variants with 'errors'

> were constructed, resulting in 84 variants of the 14 original melodies. The error types and their distribution were done according to the literature on memory errors for melodies …. (Müllensiefen and Frieler 2004 [online version]: 14)

In the course of this project, the interpolation curves discussed were expected to approximate the main patterns of melodic contour across a very large corpus (see Figure 5.2).

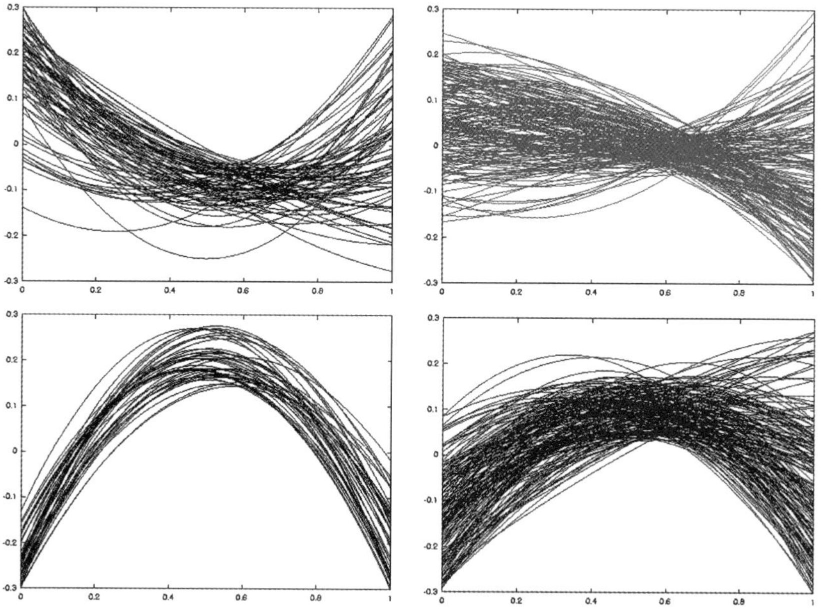

Figure 5.2 Clusters of interpolation curve contours after extracting melodic contour classes from the corpus as found by Klaus Frieler

Key: Clockwise from top left: Cluster 1 (concave-descending); Cluster 2 (mixture); Cluster 3 (small arch); Cluster 4 (big arch)

Source: Müllensiefen et al. (2008): 146. Reproduced by kind permission of Daniel Müllensiefen.

The stimuli were presented in the form of 'melodies … played from CD over suitable loudspeakers with a piano sound at a comfortable listening level (around 65 db)' (Müllensiefen and Frieler 2004: 15f.).

The intention here is to hint at the complex action sequences that this testing embraces. It combines complex listening tasks on a high-level feature, such as melodic similarity, with indications on rating scales, and it shows how elaborate are the testing procedures that address just one feature of auditory processing. Furthermore, the musical corpus chosen is close to everyday musical experiences of the subjects, and the stimulus presentation via CD also comes close to a regular music listening scenario. Post-2000 experiments finally allowed the technically mediated sounds of popular culture to be accepted as musical stimuli.

While experimental and statistical modelling has improved to a remarkable extent, it is still a long way from understanding how these features interact to generate aesthetic pleasure and musical meaning. The issue has been explored in music cognition research in a variety of ways. An integral model of music perception has been put forward by Stefan Koelsch and Walter Siebel (2005), and in a revised version by Koelsch (2011). The musical features that Müllensiefen and other MFE specialists are keen to model computationally enter Koelsch and Siebel's model as a group of components in the left area of Figure 5.3, among many others interacting during auditory perception. The prominent observation of the emotional dimension, and of the meaning dimension, too, were new and were articulated in music cognition studies only after 2000. The inclusion of somatic and physical responses manifests the growing impact of the embodied cognition paradigm that has led to a new orientation in music cognition and action studies.

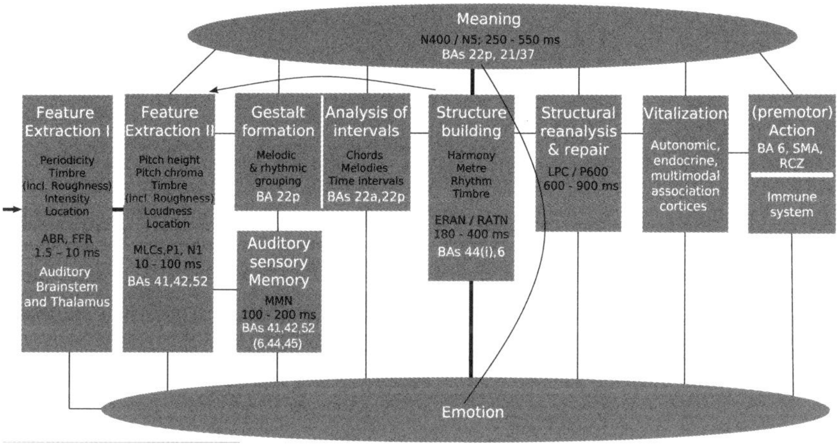

Figure 5.3 Neurocognitive model of music perception

Key: ABR, auditory brainstem response; BA, Brodmann area; ERAN, early right anterior negativity; FFR, frequency-following response; LPC, late positive component; MLC, mid-latency component; MMN, mismatch negativity; RATN, right anterior-temporal negativity; RCZ, rostral cingulate zone; SMA, supplementary motor area.

Source: Koelsch (2011): 3, as elaborated from Koelsch and Siebel (2005). Open access source, reprinted with kind permission of Stefan Koelsch.

What is of interest here is the systematic, modular presentation of all facets feeding into the music perception. It evokes the plural dimensions of the sonic saddle model, which is configured differently and does not focus on the neurocognition, but aims to capture interrelated processes much in the same way as Koelsch and

Siebel do. But this model does not disclose the temporal dynamics – meaning not the direct onset response of the listed areas and faculties, but their continuous and perhaps overlapping response to a sequence of auditory events streaming in, as in the case of listening to a continuous flow of music. This had been captured by the dynamic environment of the sonic saddle, which slowly moves on through the perceptive situation, capturing an ongoing present. How are new stimuli integrated? Considering that the model is not about auditory, but about musical perception, how is the high formal articulatedness of music represented here and processed accordingly? While Koelsch has explored similarities and differences between language and music processing elsewhere, an ideal starting point to address the problem of multi-layered articulatedness, one should note how he approaches the meaning dimension, as indicated at the top of Figure 5.3. Meaning seems to be a robust term for the cognition community, whereas in cultural, ecological and deconstructive musicology, it has received overwhelming attention.

This is how Koelsch and Siebel discuss the meaning component of music perception:

> The model outlined in this article assumes musical meaning to be closely related to a variety of aspects of music perception. Music is a means of communication, although usually used differently from language when conveying meaning information (but see also [81]). Aspects of musical meaning might comprise: (i) meaning that emerges from common patterns or forms (e.g. musical sound patterns that resemble gestures, prosodic features, sounds of objects, or qualities of objects); (ii) meaning that arises from the suggestion of a particular mood (e.g. happy, sad); (iii) meaning arising from extra-musical associations (e.g. any national anthem); and (iv) meaning arising from combinations of formal structures that create tension (e.g. when perceiving an unexpected chord) and resolution [42]. Numerous musical sounds and forms are associated with a fixed semantic meaning, for example, sounds associated with concepts like 'rough', 'warm', 'bright' or 'soft', and musical phrases that sound 'friendly', 'angry' or 'gigantic'. Because some musical forms mimic prosodic and other gestures, their meaning is possibly universal across cultures. Other musical forms have culturally determined meanings, for example a church anthem and the word devotion. (Koelsch and Siebel 2005: 581)

Among the questions prompting further research, the issue of meaning and of autobiographical memories (see below) is also addressed:

> What are the physical properties that determine the meaning of short acoustic signals, as well as of more complex musical information? Which of such properties have a universal meaning, and which are culturally determined? … How do the different modules of music processing interact with each other, and interact with different auditory memories? (Koelsch and Siebel 2005: 582)

This challenging research programme underlines the extension of the horizon of music cognition studies, and of music psychology in general, which has absorbed influences from bio-musicology, action studies, behavioural psychology and research on emotion. It also underlines the complexity of the processes under review, ranging from cultural traditions to specific autobiographical memories, all playing their part in music perception. If one contrasts these views with insights from the philosophy of music, and with positions from a historically and transculturally informed bio-musical semanticity (Cross 2009), one could even expand this agenda. Following the premise that listening takes place as a form of musical interaction, that these interactions yield contradictory situations, that music spells out and makes physically and aesthetically accessible a-logical situations and experiences (Mahrenholz 2000), that there are no fixed relationships between auditory objects and emerging meanings,[2] then the road map for future cognition studies could be substantially extended and the concept of meaning and its interrelation with acts of listening and auditory appropriation could be problematized in fruitful ways.

While music and action studies as well as the ecological psychology of music (Dibben 2002; Clarke 2005) have moved in this direction, we will turn to another development for the purpose of the present chapter, which takes up the autobiographical facet of listening.

Measuring and Visualizing Musical Autobiographical Memories

Due to the refinement of functional imaging that monitors the time dynamic behaviour of cognitive processes of auditory perception, and due to the cultural standing of cognition research that aims to anticipate future behaviours and detect moral orientations from the observed cortical activation pattern, a new genre of experimental set-up came within reach. It targets highly individualized musical experiences and tries to draw general conclusions about auditory perception. Among these, autobiographical memories triggered by music have emerged as an important topic. The pioneer in the field of cognitive modelling of these memories in music, Petr Janata, introduced it as follows:

> Despite music's prominence in Western society and its importance to individuals in their daily lives, very little is known about the memories and emotions that are often evoked when hearing a piece of music from one's past. We examined the content of music-evoked autobiographical memories (MEAMs) using a novel approach for selecting stimuli from a large corpus of popular music, in both laboratory and online settings. A set of questionnaires probed the cognitive and affective properties of the evoked memories. On average, 30% of the song

[2] This has been underlined by Ian Cross (2009) and is manifest in Shepherd and Wicke's semiological model: see Figure 5.1 earlier in this chapter.

> presentations evoked autobiographical memories, and the majority of songs also evoked various emotions, primarily positive, that were often felt strongly. The third most common emotion was nostalgia …. (Janata et al. 2007: 845)

The content orientation is familiar from MFE modelling (see above). Although the autobiographical component may capture only a portion of the complex auditory processing and meaning construction during musical listening, its theory-driven exploration has yielded insights that affect the biographical orientation in general. In order to assess how listening has been introduced in this research arena, I will pay attention here to the experimental design. It exemplifies the complex and studious efforts required in order to address a seemingly commonsense conviction – music-related autobiographical memories tend to be vivid and emotionally salient – in the realm of cognition studies. Janata is interested in the detection of a cortical network and in a time-dependent localization of these networks in the wake of autobiographically relevant listening sessions. The range of methodological and technological precautions and framings of the listening situation which is coupled with a verbal rating experiment and the sheer quantity and statistical processing of the data obtained from this series of experiments are most notable.

This is how the researcher introduces his project:

> The medial prefrontal cortex (MPFC) is regarded as a region of the brain that supports self-referential processes, including the integration of sensory information with self-knowledge and the retrieval of autobiographical information. I used *functional magnetic resonance imaging* and a novel procedure for eliciting autobiographical memories with excerpts of popular music dating to one's extended childhood to test the hypothesis that music and autobiographical memories are integrated in the MPFC. … These findings extend the results of previous autobiographical memory research by demonstrating the spontaneous activation of an autobiographical memory network in a naturalistic task with low retrieval demands. (Janata 2009: 2,579)

The stimulus selection and presentation were arranged as follows:

> Selecting the set of stimuli to play to any given subject presented a considerable challenge. … An adequate strategy consisted of selecting excerpts at random from the Billboard Top 100 Pop and R&B charts for the years when the subject was between 7 and 19 years of age. This strategy was validated in a large sample of ~300 subjects and is described in detail elsewhere (Janata *et al.* 2007). … Across the 13 subjects, 341 unique song excerpts were presented.
>
> **Stimulus Presentation and Response Collection**
>
> The experiment was controlled by Presentation software (Neurobehavioral Systems, Inc., Albany, CA) in conjunction with a Matlab engine (The Mathworks, Natick, MA) that selected stimuli from and submitted responses to

> 'Ensemble', an experiment control and database system (http://atonal.ucdavis.edu/ensemble/) .... Thirty song excerpts were presented across 2 scanning runs of 15 songs each. Each song excerpt was 30 s in song duration. The excerpts were the samples available from the Apple iTunes Music Store (Apple, Cupertino, CA) .... Prior to a scanning run, 15 excerpts were selected at random from a period of time that the subject was between 7 and 19 years of age .... Thirty stimuli were presented across 2 scanning runs via electrostatic headphones (MR confon GmbH, Magdeburg, Germany). Subjects also wore foam earplugs. Prior to the scanning runs, the volume of the music was adjusted so that is was as loud as the subject could comfortably stand but without noticeable distortion of the audio quality .... (Janata 2009: 2,580)

The information is reproduced at length here in order to appreciate the reflective and elaborate methodological investments preceding the data collection that are usually overlooked in favour of the coloured visualizations of measured activation patterns. As we progress, the level of technicological mediatedness and the division of expertise, as well as the reliance on software and specialized toolboxes, become more and more obvious.

The BOLD (blood oxygenation level-dependent) data as registered in a functional magnetic resonance imaging (MRI) scan in themselves do not carry a simple autobiographical component, but need to be calibrated with the help of a post-listening question-and-answer session. This imports a subjective aesthetic and psychological weightings into the experiment:

> **Statistical Analyses of Responses during Music Epochs, the Question and Answer Periods, and the Parametric Variation of Familiarity, Autobiographical Salience, and Valence**
>
> All analyses were performed in Matlab using a combination of third party toolboxes, for example, SPM5, the IPEM Toolbox, and custom code. Four major effects of interest were assessed with 2 models (Fig. 5.1). The first model (Fig. 5.1A) consisted of 3 sets of regressors that represented 1) the 30 s periods during which music was playing (MusPlay); 2) the question and answer period (QAP) following each musical excerpt; and 3) a set of parametric regressors that captured the variation in the familiarity, autobiographical salience, and degree of positive affect evoked by each musical excerpt. ... The parametric regressors modeling familiarity, autobiographical salience, and affective valence were constructed based on the responses to the questions following each song excerpt. Familiarity was coded with unfamiliar = -1 and familiar = 1. Autobiographical salience was coded with no association = -1, weak association = 0, and strong association = 1. Valence was coded linearly from very displeasing = -2 to very pleasing = 2. (Janata 2009: 2,581)

The visualization of activation patterns is not easy to penetrate. It requires some effort to unravel its complexity, and to understand the many methodological layers and decisions that are literally inscribed in it in the form of a technical image. Figure 5.4 is a case in point. It assembles composite data across the sample, and shows activation patterns in a variety of respects: measured data, projective statistics and the verbal statements elicited from the subject interact and are didactically presented to identify the main activation areas and their potential overlap. It synthesizes individual responses into a general cortical landscape for music-evoked autobiographical memories. Although they seem to capture 'listening' itself, turning listening into an activity that can be visualized as it plots itself upon the cortex, it needs to be pointed out that the data emerge from a sequence of well-justified strategic decisions and are therefore highly mediated in themselves. Is 'listening' identical to 'thinking', given that core areas of the cortex are involved in their processing? Or is it, in terms of functional neuro-anatomy, a mere dynamic change in the oxidation level in the affected regions of the brain? How do oxidation level changes translate into cultural meanings? Is the pop canon monumentalized in this figure in some way or the other? Figure 5.4 shows processes that are both material and constructed. The visualizations are allegories of statistical processing tied to auditory perception.

In the discussion, Janata addresses the relationship between the experimental situation and the everyday experience of music listening, anticipating a strong similarity to acts of everyday listening – an assumption that Shepherd and Wicke had been skeptical about:

> Although many further experiments remain to be performed, for example, to tease apart contributions of memory processes to the retrieval of lyrics or to relate distributed activation patterns to the content of specific autobiographical episodes, this study establishes the feasibility of studying autobiographical memory in an experimental context that closely resembles the common experience of hearing a song that evokes vivid memories and shows that the MPFC plays a central role in this experience. (Janata 2009: 2,593)

We might infer that music cognition studies really aim to achieve the reconstruction of the stimuli from the activation pattern. The refined exploration of the relationship between autobiographization and temporal localizations points in this direction. It foreshadows an equally fundamental shift for cognition studies, implying that volatile data (in this case, autobiographical memories) elicited from subjects could lead to important general insights, like the algorithmic modelling of human listening in MFE.[3] Janata's experiment makes an explicit reference to a dimension that could be considered a high-level feature within MFE: tonality.

[3] Janata's project closely observes one high-level feature, tonality, for which he develops a time-dependent tonality tracking procedure coupled with the autobiographical vector, lending extra depth and significance to this experiment. This cannot be presented here in detail. Suffice it to say that the modelling of single high-level features implicated in the proliferation of cortical networks continues to be complex and demanding.

It was expected to be enhanced in autobiographically salient listening situations. This could be of interest to future MFE modellings, as well as to the sonic saddle model, into which autobiographical states of awareness could be introduced as a new modality.

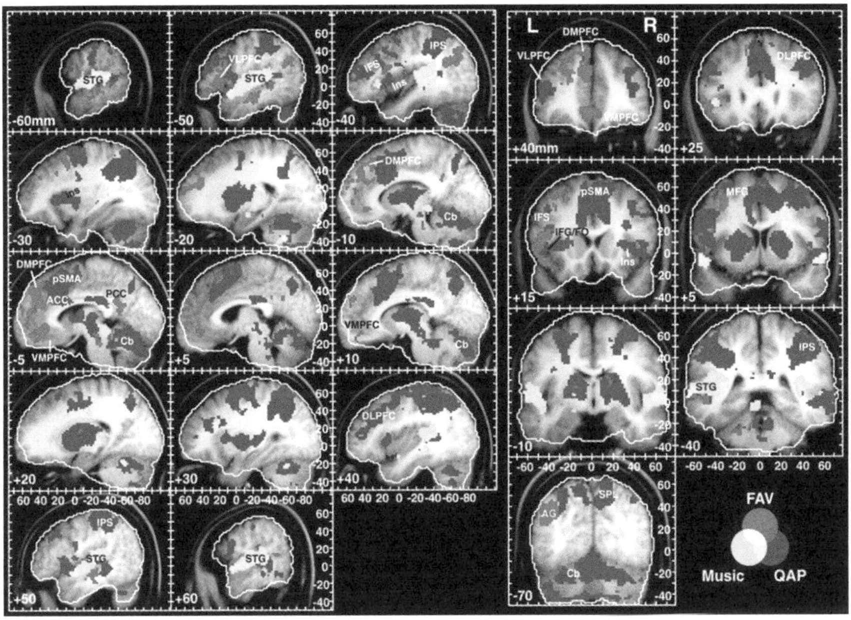

Figure 5.4 Summary of the activation patterns associated with the MusPlay, QAP, and FAV effects[4]

Source: Janata (2009). Reprinted by kind permission of Petr Janata.

[4] The beginning of original caption reads: 'The color legend for each of the effects of interest and conjunctions of effects of interest is shown at the bottom of the right panel. The statistical maps are thresholded at $P < 0.005$ (uncorrected) and a 40 voxel extent for all effects. In this and subsequent figures the following apply. The lateral displacement (mm) of the anatomical slice shown in each subpanel is indicated in the bottom left corner. Negative values for the sagittal sections in the left panel denote positions in the left hemisphere. Negative values for the coronal sections in the right panel denote positions posterior to the anterior commissure. The tick values of the scales (in mm) are given relative to the anterior commissure. The white contour lines enclose the volume in which data were available for all subjects.' See the original article for a reproduction in full colour.

Beyond Causality: A Social Systems Theory Approach to Auditory Cognition

While cognition research develops refined tools to capture human listening, moving towards everyday music as important stimulus material, sound designers and engineers have begun to create sounds that do not stem from the usual genealogy of musical instruments. Source-based modelling functions regardless of the familiar descriptive vocabularies and regardless of the possibility that listeners may infer meaning from them. Perceivable sounds are considered to be features of sound-generation procedures. Frictions, collisions, tensions, rolling objects, processes, bursting effects (Rath 2008: 221) become the raw material of these sounds, and of listening.

Physics-based sound synthesis and source-based modelling clearly revert the preconditions of culturally informed musical listening. A similar reversal can be observed in fresh approaches to music perception from outside the musicology and cognition communities. The systems theorist Dirk Baecker turned to experimental electronic music (EEM) for a penetrating revision of music's cognitive profile.[5] Instead of evoking outright references to phenomena outside of music, this genre would rather perform perception itself, thus, we may argue in extending Baecker's point of view, short-circuiting the elaborate cognition experiments sketched above. EEM enacts our very motor and cognitive capacities; this is their very material. EEM broaches both its matter and our access to this matter. EEM co-models the neural physiology of the human brain, the autopoiesis of organisms, the electrophysics of a CPU. This has substantial effects on the approach to the perceptual process: the mind must permanently adapt and accept that it is not dealing with its own sensations, but with those prompted by the music. Baecker speaks of an ecological regulation in the sense that the system cannot rely on any other actor or agency except itself in order to gauge its dynamic and ever-changing relations to its environment. But this relationship is modelled upon the operativity of the form of the sounds. The causality lying at the heart of MFE and of the autobiographical cognition research cannot be upheld here. It has been replaced by aesthetics. Aesthetics stands for experiences that we conceive as being right, without knowing why this is the case. Form stands for something that is present, reliable, and that invites distinctions to which we can relate. Baecker envisages a dispositive that would allow us to lay bare the coding rules at the heart of the coding process.

To most music cognition researchers, it is the other way around: music is already out there, and can be connected to subjects by way of a stimulus presentation. In Baecker's reading, sounds themselves are operative; as hermeneutics fails to confront these new textures and the set-up in which they gain form, (hermeneutic) analysis and content-based artistic production that aim to produce 'meaning' would need to be replaced by operational research. This research cultivates a strategy of control which is only about determining and processing the next possible auditory event. Electronic music programming of clicks and cuts is a state of permanent calculation,

5 In the following, I paraphrase Baecker (2003).

folds this calculation upon itself and exposes this double-operation, while allowing the non-calculable to take place at any time. These recursive processes do not aim to model any content which was the basis of MFE (see above).

With its continuous production of tiny differences, EEM attracts our attention. But we cannot infer meaning from it along the same lines that we make sense of other musical stylistics. Furthermore, artists in the EEM scene do not even insist that they create auditory objects to be memorized by human actors:

> The music even claims independence from any specific perception that would recognise it for itself, that could also cause it to sink into oblivion. Even so this forgetting is only a part of the power of the memory itself, the audible however, is the naked updating of particular dispositives that belong to habit. (Szepanski 1996: 18)

> The machines themselves are endlessly folded, and one cannot separate the sound machines from economical, political, physical, psychological and biological machines. (Szepanski 1996: 23)

It would be intriguing to set up an experiment that would fold such a Deleuzian, cognitively informed music upon cognition itself. Can autobiographical memories attach themselves to musical materials that defy referentiality? What are their low- or high-level features? Perhaps, and contrary to Baecker's assumptions, the sounds may carry evocations and references. It would, in fact, be hard to imagine sounds that completely elude any kind of signifying potential, so that the sonic saddle would collapse.

Distributed Listening and Technological Agency: An Outlook

To summarize: the empirical models and research paradigms reviewed here address feature extraction and autobiographical processes, seeking, as in the projects by Janata, to capture their temporal dynamics and cortical localization. Despite the advanced level of statistical expertise and high-tech data-generating devices, researchers admit that a full understanding of how the human mind and body achieve a meaningful integration of auditory information requires further studies and refined methodologies. In Koelsch's model, it becomes apparent that sound processing thus involves components of action induction and an active construction of meaning.[6] The autobiographical experiment not only underlines the active and constructive role of human subjects; it enhances a research strategy that considers music no longer as a carrier of content processed as syntactic

[6] This perception-as-action perspective has been explored at the Symposium 'From Sound to Dispositions of Musical Action – Functional, Computational and Ecological Perspectives on Music Perception', held at Istituto Storico Germanico di Roma in 2010, organized and chaired by the author and funded by Fritz-Thyssen-Stiftung.

information, but as being evocative of experiences and situations. The affordances and agencies supplied via auditory material in music-related situations thus come into focus and have been programmatically established as a research paradigm in the ecological psychology of music.[7] I suggest further expanding this aspect in order to gauge how intentions can be communicated and how presence is being produced via auditory objects in a listening situation.

In a parallel post-2000 development, social systems theories, which have pondered music cognition (Baecker 2003), experimental sound research (physics-based modelling) and artistic productions, have shifted the perspective away from auditory referentiality towards an entirely new construction of auditory objects (as a function of their perception) and towards a practice of listening as a mere auditory registration of differences. The focus has been shifted to the operativity and the knowledge dimensions of sounds, and has exposed the impossibility of understanding them by way of hermeneutics. Analysis has been replaced by control. This control oversees the minute differences that are assumed to be evocative of the modalities of perception itself.

This chapter is an attempt to characterize some of the repercussions that these shifts entail for our understanding of listening as a cultural and technological practice. Ironically, while the subjective foundation of listening is implicit yet not overtly stated within the cognition community,[8] these experiments work towards a post-subjective condition of listening: through their application of computational and statistical models leading to algorithmic judgments (MFE) and through a data-intensive processing of subject samples across the subject population that results in synthesized, quasi-collective and composite modellings of human perception ('nostalgic listening'). Listening thus emerges as a capacity distributed among human, statistical and technical actors.

The cultural field of listening has been exposed to powerful economic forces. The considerations that have been voiced here, in the spirit of an experimental variantology[9] and rearrangements, could furnish alternative approaches. The overall research situation favours richer, non-reductive contextualizations of listening and of musical practices; in fact, cognition research has exhausted the functionalistic paradigm and is beginning to modify the logic-driven and syntactic paradigms (dating back to the early years of information theory) and its strong leaning towards the processing of linguistic structures. Instead, concepts of mimetic learning and enactment (Becker and Vogel 2007) are fruitful, and may extend the agenda of music cognition studies. Furthermore, the implicated paradigms of high-level feature processing, of the localization, modularity and functionality of music

[7] See Chapter 2 in this volume by Eric Clarke, a pioneer in this field.

[8] Generally, there is little critical and meta-reflection on the terms, concepts, paradigms and ideologies of performing research.

[9] This term was coined by the media archaeologist Siegfried Zielinski in 2007. He is the co-editor of the five-volume series *Variantology: On Deep Time Relations of the Arts, Sciences and Technologies* (Cologne: Verlag der Buchhandlung König, 2005–11).

perception offer themselves to be contrasted and complemented by paradigms such as semantic depth, by auditory perception as stimulus disambiguation (Leman et al. 2008: 37). The observed multi-functionality of musical dimensions (Cross 2009), non-fixity relations and imaginative, non-modular conjunctions that are part of the rich aesthetic and affective experience of listening could thus unfold their relevance. The potential and the challenge of the latter precisely lie in the fact that they cannot be modelled or monitored with the existing toolbox of music cognition studies and computational musicology.

It has become difficult to find a critical vantage point in an age which not only technically reproduces sounds, but also simulates human judgments, knowledge forms and memorizing strategies that make up human listening, and in which musical taste recommendation systems, collaborative filtering and algorithmic empowerment have easily infiltrated the generation and appropriation of sounds. These systems have already implemented the control envisaged by Baecker (2003: 146), and have coupled it to desire and consumption. The experimentalization of life (Rheinberger and Hagner 1993) which was developed as a key scientific practice and discourse in the nineteenth century and which still marks the objectivity-committed experiments discussed here[10] has been amalgamating with the liveness and animatedness of technologies. These technologies operate in real time, achieve algorithmically based near-human judgements and emerge as eloquent actors in machine–human interactions.

Undoubtedly, critical analysis should confront the processes on the methodological and technological level on which they unfold.[11] How can Janata's fascinating tonality-tracking movies[12] and brain activation images be translated back into a consistent narrative about listening? Regressor tables, composite statistics, interpolation curves, model-based clustering, expectation-maximization algorithms, statistical approximations and composite visualizations of brain activations are the new 'scores' which frame and process the topic and the practice of listening. They generate a specificity of data and of a technologically driven evidence that needs to be balanced against approaches cultivating non-specificity while still managing to articulate inspiring and bold models.

---

[10] In Janata's experiments, aspects that are part of life – musical autobiographical memories – are exposed to experimental procedures that seek to capture them, experimentalizing this facet of life (a 'naturalistic task', Janata [2009]: 2,579; see above) by way of complex detection procedures.

[11] This could only be hinted at here, as this project implies teamwork.

[12] See http://cercor.oxfordjournals.org/content/suppl/2009/01/19/bhp008.DC1/cercor-2008-00671-File014_bhp008.mov and http://cercor.oxfordjournals.org/content/suppl/2009/01/19/bhp008.DC1/cercor-2008-00671-File015_bhp008.mov (accessed 30 June 2015).

Further cross-fertilizations that lead to new questions need to be strongly encouraged.[13] Sound engineers and artists work in similar technological environments to those used in MFE and in cognition research. Looked at in this way, the careful orchestration of research procedures such as Müllensiefen's and Janata's, with their manifold action sequences, listening and post-listening situations, trial runs and inserted mock samples, might be looked at as a choreographed performance which synchronizes various levels of expertise, social roles, technologies and expectations. Sharing viewpoints from the current theory of sciences and of mediation as exposed by Bruno Latour, Antoine Hennion[14] and Régis Debray, one could regard listening not as a subject–object relationship attached to human minds and ears from which content can be drawn analytically, but as a cultural practice that leads to peculiar arrangements of technologies, social roles, and scientific and aesthetic convictions. We would then be able to leave the theoretical humanist scenario (Debray 2003: 31) to which the research reviewed here adheres, with the exception of Baecker and EEM – a step that has long been taken by commercially aided listening technologies. They are evolving towards post-subjective distributed networks, only to re-address users on a level that evokes 'individuality' and 'personalization', although these are entirely synthetic and algorithmically based.

The volatility of the topic of autobiographical memories mentioned above prevents MRI-based cognition research aiming at 'precise' data. But is laboratory situatedness as a whole not equally volatile? If, according to Régis Debray (2003: 175), technologies need to be considered as realities *sui generis*, we are led to ask which intermediaries are at play in the complex research procedures that have been discussed. The MRI scanner used by Janata (see Figure 5.5) – unlikely to breed auditory nostalgia given its impressive dimensions and the utterly clinical set-up – is surely such a candidate. Its technical features and capabilities determine how listening is being looked at and in which cultures of measurement it is being contextualized. It easily gathers data that are irrelevant to the experiment. Such intermediaries exceed their expected functioning – a fact openly admitted and actually exploited only by Baecker and the aesthetics of clicks and cuts with respect to their intermediaries.

13 When the author approached a leading protagonist of brain and cognitive sciences, proposing that the by-now classical experiments from music cognition research of around 2000–2005 should be re-enacted under supervision, this suggested de-territorialization was met with utter disbelief.

14 Hennion regards music as a phenomenon emerging from diverse institutional, aesthetical and economical mediations. Effacing the object-centring of traditional musicological discourse, 'music', according to Hennion (1993), is the term that covers these very relationships.

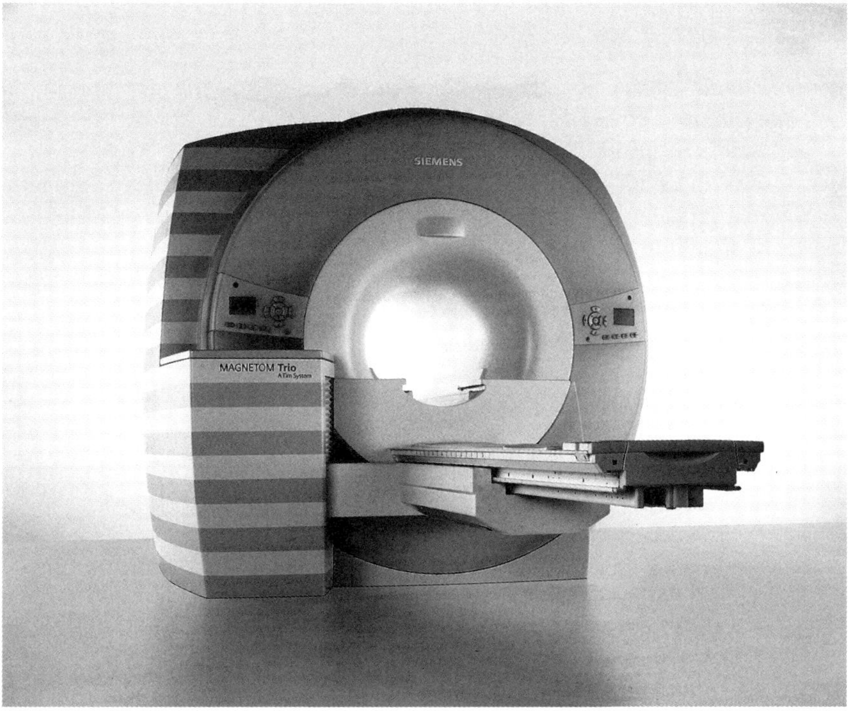

Figure 5.5 Siemens 3T MAGNETOM Trio whole-body MRI system, as used in the experiments of Petr Janata
Source: Courtesy of Siemens AG.

These considerations may inspire future research in which the problematic aspects of a culturally contested practice such as listening, largely absent from empirical research agendas,[15] could be brought to bear on them. These new investigative variants would have to fully acknowledge the operative agency and inherent relationality of sounds and the intermediary potential of technologies and the discourse systems implied. This may lead to a re-calibration of the empirical, of causality and of assumed naturalistic practices themselves. In the long run, cultural economies of listening, of music and of noise will figure in even more programmatically hybrid, consciously mediated, or with Shepherd and Wicke, dialectical research situations (see their diagram reproduced as Figure 5.1 above).

[15] This observation refers to music cognition laboratories as well as to textbooks on the auditory sense, such as Plack (2010) and Plack (2013).

References

Baecker, Dirk (2003) 'Kopfhörer. Für eine Kognitionstheorie der Musik', in *Soundcultures*. Über *elektronische und digitale Musik*, ed. Marcus S. Kleiner and Achim Szepanski, Frankfurt am Main: Suhrkamp, pp. 137–51.

Becker, Alexander and Vogel, Matthias (2007) 'Einleitung', in *Musikalischer Sinn. Beiträge zu einer Philosophie der Musik*, ed. Alexander Becker and Matthias Vogel, Frankfurt am Main: Suhrkamp, pp. 7–24.

Clarke, Eric F. (2005) *Ways of Listening: An Ecological Approach to the Perception of Musical Meaning*, New York: Oxford University Press.

Cross, Ian (2009) 'The Evolutionary Nature of Musical Meaning', *Musicae scientiae*, 13/2 (suppl.), pp. 179–200.

Debray, Régis (2003) *Einführung in die Mediologie*, Bern: Haupt.

Dibben, Nicola (2002) 'Musical Materials, Perception, and Listening', in *The Cultural Study of Music: A Critical Introduction*, ed. Martin Clayton, Trevor Herbert and Richard Middleton, New York: Routledge, pp. 193–203.

European Science Foundation (2012) *Musicology (Re-)Mapped*, European Science Foundation Standing Committee for the Humanities discussion paper, Strasbourg: European Science Foundation.

Hennion, Antoine (1993) *La Passion musicale. Une sociologie de la médiation*, Paris: Métailié.

Janata, Petr (2009) 'The Neural Architecture of Music-evoked Autobiographical Memories', *Cerebral Cortex*, 19/11, pp. 2,579–94.

———, Tomic, Stefan T. and Rakowski, Sonja K. (2007) 'Characterisation of Music-evoked Autobiographical Memories', *Memory*, 15/8, pp. 845–60.

Klotz, Sebastian (2013) 'Klang als epistemische Ressource und als operativer Prozess', in *Auditive Medienkulturen. Techniken des Hörens und Praktiken der Klanggestaltung*, ed. Axel Volmar and Jens Schröter, Bielefeld: transcript, pp. 189–205.

Koelsch, Stefan (2011) 'Toward a Neural Basis of Music Perception – a Review and Updated Model', *Frontiers in Psychology*, 2/110, pp. 131–7.

——— and Siebel, Walter A. (2005) 'Towards a Neural Basis of Music Perception', *Trends in Cognitive Sciences*, 9/12, pp. 578–84.

Leman, Marc, Styns, Fredrik and Bernardini, Nicola (2008) 'Sound, Sense and Music Mediation: A Historical-philosophical Perspective', in *Sound to Sense – Sense to Sound: A State of the Art in Sound and Music Computing*, ed. Pietro Polotti and Davide Rocchesso, Berlin: Logos, pp. 15–46.

Mahrenholz, Simone (2000) 'Logik, A-logik, Analogik. Musik und die Verfahrensformen des Unbewussten', in *Musik in der Zeit. Zeit in der Musik*, ed. Richard Klein, Eckehard Kiem and Wolfram Ette, Weilerswist: Velbrück Wissenschaft, pp. 373–98.

Müllensiefen, Daniel and Frieler, Klaus (2004) 'Cognitive Adequacy in the Measurement of Melodic Similarity: Algorithmic vs. Human Judgments',

Computing in Musicology, 13, pp. 147–76, http://www.doc.gold.ac.uk/~mas03dm/papers/CM_MullensiefenFrieler_2004.pdf (accessed 30 June 2015).

Müllensiefen, Daniel, Wiggins, Geraint and Lewis, David (2008) 'High-level Feature Descriptors and Corpus-based Musicology: Techniques for Modelling Music Cognition', in *Systematic and Comparative Musicology: Concepts, Methods, Findings*, ed. Albrecht Schneider, Frankfurt am Main: Peter Lang, pp. 133–55.

Plack, Christopher J. (ed.) (2010) *The Oxford Handbook of Auditory Science: Hearing*, Oxford: Oxford University Press.

——— (2013), *The Sense of Hearing*, London: Taylor & Francis.

Rath, Matthias (2008) 'Dynamisches Klang-Feedback in Mensch-Computer-Interaktion. Perspektiven physikalisch basierter Klangsynthese', in *Funktionale Klänge. Hörbare Daten, klingende Geräte und gestaltete Hörerfahrungen*, ed. Georg Spehr, Bielefeld: transcript, pp. 219–44.

Rheinberger, Hans-Jörg and Hagner, Michael (eds) (1993) *Die Experimentalisierung des Lebens. Experimentalsysteme in den biologischen Wissenschaften 1850–1950*, Berlin: Akademie.

Rhodes, Christophe, Lewis, David and Müllensiefen, Daniel (2009) 'Bayesian Model Selection for Harmonic Labelling', in *Mathematics and Computation in Music*, ed. Timour Kloche and Thomas Noll, Berlin: Springer-Verlag, pp. 107–16.

Shepherd, John and Wicke, Peter (1997) *Music and Cultural Theory*, Cambridge: Polity Press.

Szepanski, Achim (1996) 'This Evening a Concert Will Take Place (Gilles Deleuze)', in *In Memoriam Gilles Deleuze* (CD Booklet), Frankfurt: Mille Plateaux, pp. 18–26.

Chapter 6
Listening to Histories of Listening: Collaborative Experiments in Acoustemology with Nii Otoo Annan

Steven Feld

In the field of ethnomusicology one typically encounters a historical emphasis in discussions of sound recording technologies. Surely this follows from how the discipline's development has closely relied on the evolution of field and archive sound technologies for the documentation, analysis and dissemination of human musical diversity (for example, Christensen 2002; Hart and Kostyal 2003; Baily 2009; Myers 1992; Stock 2009; Rice 2014: 17). In this chapter I shift away from this historical emphasis to engage a contemporary conjuncture: that of listening practices and experimental field and studio recording. My interests here are to discuss dialogic recording and listening encounters with a Ghanaian musical colleague, Nii Otoo Annan, and to present how our collaborative CD recordings open up experimental formats for articulating research on listening and playback.

That sound recording can be powerfully linked both to new knowledge about African music and new possibilities for listening to it reached an unquestionable watershed moment in 1973. This was when Simha Arom introduced an experimental technique that forever changed analytic access to the music of African multi-part vocal and instrumental ensembles. Recognizing that there was a great deal of conjecture about time and interlock principles based on listening to the gestalt summary of multi-part music in Africa, Arom suggested that it was fundamentally necessary to be able to hear each of the parts separately and in contextual juxtaposition in order to analyse their relations. He proposed a brilliant analogue recording strategy to make possible the transcription of traditional African polyrhythms and polyphonies on a part-by-part basis (Arom 1973; 1976). Arom's proposal was daring, startling and original. 'The method I propose is an experimental one,' he wrote. 'It consists in applying the well-known technique of "playback recording" *in the field itself*' (Arom 1976: 483; emphasis in original). The technique exploits the possibilities of coupling two analogue stereo reel-to-reel recorders. In so doing, the left and right track material recorded on one can be re-recorded to just one track of the other, thus leaving a synchronous open track which can be overdubbed to playback. This makes it possible to record an ensemble, and then to record each component part of the ensemble sequentially. To do this, each player or vocalist records his or her unique solo part while listening to playback of the whole ensemble, or to one or more other parts of that whole.

Arom's method relies on both a rigorous technological procedure with the paired stereo recorders and the ability of the researcher to work in a highly structured and artificial way with his or her interlocutors. In effect, the researcher trains the interlocutors in the technique of playback, which is to say, trains them to become adept at re-recording, a new overdub way of listening to and performing with themselves. Even if the emphasis is largely technical, methodological reflections on the complexities and intricacies of this approach are found in Arom's initial articles on the technique (1973; 1976), in his later major analytic works (Arom 1985; 1991), as well as in works written with and by his students (for example, Arom and Fürniss 1992; Fernando-Marandola 2002; Fürniss 1993; 2006).

The key methodological goal of Arom's technique has been to access sonic structures through a sequential part-by-part transcription that allows for preparation of an analytic musical 'score'. Indeed, the *raison d'être* of the playback technique is described as methodological and linked to the necessity of accuracy in transcribing part-to-part relations with a reference pulse. Despite this dominant focus, however, Arom recognized the deeper potentials in the procedure for a multi-dimensional collaborative practice, particularly through the value of dialogic presentation. He concluded:

> The method described changes deeply the usual relationship between the ethnomusicologist and the musicians during fieldwork: the musicologist is no longer on one side, with his informants on the other. On the contrary, its application requires very active participation from the musicians; they become true scientific collaborators. It is necessary that they not only understand what they are asked to do in the experimental conditions, but also that they assume the determination of the successive stages of the experimental work, decided upon jointly with the ethnomusicologist. (Arom 1976: 495)

I have never directly experimented with these techniques in the field, even though I have been aware of them since 1974, when, during a student semester in Paris, Arom generously gave me an offprint of his first article (1973) about playback. But as a studio session musician I had a number of experiences of recording to playback. And as an improviser I had a number of experiences of live performance with experimental playback and feedback from prepared tapes, electronics and self-sampling. In addition to these experiences as a performer, I was also familiar with the techniques from the point of view of the recording engineer.

The combination of my recording studio experience with playback, my use of dialogic techniques playback in linguistic and ethnographic research and CD production (for example, Feld 1987; 2011), and a fascination with the radical collaborative possibilities in Arom's method came together for me in a new way during my first week in Accra, Ghana, in 2004. This is when I both met the Ghanaian multi-instrumentalist Nii Otoo Annan, and heard the sounds of the ubiquitous gutter toad, *Bufo regularis*. Four years later, this conjuncture led to the experimental CD music project *Bufo Variations* (Annan and Feld 2008).

The process that unfolded during those four years, from first encounters through the CD recording and production, exemplifies what I have called acoustemology – the study of sound as a way of knowing (Feld 2012; 2015). Acoustemology is an inquiry into what is knowable, and how it becomes known, through sounding and listening. Acoustemology begins with acoustics to ask how the physicality of sound is so instantly and forcefully present to experience and experiencers, to interpreters and interpretations. It joins that concern to epistemology to investigate sounding and listening as a knowing-in-action, a knowing-with and knowing-through the audible. Listening to histories of listening is one methodological approach to making connections between acoustics and epistemology.

That listening work began with the first recordings I made in Accra, the midnight interactions of the gutter toad *Bufo regularis*. Emanating from two-foot-deep concrete sewers flanking city roads, the toads' voices are intensely amplified by the cement walls of their foetid amphitheatres, the ratcheting sounds broadcast far and wide. The space–time interplays of the toads, both within particular gutters and across the roads, were acoustically rich and unlike recordings I knew of toads and frogs in rural or urban environments. They exhibited many polyrhythmic dynamics with which I was unfamiliar. Recording multi-channel to a digital hard drive recorder in real time with DSM head-worn recording technology,[1] I began each recording with a metronomic figure, the sound of my walking along the asphalt into the spatial surround of the *Bufo* sound-field, and proceeded to allow numerous rhythmic interaction patterns to emerge in the density of repetitions.

In the months after leaving Ghana I mixed several experimental short soundscape composition pieces from this material, and ultimately presented a brief one as a multi-channel mix for the 2006 Ear to the Earth concert in New York City. Then, in 2008, after regular returns to Ghana and lengthy study of percussion and timeline principles with the acclaimed musician Nii Otoo Annan, I played for him a 6 minute 38 second piece I called 'Bufo Aria'.

Taking his headphones off, Nii Otoo said:

> You hear, Prof, it is like what I have been showing you in our music. The crickets are sounding everywhere like the bell with very strict time, and the *kawkawdene* [the toad's name in Ga, Nii Otoo's first language] are master drummers, making many rhythms that cross on top and sit below.

'Sounding everywhere', 'crossing on top', 'sitting below': how might the metaphoric space–time concepts that Nii Otoo used in English be shaping forces of musical imagination? A first revelation was the way Nii Otoo complicated my listening. The multi-track mix I had made focused on the left-to-right, foreground-to-background, immediate-to-deep layers of rhythm that I could hear in the toad interactions. But Nii Otoo was juxtaposing all of that to the additional height and depth layers of

---

[1] For details of DSM Microphone Systems, see http://www.sonicstudios.com (accessed 30 June 2015).

the cricket pulsation. In effect, his listening blew up a larger 3D acoustic picture from the one I created, making clear that the figure–ground relationships that I was hearing could all dissolve into another figure against another ground.

A second revelation was the spatial use of 'crossing on top' to signify side-to-side changing rhythmic motion. 'Crossing on top' is a way a drummer might speak about additive improvisation, about pattern embellishment or ornamentation layered as an upper auditory layer onto the 'sitting below' ground of intermediate and lower-level rhythm-defining pattern repetitions. And 'sounding everywhere' listens to how sound fills and defines space as a density of simultaneous height–depth, foreground–background, and side-to-side interplays.

Over time I considered and queried Nii Otoo's thoughts on 'sounding everywhere', 'crossing on top' and 'sitting below', both as we were listening and as we were playing together. My desire deepened to communicate something about the intricacy and richness of his listening, his sonic knowing, his acoustemological way of hearing 'companion species' (Haraway 2003) in his acoustic environment.

But there are real linguistic limitations here, and neither Nii Otoo nor I understand the other's language with the degree of precision necessary to get into the deeper dimensions of listening. Besides, we were more used to playing together and listening together than talking. So I proposed that we collaborate on an experiment in listening and playback, one where I might more directly listen in on his way of listening to *Bufo* toads. And one where he would be able to direct the course of collaboration, and employ my recording, video and recording studio skills to present the musicality of his listening. In other words, what opened up here was an opportunity to use playing and recording, rather than verbal interchange, to represent the beneath-the-surface complexity of our acoustemological dialogue.

This led to a playback and overdub recording experiment where Nii Otoo improvised, sequentially, on 10 percussion instruments or instrument sets, while listening in headphones to playback of a repeated six-minute toad and cricket soundscape recording. These recordings open up new lines of inquiry into how routine listening to the environment forms a creative backdrop for knowledge of sonic space and time, for improvisation, for music perception, and specifically for a local understanding the concept of musical variation. Listening with headphones, Nii Otoo's synchronous performances feed back his musical responses by recording overdub tracks, each overdub an original variation on a different instrument or set. What is revealed by this listening-in acoustemology is the relational epistemology of how Nii Otoo uses the toads simultaneously as a metronomic click-track, stimulus, calculator and companion species musical interlocutor.

His overdubs feed back the polyrhythmic math that reveals a simultaneous hearing in patterns of three against two, four against three and six against four. They feed back the articulateness of hearing space–time interplays as 'crossing on top', 'sitting below' and 'sounding everywhere'.

Some details are required to make clear just what is at stake here. Nii Otoo improvised each of his variations in a complete take, without additional edits or overdubs. Variation 1 is performed on tenor and bass *gyil* xylophones. Variation 2 is performed on the *gome*, a seated bass drum played with heels and hands. Variation 3 is performed on a *brekete*, a snared bass drum played with palm and curved stick. Variation 4 is performed on the *odonno*, an under-arm pressure drum played with palm and a curved stick. Variation 5 is performed on *gome*, *brekete* and *odonno* drums. Variation 6 is performed on electric guitar. Variation 7 is performed on an *ashiwa*, a seated rhythm-box bass with three metal keys. Variation 8 is performed on a mix of *gome*, two *kpanlogo* and two *apentemma* drums, played with mallets and hands. Variation 9 is performed on the 'gangofone', Nii Otoo's experimental rack of seven *gangokui* double bells, played with mallets and sticks.

Variation 10 is different from all the others. For our last session, Nii Otoo set up a combination of *kpanlogo*, *gome* and *brekete* drums, hi-hat and ride jazz cymbals, and with jazz brushes played not to the toads, but to a previous overdub of the same toad track. This prepared overdub was played by a trio of the jazz saxophonist Alex Coke, vocalist Tina Marsh and myself on *ashiwa* rhythm box bass. For that trio recording Alex, Tina and I simultaneously improvised to playback of the toad piece, but each in different rooms, and with no eye or ear contact, hearing only the toads in our headphones, with no auditory or visual clue as to what each other was playing. Only afterward, at the recording console, with the toads removed, did we hear the live interplay of our collective conversation and mix it into a trio track (Coke et al. 2008). Nii Otoo's overdub of that track listens in and feeds back on our trio composite track, adding an African free-jazz overhearing of our trio overhearing of the *Bufo* toads.

For the *Bufo Variations* presentation CD recording, we begin with the unaccompanied 'Bufo Aria', the basis of my original listening to Accra's gutter toads at midnight, and of Nii Otoo's listening to my constructed listening. We then proceed with Nii Otoo's 10 variations, and end with 'Bufo Aria' again, in a slightly different mix. On 9 of the 10 overdubs the toad tracks are taken away so that Nii Otoo's total musical response is fully exposed. This is meant to encourage the listener to focus on Nii Otoo's musical improvisations, but also to either listen again just to the 'Bufo Aria', or to use the computer to listen simultaneously to the 'Bufo Aria' and to any of Nii Otoo's responses. To clarify this process midway, to expose the significance of removing the toads from the mix and to heighten the listening experience, we retain the ambient 'Bufo Aria' track together with Variation 6 for electric guitar, making it possible to hear Nii Otoo playing along with what he was listening to in the moment, in his headphones.

Nii Otoo's improvisations sound the generative mathematics of many rhythm families. They also map his histories of musical absorption, linking national, ethnic, regional and over-the-border patterns that reach from Ghana into Nigeria, Togo and Burkina Faso. They also head in the direction of jazz. In this way, Nii Otoo's cosmopolitan listening feedback speaks to how numerous Ghanaian rhythm families sound the historical and musical space and time of place, nation and the interpenetration of international musics.

Consider some of these dimensions track-by-track through Nii Otoo's playback annotations and comments as we listened together to the composite recordings.

His attention to detail reveals much about the complexities of his listening practice and how it feeds back into performance.

In Variation 1, for two *gyil* xylophones, Nii Otoo says the introduction has 'the left hand walking' to my footsteps, and the right 'coming in' to trill like the crickets. After the introduction, the left hand states patterns and the right embellishes. Playing the left with two mallets and the right with one, Otoo uses echoing and mirroring in a musical mimesis of the left–right, forward–backward sounding space of the frogs and the up–down sounding space of the crickets. Listening to his composite, he called his playing 'Kakraba Lobi' after the famous Ghanaian northern master player who was a frequent performer on national radio and a much-noted teacher in residence at the Institute of African Studies, University of Ghana (1962–87). Nii Otoo never studied with Kakraba, but said that after seeing him play he wanted to take the energy of his left–right hand interactions and do something less traditional with the technique, where independence of the hands can be spread to multiple instruments and improvisations against ostinatos played with a jazz touch. He credits his use of volume dynamics on this track to the jazz drumming techniques of Elvin Jones and Rashied Ali. Ghanaian instrumentalists more typically play at one dynamic level from start to finish.

In Variation 2, for *gome* bass drum, Nii Otoo begins with a Shai East rhythm associated with the inland Ga-Adangme people, but in a jazz-inflected form. This transforms to *otofo*, another Ga-Adangme rhythm. Otoo notes hearing the bell pattern in his head throughout (in $\frac{12}{8}$ the count is 1-1-1-1-3-2-3). Slowing down at two points, Otoo brings in rhythms of Bamaaya, the social music of the Dagbamba, widely heard at funerals and festivals in northern Ghana. While describing these rhythm fusions, Nii Otoo talked frequently about 'topping it' in relation to all rhythms, meaning playing all the interacting dance parts and adding what jazz drummers call 'fills', both connecting implied beats and rhythmically underlining overt and non-overt connections.

In Variation 3, for *brekete* drum, Nii Otoo again uses Dagbamba rhythms from the North, *takai*, a royal dance for festive occasions, and *bamaaya*, and uses drum-speaking to interject phrases, 'Turn yourself!', 'Stand!', 'Wave!', 'Bless you!', 'Strut like a king!', all in relation to rhythms associated with kings and princes.

In Variation 4, for *odonno* 'talking' drum, Nii Otoo simultaneously draws on portions of the drum, bell and rattle parts from *tikali*, again from the North, a ceremonial music for the gods, mixed with sounds from *Ipala*, a Nigerian sounding of drums talking to gods, telling how to dance. The ending swells back to Ghana, with a familiar formulaic phrase, the rhythm call to assemble of 'Ghana muntie!' ('Listen, Ghana!').

In Variation 5, for *gome*, *brekete* and *odonno* drums, Nii Otoo uses *sisala*, another Northern rhythm, which usually involves four drum parts. Here he plays five drum parts on three drums, no bell part, with the rhythm keyed to the timing of the dance. When I asked at this point why so many of the rhythm package choices came from the North, Nii Otoo said: 'They are heavy, more heavy, spiritually. We feel them reaching down to us here. Nigeria too, they are more heavy with spiritual music, dance music. We must take from them.'

In Variation 6, for electric guitar, Nii Otoo plays off the metronomic pulse of crickets, using them as a background timeline bell. He calls the first song, an original for himself, 'Otoo *kwao*', *kwao* being short for *kweku*, the day name for those born on Wednesday. The second song is a re-versioning from 1960s palmwine and highlife guitar band rhythms he associates with the famous Kumasi guitarists Koo Nimo and Kwa Mensah.

In Variation 7, the *ashiwa* box bass is played in the style of *otoome*, typically a large frame drum played by stick and hand. But Nii Otoo transfers the typically right hand on frame skin and left hand on frame shell pattern to alternations of hand on wood and hands on metal keys.

In Variation 8, for *gome*, *kpanlogo* and *apentemma* drums, Nii Otoo begins with sticks playing the wooden drum shells to indicate walking and shuffling sounds in the night, and then moves to a rolling and tumbling 'thunder' sound that he says he picked up by listening to Elvin Jones and Rashied Ali, the famous jazz drummers who worked with saxophonist John Coltrane. Then he goes into fast *waka*, in a jazz form fusing elements of *kpanlogo*, with common pulse bell pattern (in $\frac{12}{8}$ the count is 2-2-3-2-3) and then develops a solo with different speed alternations, but coming back constantly to phrases that reference the underlying bell pattern.

In Variation 9, for his invented gangofone, Nii Otoo uses Ewe *atsiagbekor* rhythm, from southern Ghana, Togo and Benin, mixing two and three bell parts. *Atsiagbekor* is a well-known social dance form, its dance movements closely keyed to drum motifs. To shifting middle ground parts, new 'tops' are added in the form of what Nii Otoo calls 'speaking' parts, with evocations of the phrases 'Come here', 'Stay here', 'Where are you going?', 'Just stay, don't move!', 'I'll come back and see you!', 'Stay on it, I'm with you!', 'I'm going and coming!'. Here Otoo plays with tympani mallets. The second half of the piece shifts from mallets to curved sticks and to Ga *kple*, a stately rhythm of spiritual songs, playing both bell and drum parts and 'speaking on top'.

These improvisations speak to how Nii Otoo utilizes musical geography as a listening topography and history of ethnic, national and international cosmopolitan dialogues. They also take us into a distinctive musical conceptualization of variation and its basis in rhythm weaving. Could this be an intimation of musical infinity? Trying to speak more deeply with Nii Otoo about variation, I found myself playing different musical examples to elicit his thoughts as well as playing along with him on *ashiwa* box bass. While a respected master of both traditional Ghanaian percussion and popular and jazz musics, Nii Otoo has had little exposure to concepts of variation in Western European art music. As he had never heard the name of Johann Sebastian Bach, I made the introduction, by way of Bach's *Goldberg Variations*.

While completely self-taught, Nii Otoo has considerable knowledge of Western harmony and melodic motion from playing guitar and bass. Not surprisingly, he noticed the repeating patterns of Bach's bass line motion from one variation to the next, and at one point, stopped to sing the down-and-back line

G–F♯–E–D–B–C–D–G. But listening in to the density of Bach's keyboard music, Otoo's main auditory focus was on something more familiar in West Africa: the interdependence created by independent yet interlocking left and right hands. Nii Otoo asked me to pause the playback several times to listen again to the left–right and front–back play on the double manual keyboard. He greatly enjoyed much of what he heard. All the same, it was the harpsichord's shimmering timbres that he responded to most immediately while hearing Bach's music, qualities he likened to the snare of the *brekete* drum, the rasping interplay of crickets and toads, and the buzz of his xylophone's resonators.

Take a moment to fantasize what the *Goldberg Variations* might sound like had Bach been born in Ghana, gone to sleep each night listening to *Bufo* toads, and devoted himself to the mastery of polyrhythms with the same dedication he showed to harmony. The first of Nii Otoo's variations addresses this fantasy in a rather good-humoured way, using tenor and bass gourd-resonated *gyil* xylophones in a G major pentatonic, the instruments tuned G A B D E, Nii Otoo realizing G major as home key of the *Goldberg Variations*. Nii Otoo plays the left one-octave bass xylophone with two mallets, and the right three-octave tenor xylophone (one octave overlapping) with three. He uses echoing and mirroring in a musical mimesis of the side-to-side left–right and front-to-back forward–distant toads, and the up–down crickets. As in the other variations, you'll hear his interdependent interlocking as a 'crossing on top' and 'sitting below', both in the ways he separates and links the two instruments, and the ground-to-figure ways ostinato layers and rhythmic phrase repetitions intersect fragments of newly emergent melodic improvisation.

Nii Otoo has never touched or even seen a double manual keyboard, but Bach's extensive use of hand crossing was intuited by him solely on the basis of the performance recording. You can also hear a great deal of play between 3 and 2 in Otoo's rhythmic parsings, and as is well known, the *Goldberg Variations*' grand ternary form, with canon in ascent every third variation from numbers 3 to 27, is matched by contrastive binary symmetries on the multiples 2, 4, 8, 16 and 32.

In his *Bach: The Goldberg Variations*, Peter Williams notes many of the work's recurring patterns, and some of his phraseology stands in perfectly in a descriptive lexicon of Nii Otoo's improvisational playfulness: angular lines and inversion (Williams 2001: 56), anticipation in the bass (57), 'cascading' and disappearance becoming reappearance (61), 'patterns crossing, chasing and coming together' (68), 'lines appear to go their own way' (74), 'many tied notes over the bar-lines' *in re* Variations 18 and 19 (75), 'bubbling lines testing the player's hand-positioning' (76), and 'lines tumbling over each other, answering or running against each other, both up and down' (79).

Bufo Variations opens up these many listening possibilities, ones that cross and route back and forth between African traditional and popular dance forms, jazz and European art music. The goal of the project is thus to use playback dialogic techniques to record in a way that encourages playful, expansive and creative listenings, ones that make musical connections, rather than ones that reproduce musical partitions. And while none of this was meant to record systematically in order to lead to a score for musical analysis, the presence of real-time *Pro Tools* tracks with reference pulse timelines certainly makes possible many additional analytic exercises with the same materials. Like Arom, I take as an ultimate goal the invention of techniques that reveal the musical intelligence and creativity of African musicians. Unlike his playback technique, however, this one emphasizes forms of direct access to the distinctly sensuous and creative character of African experimentalism, ranging from cross-species conversation beyond the human to distinctly avant-garde musical conversation with an improvising trio at a distant studio location.

A second CD project, *Ghana Sea Blues* (Annan and Feld 2012), continued my dialogic experiments in listening and playing with Nii Otoo Annan. But it emerged differently and with more direction and control from Nii Otoo himself. In January 2010 Nii Otoo asked me to record 13 of his compositions for solo electric guitar. Ten months later he came to New Mexico for a teaching and performance residency at my university. During his stay we spent several nights in a recording studio, where, listening to playback of his solo recordings, he sequentially overdubbed each of the 13 pieces with 7–10 additional tracks.

In each instance Nii Otoo would select a song. Then, listening to the playback of his original guitar solo over headphones, he first overdubbed himself start to finish with the finger bell *ododompo*. Then, listening to a mix of the guitar and *ododompo* tracks, he overdubbed a second time from start to finish with *gangokui*, a double bell. Then, listening to that composite, he laid down a start-to-finish track on *shekere*, a beaded gourd rattle. And then a track with a pair of conga-type hand drums called *apentemma*. Then, to fill out the bottom, he overdubbed a track on *gome*, a bass drum played with heels and palms, and finally, a track on electric bass. For 10 of them he also overdubbed lyrics he composed.

In the studio we listened back to the multi-track compilations in the *Pro Tools* editing program, which provides time-coded grids superimposed on the vertical tracks. Nii Otoo and I moved the mixing board sliders up and down as we listened, to simulate ways tracks could be taken in and out of a mix, thus exposing different kinds of juxtapositions of the top and bottom layers of the percussion, and different interactions between timelines and the guitar melodies. Departing for Accra a few days later, Nii Otoo slapped my hand vigorously, and with his infectious grin, said: 'Ok Prof, you hear the music. Now make the arrangements!'

In effect, Nii Otoo had these multi-part grids in his head for those ten months between recording the guitar leads and adding the bell, rattle, drum and bass parts. In the course of these overdub sessions, he gave me the gift of another kind of conversation beyond talk or music performance: acoustic entrée to his mind, and with it the challenge to take his recorded overdub track materials and to make musical arrangements for each song in order to expose something about their inner workings.

Studying the 13 pieces consumed me for the next year. I analysed and played with the songs, track by track, phrase by phrase, groove by groove, and using the *Pro Tools* audio suite constructed musical arrangements that bring the overdubbed layering of instruments in and out to expose Nii Otoo's engagements with many

Ghanaian and international pop and jazz idioms. In 2011 I twice took rough mixes back to Accra to review with him. And in January 2012, when the work was finished, we released the CD *Ghana Sea Blues*.

To give an example of the experimental questions and ideas opened up in the process of playback listening and making the final CD, I offer a brief story about one of the three all-instrumental tracks, titled 'Africa Take Five'. When I recorded the guitar solo in 2010, I asked Nii Otoo what he meant by this title, and he tersely replied: '"Africa Take Five". *Um bomp-a-bomp Um bomp Um bomp-a-bomp Um bomp*. You know it, Prof. You know the name. Dave Brubeck. But Africa way.'

The composition 'Africa Take Five' is one of three instrumental pieces on the CD. The underlying title it quotes and references, 'Take Five', is a composition by saxophonist Paul Desmond, made famous in 1959 on The Dave Brubeck Quartet's Columbia Records LP *Time Out* (1959). 'Take Five' became the Brubeck group's theme song, and *Time Out* became the first jazz LP to achieve platinum sales status in the USA. In 2005, after years of just about every other kind of commercial and artistic recognition imaginable, *Time Out* entered the US Library of Congress National Recording Registry. It can only be described as among the most widely circulated, broadcast, known and cited recordings in jazz history, worldwide. An experimental mix of the 1950s West Coast cool style and what were then completely unconventional time signatures in jazz, *Time Out* opened the possibility that jazz could be improvised – indeed, could swing – in time signatures beyond those conventionally based on three- or four-pulse cycles. 'Take Five' was notably the first song to demonstrate this in the time signature of $\frac{5}{4}$.

What Otoo sang to me as '*Um bomp-a-bomp Um bomp Um bomp-a-bomp Um bomp*' sounds out the way jazz ears typically count out that five-pulse cycle: 1, 2 and 3, 4, 5 | 1, 2 and 3, 4, 5. That cycle and accent structure is what is famously announced and repeated throughout Dave Brubeck's piano part on 'Take Five', a L-R-L-R-L-R hand alternation of the repeated chordal vamp from E♭m to B♭m7 over the introduction and A phrase of the song.

Nii Otoo's 'Africa Take Five' transforms this into an Afro Escher sketch with an inside-out gestalt. Listening to the composite and the breakdown of bell and rattle parts, we hear how he plays in an underlying pulse cycle of 6 while maintaining the feel and implication of an accent cycle in 5. He does this by off-setting the Brubeck piano vamp rendering of the five-pulse cycle to stretch the gestalt: 1 and 2 and 3, 4, 5 | 1 and 2 and 3, 4, 5. In effect, he simultaneously references and evokes the $\frac{5}{4}$ groove of the Brubeck Quartet's 'Take Five' (particularly with the strong push of pulses 4, 5 and across the bar line to 1) but in the push–pull of a more danceable and Afrocentric, even six-pulse groove.

What we hear in 'Africa Take Five', then, is an African listening history and a new way of listening to and with the time experiment of swing in $\frac{5}{4}$ offered in Brubeck's 'Take Five'. This is one way that listening to African histories of listening, and engaging them through recording, opens us up to other ways of thinking about the play of time, groove and multiple metre. These listening histories also help excavate and query entrenched narratives that position African ways of hearing in relation to those of the West. In this specific case, one of those narratives is distinctly political, because 'Take Five' was, in its time, very much racialized as the cool jazz played and listened to by whites, Europeans and educated elites. Nii Otoo's creative Africanization of 'Take Five' opens up the possibility that the song was heard differently in Africa. And it reminds us that 'Take Five' was also enjoyed by many people who had no idea whether the members of The Dave Brubeck Quartet were white or black. This is highly ironic, of course, given that the nationalist US jazz narrative that polemicized cool/white versus hot/black stylistics was the same discourse that relegated Africans to the position of jazz ancestors, actors only in the music's distant historical past, and not players or listeners engaged with the music in a historical present (Feld 2012).

Listening with Nii Otoo, and listening to his history of listening, also helps us pose another question: Why did Africans like this song so much? Certainly, Voice of America radio, which is where Nii Otoo first heard 'Take Five' in his youth, had great prestige, power and wattage in West Africa. We know that Willis Conover, and then his successors, programmed a great deal of West Coast cool jazz for airplay on Voice of America. And we know that this music even became more popular when white artists arrived to play in West Africa as 'jazz ambassadors', following Louis Armstrong's 1960 success in that role (Von Eschen 2006). Still, very few songs with high Voice of America radio rotation ever became as popular, or remain as memorable as 'Take Five' in West Africa, especially among musicians, who love to cover it. Why?

Part of the answer now strikes me as rather straightforward, even if it partially resists the cultural imperialism framework that is most typically invoked to address the matter. Namely: African artists and audiences appreciated Brubeck as a musician who experimented with time and rhythm, even when it was with time and rhythm quite foreign to their own local music. It may come as a shock that working-class, uneducated and musically non-literate Africans enjoyed 'Take Five', enjoyed the way the Brubeck Quartet was playing with time. But 'playing with time' is exactly what Brubeck embraced experimentally, and that is also what many musicians in West Africa know how to do well and enjoy. Indeed, this is just what Nii Otoo says he loves about 'Take Five', and why he wanted to make a composition dedicated to the song. Ironically again, as I was visiting Accra in December 2012, it was also Nii Otoo who informed me about Brubeck's passing, after he heard the news broadcast by Voice of America.[2]

This is the kind of 'roots and routes' soundtrack that James Clifford's *Routes* (1997) alerted us to listen for: the sound of discrepant cosmopolitanism. For an African like Nii Otoo Annan, playing with time, loving and mastering the playfulness of 'Take Five' and matching it with his own, also tells a deep story about music as a site of black pride and accomplishment. It tells a story of imagined and criss-crossed

[2] Doug Levine, 'Pioneering Jazz Musician Dave Brubeck Dies', *Voice of America*, 5 December 2012, http://www.voanews.com/content/jazz-musician-dave-brubeck-dies/1559095.html (accessed 30 June 2015).

alliances in sound. It's a story born of the recognition that musicians playfully engage the complexities of rhythm and that there's a good conversation waiting. It's a story about wanting to meet that playfulness on a level field where desires for expansive agency, for mobility, connection and intimacy, can be realized.

Listening this way to Nii Otoo's histories of listening is how I hear 'Africa Take Five' as a dense chord of discrepant cosmopolitanism, a chord that sounds a desire to own, to inhabit, to converse with wondrous music from beyond as much as he could own, inhabit and converse with multiple layers of Ghanaian and West African idioms that were so close by. Discrepant cosmopolitanism: how else to describe the musical revelation packed into Nii Otoo crossing two bell parts to trick our ears into hearing 5 in 6 and 6 in 5? Discrepant cosmopolitanism: how else to describe the social revelation that an African musician, one unaware of the polemically racialized past of 'Take Five', can pulverize the imagined incommensurability of its cool $\frac{5}{4}$ timeline and a rhythmically hot $\frac{6}{4}$ West African dance groove?

Bufo Variations and *Ghana Sea Blues* use aspects of field and studio playback technologies to engage the importance of collaborative and dialogic listening experiments. These experiments can have important musical and social implications for performance, recording, analysis, technological mediation, representation and publication. They can also help realize a decolonized and reimagined 'ethno'-musicology, an ethnomusicology where, as Arom proposed long ago, sound recording technologies and techniques could figure in more collaborative forms of knowledge production that reach across and beyond musical and cultural difference.

References

Annan, Nii Otoo and Feld, Steven (2008) *Bufo Variations* (CD), Santa Fe: VoxLox.

Annan, Nii Otoo and Feld, Steven (2012) *Ghana Sea Blues* (CD), Santa Fe: VoxLox.

Arom, Simha (1973) 'Une méthode pour la transcription de polyphonies et polyrhythmies de tradition orale', *Revue de musicologie*, 59/2, pp. 165–90.

——— (1976) 'The Use of Play-back Techniques in the Study of Oral Polyphonies', *Ethnomusicology*, 20/3, pp. 483–519.

——— (1985) *Polyphonies instrumentales d'Afrique centrale: structure et méthodologie*, 2 vols, Paris: Selaf/Collection Ethnomusicologie.

——— (1991) *African Polyphony and Polyrhythm: Structure and Methodology*, Cambridge: Cambridge University Press.

——— and Fürniss, Susanne (1992) 'The Pentatonic System of the Aka Pygmies of the Central African Republic', in *European Studies in Ethnomusicology: Historical Developments and Recent Trends*, ed. Max Peter Baumann, Artur Simon and Ulrich Wegner, Wilhelmshaven: Florian Noetzel, pp. 159–73.

Baily, John (2009) 'Modi Operandi in the Making of "World Music" Recordings', in *Recorded Music: Performance, Culture and Technology*, ed. Amanda Bayley, Cambridge: Cambridge University Press, pp. 107–24.

Christensen, Dieter (2002) 'Berlin Phonogramm-Archiv: The First 100 Years', in *Music Archiving in the World: Papers Presented at the Conference on the Occasion of the 100th Anniversary of the Berlin Phonogramm-Archiv*, ed. Gabriele Berlin and Artur Simon, Berlin: Verlag für Wissenschaft und Bildung, pp. 19–31.

Clifford, James (1997) *Routes: Travel and Translation in the Late Twentieth Century*, Cambridge, MA: Harvard University Press.

Coke, Alex, Marsh, Tina and Feld, Steve (2008) *It's Possible* (CD), Santa Fe: VoxLox.

Dave Brubeck Quartet (1959) *Time Out* (LP), Columbia Records.

Feld, Steven (1987) 'Dialogic Editing: Interpreting How Kaluli Read *Sound and Sentiment*', *Cultural Anthropology*, 2/2, pp. 190–210.

——— (2011) *Voices of the Rainforest* [1991] (CD), Washington, DC: Smithsonian Folkways Recordings.

——— (2012) *Jazz Cosmopolitanism in Accra: Five Musical Years in Ghana*, Durham, NC: Duke University Press.

——— (2015) 'Acoustemology', in *Keywords in Sound*, ed. David Novak and Matt Sakakeeny, Durham, NC: Duke University Press, pp. 12–21.

Fernando-Marandola, Nathalie (2002), 'New Perspectives on Interactive Field Experiments', *Yearbook for Traditional Music*, 34, pp. 163–86.

Fürniss, Susanne (1993) 'Rigueur et liberté: la polyphonie vocale des Pygmées Aka (Centrafrique)', in: *Polyphonies de tradition orale: histoire et traditions vivantes*, ed. Christian Meyer, Paris: Créaphis, pp. 101–31.

——— (2006) 'Aka Polyphony: Music, Theory, Back and Forth', in *Analytical Studies in World Music*, ed. Michael Tenzer, Oxford: Oxford University Press, pp. 163–204.

Haraway, Donna (2003) *The Companion Species Manifesto: Dogs, People, and Significant Otherness*, Chicago, IL: Prickly Paradigm Press.

Hart, Mickey and Kostyal, Karen (2003) *Songcatchers: In Search of the World's Music*, Washington, DC: National Geographic Books.

Myers, Helen (1992) 'Ethnomusicology', in *Ethnomusicology: An Introduction*, ed. Helen Myers, New York: W.W. Norton.

Rice, Timothy (2014) *Ethnomusicology: A Very Brief Introduction*, Oxford: Oxford University Press.

Rödel, Mark-Oliver (2000) *Herpetofauna of West Africa*, vol. 1: *Amphibians of the West African Savanna*. Geneva: Edition Chimaira.

Stock, Jonathan (2009) 'Recordings as Research Tools in Ethnomusicology', in *Recorded Music: Performance, Culture and Technology*, ed. Amanda Bayley, Cambridge: Cambridge University Press, pp. 187–205.

Von Eschen, Penny (2006) *Satchmo Blows Up the World: Jazz Ambassadors Play the Cold War*, Cambridge, MA: Harvard University Press.

Williams, Peter (2001) *Bach: The Goldberg Variations*, Cambridge: Cambridge University Press.

PART II
Remediations

Chapter 7

Remediation or Opera on Screen? Some Misunderstandings Regarding Recent Research

Michele Girardi

My remarks in this chapter on the concept of remediation – an apt neologism that gave the title to a hefty volume (Bolter and Grusin 1999) – will start from Marshall McLuhan's renowned maxim, formulated forty years ago in a bible on the sociology of mass communication, *Understanding Media* (1964): 'the content of a *medium* is always another *medium*'. It is the representation of a means of mass communication within another, or rather, the use of some characteristics of the first within another. Opera – a true semiological *monster* in itself – seems to be suitable for studies in the field of remediation, considering that this genre is today growing in popularity and has considerably expanded its own boundaries of reception, thanks to new media.

I am borrowing the definition of 'opera on screen' from Emanuele Senici's fine 2009 article because I find it flexible at the right point: it encompasses 'film, opera in the studio, films of opera in the theatre' on different media, from the PC to home video, which can be acquired in stores, supermarkets, service stations, kiosks, but also especially via YouTube, the Library of Alexandria for moving images of our time (Senici 2009: 278).[1] Senici wrote his essay when musical theatre, film and other material were available only in clips of ten minutes or so, whereas now we can view them one after another, and even download (in accordance with copyright laws) complete operas such as the *Götterdämmerung* (more than four hours of music). This immense and vibrant archive offers complete operas of any genre, including special stand-outs such as the most recent productions of the theatrical season and festivals, as well as historical recordings of great interest: for example, *Lulu*, with Act III completed by Cerha and directed by Boulez (Paris, 1979), films linked to the operatic repertory of unquestionable precocity such as *Carmen* by Cecil B. DeMille (1915), the last production in the field of *Regietheater* recorded for a television broadcast and made available on a website with free access.

[1] For an updated bibliography, see Senici (2009): 275–7 (nn. 4–6). See also: Senici (2010), Esse (2010), Morris (2010), Will (2011), Scognamiglio (2011), Senici (2011), Wells (2012), Cenciarelli (2013) and Grasso (2013).

I would like to start with a question: Who is the author of the production of an opera on screen? Does a name such as Humphrey Burton mean anything? Burton, with a solid music training, outstanding biographer of composers such as Bernstein (Burton 1994), is one of those pillars of opera on screen that enthusiasts are not well acquainted with, and of whom no critic speaks. Together with other legendary figures such as Brian Large, and with Kirk Browning, Peter Maniura, Tony Palmer, or with the younger generation such as François Roussillon (Robert Carsen's regular collaborator), as a director and producer Burton created the most significant opera DVDs on the market, but also documentaries, films of concerts.

The role of these silent protagonists is the first theme to highlight. According to the well-known Brian Large, musician *in primis* and omnipresent television director (who has filmed more opera productions than anyone else): 'The television director must translate a production conceived by a stage director into a video production. As always, the video director begins by preparing a storyboard from the score, although changes will be made after the stage version has been seen.'[2] Large also describes the method used:

> The different shots are joined in a sequence, the pacing of which is determined by the types of shot used and the length that each lasts. Visual interest is created by the frequency of cuts: a quick succession can increase the pace and excitement, while a wide-angle shot may be used to set a mood or relax the pace. Directors often derive the usual pacing from the rhythm of the music itself, as determined by the harmonies, chord structure, orchestration and other factors. In choosing the shots and the pacing of cuts, the director may also be influenced by the opera's period and style, aiming to create a visual style appropriate to the artistic period in which the piece originated or is set.[3]

Hence, the television director begins working independently of the theatre director, finding later a point of convergence and translating to the screen what has been conceived for the stage.

One would then state that the author is the one who films a production, which might be a live staging or realized in the studio and so on. Without going back to the theoretical formalization of *Remediation* (Bolter and Grusin 1999; see also Chapple 2006), it is easy to agree on the fact that an opera on screen is very different from a theatrical production. On the other hand, the two scholars seem reluctant to treat music and specific problems concerning opera, as they discuss the immediacy of hypermediation by referring to video editing in the field of popular music. And if we obviously agree with someone who writes that 'performance's only life is in the present', it is not taken-for-granted to agree with its consequent corollary, that a 'performance cannot be saved, recorded, documented' (Phelan 1993: 146) –

2 Brian Large, 'Filming', *Oxford Music Online*, http://www.oxfordmusiconline.com:80/subscriber/article/grove/music/0901619 (accessed 30 June 2015).

3 Ibid.

in any event, 'television director' refers to a staging, whose peculiarity does not disappear at all in the transposition, but becomes re-elaborated. Moreover, to give credit to Brian Large's method, the hypotext always remains the point of reference, when a score of music theatre is performed on stage, and when it is recorded there for the visual medium. If the recording for the screen indeed follows its own rules, complex and very articulated, which put the language of the image in relationship with the musical differently from what the director does onstage, the object in the limelight remains the same. This canon is well summarized by Lionel Salter:

> Fewer changes of image accord with the tempo and mood of slow-moving music: quicker changes can underline the excitement or agitation of fast movements. These changes of shot should take place only where the musical structure allows, never in mid-phrase: camera cuts are appropriate at starts of clean-cut phrases (in which case they need to be made with precision, neither too early nor – even worse – too late); but, if the music is fluid, dissolves correspond better (slow lingering cross-fades, however, only draw attention to the technique employed): after a series of mixes, a cut can have the effect of a sudden *sforzando*. A camera tracking in usually suggests an increase in tension or a crescendo, as does a panning or tracking shot across a section of the orchestra (as for a Rossini build-up); quick zoom-ins look melodramatic and should be used only in exceptional circumstances: a zoom-out, at whatever speed, is better avoided, as it gives the impression of retreating or fleeing from the music. Superimposition of images of instruments is usually undesirable musically except, for example, in ostinatos such as in Ravel's *Bolero* or Holst's 'Mars'. Some emphasizing of the structure of, for example, a sonata form movement can be achieved by adopting for the recapitulation the same image sequence as in the exposition. All this of course necessitates the director's planning his or her camera treatment from the score. All shots should be musically motivated: those made purely for pictorial effect, or cutaways to members of the audience, detract from concentration on the music and suggest that the director has lost interest in it. Works with colourful orchestration (e.g. Rimsky Korsakov's *Spanish Capriccio)* and concertos are the musical forms most adaptable to television, the interplay between soloist, orchestra and conductor in the latter offering quasi-dramatic interest.[4]

Prelude: Rewriting a Musical Dramaturgy

The *Candide* production directed for the theatre by Robert Carsen and filmed for television by François Roussillon, which premiered at the Théâtre du Châtelet in 2006 and went to the Teatro alla Scala of Milan in 2007 in the wake of bitter

---

[4] Lionel Salter, 'Television', *Oxford Music Online*, http://www.oxfordmusiconline.com:BO/SJbscriber/article/grove/music/41850 (accessed 30 June 2015).

polemics and with some politically motivated censorship,[5] seems to me a good way to introduce the subject of this chapter.

> When the conductor enters, we see a television screen already positioned before the curtain (Candide 2006; Figure 7.1) and the overture accompanies a broadcast dated 1956 (but already in Technicolor!) of VOLT-AIR TV; the *Allegro molto con brio* starts (*Candide* 1957: 2) on the opening rolling credits of the theatrical production; at the Cantabile (15; bar 95) a film begins on the United States during the 1950s–60s prosperity, reassuring images of healthy families with well-nourished children, electric appliances, well-stocked supermarkets, military parades; then, missile launches into space towards the moon in the Apollo mission, John Kennedy dancing with Jacqueline Bouvier on their wedding day (1953), then they are amid a sea of adoring people; Broadway with parades of famous stars including Marilyn Monroe and Ronald Reagan, glittering Las Vegas, Elvis Presley in military uniform; the screens goes off and Lambert Wilson, in the role of Voltaire, starts off the performance.

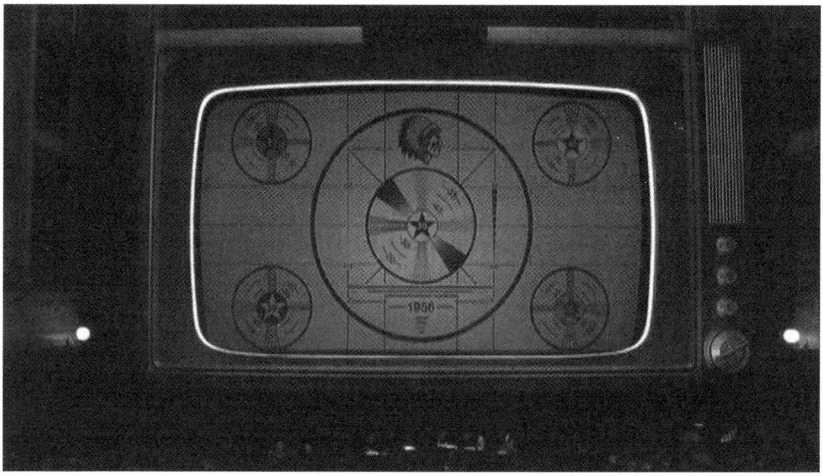

Figure 7.1 *Candide* (2006)

Bernstein and Carsen's *Candide* is a real semiological *monster* because, in addition to the natural complexity of opera itself, there is a rewriting of the theatrical text and a massive use of technology in an interactive relationship between *media* realized onstage, such as the film described above. There is nothing irregular, after all,

5 See: 'My Big Fat Candide Review', *Opera Chic*, 22 June 2007, http://operachic.typepad.com/opera_chic/candide/ (accessed 30 June 2015); see also Anna Cirillo, 'E il Candide taglia la satira sui preti', 19 June 2007, *la Repubblica.it Archivio*, http://www-5.unipv.it/girardi/saggi/2007_Candide_press.pdf (accessed 30 June 2015).

in Carsen and his dramaturg Ian Burton's operation: this libertarian opera had undergone rewriting by the author himself until 1989, the year before Bernstein's death, when he directed a performance in concert form at the Barbican with a stellar cast (*Candide* 1989), directed by the same Humphrey Burton.

In the following pages I will analyse four operatic sequences, connecting the musical dramaturgy with its theatrical staging and version on screen.

Fidelity to Performance?

A review of the video recording of Act II of *Tosca* from Covent Garden in 1964 will help us understand the communicative power of a television production at the dawn of its history, celebrated among the aficionados for the epic encounter between Maria Callas and Tito Gobbi (*Tosca* 1964). As the curtain opens, the zoom focuses on Scarpia. The camera remains fixed until Spoletta enters, then follows the action. The frame recaptures the entire stage only when Tosca has killed Scarpia, then the curtain closes.

The producer Bill Ward followed the instructions of the director Franco Zeffirelli, who at the time was also launching his cinema career. The film's intention is to affirm emphatically that we are in the theatre, considering that the playbill of the show scrolls after the first frame. At the same time, a formal strategy emerges and highlights the macro-structure of the act: only when Tosca commits the crime, saving Rome from a monster, does the camera return to frame the entire stage until the curtains close. Precisely this last shot demonstrates how the issue of fidelity to performance, which could be achieved with a fixed onstage camera, is pure Utopia: not once did my eyes abandon Floria Tosca's actions in this finale, not least because of the structural connection with the stage music studied with meticulous care by the composer (Girardi 2002: 181–7).

This technical perfection allows the fruition of details that otherwise would not be noticed in the theatre. For example, thanks to the enormous progress in sound technology, in a recording of *Věc Makropulos* we can hear the viola d'amore, nearly inaudible in the theatre, which Janáček uses more for the semantic implications of the name than for its specific timbre (Girardi 2013: 33). Likewise, the camera eye can bring details into focus that enrich the reception, as described by Salter: 'Television's ability to focus closely on small but important details of the action, such as Michele lighting his pipe in *Il tabarro* or the Count pricking his finger on a pin in *Le nozze di Figaro*, increases their significance.'[6]

[6] Lionel Salter, 'Television', *Oxford Music Online*, http://www.oxfordmusiconline.com:BO/SJbscriber/article/grove/music/41850 (accessed 30 June 2015).

Details in the Foreground

However, I would like to focus on a performance I personally attended and can directly compare with its video transposition. *La traviata*, opening the 2004 season of the Teatro La Fenice (after the 1996 fire), is a perfect example of the interaction between two different visions (stage and screen), both in general and in detail. Even if the television director does not sign off and has often worked with the most renowned directors (from Brian Large to François Roussillon), on this occasion Robert Carsen's choices made for the theatre prevail over any request by Renata Carmine, director of the DVD that 'textualizes' the performance.[7] The key moment of Act II is no doubt the encounter between Violetta and Germont: Carsen sets up a double strategy, to benefit both theatrical and televised action, in which the details can be managed to create meaningful associations.

'Sarà lui che attendo.' Violetta pulls out a red book while Germont enters and throws it to the ground (*La traviata* 2004; Figure 7.2), which will be framed soon after ('a tutti fia mistero quest'atto'). While she sings 'non sapete quale affetto', Germont-*père* picks up the book, singing 'È grave il sagrifizio' (Figure 7.3). 'Lui solo amar vogl'io': Violetta tears the book from his hands, and we catch a glimpse of the title ('Poiché dal cielo non furono | tai nodi benedetti'; Figure 7.4). 'L'uomo implacabil per lei sarà': the woman hurls the book to the floor and is framed by the camera: it is *Manon Lescaut,* or, more precisely, *L'histoire du Chevalier Des Grieux et de Manon Lescaut* by Abbé Prévost (Figure 7.5). 'Conosca il sagrifizio': the protagonist picks up the book to slip in the party invitation, in the guise of a bookmark, probably because it will be found by Alfredo … (Figure 7.6). 'Non ci vedrem più forse': who will she not see again, Germont or Alfredo? 'Addio': she blows a kiss to the book, but in truth to Alfredo (Figure 7.7) and, caressing it, lays it on the floor (Figure 7.8). Saying farewell, Violetta stares at the book, shortly after found by Alfredo, in the duet with the father ('un padre e una suora t'affretta a consolar'). Alfredo discovers the invitation in the book (Figure 7.9), which he angrily throws it to the floor before hurrying off to Paris.

7 The filmed version shows the premiere at the Teatro La Fenice in 1853, based on the critical edition (*La traviata* 1997).

Figures 7.2–7.9 *La traviata* (2004)

The theatre spectator can follow only part of the action: the spectator notices a hand-bound book in her hands, perceives that the soprano picks the book from the floor and slips the party invitation into it, and that Alfredo, at the end of the duet with his father, opens it, finds the invitation and exits in fury to follow his love at Flora's home.[8] Therefore, the protagonist left the book there, hoping that her lover would find it and hopefully take it with him, just like the flower in the preceding act – but the consequences of this act of love will be tragic. Before the book ends up on the floor, it changes hands, it is brandished by the father, and so on. This part of the action, setting up an intertextual relationship between Violetta and another celebrated prostitute of the eighteenth century, Manon Lescaut

[8] Alfredo exclaims: 'Ah! … ell'è alla festa! … volisi | l'offesa a vendicar.'

(and, on a second level, involving Verdi, Massenet and Puccini), can only be understood in full by those who see the DVD and read the book's title. This is not only a case of amplifying a detail of the text, but of adding meaning to the action by re-reading the stage directions of libretto and score.

In Agreement with the Score

However, attention to detail is not always useful to opera on screen. Let us return to Tosca and consider the finale of Act I. Usually, the television director is drawn to Scarpia's Satanism, showing this in a monologue at the proscenium, where Scarpia mixes the devil with the holy water according to the instructions of the score (bells ostinato versus chromatic harmonies in a ninth interval). He forgets that in the background a religious ceremony is unfolding, which is primary to the economy of the event: this is why the television director usually chooses to put the protagonist in the foreground. In a recent recording at Covent Garden, television director Jonathan Haswell attempted to separate the two spheres.

> Floria exits after the duet: Scarpia does not hide his passion for the female sex (*Tosca* 2011; Figure 7.10), a passion that obsessively extends to the vivid depictions (Figure 7.11) – the television director indulges in the protagonist overwhelmed by his fantasies, leaving less space to the entire stage (Figure 7.12). A few instants to extol the suspicions of his erotic idol and to take a look at the ceremony taking place above his delirium (Figure 7.13), which requires a close-up of the baron while the erotic tension grows glaringly, almost until the liberating orgasm (Figure 7.14). Only in the concluding section, eros and religion unite dramatically in the sign of the cross (Figure 7.15).

Figures 7.10–7.15 *Tosca* (2011)

This penalizes the authors' will, calling for two simultaneous actions because they represent a single sign: on the one hand the *eros* of the individual, on the other the bigotry, which is also a manifestation of religious power. The bishop and crowd in prayer must be mixed into the monologue and the scene must be viewed in a general frame. I find Lehnhoff's direction of this scene (Amsterdam, 1998), conceived basically also for the video recording, more in agreement with the score. The lighted candles symbolize the ceremony.

Scarpia (Terfel again) leaves Tosca at the end of the duet, not without gallantry and begins his monologue: the promise of 'un pronto sospetto' triggers the devotion, and the candles together with the cannon's boom (faith unites with suspicion; *Tosca* 1998; Figure 7.16). The choir begins to pray: a row of candles is lit ('Auditorjum nostrum | in Nomine Domini'; Figure 7.17). In the *Te Deum*, the fire embodies Scarpia's theme (major triads of B♭ > A♭ > E♮ trace the arc of a tritone also at the finale of the act, with enormous emphasis), his faith and his perversion: the demon (or *diabolus*) invades the scene (Figure 7.18).

Figures 7.16–7.18 *Tosca* (1998)

Between Video and Stage

I would now like to consider a theatre director and cinematographer who filmed his own productions, giving us unbeatable hermeneutic perspectives, such as with *Theodora*, Handel's penultimate oratorio (Glyndebourne, 1996; see Martino 2004–5). Peter Sellars has received somewhat more critical attention than his colleagues, as noted by Senici, because his case is not unique (one may recall Jean-Pierre Ponnelle; see Bendikas 2004; Faroni 2014) but not that frequent – 'the director of the performance and that of the video identify with one another' (Senici 2009: 275; for a glance at the collective body of his work and his Mozart productions, see Citron 2000). In his celebrated Mozart trilogy, the overtures are treated as in a film (on the staging, see Littlejohn 1990): New York is the protagonist here, both for *Le nozze di Figaro* and *Don Giovanni*, in the first case with scenes of the luxurious city centre (Manhattan), in the second showing the desolate suburbs, the ideal background for a degraded hero. Events have been modernized (for a comparison with similar stagings, see Porter 1992) and take place in a space that is not entirely defined, yet still recognizable, as in the *Nozze*, where the characters come together at the entrance to a skyscraper (for a critical account of the rehearsals, see Trousdell 1991). The audience legitimately think they are attending a film-opera up until the third scene, when this misconception creates problems ('Is this a video of a live performance, or in the studio?'; Senici 2009: 288). This happens in three distinct situations during the first and second acts of *Così fan tutte*, which establish a precise musical relationship with the baritone's two arias and propose a dramatic suggestion tied to Don Alfonso's expression. After Fiordiligi's firm refusal in her grand aria 'Come scoglio', it is in fact her fiancé who starts off the courtship. With its ruffian tone, the orchestra proclaims the high jinks and the baritone listens to the sound supporting him.

I.11, no. 15: Guglielmo goes to the proscenium to sing his aria 'Non siate ritrosi, occhietti vezzosi' (the substitute aria, now in current use), and here, suddenly, the pit appears (*Così fan tutte* 1990; Figure 7.19), just when the orchestra plays the first bars of the aria and Guglielmo listens satisfied (Figure 7.20). In the next act, the two 'Albanians' are making their final attempt at seducing the two ladies of Ferrara: II.4, *recitativo* after no. 21, 'Il tutto deponete sopra quei tavolini'. Don Alfonso should turn 'ai servi che portan un bacile di fiori', but instead once again violates the film fiction and returns to the theatre, speaking to the orchestra from the stage ('cos'è tal mascherata?'; Figure 7.21). In closing II.8, recitative after no. 25: the 'winning' baritone (Guglielmo has just succeeded in courting Dorabella), unable to console the tenor's broken heart, performs the accompanied recitative, and little by little, reveals the production's features. 'Certo caso quest'è da far stupore': The image reverses for an instant, as if the perspective itself has been turned upside down. Guglielmo, meanwhile, first approaches the cameras that are filming the scene (Figure 7.22), and then, with a microphone sings aria no. 26 'Donne mie la fate a tanti', moving among the music stands (Figure 7.23). 'Io vo' bene al sesso vostro, ogni giorno ve lo mostro' (Figure 7.24). Some other gags involve the audience, then Guglielmo sings the finale of his aria assuming the camera's perspective, after passing again in front of the orchestra. At the end, the image reverses once again: the situation goes back to 'normal'.

Figures 7.19–7.24 *Così fan tutte* (1990)

When in the following act Alfonso sends the two men away (and Guglielmo will soon achieve the first success), the orchestra takes over. The puppeteer here begins the decisive phase of the seduction that began with aria no. 15, and the two appear in striking disguise, leaving speechless the two women – who in the preceding three scenes had decided to surrender. But even more important is what happens while Guglielmo performs the accompanied recitative and aria no. 26, 'Donne mie la fate a tanti': also, in this case, after Fiordiligi has sung a solo – the rondo no. 25, 'Per pietà ben mio perdona' – what emerges is the fragility of a rock that is no longer so immovable (on Sellars's direction, see also Robinson 1986). The director's choice seems to support the characteristics of the only didactic aria of the opera with a transversal artifice overlapping theatrical staging, screen and audience. The first meta-theatrical artifice is the microphone, contextualizing a meta-aria as if it were stage music. Then the perspective turns to the encounter between the baritone and the camera in the wing, again while it passes in front of the orchestra in the pit, and finally when it reaches the audience on the risers, involved by the performers in a gag that is intentionally predictable. Sellars thus proposes *Così fan tutte* as a masterpiece of artifice, the disguise being more real than reality itself and turning it upside down. At the same time, it declares the rules of a theatrical game that involves the spectators, also retrospectively. The illusions achieved through remediation – which reappropriates the theatrical dimension from the opera film – become purely vertiginous and reveal the aesthetic potential of the entire trilogy (for an in-depth analysis of Sellars's conception of opera in the television production, see Citron 2002).

Is Remediation a False Problem?

The final case does not concern the relationship between a theatrical production and its recording on video, but it allows us to broaden the view and to understand the real possibilities of video to communicate aesthetical messages connected to opera: *Leonard Bernstein Conducts 'West Side Story': The Making of the Recording* (1985). The title places the author and his creation in the foreground, and as a subtitle, the dual natures of the work itself – opera and document – are immediately combined. The DVD was directed by Christopher Swann and produced by Humphrey Burton, whose undisputed authority is evident in how strongly he influences every aspect, from the visual choices to the narration. Even if this does not concern the recording of an opera for the screen, there is a tight connection between the rehearsals conducted by the composer and the events recounted by Leonard Bernstein, Stephen Sondheim and Arthur Laurents, who straddle different media and genres, from Broadway to the multi-award-winning film with Jerome Robbins' choreography (the architect of this modern *Romeo and Juliet*, about the gang wars that haunt New York's slums). The *Making* provides us with new perspectives for *West Side Story*'s reception, recorded in a complete audio version in 1985 (for an in-depth study on the opera, see Simeone 2009; for an updated and more general view of Bernstein's musical theatre, see Smith 2011). Bernstein had never conducted his masterpiece during his successful 30-year worldwide career: thanks to this project supported by Deutsche Grammophon, he could enjoy a full orchestra, compared to the 32 musicians crowding the Broadway stage at the 1957 premiere. The cast of *West Side Story* (1985) also recorded the opera and this was released as a CD by Deutsche Grammophon Gesellschaft (457 199–2), with only one difference: no. 13d, 'Somewhere', is sung by Marilyn Horne, whereas in the *Making* it is sung by Kiri Te Kanawa (who obviously cannot perform both the offstage voice and Maria's role in the opera).

Maria and Tony, that is, Kiri Te Kanawa and José Carreras are performing the Balcony Scene no. 6: suddenly, after the two sing the last verses of 'Tonight' ('But here you are | And what was just a word is a star | Tonight!'; *West Side Story* 1985; Figure 7.25) and before the concluding dialogue of their scene, the camera cuts to the recording studio, until then full of life, now gloomily empty. Bernstein enters and performs a sort of 'epilogue'[9] while leafing through a score (Figure 7.26). He says: 'At the beginning of this project I was not all that secure about what was going to happen. It was an extraordinary idea. I thought it might for one thing seem dated. It is fifties music, and what I found out of all that insecurity is a tremendous feeling of security. This poetic language of Jets and Sharks that was created by Arthur Laurents is something truly poetic in a sense that it lasts as a poem lasts. I feel that this piece is, in its funny little crazy way, a classic.'

The music starts again in the orchestra and while the two lovers take leave of one another ('MARIA: What does Tony stand for? | TONY: Anton. | MARIA: Te Adoro Anton. | TONY: Te adoro Maria'), the camera borrows a shot from Robert Wise's film (*West Side Story* 1961) of the stage set where the love story takes place (*West Side Story* 1985; Figure 7.27), that already appeared at the beginning of the *Making*, before the opening titles. The end-to-end cross-reference of the video emphasizes the milieu in relationship to Romeo and Juliet's love, looming over all, contexts and epochs. The scene closes and with it, the entire *Making*, with Te Kanawa and Carreras singing the last four verses of their duet ('Good night, good night, | Sleep well and when you dream, | Dream of me | Tonight').

[9] I use this term in the accepted meaning of 'finale of a comedy … common … in certain modern dramaturgy that is fond of declaring the theatrical, fictional character of the work'. See 'Commiato (Congedo, Licenza)', in *Enciclopedia dello spettacolo* (Rome: Le maschere, 1954–65). An example in opera is illustrated by the spoken epilogue in Puccini's *Gianni Schicchi* (see Girardi 2002: 433–44); Bernstein's statement also performs the function of an authorial epitext (Genette) commenting upon the primary text. Thanks to Laurie Schwartz and David Rosen for the stimulating discussion regarding this passage.

Figures 7.25–7.27 *West Side Story* (1985)

Bernstein's poetic and aesthetic intent with this video was to affirm the classicism of his creation, since he had under his baton both a talented orchestra and a stellar *belcanto* cast, thus affirming the true nature of his work, from a Broadway production to opera (it was with this label that *West Side Story* arrived in 2000 at the Teatro alla Scala in Milan). One only has to take a look at the index of the DVD (booklet of *West Side Story* 1985: 3–4) and compare it with that of the score (*West Side Story* 2000: ix–x) to realize that the new order of the pieces aims to communicate, almost quintessentially, the transcendent power of love binding the two protagonists by using the power of Bernstein's musical bonds which are revealed (see Figure 7.28). 'Tonight', no. 10, is rehearsed as an ensemble piece anticipating the conflict between the rival gangs [4], but soon after Carreras sings with the piano accompaniment [7] as in the Balcony Scene. Immediately after, 'Something's Coming' [8] expresses Tony's presentiments of love, in its *incipit*, with the interval of the descending augmented fourth, ('Who knows?'), which in reverse generates Maria's theme. The lover's anxiety is a long-lasting wait (00:10:10) in the *Making*: when Carreras rehearses 'Maria' [20] and begins to record it, the $B\flat_3$ unfortunately breaks, discomforting an author who is extremely participatory and affectionate to him [21]; Carreras immediately repeats it, giving his best [22], thus confirming that the part, when entrusted to an opera tenor, acquires depth.

A tragic destiny weighs on Tony and Maria's love: while this remains the pessimistic conclusion of the work, in the *Making* it is realized in a less tragic manner, keeping in mind the thematic references that the score puts into action.[10] The Balcony Scene ends with a short motif that reaches towards an ideal breath of life (see Example 7.1), sounding like a premonition of the following events. After Bernardo's murder, Tony and Maria sing in despair, 'Somewhere there's got to be some place for you and for me' (no. 13a, Ballet Sequence); shortly after, a girl answers (an offstage voice, no. 13d, 'Somewhere'): 'There's a place for us | Somewhere a place for us' (see Example 7.2). In the final bars of the opera, during the funeral procession, the same motif returns to recall the fulfilment of the sorrowful destiny (see Example 7.3).

Example 7.1 Leonard Bernstein, *West Side Story*, no. 6, measure 151
Source: West Side Story (2000): 167.

Example 7.2 Leonard Bernstein, *West Side Story*, no. 13d, measures 123–6
Source: West Side Story (2000): 369.

[10] The many intertextual connections in *West Side Story* score would require a separate chapter (see Simeone 2009); one may recall only that the melody of no. 15, 'I Have a Love' (*Andante sostenuto*, from bar 68, *West Side Story* 2000: 440), contains two references: the first to the so-called theme of Brünnhilde's glorification ('Im Feuer Leuchtend') that celebrates the sacrificial rite in the finale of the *Götterdämmerung*; the second, 'I love him', refers instead to Delilah's sensual phrase in *Samson et Dalila* ('Ah! Réponds à ma tendresse!').

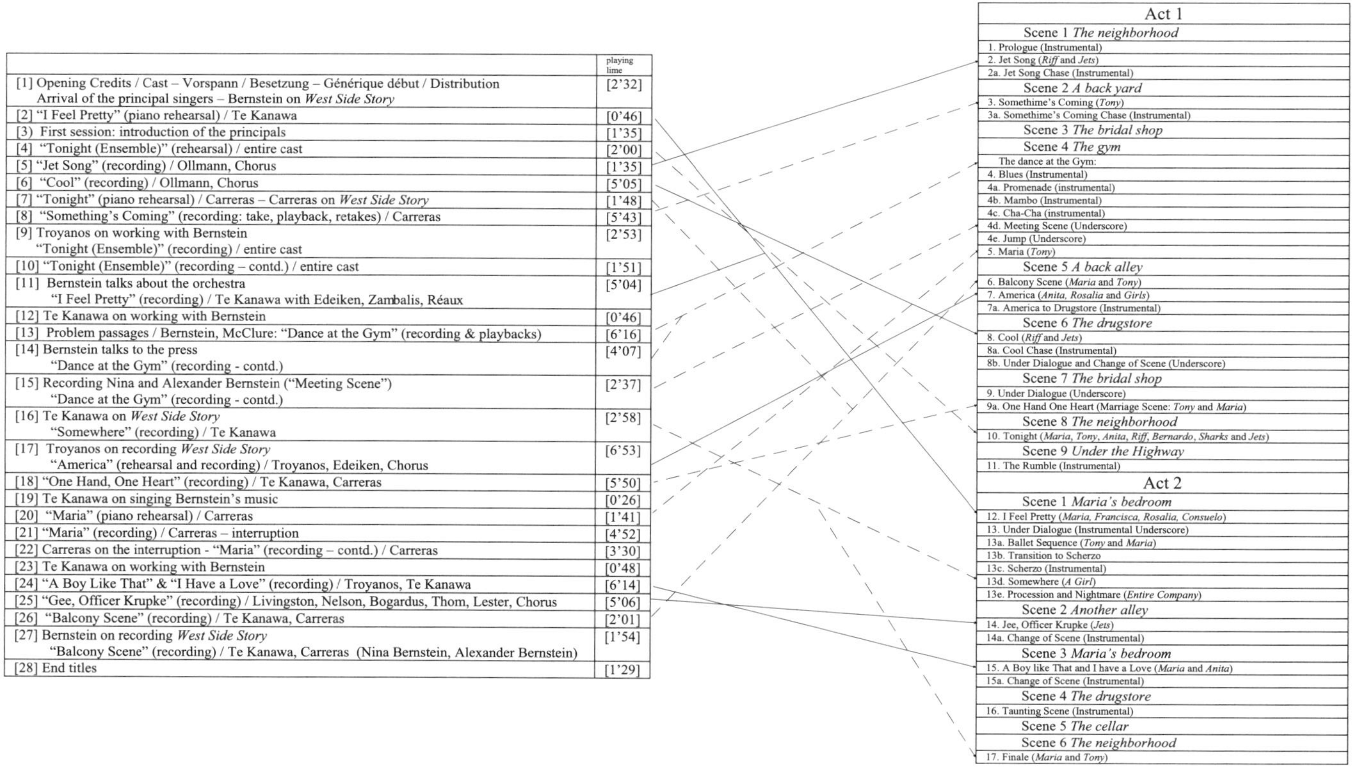

Figure 7.28 In this comparison, the dashed lines highlight the articulation of the plot; the solid lines indicate the point of reference from *West Side Story* (1985) to *West Side Story* (2000)

Example 7.3 Leonard Bernstein, *West Side Story*, no. 17, measures 22–7
Source: West Side Story (2000): 474.

In the *Making*, Bernstein also asked Kiri Te Kanawa to sing 'Somewhere' [16], explaining this as the pure joy of recording the piece with this soprano. This choice is important for whoever follows the video until the end, when in the final images of the Balcony Scene, after Bernstein's epilogue, the motif of Example 7.1 returns and ends, no longer as the sign of a tragic premonition, but as the attainment of the endless sorrow of two lovers.

The articulation of the *Making* is that of creating a new perspective for *West Side Story*'s reception, derived from the re-editing of its structure. This video leads us towards an aesthetic statement, based on specific relationships with the motific texture of the work: *West Side Story* was created as a musical, but thanks to opera singers, it could also enter the repertory of the great opera houses and become a classic, as Bernstein himself claimed. This last example reinforces the way of thinking that I began with: Bolter and Grusin's concept of remediation is actually a false problem. In fact, I do not believe that remediation creates anything truly autonomous in musical theatre. In crossing between media, not even *'West Side Story': The Making of the Recording* – the most radical of the above-mentioned examples – betrays the hypotext, but reformulates its message. In the other cases, the perspective of the stage production remains decisive for reception, and the video fulfils an extremely important task in a modern society so conditioned by images: it allows us to study masterpieces of the past from many different standpoints, confronting us with the art of direction, which is at present in full development.

Translated by Laurie Schwartz

References

Bendikas, Kristina (2004) *The Opera Theater of Jean-Pierre Ponnelle*, Lewiston, NY: Edwin Mellen Press.

Bolter, Jay David and Grusin, Richard (1999) *Remediation: Understanding New Media*, Cambridge, MA: MIT Press.

Burton, Humphrey (1994) *Leonard Bernstein*, New York: Doubleday.

Candide (1957) *Overture to 'Candide' by Leonard Bernstein* (score), New York: Schirmer, © 1955, 1957, pp. 2, 15; New York Philharmonic Leon Levy Digital Archives, http://archives.nyphil.org/index.php/artifact/3e251523-480c-438d-8999-78981c23b775/fullview#page/1/mode/2up (accessed 30 June 2015).

——— (1989) Leonard Bernstein, *Candide*, staged by Humphrey Burton; Jerry Hadley (Candide), June Anderson (Cunégonde), Adolph Green (Dr. Pangloss/

Martin), Christa Ludwig (Old Lady), Nicolai Gedda (Governor/Vanderdendur/Ragotski), Della Jones (Paquette), Kurt Ollman (Maximilian/Captain); conducted by Leonard Bernstein with the London Symphony Orchestra and the London Symphony Chorus; orchestrations by Leonard Bernstein and Hershy Kay.

——— (2006) Leonard Bernstein, *Candide*, mise-en-scène de Robert Carsen; comic operetta en deux actes; livret de Hugh Wheeler, d'après la satire de Voltaire, librement adapté par Robert Carsen et Ian Burton, choréographie de Rob Ashford, dramaturgie de Ian Burton; conception vidéo François Roussillon, costumes de Buki Shiff, décors de Michael Levine, lumières de Robert Carsen et Peter Van Praet; produit par le Théâtre du Châtelet, le Teatro alla Scala de Milan et l'English National Opera de Londres; direction musicale de John Axelrod; chef de chœur Stephen Betteridge; avec l'ensemble orchestral de Paris et le chœur du Théâtre du Châtelet; avec Lambert Wilson (Voltaire/Panglos/Martin), William Burden (Candide), Anna Christy (Cunégonde), Kim Criswell (la Vieille Dame), John Daszak (Le Grand Inquisiteur /le Capitaine/le Gouverneur/Vanderdendur/Ragotski), Jeni Bern (Paquette), David Adam Moore (Maximilien), Ferlyn Brass (Cacambo); Paris, Théâtre du Châtelet (Jean-Luc Choplin), 12 November.

Cenciarelli, Carlo (2013) '*At the Margins of the Televisual: Picture Frames, Loops and "Cinematics" in the Paratexts of Opera Videos*', *Cambridge Opera Journal*, 25, pp. 203–23.

Chapple, Freda (2006) *Digital Opera: Intermediality, Remediation and Education*, in *Intermediality in Theater and Performance*, ed. Freda Chapple and Chiel Kattenbelt, Amsterdam: Rodopi, pp. 81–100.

Citron, Marcia (2000) 'A Matter of Time and Place: Peter Sellars and Media Culture', in *Opera on the Screen*, New Haven, CT: Yale University Press, pp. 205–48.

——— (2002) 'The Performance of Vision in Peter Sellars' Television Production of *Così fan tutte*', in *Music, Sensation, and Sensuality*, ed. Austern, Linda Phyllis, New York: Routledge, pp. 213–30.

Così fan tutte (1990) Wolfgang Amadeus Mozart, *Così fan tutte*, directed by Peter Sellars; set designer Adrianne Lobel, costume designer Dunya Ramicova, lighting designer James F. Ingalls; Susan Larson (Fiordiligi), Janice Felty (Dorabella), Frank Kelley (Ferrando), James Maddalena (Guglielmo), Sue Ellen Kuzma (Despina), Sanford Sylvan (Don Alfonso); Arnold Schönberg Chor, Wiener Symphoniker, conducted by Craig Smith, original production: Pepsico Summerfare Festival (1986), © 1990 ORF, © 1991 Decca; the dramaturgy for this production can be read in Peter Sellars, *Synopsis (booklet)*, pp. 7–14.

Esse, Melina (2010) 'Don't Look Now: Opera, Liveness, and the Televisual', *The Opera Quarterly*, 26, pp. 81–95.

Faroni, Paolo (2014), 'L'opera in televisione secondo Jean-Pierre Ponnelle', master's thesis, Università degli studi di Pavia, Facoltà di musicologia.

Girardi, Michele (2002) *Puccini: His International Art*, 2nd edn, Chicago, IL: University of Chicago Press.

——— (2013) 'Una lunga vita sarebbe terribile, terribile … e dopo …?', in Leoš Janáček, *Věc Makropulos/La caso Makropulos*, *La Fenice prima dell'opera*,

2012–13, 4, Venice: Fondazione Teatro La Fenice, pp. 13–36, http://www.teatrolafenice.it/media/3usbj1362990961.pdf (accessed 30 June 2015).
Grasso, Aldo (ed.) (2013) *Storie e culture della televisione Italiana*, Milan: Mondadori.
La traviata (1997) *La traviata*, Melodramma in tre atti/Melodrama in Three Acts, libretto by Francesco Maria Piave/Libretto di Francesco Maria Piave, edited by Fabrizio Della Seta, Chicago, IL and Milan: University of Chicago Press and Ricordi, 1997 (*The Works of Giuseppe Verdi/Le opere di Giuseppe Verdi, Series I: Operas/Serie I: opere teatrali*, 19).
——— (2004) Giuseppe Verdi, *La traviata*, directed for the stage by Robert Carsen; sets and costumes Patrick Kinmonth; dramatic adviser Ian Burton; choreography Philippe Giradeau: lighting design Robert Carsen and Peter van Praet; Patrizia Ciofi (Violetta Valéry), Roberto Saccà (Alfredo Germont), Dmitri Hvorostovsky (Giorgio Germont), Eufemia Tufano (Flora Bervoix), Elisabetta Martorana (Annina), Salvatore Cordella (Gastone), Andrea Porta (il barone Douphol), Federico Sacchi (il dottore Grenvil), Vito Priante (il marchese d'Obigny), Luca Favaron (Giuseppe), Salvatore Giacalone (Un domestico), Antonio Casagrande (Un commissionario); orchestra e coro del Teatro La Fenice, conducted by Lorin Maazel; recorded live at Teatro La Fenice, Venice, 18 November; directed for TV and video by Patrizia Carmine.
Littlejohn, David (1990) 'Reflections on Peter Sellars' Mozart', *Opera Quarterly*, 7/2, pp. 6–36.
Martino, Maria (2004–2005) *'Un'interpretazione registica di Peter Sellars: "Theodora" di Händel'*, thesis, Università di Pavia, Facoltà di musicologia.
McLuhan, Marshall (1964) *Understanding Media: The Extensions of Man*, New York: McGraw-Hill.
Morris, Christopher (2010) 'Digital Diva: Opera on Video', *The Opera Quarterly*, 26, pp. 96–119.
Phelan, Peggy (1993) *Unmarked: The Politics of Performance*, London: Routledge.
Porter, Andrew (1992) 'Mozart on Modern Stage', *Early Music*, 20/1, pp. 132–8.
Robinson, Marc (1986) *'Crime and Punishment – The Robbers – Così fan tutte'*, *Performing Arts Journal*, 10/2, pp. 72–81.
Scognamiglio, Renata (2011) 'Film operistici: un profilo analitico', in *La musica nel cinema e nella televisione*, ed. Roberto Giuliani, Milan: Guerini, pp. 77–102.
Senici, Emanuele (2009) 'Il video d'opera "dal vivo". Testualizzazione e "liveness" nell'era digitale', *Il Saggiatore musicale*, 16/2, pp. 273–312.
——— (2010) 'Porn Style? Space and Time in Live Opera Videos', *The Opera Quarterly*, 26, pp. 68–80.
——— (2011) 'L'opera e la nascita della televisione in Italia', *Comunicazioni sociali*, 33, pp. 26–35.
——— (2012) 'Opera on Italian Television: The First Thirty Years, 1954–1984', in *Opera and Video: Technology and Spectatorship*, ed. Héctor J. Pérez, Bern: Peter Lang, pp. 45–70.
Simeone, Nigel (2009) *Leonard Bernstein: "West Side Story"*, Farnham: Ashgate.

Smith, Helen (2011) *There's a Place for Us: The Musical Theatre Works of Leonard Bernstein*, Farnham: Ashgate.

Tosca (1964) Giacomo Puccini, *Tosca*, from the Royal Opera House, London, 9 February; new production by Franco Zeffirelli (Director); Maria Callas (Tosca), Tito Gobbi (Scarpia), Renato Cioni (Cavaradossi), Orchestra and Chorus of Royal Opera House, conducted by Carlo Felice Cillario, ATV Production, http://www.youtube.com/watch?v=rT-86OtwzDI, 22 April 2011 (accessed 30 June 2015).

——— (1998) Giacomo Puccini, *Tosca*, directed for the stage by Nikolaus Lehnhoff; scene Raimund Bauer; costumes Falk Bauer; lighting Wolfgang Göbbel; Catherine Malfitano (Tosca), Bryn Terfel (Scarpia), Richard Margison (Cavaradossi); Royal Concertgebouw Orchestra; director Riccardo Chailly; directed for TV and video by Misjel Vermeiren; Amsterdam, 1998; © 2007 Decca.

——— (2011) Giacomo Puccini, *Tosca*, directed for the stage by Jonathan Kent; designer Paul Brown, lighting design Mark Henderson; Angela Gheorghiu (Tosca), Jonas Kaufmann (Cavaradossi), Bryn Terfel (Scarpia), Hubert Francis (Spoletta), Lukas Jakobski (Angelotti), Jeremy White (Sacristan), Zheng Zhong Zhou (Sciarrone); Orchestra and Chorus of the Royal Opera House Covent Garden, conductor Antonio Pappano; directed for TV and video by Jonathan Haswell, 2011 EMI DVD 4040639.

Trousdell, Richard (1991) 'Peter Sellars Rehearses *Figaro*', *The Drama Review*, 35/1, pp. 66–89.

Wells, Brianna (2012) '"Secret Mechanism": *Les Contes d'Hoffmann* and the Intermedial Uncanny in the Metropolitan Opera's Live in HD Series', *Nineteenth-century Music*, 36/2, pp. 191–203.

West Side Story (1961) Leonard Bernstein, *West Side Story*, a Robert Wise production, directed by Robert Wise and Jerome Robbins, screenplay by Ernest Lehman, choreography by Jerome Robbins, music by Leonard Bernstein, starring Natalie Wood, Richard Beymer, © 1961 Metro-Goldwyn-Mayer Studios.

——— (1985) *Leonard Bernstein Conducts 'West Side Story': The Making of the Recording*, directed by Christopher Swann, produced by Humphrey Burton and Thomas P. Skinner; film edited by Howard Billingham; Dame Kiri Te Kanawa (Maria), José Carreras (Tony), Tatiana Troyanos (Anita), Kurt Ollmann (Riff); recorded New York, September 1984; © 1985 Unitel, © 1988/2001 Deutsche Grammophon 0373 017-9; Burton is the author of the introductory text for the booklet (pp. 5–10).

——— (2000) Leonard Bernstein, *West Side Story* (study score), New York: Boosey & Hawkes, 2000, HPS 1176.

Will, Richard (2011) 'Zooming In, Gazing Back: *Don Giovanni* on Television', *The Opera Quarterly*, 27/1, pp. 32–65.

Chapter 8
Between Mediatization and Live Performance: The Music for Giorgio Strehler's *The Tempest* (1978)

Emilio Sala

During the 1960s and 1970s (the years of the 'performance art', of Grotowski and Barba, but also of the Théâtre du Soleil, Strehler and so on), the emphasis was placed on the 'live' dimension that we believed was innate to performative events, thus assuming an aesthetic and ideological connotation whose influence in the theoretical arena can certainly not be underestimated. In his book *Per un teatro umano* ('Towards a Human Theatre') (1974: 231), Giorgio Strehler defends and longs for the use in theatre of 'live music which is a completely different thing than *canned music*, even if it is perfect'.[1] In 1977 the critic Henry Rabine declared in no uncertain terms:

> Everyone has their own opinion on this point. But theatre being, unlike cinema, the art of the present, of life, of living, one must admit that the music that sometimes accompanies it unwillingly swallows it, like canned food. Notes, too, must be picked from the tree. In the end, it is a question of ecology, isn't it? (Rabine 1977: 17)

Throughout the history of recorded music, one can observe the pervasiveness and the insistence of the expression 'canned music', a deprecating metaphor that implies a reactive, even defensive attitude towards the ever-expanding phenomenon of 'technical reproduction'; however, what matters more – in our context – is the interpretation of the performance as a 'live' ontological event. As Peggy Phelan wrote:

> Performance's only life is in the present. Performance cannot be saved, recorded, documented, or otherwise participate in the circulation of representations *of* representations: once it does so, it becomes something other than performance. To the degree that performance attempts to enter the economy of reproduction, it betrays and lessens the promise of its own ontology. (Phelan 1993: 146)

[1] My emphasis. The passage is taken from an undated letter to Fiorenzo Carpi (Strehler 1974: 230–34).

This theoretical discourse has moved radically to the fore during the last decade. One important contribution in this respect was undoubtedly Philip Auslander's book *Liveness: Performance in Mediatized Culture*, published for the first time in 1999 (2nd edn, 2008). But Michel Chion had already touched the problem in 1990: in *L'audio-vision. Son et image au cinéma* he wrote that 'the more we use recorded and/or transmitted sound, the more we mythify its contrary: a natural acoustical experience that we actually have less and less frequently' (Chion 1994: 104).[2] This is the point. In Auslander's words: 'historically, the live is actually an effect of mediatization, not the other way around. It was the development of recording technologies that made it possible to perceive existing representations as "live"' (2008: 56). According to Auslander, the relationship between live performance and mediatized performance should not be approached from an ontological perspective, but rather within the historical and cultural contexts which, from time to time, inform and redefine it. Despite some criticism – for example, by Erika Fischer-Lichte (2008: 69–71)[3] – Auslander's position proves to be quite useful when dealing with the audiovisual reproduction of events in which the music is already an element of the representation. Moreover, such a position 'against ontology' (to cite Auslander again)[4] is often echoed in Jay David Bolter and Richard Grusin's book *Remediation: Understanding New Media* (1999), which should not be omitted here. When Bolter and Grusin, for example, speak of the double logic of remediation, they emphasize that 'Immediacy depends on hypermediacy' (1999: 6) – in the same way that, according to Auslander, liveness is a consequence of mediatization. The correspondence is evident, and demands a type of conceptualization that, in recognizing the 'secondariness' of immediacy and liveness, rejects binary oppositions of an overly rigid and structural type. Thus, just as 'the historical relationship of liveness and mediatization must be seen as a relation of dependence and imbrication rather than opposition' (Auslander 2008: 56), the two logics that carry out the process of remediation – immediacy and hypermediation – appear to be complimentary and strongly interconnected. As Bolter and Grusin write: 'even the most hypermediated productions strive for their own brand of immediacy. Directors of music videos rely on multiple media and elaborate editing to create an immediate and apparently spontaneous style' (1999: 9).[5] In this context, it is quite useful to confront the relationship between

2 Evan Eisenberg also highlighted that the musical event originally recorded or reproduced by the disc is a 'myth' (1987: 51), as much as the secondary dimension of 'liveness', for example in rock music: 'Rock music in concert tends to sound like a crude impersonation of a record' (1987: 110).

3 The concept of the 'autopoietic feedback loop' between actors and spectators, which is at the core of Fischer-Lichte's critical discourse, obviously tends to value the relationship between liveness and performance.

4 This is the title of a chapter in Auslander (2008).

5 Bolter and Grusin refer here to videos of popular music, but their discourse can be obviously extended to any type of audiovisual remediation.

live performance and its video version in a circular sense, while also trying to reveal the influence of mediatization on *liveness*. Let us recall, with Emanuele Senici, that 'the majority of videos available on DVD [Senici is speaking of opera videos] classified as "live" are montages of recordings that are made not only during single performances but also during the rehearsals' (2009: 288); in addition, during post-production one also proceeds 'to re-mix the audio tracks in such a way as to balance the relationship between the voices and the orchestra' (2009: 288). The video is obviously not a mere 'replica' of the performance, but one of its reconstructions/remediations; moreover, admittedly, if it would make sense to speak of the former as a true reproduction of the latter, 'there could probably not be a less "objective" choice than that of the stationary video camera' (2009: 300), positioned in the middle of the space and thus assuming the completely abstract point of view of a theatre spectator.

Returning to Strehler and to the videos of 'live' performances, I will now examine the 1978 celebrated production of *The Tempest* with theatre music composed and arranged by Fiorenzo Carpi. Here is a brief chronological outline:

Season 1977–78
Rehearsal opening (at the Teatro Lirico, Milan): 6 March 1978
Première: 28 June 1978

Season 1978–79
Repeat performance (again at the Lirico): opening 28 October 1978
The television version was taken from this repeat performance from the fall 1978
(directed by Carlo Battistoni, broadcast on RAI 2, 14 December 1981)

As we have seen, Strehler, with his 'human' theatre, strenuously opposed the 'multimedial' trend clearly becoming widespread in theatre during those years, which had quite rapidly assumed, not coincidentally, a strong 'post-human' valence. More precisely, in this period Strehler seems to be waging a battle against the tendencies towards mediatization in the theatre of Luca Ronconi and Carmelo Bene. As is well known, the latter gave more and more importance to the technical tools of sound reproduction and amplification in his performances. Ronconi's famous 1968 production of *Orlando furioso* reached television in the mid-1970s with great success, and whereas Ronconi comes out in favour of 'an expressive use of cinematography and television in the theatre' (Balzola and Prono 1994: 124), Strehler declares:

> The return of theatre in TV? In what sense? … A work of theatre transposed into TV can't become a pure and simple *subject*. It must remain integral and not manipulated. … TV can be a means for getting close to theatre but not a means for taking advantage of it, clouding the works. (Balzola and Prono 1994: 107–8)[6]

Nonetheless, an increasing influence of technological mediation can be observed in the production and diffusion of 'music for theatre' in Strehler's late dramas (culminating in *Faust I* and *II*). After all, even if in a somewhat forced way, the tape recorder was commonly used at the Piccolo Teatro as early as the 1950s; with *The Tempest*, it would be laboured to consider the 'sonic landscape' as a case of 'mixed-media performance' according to Auslander's (2008: 40) definition. Let us recall Fiorenzo Carpi's statement, transcribed by Amleto Ravedoni in his undergraduate thesis:

> The real effect of the [opening] tempest was recorded at the 'Piccolo' with four groups of percussionists positioned in the corners of the hall, while the recording was made by a tape recorder positioned in the centre of the hall. During the performance, in addition to the pre-recorded tape, two percussionists, live, positioned in backstage, were also included. (Ravedoni 1987: 124)

The percussionists performed on various instruments: in addition to the bass drums, a flexatone (presumably), an instrument made of metallic strips imitating rushing water, a thunder sheet and a wind machine; the recorded part also included a mixed choir (without text) and an organ pedal.[7] Perhaps the most interesting thing was the spatialization of the recorded sounds: loudspeakers were positioned in the hall in such as way as to envelop the audience. It is worthwhile to see and listen to this first scene as reconstructed/remediated in the television version (now available also on the DVD included in Colombo 2007) directed by Carlo Battistoni, Strehler's close collaborator and the future husband of Giulia Lazzarini (performing the role of Ariel).

---

6 In an article that first appeared in *Sipario* in 1971, Strehler seemed less negatively inclined with regard to an active role for theatre in television: 'Does the attempt to transport a theatrical performance "via television" have sense? Today, it seems to me that it does have a sense, even at the aesthetic level. It obviously always has to do with an adaptation, of seeking a kind of compromise minute by minute, but is not at all sterile' (2002: 260).

7 I was unable to consult some tapes created for *The Tempest* and held in the archives of the Piccolo Teatro di Milano (Archivio Fonici section).

Figures 8.1a–d Four frames from the DVD (Colombo 2007) taken from *The Tempest*, Scene I (from backstage)

In an interview, Battistoni emphasized that his television film represented 'one of the few times I took the liberty of showing things that are hidden in theatre' (2002: 241). The framing from backstage and the attention directed towards the sounds of the production are also present in Ingmar Bergman's *Magic Flute* (1975), an opera that was filmed firstly for television, and was much discussed at the time.[8] Furthermore, since the meta-theatrical and self-reflective dimension already played a fundamental role in Strehler's production, it was easy for Battistoni to show some of the goings-on backstage as a choice of 'free interpretation in fidelity' (2002: 243). From the perspective of remediation and of complementariness between mediatized performance and live performance, Strehler and Battistoni's anxiety about fidelity and 'non-manipulation' appear to be secondary yet significant as to the history of theatrical poetics: the possibility offered by video of re-examining the relationship between recording and *mise-en-scène* takes priority over all else. If we consider the *mise-en-scène* as a *process*, what Battistoni recounts in the interview mentioned above is very interesting. He had shown a first version of the video to Strehler, who was satisfied but nevertheless asked him to re-record it from the beginning:

> I was speechless and he added that I hadn't noticed that Carraro's hair was too long behind and that his robe was short in the front and 'touched up' in the back.

---

[8] For the occasion, Bergman re-created the theatre of Drottingholm Castle in the Filmhuset studios in Stockholm: the audience had the impression of being in a small eighteenth-century theatre (in Drottingholm), but everything was actually re-created in the studio (again, immediacy depends on hypermediation). On Bergman's attitude towards intermediality, see Törnqvist (2003).

> Being on a stage that was very inclined, the costume didn't fall straight down. I filmed everything again, I edited, and I informed Strehler .... (Battistoni 2002: 240)

If this anecdote is true, we are facing a clear case in which the video influenced the live performance. Strehler adjusted his direction after seeing Battistoni's video, and the latter re-filmed the performance, indulging the director's perfectionism. All of this supposedly occurred during the repeat performances of the filming of *The Tempest* in the fall of 1978. To quote a further comment of Battistoni, Strehler's reaction implies his rapprochement 'to the performance by means of television recording, that is, in the televised performance [Strehler], recognized his theatrical direction' (Battistoni 2002: 241). This intermedial process is quite revealing – once again – of the secondary nature of liveness in the era of technological reproducibility. The intermedial approach intends to consider the 'specificity of the medium' (here, the live performance) not as an essence, but as a cultural construct implying a relationship in continuous redefinition with other media.

Battistoni's video is obviously a valuable source in studying Strehler's *mise-en-scène* as well, a source that researchers should compare with all other available documents. The study of theatre music is still in its early stages, but the Carpi-Strehler collaboration was recently the subject of an important doctoral thesis written by Davide Verga: 'Musiche di scena e teatro di regia. Fiorenzo Carpi e gli spettacoli goldoniani di Giorgio Strehler' (2012).[9] Among many sources, Verga highlighted those belonging to the composer's private archive held at the Piccolo Teatro in Milan. In the two folders regarding *The Tempest*[10] there are lists of the music pieces planned during the performance. One of these outlines the plan for the musical accompaniment of the 'prologue' in a version quite close to the final *mise-en-scène* (Figure 8.2).

The use of a pre-recorded tape and sound effects added live is repeated; the handwritten note inside the rectangle ('+ pedal Lear') refers to the tempest in *King Lear* that Strehler staged in 1972, from which some effects were probably taken (following an intertextual practice typical of Carpi and Strehler's work).[11]

---

[9] See also Verga (2010): 73–119.

[10] This concerns two mauve-coloured folders marked 'C. 30 (1–2)'.

[11] In Colombo (2007) there is an interesting comment by Strehler (dated 15 November 1977): '*The Tempest* starts with *Lear* and keeps going' (2007: 354); with regard to the scene of the opening tempest, at the same point, the possibility of the 'support of an abstract tape like [in] Lear' (2007: 355) is invoked.

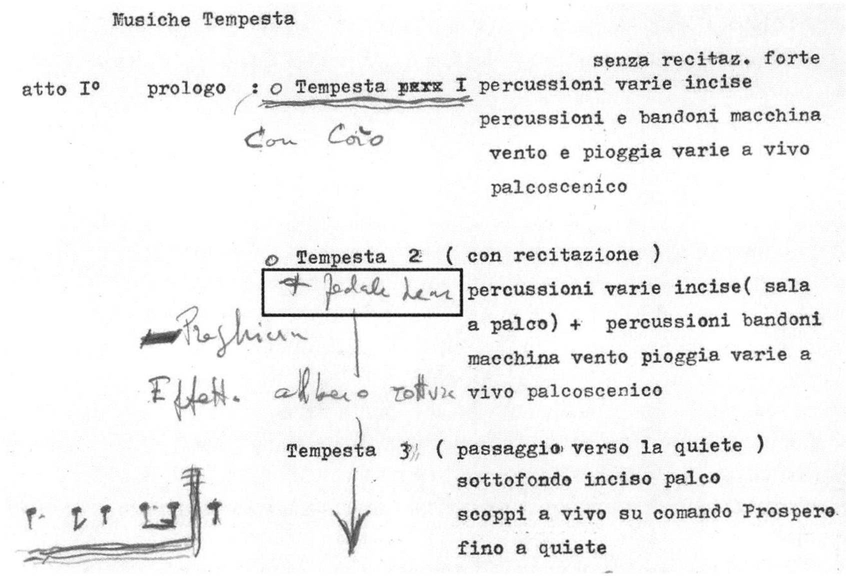

Musiche Tempesta

atto I° prologo : o Tempesta ~~parx~~ I senza recitaz. forte percussioni varie incise percussioni e bandoni macchina vento e pioggia varie a vivo palcoscenico

Con Coro

o Tempesta 2 (con recitazione) percussioni varie incise(sala a palco) + percussioni bandoni macchina vento pioggia varie a vivo palcoscenico

Preghiera

Tempesta 3 (passaggio verso la quiete) sottofondo inciso palco scoppi a vivo su comando Prospero fino a quiete

Figure 8.2 *The Tempest*, folder C. 30 (2) from Fiorenzo Carpi's archive (Piccolo Teatro, Milan): musical plan (preparatory) for the opening tempest

Source: Thanks to Martina Carpi for allowing the reproduction of this document.

Another example of the mutual relationship between mediatization and live performance concerns the preliminary stage of Strehler's directing. In his recently published letters to Agostino Lombardo (a Shakespearian translator), Strehler frequently speaks of the problem of the music in *The Tempest*. (He spoke of it as early as six months before the beginning of rehearsals!) In a crucial letter dated 25 August 1977, he imagines Ariel's voice singing like 'a small childlike voice, almost in falsetto', then deals with Ariel's first two songs (from Act I), emphasizing that these

> are to be set into music together with Fiorenzo. Like we always do. I throw in a rhythm track, of verses or something else and rhymes if there are any. He tries to understand, throws in a theme, then we mould it [si fa il 'mascherone'] with the consequent confusion and muddle. … But I believe that 'stylistically', the music will not have an Elizabethan taste at all. Looking here and there, as far as I could, I would definitely reject the virginals, lutes and the rest. And I'd look for even earlier music. I found some vocal music (such as *Angelica biltà*, an anonymous piece dated 1300).[12]

[12] Colombo (2007): 35. Included with this volume is a DVD of the television version of Strehler's *The Tempest* filmed by Battistoni which I used for this research.

The importance of early music recordings in creating the sonic landscape of the performance is of course very significant. The fact that Fiorenzo Carpi was already involved during the first stage of the directing choices is revealing. 'Angelica biltà' is not an anonymous piece, but Francesco Landini's two-voice ballad preserved in the celebrated Squarcialupi Codex. Armed with an LP recording, Strehler gathered his friends to listen to it, 'without saying what era it was from, and where it came from, saying: could this be *The Tempest*? There was not one who, wonderstruck, did not agree. I don't know why (or maybe, I know, but on a different note) the music has to be very backdated' (Colombo 2007: 35).

After many attempts, I have been able to identify the record Strehler referred to. It was an anthology released in 1976 by the Gruppo Musica Insieme entitled *Musiche medioevali e rinascimentali* ('Medieval and Renaissance Music') (EDIPAN, PAN DX-MA 52 stereo). Considering the close relationship between Carpi and Edipan, it is not surprising that this would be one of the first records used by Strehler to try to imagine the music for *The Tempest* production.[13]

Francesco Landini's 'Angelica biltà', sung by a solo female voice (Ille Strazza), appears as the fourth piece on the B-side in an arrangement by Antenore Tecardi: in addition to a flute doubling the melodic line, the second voice calls for an instrumental accompaniment (with a dulcimer and a lute). Fiorenzo Carpi's personal archive contains a transcription of this version, from which Ariel's first song ('Come unto these yellow sands') was further rearranged with the following new text: 'A queste sabbie dorate, su, vieni. Qui dolci spiriti hanno danzato, le mani intrecciate. Con un bacio e un inchino ecco calmate le acque infuriate. A queste sabbie dorate, su, vieni' ('To these golden sands, come. Here is where sweet spirits danced, their arms interlocked. With a kiss and a bow, the furious waters are calmed. To these golden sands, come'). The discographic source was thus transformed into a live performance – Giulia Lazzarini giving voice to Ariel, transformed into an invisible water nymph by the magic of Prospero (Tino Carraro). It is worth taking a look at the revised version of Antenore Tecardi's 'Angelica biltà' held in Fiorenzo Carpi's archive (Figure 8.3)[14] and listening to Ariel's first song as it appears in Carlo Battistoni's video (Figure 8.4).

---

13 It should be said (at least in passing) that Strehler had already staged *The Tempest* for the Maggio Musicale Fiorentino festival (Giardino di Boboli, 6 June 1948) with the collaboration of Fiorenzo Carpi, but in an interpretative and musical context that was completely different.

14 The lute part is of course read a minor third higher.

Figure 8.3 *The Tempest*, folder C.30 (1) from Fiorenzo Carpi's archive (Piccolo Teatro, Milan): 'Angelica biltà' by Francesco Landini in Antenore Tecardi's arrangement

Source: Thanks to Martina Carpi for allowing the reproduction of this document.

Figure 8.4 A moment from Ariel's first song in the DVD included in Colombo (2007)

Figure 8.5 A moment from Ariel's second song on the DVD included in Colombo (2007)

By contrast, Ariel's second song (Figure 8.5),[15] which follows shortly after, was composed by the same Fiorenzo Carpi in an archaic music style and in the Dorian mode – that is to say, maintaining the 'backdated' patina that Strehler wanted.[16] In the composer's sketches this piece is always indicated as 'Metamorfosi' (Figures 8.6a and 8.6b), and refers both to the transformation of Alonso's body into something precious and mysterious and to Ariel's metamorphosis from a spirit of the air into an aquatic creature. The 'don, din' onomatopoeias are sung by the invisible and disembodied voices of the water nymphs, which, as the text says, 'una campana, fanno rintoccare' ('ring a bell').[17] Ariel's second song is repeated in an instrumental version when the spirit of the air is set free at the end of the opera: in Strehler's interpretation, Ariel's liberation indeed coincides with her 'metamorphosis' into a human being. The magic of Prospero is completed.

Ariel's first song is preceded by (and in part mixed with) another piece characterized by the presence of a voice in falsetto.[18] This piece recurs many times during the performance, and cannot be associated with the letter in which Strehler talks about Ariel's voice 'almost in falsetto'. Nevertheless, it also concerns a piece that primarily refers to the magical-archaic sound atmosphere of the island. As Strehler himself wrote, *The Tempest* 'should be a play that is transparent but full of mystery. Representations, images [and music, I would add], must appear primitive, absolutely clear, but at the same time completely incomprehensible [not completely comprehensible]. There is a zone of the unknowable and inexplicable in *The Tempest*' (Colombo 2007: 354–5). Ettore Gaipa, in his invaluable chronicle of the rehearsals for *The Tempest*, significantly refers to this piece as 'celestial music'.[19] It appears for the first time when Prospero takes off his magic cloak, shortly after the opening tempest (Figure 8.7).

---

15 In the final version, a dulcimer (performed by Cecilia Chailly) was used instead of the harp to save some space, as the instrumental group was placed in a very narrow angle of the pit. Thanks to Cecilia Chailly for this information.

16 Ariel's second song was also included in the anthology *40 anni di musiche per il Piccolo Teatro: 1947–1987* (CD Fonit Cetra, CDC 34).

17 As can be seen in Figure 8.6b, the 'don, din' onomatopoeias are written for two voices, but were both performed by Margherita Vivian, as she pre-recorded one of the two parts. Thanks to Margherita Vivian for this information.

18 Ettore Gaipa (2012) also speaks about the mixing of the two pieces in his chronicle of the rehearsals for *The Tempest*, relating some of Strehler's orders to the sound technician Roberto Piergentili: '"Robertino, put the castrato in! … Mix in the castrato with *Angelica biltà*, one in front, the other, high, in the back!" And the magic of sounds, mixtures, contrasts is born. Born, in a flash, the mystery of the island' (chronicle of 30 May). What Strehler calls 'the castrato' is the piece with the voice in falsetto.

19 Some pages from this chronicle (the typescript is held in the archive of the Piccolo Teatro) have been published in Colombo (2007): 357–61, though this important document has recently been published in its entirety (Gaipa 2012).

Metamorfosi
Andante
[In fon-do al ma - re Gia - ce tuo pa - dre]
Flauto
Arpa
Liuto
Crotali Re
Vibraf. Camp.
(Vibraf)
2 Voci
Don
Din
(simile)
Don
din
Don
din

Figures 8.6a and 8.6b *The Tempest*, folder C.30 (1) from Fiorenzo Carpi's archive (Piccolo Teatro, Milan): a preliminary version (instrumental) of Ariel's second song ('Metamorfosi')

Source: Thanks to Martina Carpi for allowing the reproduction of this document.

Figure 8.7 A moment from the first occurrence of the 'celestial music' on the DVD included in Colombo (2007)

Once again, we come across the use of a discographic source and, more precisely, a troubadour-like *cansó* by Peire Vidal ('Baron, de mon dan covit') recorded in 1970 by the Studio der Frühen Musik for the series *Das alte Werk* ('Ancient/Early Works') by Telefunken; it was included as the first piece on side A of the LP titled *Chansons des troubadours* (6.41126 AS). Countertenor Richard Levitt interprets this piece.

The piece was not transcribed and performed live again – as in the case of 'Angelica biltà' – but used (with added effects) as acousmatic music. In the liner notes to the record, Thomas Binkley, conductor of the vocal and instrumental group, emphasizes that in order to re-create the complete sound of the troubadour-like music, it was necessary to take inspiration from Arabic music; he associates the *lira da braccio*, chosen to accompany Vidal's *cansó*, with the *rebab* of the Middle Eastern tradition. As Vincenzo Borghetti (2011) has clearly pointed out, in the 1960s and 1970s the sonic concept of medieval music deliberately distanced itself from 'classical' performance practice in order to assume a strong ethnic-oriental connotation. The 'backdating' of the music for *The Tempest* realized by Strehler fits into this change of landscape, the cultural implication of which is a 'de-familiarization of the medieval into a "popular" direction' (Borghetti 2011: 44). In this context, it will seem less surprising to read in an article that appeared in *L'Unità* of the presence 'of a *fedayn* song (all of the musical works in the play are re-elaborations of oriental songs or troubadour-style compositions)'.[20] But what matters more for our discourse is – once again – the centrality of technological mediation (in this case, discographic) in defining the sound landscape of a performance which on the one hand is firmly anchored in the aesthetics (and the

20 Tiziana Missigoi, report of Giorgio Strehler's *The Tempest*, *L'Unità*, 6 June 1978.

ideology) of liveness, while on the other continually practices remediation and mixed-media performance. It is an intermedial *modus operandi* which certainly cannot be ignored when studying in depth the *mise-en-scène* and the *mise-en-musique* of this fascinating performance, and above all Strehler's 'late style'.

Translated by Laurie Schwartz

References

Auslander, Philip (2008) *Liveness: Performance in Mediatized Culture*, 2nd edn, New York: Routledge.

Balzola, Andrea and Prono, Franco (eds) (1994) *La nuova scena elettronica. Il video e la ricerca teatrale in Italia*, Turin: Rosenberg & Sellier.

Battistoni, Carlo (2002) 'Il lungo sodalizio con Strehler' (interview), in Tabanelli (2002), pp. 215–58.

Bolter, Jay David and Grusin, Richard (1999) *Remediation: Understanding New Media*, Cambridge, MA: MIT Press.

Borghetti, Vincenzo (2011) 'Purezza e trasgressione: il suono del Medioevo dagli anni Cinquanta ad oggi', *Semicerchio*, 44/1, pp. 37–54.

Chion, Michel (1994) *Audio-vision: Sound on Screen*, trans. Claudia Gorbman, New York: Columbia University Press.

Colombo, Rosy (ed.) (2007) *'La tempesta' tradotta e messa in scena 1977–1978. Un carteggio ritrovato fra Strehler e Lombardo*, Rome: Donzelli (the book includes a DVD of the performance, directed for TV by Carlo Battistoni).

Eisenberg, Evan (1987) *The Recording Angel: Explorations in Phonography*, New York: McGraw-Hill.

Fischer-Lichte, Erika (2008) *The Transformative Power of Performance: A New Aesthetics*, trans. Saskya Iris Jain, New York: Routledge.

Gaipa, Ettore (2012) 'Il metodo Strehler', *Diari di prova della Tempesta scritti da Ettore Gaipa*, ed. Stella Casiraghi, Milan: Skira.

Phelan, Peggy (1993) *Unmarked: The Politics of Performance*, London: Routledge.

Rabine, Henry (1977) 'Au français il y a aussi des musiciens et des chanteurs', *Comédie-Française*, 61, pp. 16–17.

Ravedoni, Amleto (1987) 'La musica teatrale dei teatri stabili di Milano, Torino e Genova nei primi vent'anni della loro esistenza', graduate thesis, Università Ca' Foscari di Venezia.

Senici, Emanuele (2009) 'Il video d'opera "dal vivo". Testualizzazione e *liveness* nell'era digitale', *Il Saggiatore musicale*, 16/2, pp. 273–312.

Strehler, Giorgio (1974) *Per un teatro umano. Pensieri scritti, parlati e attuati*, ed. Sinah Kessler, Milan: Feltrinelli.

——— (2002) 'Ha senso fare teatro in tv?' [1971], in Tabanelli (2002), pp. 259–62.

Tabanelli, Giorgio (ed.) (2002) *Il teatro in televisione*, vol. 1, Rome: RAI-ERI.

Törnqvist, Egil (2003) *Bergman's Muses: Aesthetic Versatility in Film, Theatre, Television and Radio*, Jefferson, NC: McFarland.

Verga, Davide (2010) 'Il "grazioso" e "umano" di Fiorenzo Carpi. Appunti sulle musiche di scena per *Arlecchino servitore di due padroni*', *Stratagemmi. Prospettive teatrali*, 15, pp. 73–119.

——— (2012) 'Musiche di scena e teatro di regia. Fiorenzo Carpi e gli spettacoli goldoniani di Giorgio Strehler', doctoral thesis, Università degli studi di Milano.

Chapter 9
The 'Remediated' *Rite of Spring*

Gianfranco Vinay

This chapter investigates the remediation of a ballet performance, beginning with an analytical comparison of three different remediations (produced as DVDs and/or to be broadcast via several audiovisual channels – television or the Internet) of three different performances of a single choreography of the *Sacre du printemps*: the so-called 'reconstruction' of Nijinsky's original version by Millicent Hodson and Kenneth Archer. In order to deepen my understanding and assemble my own approach, I have welcomed suggestions and ideas from various sources, in particular Giovanni Morelli's essay 'Il postiglione Cronos. *Barry Lyndon* e ancora il "cinema del Settecento"' (2011). This will be useful to illuminate a fundamental aspect of the *Sacre*'s choreomusical dramaturgy.[1]

I will limit my analysis of the three remediations to the first scene: 'Les augures printaniers – Danses des adolescentes',[2] but giving some consideration to the introduction preceding it. The primordial impulse is provided by the famous obsessive and asymmetric repetition of two dissonant and percussive chords (the dominant seventh of A♭ major combined with an F♭ major triad), which can be interpreted either as an octatonic fusion or as the conflict of two tonalities (motif B). This ambivalence (between unification and laceration), which affects not only the harmony but all the components of musical composition, is one of the fundamental dramaturgical elements of the *Sacre* – a sonorous expression of a ritual which, through a human sacrifice (therefore a laceration), celebrates a unification (between men and nature, individuals and collectivity).

Throughout the first part of the scene – up to rehearsal number [26]+6 – the main character is the 300-year-old Woman. Her presence is signalled by the sound of the piccolo motif at rehearsal number [15] (motif C), and she is the principal animator, awakening the groups and inviting them to follow her in her adventures and ritual actions. However, from rehearsal number [26]+7 until the end of the scene, the stage action is inspired by the groups' movements and figurations. The various motifs are not used to identify characters, actions or movements, but to provide a rhythmic and sonorous support to movements and figurations.

---

1 I mention this at the opening of this chapter as a personal tribute to the memory of my dear friend and colleague, who passed away on 12 July 2011.

2 The edition I refer to in the following pages is Igor Stravinsky, *The Rite of Spring (Le Sacre du printemps)* [1911–13, rev. 1947], Full Orchestral Score, London: Boosey & Hawkes, 1967.

The three remediations are:

1. the version staged on 11 February 1994 at the Opéra de Paris, with its *corps de ballet* and orchestra directed by Jocelyne Genet;
2. the Joffrey Ballet version, this being the company with which Hodson and Archer's 're-creation' came into being; the Prague National Theatre Orchestra directed by Allan Lewis; 300-year-old Woman: Carole Valleskey. This version was produced by Judy Kinberg and Thomas Grimm in 1989 for a television programme dedicated to the reconstitution of the *Sacre du printemps*: *The Search for Nijinsky's Rite of Spring*;[3]
3. the Marinsky Theatre version, with its *corps de ballet* and orchestra (300-year-old Woman: Yelena Bazhenova), filmed in June 2008 by video director Denis Caiozzi.

In the following synoptic table I have summarized and compared the key musical and choreographic elements as well as aspects of the filmic sequences of the three videos. In doing so, I have used abbreviations to indicate the musical motifs, groups and characters, as well as to indicate the cinematic shots.[4]

Synoptic Table

Les Augures Printaniers – Danses des Adolescentes

[12]+10: The curtain rises on the repetition of the *ostinato* consisting of two intervals, a minor third and a perfect fourth in the first violins (motif A): two groups of dancers – a *côté jardin* consisting of five young men with red hats on their heads and skins on their shoulders (YM1), and a *côté cour* consisting of 11 young men, five with hats and beards and six shaven and hatless (YM2) – and two groups of ballerinas – one in the centre, consisting of seven ballerinas dressed in white and blue (YF1), and another, *côté cour*, consisting of three ballerinas dressed in red (YF2). A fifth group of seven ballerinas dressed in red (YF3) joins the others when the 300-year-old Woman comes on stage. The 300-year-old Woman (OW) bends over in the centre, closer to the proscenium.

[3] In collaboration with WNET of New York, Danish Radio, Czechoslovakia television, the BBC, La Sept and NOS television; Dance Director: Thomas Grimm; lights: Jœrgen Johannessen and Tim Hunter; camera: Leif Larsen, Knud Pedersen, John Anderson Dahl; video: Knud Boe, Karl Jœrgensen, Michel Wad Larsen.

[4] For the Marinsky Theatre version I produced an analysis of the complete ballet in a recent volume on the Ballets Russes (Vinay 2013). In that case, being only one version, I noted the timing of the sequences in addition to rehearsal numbers. But in this case, comparing three different versions, each sequence corresponds to a different timing: for clarity's sake and to avoid an excess of data, I use rehearsal numbers as common reference points.

Table 9.1 Synoptic table

Music and choreography	Opéra de Paris	Joffrey Ballet	Marinsky
[14]–[14]+4: Over motif A in the English horn, bassoon and cello, YM1 spin around on one foot only, whereas the hunched OW holds a faggot in her arms.	[14]: FS first on OW with shaking hand, then on YM1, excluding their heads		
[14]+5–[14]+8: Over the return of motif B, YM1 resume making small leaps on two legs dragging the feet back and forth with upper arm movements on each of the syncopated chords in the horn.			[14]+5: MS on OW, with her right arm outstretched and her hand hooked
[15]–[15]+6: With motif C in the piccolos, clarinets and pizzicato first violins, and the answer to it in chromatically descending triplets in oboe, C trumpet and first violins, the OW in yellow and orange costume makes two leaps (while the YM1 continue their moves forward/backward and in a circle), and then starts to run.	[15]: Travelling shot towards the centre of the scene [15]+5: SLS on OW and four groups	[15]+1: SLS on OW and all the groups.	[15]: FS on OW, who leaps around YF1
[16]–[17]+5: With the bassoon trill accompanying motif A and with more sonorous variants of motif C, the OW continues to run and make leaps around the central group and next to YM2, who wake up and begin to dance in circles. The OW, her back to the audience, bends forward and lifts her leg, showing her backside to the public.	[16]+2: SLS closer on OW and on the four groups [16]+6: LS on OW, who leaps among the groups and then, her back to the audience, bends forward and lifts a leg	[16]+5: FS on OW, who awakens YM2	[16]+5: MS on OW, who leaps around YM2 awakening them [17]+3: FS on OW, who returns towards YM1 and bends forward, raising her leg

Table 9.1 *continued*

Music and choreography	Opéra de Paris	Joffrey Ballet	Marinsky
[18]–[20]+8: Over the return of motif B, and with the addition at [19] of fragments of ascending/descending scales (motif D), the OW invites the two male groups to follow her, lays the faggot on the ground, and spins in circles.	[18]+4: SLS on OW and the four groups	[20]+5: LS on OW and three groups: YF1, YF2 and YM2	[18]+3: MS on OW, who with a hand gesture invites the men's groups to follow her [18]+6: FS on OW, who invites the groups to follow her [19]: CS on OW [19]+5: FS on OW and YM2, who leap [20]+5: LS on OW and all groups
[21]–[21]+12: With the canon-like return of motif D between the bassoon, contrabassoon and oboes with grace notes, the OW leaps on either side of the faggot on the ground and nods her head, imitated by the groups. Then she leads the two *côté jardin* groups. Over the final drumming cadence, the two groups leap and then bend to the ground.	[21]: LS to OW, who leaps and nods head among the groups [21]+12: SLS on OW and all the groups	[21]: FS on OW, who leaps and nods head in agreement among the groups [21]+11: LS on OW and the male groups who are leaping	[21]: FS on OW and YM2, who respond to each other with their heads nodding in agreement [21]+7: CS on OW, who goes towards the *côté jardin* with a bundle of branches under her arm [21]+11: Zoom on OW and then FS on OW and YM1, who leap and then crouch [21]+12: SLS on the whole troupe crouching

Music and choreography	Opéra de Paris	Joffrey Ballet	Marinsky
[22]–[24]+6: Over the return of motif A accompanied by trills and with the accents on strong beats at [23], the OW lies down with her legs in the air and single dancers leap from one side of the faggots to the other, before returning to the crouching OW.	[23]+5: FS on OW and on the leaps of two male dancers either side of the faggots surrounded by companions [24]+5: SLS on all the groups	[22]: FS on OW and some dancers of YM2, then zoom back to LS [23]: LS on the leaps from one side of the faggots to the other [23]+5: FS on OW crouching [24]+3: SLS on OW and all the groups	[22]: FS on OW with her legs in the air and YM1 [22]+2: SLS on all [23]+5: FS on the young men with bare heads who make the last leap from one side of the faggots to the other [24]+5: CS of OW crouching
[25]–[26]+6: Over a new folk-like motif played by the horn (motif E) and quickly taken up in varied form by the flute, the two male groups walk, first crossing each other's path and then in the opposite direction, shuffling their feet. The OW draws a circle with the faggots, leaps at the conclusion of the triplets in the oboe ([26]–[26]+6), then leaves the stage.	[26]: FS on 6 young men and on OW, who, after two leaps, leaves the stage	[26]: FS on YM1 crouched down and OW, who traces a circle on the ground with the faggot and leaps before leaving the stage [26]+6: LS at the entrance of YF3 *coté cour* and a short zoom forward	[25]+3: MS on young men with bare heads crouching down and OW, who traces a circle on the ground with the faggot
[26]+7–[28]: The return of motif E, this time in the alto flute, then in the three flutes in a more sonorous variation. [28] –[28]+4: Seven red-clad teenagers (YF3) enter *côté cour*, holding hands with their arms raised and left leg forward, then forming two rows and moving laterally, tilting their heads to both sides.	[26]+7: SLS on YF3, who enter the scene *côté cour*, and on the other groups	[27]+2/3: FS on YF1 crouched down and YF3 dancing in circles and then sideways	[26]+7: SLS on all while YF3 enter the scene *côté cour* [27]: FS on YF3 lined up holding hands with arms raised, then forming into a circle while a shot zooms forward [28]: LS on four groups with YF2 in close-up

Table 9.1 *continued*

Music and choreography	Opéra de Paris	Joffrey Ballet	Marinsky
[28]+5–[29]+8: Over the repetition of another folk motif introduced by the trumpets (motif F), the YF2 get up and move, leaning on both sides with their arms bent on one side or the other, to rejoin YF3.		[28]+5: SCS of YF3, who bend their heads to one side and the other [28]+8: FS of YF2 in close-up, getting up and then moving to reach the red-clad companions of YF3 [29]+4: SCS of YF3 bending their heads to the side [29]+6: FS on YF3+YF2 and awakening of YF1	[28]+5: AS of YF3, who tilt their heads to both sides [28]+9: LS on four groups with YF2, who stand up [29]+3: AS of YF2, who bend to one side to the other to reach YF3
[30]–[30]+8: With motif A enriched by semiquaver counterpoints and offbeat accents in the clarinets in syncopation, the two female groups of red-clad teenagers arranged in a single row beat out the rhythm, tapping their feet on the ground with folded arms. At [30]+4 the YF1 come alive, first raising their arms on their knees in time, then standing up.	[30]: LS on YF3 and YF1 to the right [30]+7: SLS on all the groups	[30]+7: SLS on all the groups	[30]: LS on YF1 and part of YM1, who are crouched, behind the red-clad teenagers and tap their feet on the ground with folded arms [30]+4: FS on YF1, who are about to rise, behind which the red-clad teenagers continue to tap their feet
[31]–[31]+8: Over a variation of motif E played by the oboes and piccolo and accompanied by semiquaver *ostinati* of the strings, all four groups dance, each with different movements and gestures, moving in various directions.	[31]+7: FS on YF3 running around like dervishes with YM1 behind them.	[31]: FS on YF1 and YF2+YF3. [31]+5: SLS on all the groups.	[31]: Dance of YF1 and of part of the red-clad teenagers

Music and choreography	Opéra de Paris	Joffrey Ballet	Marinsky
[32]–[32]+8: At the beginning of the crescendo achieved by the progressive addition of *ostinati*, the ballerinas of the group of red-clad teenagers begin to spin on themselves like dervishes.		[32]+5: FS on all the red-clad teenagers spinning on themselves like dervishes and zoom forward	[32]: AS on the red-clad teenagers spinning on themselves [32]+2: LS on all the groups dancing [32]+3: AS on the red-clad teenagers spinning on themselves
[33]–[36]+4: Over the continuation of the crescendo, the four groups placed with gaps between male and female groups (*côté jardin* YM1 in the front row, YF1 back row; *côté court* YF2+YF3 in the front row and YM2 in the back row) come and go, approaching and withdrawing from one another with downward arm movements, the male groups throwing up their fists on the beats of the timpani and bass drum, foreshadowing the violence of the next scene.	[33]+2: SLS on all the groups	[33]: FS on the red-clad teenagers [33]+3: SLS on all the groups [34]+2: FS on a group of white-clad teenagers [34]+4 SLS on all the groups [35]+4: FS on a group of white-clad males [36]: FS on the group of red-clad teenagers and some young men in hats [36]+3: SLS on all the groups	[33]: SLS on all groups approaching and withdrawing from one another [34]+4: FS on the teenagers throwing up their arms with clenched fists on the beats of the timpani

Abbreviations and descriptions of shots:

CS: close shot or close-up (the head to mid-bust)
SCS: semi-close shot (half-figure)
MS: medium shot (from waist to head)
AS: American shot (head to the knees)
FS: full shot (whole figure visible in the centre)
SLS: semi-long shot (wide, with actors in the middle of the stage)
LS: long shot (actors in the centre, surrounded by the entire set)

Before going into an analytical comparison of these versions, let us clarify some fundamental premises. The remediation of a ballet might well use the same filmic techniques as a cinematic performance, but must not be confused with it. Instead, it should be considered more as a documentary – with greater or lesser artistic value – having as its primary function that of reporting, divulging and observing a phenomenon from a certain point of view and hearing – from a certain *audiovisual perspective*. ‘Perspective’ here is used in the philological sense of the term, adopted by Bolter and Grusin in their volume on remediation (Bolter and Grusin 1999).

This is a very different perspective from that of a spectator in a theatre attending a performance. Rather than having a global perception and being able to freely organize their watching, listening and mutual interactions, film viewers must deal with a partial perception imposed by others. Alternations of different shots, camera positions and movements, editing, as well as the visual articulation of the music and the cuts between different sequences – all of this creates a filmic narration: the story of a journey through the performance’s audiovisual components, but a journey, so to speak, organized and presented by a guide, not a discovery voyage or a free exploration, with all of the risks such a voyage implies.

The metaphor of the journey, discussed by Morelli in his essay on *Barry Lyndon* (2011), is a true audiovisual reality. As an example, let us examine the DVD *Stravinsky and the Ballets Russes*, which includes in its second part *Le sacre du printemps* in Marinsky’s version and in its first part *L’oiseau de feu*. It begins with the first four rehearsal numbers of the introduction of the *Sacre*’s second part, used as a musical commentary to a 40-second trip along the Neva and through the canals of St Petersburg towards the Marinsky Theatre. Waiting for us here we find Valery Gergiev, at the helm of the theatre orchestra, one hand already outstretched towards the orchestra, ready to begin.

The journey continues inside the orchestra in the introductions to both *L’oiseau de feu* and the *Sacre du printemps*. The beginning of different filmic sequences coincides with the beginning of some of the instruments’ principal motifs, so that the viewer is guided through a sort of analysis of the music and its performance. As such, this is a quite different journey from that of a spectator listening in an auditorium. Such a listener, transported by the stream of sound, can freely fantasize about the motific germination and its symbolic relationships with the subject of the ballet, while waiting for the curtain to rise. From a ‘political’ point of view, focusing the attention on Gergiev, conductor and Artistic Director of the Marinsky, after the entry into the theatre following the boat trip along the canals of St Petersburg highlights emphatically the fact that he is the master of the house.

In the other two videos, the introduction of the *Sacre* is used as a musical background to the scrolling of the titles and names of the production and performance staff. However, there is a difference: in the Opéra de Paris video, the background is dominated by the figure of Nijinsky in a green costume, a blue scarf around his neck and a blue belt around his waist, as portrayed in a drawing which is a bit naive and perhaps not of great value, while in the one performed by the

Joffrey Ballet, the camera films very closely the background painted by Roerich for Part 1 of the ballet, wandering among its details.

Among the three videos, the Opéra de Paris uses semi-long shots with a fixed camera more continuously, except for some sequences (full shot or long shot), showing some of the 300-year-old Woman's actions (but not all: for example, when she throws herself to the floor and lifts her legs), and one of the groups as it awakens and begins to become active. The 'audiovisual perspective' simulates that of a spectator sitting in a central position of the auditorium, slightly higher than the stage, and using binoculars now and then to capture details of the action and the groups' movements. The cuts from one shot to another anticipate by a few beats (or a few seconds) the appearance of new motifs or the re-stating of previous motifs. However, this is not a systematic attempt to create connections between musical and choreographic sequences. Often the camera is fixed on a shot during several audiovisual sequences, and the cut from one shot to another is principally used to show the *corps de ballet*'s movements and gestures more closely. The lack of camera zoom or shots from other perspective angles suggests that the primary function of this video (produced in 1994, three years after the Opéra de Paris introduced Hodson and Archer's so-called 'reconstruction' into its repertoire) is documentary-like and educational. Its aim is to record a production of the performance, offering at times an overview, at other times a more detailed perspective.

In the Joffrey Ballet video (the first of the three), made in 1989, two years after the première of the 'reconstructed' Nijinsky version, the exact opposite is the case. The scene begins with a travelling shot from low to high of the 300-year-old Woman in a very tight close-up, at the first introduction of the *ostinato* of minor third and perfect fourth introduced at rehearsal number [12]+4, immediately after the opening Lithuanian motif played a semitone lower. In the stage version of the ballet, that *ostinato* is still part of the introduction and is therefore played before the curtain rises. Here, instead, it accentuates the leading role of the 300-year-old Woman, immediately identified with her main function – awakening the different groups and turning them into disciples.

Most of the sequences of the scene are filmed in full shot and long shot, incorporating the Old Woman's actions and the groups' reactions. With the disappearance of the Old Woman and the emergence of the group of red-clad teenagers, the disposition of the groups with respect to one another becomes even more important in grasping the essence of the choreography and of the relationship between music and ballet. Thus the semi-long shots continue to be sporadic. More frequent, however, are the full shots and long shots capturing the groups in particular and the particularities of the groups: for example, the movement of the leader of the red-clad teenagers or the aggressive attitude of the male groups, which at the end of the second part of the scene already prefigure the following 'Jeu du rapt'. This insistence on closer shots, as well as the alternation of higher/lower shots and the moderate use of zooming, puts the spectator in an audiovisual perspective which is more internal to the scene and implies a travel through the dancers' actions and movements.

Even the Marinsky video, made more recently in 2008 – the only one commercialized as a DVD – favours the use of close-up shots of the Old Woman and of the groups, instead of long shots of the overall actions and movements of the groups. The latter appear in brief flashes, reminding us of their presence in a global perception of the performance. Even the shots from above play a similar role, acting as rememorative flashes. This is especially true for certain sequences, particularly significant with regard to the figures and movements of the groups. Such a shot seems to suggest that 'while we are observing certain details, this is what is going on in the whole scene'.

In comparison to the other two remediations, this one is livelier. It is based on a continuous alternation of shots and camera movements, some of which are closer than others. Such an alternation communicates the dynamic nature of the audiovisual plot to a much greater degree. This version is also the fastest in terms of pacing: minim = 59, compared to 50 for the Opéra de Paris version and 56 for the Joffrey Ballet version. The Joffrey version, however, is more vigorous and energetic as to the *corps de ballet*'s gestures and movements.

In these three videos, with different proportions and combinations, we see a coexistence of the three main functions of a filmic remediation of a performance:

1. the documentation of a performance or a production;
2. the promotion of that performance or production;
3. the search for an in-depth analysis of the dramaturgical and staging components of the performance through the shooting and editing of the film.

One essential question remains: Through their remediated audiovisual images, what do these different journeys offer us as about the essence of the work, and in this specific case, of ballet and *Le sacre du printemps* in its ballet version?

This may seem like a naive question. Clearly, any kind of intervention (involving staging, dramaturgy, choreography, directing or cinematography) modifies the nature and the character of an original theatrical work. One should, however, bear in mind that Hodson and Archer's *Sacre* was internationally recognized as *the* reconstruction of Nijinsky's original. Given that the remediated versions – especially Marinsky's, which is now commercially available – have brought it to audiences worldwide, attempting to understand which aspects of a hypothetical original version have been more or less respected or betrayed can be of great help in acquiring further awareness of the problematic nature of any kind of re-creation of an 'original' (including the mystifications that may have been derived from it along the way). An accurate analysis of the relation between the sources and Hodson and Archer's reconstruction would not only require a great deal of space, it would also lead us away from the main topic of this chapter: remediation. I will therefore consider a single aspect of the dramaturgy that to my mind reflects an essential element of Nijinsky's choreography, as the latter can be inferred after having reflected on numerous sources.

Again, I draw inspiration from Morelli's aforementioned 2011 essay and the heuristic fertility of one its principles: the question of 'anti-narrative narrativity'.

Morelli refers to the French and English philosophical novel of the Enlightenment (Voltaire, Rousseau, Diderot, Sterne). This can be seen as a precursor to the renewal of narrativity that was to radiate across many currents through to twentieth-century experimentations and beyond. But it also becomes a fundamental aspect of modernity if understood as an *overcoming of* or an *alternative to* narrativity taken in a more linear sense. Hence, the essence of this issue is one of the fundamental aspects of *Le sacre du printemps*. Musically speaking, Stravinsky spent a good part of his life denying the traces of the *Sacre*'s narrative content, understood in a broad sense. He carried forward his argument that the *Sacre* was a purely formalist work, an expression of a pure game of forms entirely based on themes of his own invention, apart from the opening Lithuanian motif. Taruskin has shown the extent to which this argument is fallacious, linked as it is to many political, economic and aesthetic factors (Taruskin 1996).

Hodson and Archer's reconstruction of the Nijinsky version opened up a new area of interpretation. Such a reconstruction is not a posthumous exhumation of the Nijinsky version, but a puzzle offering several solutions (some more plausible than others). However, its impact on critical reception has been huge. This is partly because it contributed to invalidating the theses of the music's aniconicity and Nijinsky's amateurism as a choreographer, which for many decades had been taken for granted.

Now, whether Hodson and Archer's reconstruction is considered good or not is one thing. Taking into account only its sources (graphic, photographic, iconographic and musical documents with annotations), however, it is evident that Nijinsky developed his choreography with the same method of 'antinarrative narrativity' used by Stravinsky for the music. He started with a plot developed together with Stravinsky, but above all with Roerich, painter and set and costume designer. However, Nijinsky reduced to a bare minimum the characters, gestures and movements tied to the ritual plot. Furthermore, he conceived a performance in which the movements and gestures of the various groups of dancers played a fundamental role, thus creating a sort of choreographic symphony that resembled Oskar Fischinger's experimental films (then still to come) more closely than previous ballets, even modernist ones such as *Petrushka*.

In this latter work, Stravinsky had already introduced innovations that were to appear in the *Sacre* as well, such as the scansion of musical time in short phrases, periods and sequences. This resembled the alternation of frames in cinema more than the classical/romantic style in vogue at the time in ballet music. Another innovation is the technique of overlapping and juxtaposing elements, similar to that of film editing. Lastly, musical composition was given priority over choreographic composition, as Alexandre Benois stated in his autobiography:

> Today, when I listen to the music of the second scene of *Petrushka* and observe what the gestures and miming of the dancer on the stage express with greater or lesser success, it's hard for me to believe that, faced with this perfect congruence of action and music, the latter had not been written before the programme.

> This is because the program was adapted to a pre-existing piece of music. In this case, the process of creation took place in the opposite manner with respect to a normal and natural path. (Benois 1980, vol. 2: 523)

The 'normal and natural path' is that set by a libretto, a series of choreographic gestures to which the music must comply, as in the case of the collaboration between Stravinsky and Fokine for *L'oiseau de feu*. In *Petrushka*, Stravinsky started instead from the draft for a piano concerto and created a scene in which, through a concatenation of musical motifs and gestures, he expressed the contradictory personality of the protagonist and, in the outer scenes, the crowd's actions and movements. In the same passage from his autobiography, Benois mentions the 'perfect congruence of action and music': this does not derive from the fact that Stravinsky had composed the music of this scene imagining in detail the correspondence between musical and choreographic gestures. Actually, it derives from the alternation, within an extremely limited lapse of time, of short episodes differentiated in terms of their metric-rhythmic-dynamic-kinetic characteristics. Such characters can be translated into pantomimic gestures and movements without calling on any kind of leitmotif.

A few reviewers at the time of the *Sacre*'s 'scandal' did not fall into being (overly) scandalized. They tried to understand its originality without overlooking its relationship with that which had already been accepted as innovative (Fokine and *Petrushka*). For example, here is Jacques Rivière, who speaks precisely of this new way of conceiving the movement of bodies and groups:

> Throughout the choreography of the Sacre there is an asymmetry that is part of the essence of the work. Each group starts by itself; none of the gestures are caused by the need to respond, to compensate, to restore balance; each group is moved with emotion and each recoils and stands to the side, slipping away and forcing us to follow it. We end up recapturing it, but that's because it has been possessed by another, which has gotten the better of it. It isn't that composition is lacking; on the contrary, there is indeed composition of a more subtle kind, in the encounters, the confrontations, the mélanges and the struggles of these strange battalions. But this does not take precedence over the detail; nor does it determine it; it copes with it as it can, in all its diversity. The impression of unity that we never cease to feel is that which one experiences seeing inhabitants of the same world circulating, crossing, approaching and separating, according to their specific intentions, at the same time familiar and oblivious to one another. (Rivière 1913, in Lesure 1980: 44)[5]

---

[5] 'Il y a dans toute la chorégraphie du *Sacre* une asymétrie profonde qui fait partie de l'essence de l'œuvre. Chaque groupe commence par soi; il ne fait aucun geste qui soit suscité par le besoin de répondre, de compenser, de rétablir l'équilibre; il s'émeut et s'ébranle à l'écart, il glisse de son côté et tire notre attention à sa suite. Nous finissons bien par la lui reprendre, mais c'est parce qu'un autre s'en est emparé et l'emporte avec lui.

Therefore, the *Sacre* is an 'anti-narrative narration' in two ways. First, it does not tell a story interpreted by leading characters, but rather presents a group ritual whose characters are integrated within the group (such as the 300-year-old Woman, or the Wise Old Man). Secondly, the way in which it creates a choreo-musical symphony is based on the movements of bodies and groups dressed in different colours rather than on what is narrated according to the liturgy of a prehistoric, collective and sacrificial ritual. Thus, the *Sacre* is situated precisely within this kind of narrative/anti-narrative oxymoron.

'Anti-narrative narration' – like all concepts, in the end – is a historical category. Today, following Proust, Joyce, Beckett, the *nouveau roman*, experimental cinema and cinema *tout court*, modern dance, the happening, indeterminacy and so on, the concept of 'anti-narrative narration' is quite different from the one in vogue a hundred years ago. One could go so far as to say that this latter concept has disappeared: today everything becomes narrative, even that which appears to be abstract and fragmentary. Instead, a hundred years ago a score conceived for ballet and a choreography without an obvious plot were strange and bizarre. In the realm of dance, there was no lack of new, non-narrative proposals: one thinks of Loïs Fuller and Isadora Duncan. But non-narration is one thing; anti-narrative narration is another. The success of the second *Sacre*, the one choreographed by Massine using the *décor* and costumes of the first *Sacre* created by Roerich, depended on two things. The first was, in accordance with the logic of the time, its anti-narrativity as revealed by the absence of characters and gestures (the presence of which would have suggested traces of narration), thus emphasizing the purely ritual and anthropological aspect of the subject. And of course, the second was the fact that, in the mean time, the *Sacre*, in its concert version, had been established as one of the most exciting expressions of musical modernity.

In the framework wherein the three remediations were analysed above, the narrative plot is primarily entrusted to the ritual actions of the 300-year-old Woman teaching and animating the young people. Because these actions are often shot using close-ups, they assume a greater prominence than if they had been integrated into the overall perception of the scene.

Between the narrative and the non-narrative, one could place the group movements and the combinations of figures and colours that make up the choreographic symphony admired by the more sensitive and acute critics. That symphony is created by co-ordinating the sequences of Stravinsky's music with the gestures, movements and colours of the costumes of the various groups. The year was 1913; Delaunay had begun painting his coloured circles, Kandinsky created

---

Non pas manque de composition; il y en a une au contraire, et des plus subtiles, dans les rencontres, les affronts, les mélanges, les combats de ces étranges bataillons. Mais elle ne précède pas le détail; elle ne le commande pas; elle s'arrange comme elle peut de sa diversité. L'impression d'unité que nous ne cessons pas un instant de ressentir, c'est celle qu'on éprouve à voir circuler, se croiser, s'aborder et se séparer, selon leurs intentions particulières, à la fois familiers et oublieux les uns des autres, les habitants d'un même monde.'

his famous *Komposition VI* and several other artists from different nations were gravitating towards abstraction. Nijinsky would later obsessively dedicate himself to creating colourful geometric designs. However, already at this time Nijinsky admired the art of Bakst. He shared – whether knowingly or not one cannot tell – this new kind of perception concerning the relationships among sounds, shapes and colours that was radically renewing the principles of artistic creation.

This aspect of Nijinsky's choreographic art cannot be grasped without constantly considering the entire ensemble of audiovisual elements that compose the choreographic scenes. Translated into cinematic terms, this implies a continual need to use long shots and/or shots from above. But, as seen in the filming of the Opéra de Paris performance, what is gained in this way is lost in cinematic rhythm.

The challenge remains open to filmmakers who are more creative and less didactic than those who produced these three versions. Perhaps frames could be opened simultaneously instead of passing ceaselessly from one shot to another; in any case, it is evident that the more educational a version is, as in the case of the Opéra de Paris and the Joffrey Ballet remediations, the more clearly the didactic and compiled character of Hodson and Archer's so-called 'reconstruction' emerges. This was already in itself more in the spirit of a documentary than a true re-creation. And a documentary of a documentary is difficult to transform into a 're-creation'.

Translated by John O'Donnell

References

Benois, Alexandr (1980) *Moi vospominanija*, ed. N.I. Alexandrova, 2 vols, Moscow: Zakharov.

Bolter, Jay David and Grusin, Richard (1999) *Remediation: Understanding New Media*, Cambridge, MA: MIT Press.

Lesure, François (1980) *Igor Stravinsky, Le Sacre du Printemps. Dossier de Presse*, Geneva: Editions Minkoff.

Morelli, Giovanni (2011) 'Il postiglione Cronos. *Barry Lyndon* e ancora il "cinema del Settecento"', in *Prima la musica, poi il cinema. Quasi una sonata: Bresson, Kubrick, Fellini, Gaal*, Venice: Marsilio, pp. 47–85.

Rivière, Jacques (1913) 'Le Sacre du Printemps', *Nouvelle revue française*, 5, pp. 706–30.

Taruskin, Richard (1996) *Stravinsky and the Russian Traditions: A Biography of the Works through 'Mavra'*, Berkeley, CA: University of California Press.

Vinay, Gianfranco (2013) 'Un Sacre per tutti e per nessuno', in Veroli, Patrizia and Vinay, Gianfranco, *I Ballets Russes di Diaghilev tra storia e mito*, Rome: Accademia Nazionale di Santa Cecilia, pp. 65–84.

PART III
Listening with Images

Chapter 10

Listening to Images: A Historical Overview of Theoretical Reflection

Roberto Calabretto

Jean-Paul Sartre's early memories inspired him to dedicate a beautiful passage to the films that had deeply moved him as a child, describing as follows the associations between music and the emotions felt by those watching the moving images onscreen:

> The pianist would attack the overture to *Fingal's Cave* and everyone understood that the criminal was about to appear: the baroness would be frightened out of her wits. But her beautiful, sooty face would make way for a purple show-card: 'End of Part 1.' The lights would go on, it was a sudden awakening. Where was I? (Sartre 1964: 120)

In Sartre's memories film music played itself out according to easily foreseeable associations: sinister chords foreshadowed a murder, while 'the demonic movement of the "Race to the Abyss," an orchestral selection from *The Damnation of Faust* adapted for the piano, was always one and the same: it was Destiny' (Sartre 1964: 124). Played by a worn-out piano that 'whinnied' under the screen, the music was always a warning as to the destiny of those characters: 'An unbroken song blended with their lives, led them on to victory over death by moving toward its own end' (Sartre 1964: 124). These speechless heroes expressed 'the sound of their inner life' (Sartre 1964: 123) with silence. Chopin's *Funeral March* – a reliable leitmotif taken for granted and used in a predictable way, as dictated by the stereotypes of the time – was also, to his eyes, a way of arousing emotion and leading him to identify himself with what was happening onscreen:

> I would perceive by ear the proud grief that remains silent. I was compromised; the young widow who wept on the screen *was not me,* and yet she and I had one and the same soul. Chopin's funeral march; no more was needed for her tears to wet my eyes. (Sartre 1964: 124)

The constellation of metaphors that shaped Sartre's experience bears witness to the impact that music had on many cinema-goers, and can be taken as a first assessment of the relationship between musical accompaniment and moving images. However, he was not alone. Robert Musil, for example, underlined in

The Man without Qualities (1996) how the driving force of music constantly stimulated the magic of cinema,[1] and while Theodor Heinrich Mayer (2000: 82) observed in astonishment how the public gave greater attention to the music than to the images on screen, Giovanni Papini (1951: 28) mentions a film that kept him within 'the Wagnerian darkness of the theatre'.

Film music was often strongly criticized for its inconsistent quality in long and monotonous *cahiers de doleances*,[2] something to which Giuseppe Becce gave particular attention in several reviews. The musician Becce, who was Italian by birth and a Berliner by adoption, was well aware of the random character of film music and grasped its vocation as an illustration that rendered moving images functional. For this reason, in the *Allgemeines Handbuch der Film-Musik* (Erdmann et al. 1927) Becce confirmed the non-existence of true film music, which would derive from a free creative act rather than being limited by its connections to words and the scene. For him, the definition of 'film music' was in itself ephemeral, and for this reason he preferred to use the term 'auteur illustration' (Erdmann et al. 1927: 6).

Music for the Eyes

The difficulties involved in defining film music might explain why it took some time to situate it within certain categories of theoretical discourse. Some attempts were made during the age of silent cinema. Then, with the advent of sound, clear steps were made towards the elaboration of ideas and reflections of film music, and theories were formulated as to cinema's innate musicality, which, according to the celebrated Sebastiano Arturo Luciani, was 'like music for the eyes [*musica ottica*], which was also sustained by rhythm; but with a rhythm of its own, that takes place in time and space …' (1920b: 19–20). In electing music as inspiration of the seventh art, two opposing currents can be distinguished. The first is more radical, and appeals to a minority. Its concrete claims to an analogy with music refer exclusively to non-narrative and non-figurative cinema, based on a rhythmic sequence of moving abstract forms. The second is more widespread, and uses the notion of 'music for the eyes' in an unselfconscious and metaphorical manner, applying it to concepts pertaining to narrative film borrowed from the meta-language of music theory, such as melody, counterpoint and above all rhythm. This latter analogy was criticized by Jean Mitry, who underlined the radical difference between the rhythmic organization of sonorous and cinematographic material: 'The linear development of music creates its own meaning; now, since visual forms have no sense in themselves, neither can the way in which they follow one another make sense' (1974: 199).

---

[1] 'But physical movement in itself is so magical that we can't stand it without some kind of buffer. You can see that in films when there's no music. Music is inward motion, it supports the kinetic imagination' (Musil 1996: 459).

[2] Ernst Bloch's are particularly famous for their criticism of the foreseen equations on which similar performances were based (1974: 185–8).

Moreover, the authors of the *Allgemeines Handbuch der Film-Musik* distinguished between different levels in the use of the parameter of rhythm, beginning with the slowest 'beat' defined as a simple rhythmic pattern occurring within both physical and musical movement, and reaching a more extended rhythmic tension which is given the name 'eurhythmics'. This concept does not only involve the sphere of movement, indicating on the contrary the dramaturgical structure's moments of high and low tension.

The concept of the leitmotif has been borrowed very often and mediated in a very superficial way through Wagnerian dramaturgy, heavily conditioning the development of film music for a long period. On the other hand, it was only natural for the *Gesamtkunstwerk* to provide a framework for cinema, whose 'visual poetry' was enriched by 'a subtle depth of musicality, capable of creating an internal dynamism rich with nuance' (Luciani 1920a: 12), compared to the traditional – and inadequate – function of 'accompaniment' normally assigned to music (Gianoglio 1980: 361). The music no longer simply followed the action scene by scene: its role was now to determine its development, evoking images without translating them into sound, according to the usual procedures of mimesis. Thus, its function could not be reduced to a simple search for synchronicity with the film's editing, and aimed instead to provide a connection between the various scenes.

The reflections that appeared over the first few decades of the century suffer on the whole from their excessively abstract nature. The underlying idea itself, which consists in a hypothesis concerning analogies between acoustic and visual perception supported by vague or pseudo-physiological lines of reasoning, is entirely unsustainable. Ultimately, any comparison with music can only seem to find legitimacy within the historical process that led to cinema's ennoblement and that in the years in question was searching for support from some of the best-known figures of the literary milieu. The reality of film, in any case, was quite distant from its theoretical elaboration, and the use made of musical commentary in theatres themselves only rarely produced the structural interrelations that sustain any reflection, whether theoretical or technical, concerning the linguistic affinities obtaining between cinema and music. Music allowed cinema to do away with the silence that previously reigned in theatres, compensating for the images' illusiveness and offsetting their phantasmagoric nature, which may have unsettled audiences; aesthetically speaking, however, music was only rarely put on a par with the formal structure of a given film.

Music as a Component of a Film

At the time, an important contribution helped to establish an adequate viewpoint for this investigation, privileging specific aspects of film music at the expense of more global or all-encompassing ideas. The arrival of sound film led to a radical change in the status of film music, which became more of a fully textual component of film and less of a performance, as was the case with the accompaniments set up alongside the screen in the years of silent cinema. The dimension of sound now became a constant feature of moving images, its primary importance became clear and the close interrelations between the two languages began to transform cinema itself, as was quite evident to the first theoreticians to study its aesthetic and linguistic components.

Sergei Eisenstein, Vsevolod Pudovkin and Grigori Aleksandrov had developed the so-called 'Asynchronism Manifesto', which identified, if only in an embryonic form, a series of elements that were to become incorporated into a new cinema based on editing as well as technical and formal factors that carried with them a new artistic potential. Here, as is well known, the authors elaborated their idea of counterpoint, which was to enjoy great success in the history of film music. Even if this notion was still understood as a musical metaphor, it was nevertheless a question of a 'method of construction' in so far as it was not fully based on theoretical experience – a point argued by Michel Chion (1994: 58–62) and later by Sergio Miceli (2009: 507–9). Chion's doubts correspond with those of Rudolph Arnheim, who soon underlined that while this theory was indisputable, it was difficult to apply on a practical level. For this reason, his aesthetic conception, born in the realm of experimental psychology in Berlin (the *Gestalttheorie*), called for the editing process to perceive sound and image as inseparable – something that asynchronism brought into question (Arnheim 1979: 78–81).

However, all of these positions, while difficult to contradict, forget that Eisenstein's reflections did have a practical influence on filmmaking, unlike other ideas that did not go beyond an abstract formulation. Suffice it to consider the notion of *vertical montage*, which was to remain one of the cornerstones of film theory for many years, and which can be an extremely useful analytical tool even today.

Not by chance, Béla Balázs concludes: 'In an asynchronous sound film the action can move on two parallel levels at the same time, in the sphere of sound and in the sphere of visual images' (1952: 219). This formed the basis for the important notion of audiovisual combination, which goes beyond the composition of the elements of an image and has a surprising affinity with a celebrated and masterly adage by Pier Paolo Pasolini (1984), who identifies music as 'the physical "elsewhere" due to its "deep" nature [that] breaks the one-dimensional images, or gives the illusion of their depth on screen, opening up a confused depth where life's limitations do not exist'.

From a historiographical perspective that considers cinema's development as a form of popular spectacle, from this period on there is no doubt that film music made a fundamental contribution to the way in which cinematic genres evolved, and was responsible for aesthetically important formal choices. Within the so-called 'Hollywood film language' – which was to influence other cinematographic schools for decades – music played on an equal footing with dialogue and images. Musical structures turned out to be fundamental in identifying the *topoi* that were typical of the genres themselves, as was the case with film noir, or the western in particular, or again in sophisticated comedies and *mélo* that turned to music for dramaturgical results unattainable by dialogues.

The Unclear Identity of Film Music

Since the 1950s the theoretical debate surrounding film music has been enriched by multiple and complex aspects that nevertheless focus on a few central points. The 'functions' of film music are insistently discussed – functions that Siegfried Kracauer circumscribes within well-defined routes, denying at the same time the ambition of music to attain dramaturgical potential and to engage in an active dialogue with moving images.[3] In order to examine the problematic relationship with moving images, the synaesthesia of music is also called into question.

Georges Hacquard (1959) underlined the contribution made by *musique concrète* to cinema's soundscape. Shortly after, Zofia Lissa demonstrated how to face with greater awareness the problems cinema posed to music, and later on she focused on cinema's innate syncretism, where music assumes a different and temporary 'statute', having to follow also the visual, and where its innate semantic ambiguity is resolved. This is surely one of the most important findings of Lissa's Ästhetik der Filmmusik (1965), which offers the first comprehensive systematization of the functions of film music. While later developments and analytical orientations brought about a reduction of the functions theorized by Lissa, her text is nonetheless exemplary for its methodological rigour, its documentation and references that are only rarely found in contemporaneous reflections.

Leaving aside a number of texts whose success does not correspond in the least to the real consistency of their theoretical weight,[4] we should dwell upon another important volume: the famous *Komposition für den Film* by Theodor W. Adorno and Hanns Eisler (1969). Its limitations are evident from the beginning, where the authors postulate cinema's full integration into the realm of mass culture. This is an incorrect and crude evaluation, which on the one hand fails to recognize that films of that time could be considered as true works of art, while on the other hand affirming the prosaic character of a seventh art incapable of symbolism, inasmuch as its goal is to depict reality. The two affirmations are both misleading and can easily be proven false: the first by quite simply taking note of the masterpieces created during the years in which Adorno was formulating his reflections, and the second by what figures such as Christian Metz, Roland Barthes, André Bazin, Jean Mitry, Gianfranco Bettetini or Étienne Souriau were to theorize in the years to come. Its own high degree of prejudice was to affect the volume's theoretical vision, denying film music both the possibility of developing its own standards and any ability to establish its own style.[5]

---

[3] Among his texts, Kracauer (1964) features strongly.

[4] It is enough to consider the superficiality of two volumes, justified by its attitude towards divulgation: London (1936) and Manvell and Huntley (1957).

[5] On this perspective, see Hansen (2012).

From 'Film' Music to 'Music for the Cinema': The 'Real Laws' of Film Music

The new systems of production and mechanical reproduction that coincided with film music's development created the basic conditions required to define an aesthetics of listening. Film music was born from the dialogue between the elements that merged in a soundtrack, thus undergoing a metamorphosis. Film music's unclear identity might easily evoke the image of a large workshop whose artisans rely on communication with the composer, who in turn must understand their needs. The way in which film music produces meaning, therefore, appears to be conditioned by a closely woven network of connections and relationships whose discourse is dynamic and constantly open, calling into question the public's 'listening' (Calabretto 2010: 47–56).

Since the 1970s, aesthetic reflection has approached such problems. The empirical approach, strongly conditioned by historical and cultural factors, was gradually replaced by a scientific or analytic approach that overcame the 'impressionism' and prejudice previously found in criticism. Directors were aware of and sensitive to the role of a film's soundscape when editing, and endorsed alternative stances in terms of 'dismantling the audiovisual text', thus making eye-catching and appealing observations. Inspired masters, such as Robert Bresson, Andrei Tarkovsky, Werner Herzog and Michelangelo Antonioni, have insistently attempted to concretely define what film music is, reaffirming a specificity which treasures its own law and avoids influence from other areas. Such autonomy had simply not existed during previous decades. On more than one occasion Antonioni firmly states that film music must be 'a part of unique sensory experience' (1994: 134)[6] in combination with images, thereby losing its own autonomy, which is why the scores of his films are completely lacking in rhetoric. Tarkovsky widened the semantic field of film music by introducing electronic compositions that he himself defined as 'organic reverberations of the world', in opposition to acoustic music, which he considered alien to the needs of moving images.[7] Subsequently, both Antonioni and Tarkovsky, as well as Bresson,[8] underlined 'noise' as a fundamental presence in editing a film – and if this noise is used poetically, then it is the 'real' music of moving images.

A more interesting element as regards our historical outline, however, is the fact that thanks to this awareness, new theoretical perspectives opened up that further delimited the functions of sound within an interweaving of audio and visual

[6] In a famous statement the director says: 'It is not sound: word, noise, music. It is not image: landscape, attitude, gesture. But *the indecomposable, stretched out in a singular length of time which penetrates and determines its essence*' (Antonioni 2002: 21–2; my italics).

[7] 'Electronic music must be purged of its "chemical" origins, so that as we listen we may catch in it primary notes of the world' (Tarkovsky 1986: 162).

[8] 'Reorganize disorganized noises (what you think you hear, is not what you are actually hearing) in a street, in a train station, in an airport … to retrieve them in silence one by one and measure out their blending' (Bresson 1975: 52).

languages. Bresson, from this point of view, represents a magisterial example of how to overturn that which had long been widely accepted as a universal truth. Music, in his opinion, should in no way comment on the events occurring in a film, and still less should it underline or reinforce the movements within each single scene or frame. Sound is extraneous to the laws of cinema to such a point – as many directors, such as Rohmer, have insistently reaffirmed – that its functions are projected in radically different directions than those set out by Lissa. Music is no longer used for its alleged semantic codes, nor is it subservient to a succession of images, and does not support narrative functions: rather, it is an element of cinematographic language that must be used with a great deal of prudence: pure listening and pure vision, in the words of Tarkovsky, who was inclined to use acoustic music during the opening and closing credits of his films, leaving room for electronic music during the film itself, while Antonioni went as far as to say that only diegetic music is fully legitimized within a cinematic narration.

The notion of soundscape as sketched out at that time had already been discussed in Balázs's theoretical writings. His version is perhaps more poetic, but equally portentous as regards the role of sound in film:

> It is the business of the sound film to reveal for us our acoustic environment, the soundscape in which we live, the speech of things and the intimate whisperings of nature; all that has speech beyond human speech, and speaks to us with the vast conversational powers of life and incessantly influences and directs our thoughts and emotions. (Balázs 1952: 197)

The Hungarian theorist, unconstrained by the limits of speech as a culturally defined language, clearly expressed his wishes: the use of sound would not be limited to well-consolidated naturalistic or literary conventions, but on the contrary would liberate itself from the legacy of common symbolism and stimulate the spectator's thoughts and emotions. This is how sound film could teach the spectator on the one hand 'to analyse even chaotic noise', and on the other to 'read the score of life's symphony' (Balázs 1952: 198). If it were possible to realize a perfect collocation of sound within a layered space, similarly to the interplay of images, and to attain a sound editing process as significant as that applied to the sequence of frames, then sound could assume a leading role in film language.

New Approaches to Film Music

This was springtime for film music studies, a season when many and diverse approaches were established. The semiological approach, thanks to its linguistic grounding in literary analysis, detected two notable functions – diegetic and extra-diegetic (at an internal and external level) – that were further enriched by Sergio Miceli with the so-called 'mediated level', in which we find the maximum potential for interaction between the soundtrack and the images (1994: 517–44).

Here, verbal language is replaced by musical language, and a double reinforcement emerges: firstly regarding music, which has an effect on the listener that goes beyond the contingent narrative, and secondly concerning the outcome of this interaction between the spectator and the interior experience of the characters, who themselves become musical instruments. The presence of this level allowed Miceli to consider music to be one of the film's characters, endowed with a specific narrative valency – a function that was magnified by a few particularly inspired directors, such as Federico Fellini or Sergio Leone.

A similar approach also characterized *Unheard Melodies* (1987), a distinguished work written by Claudia Gorbman: based on linguistics (Gérard Genette, Étienne Souriau and Christian Metz, as regards its filmological premises), this book gave life to an analytical model that emphasizes narrative mechanisms and phenomena as its paradigmatic elements, above all as regards temporality. Gorbman succeeds in avoiding the 'systematizating fury' that Hansjörg Pauli found in Zofia Lissa and that can also be seen in Cristina Cano and Giorgio Cremonini's *La musica nel cinema* (1990). In this latter volume, the two authors enumerate the many ways in which music appears during a film; however, their findings are difficult to apply, thus suggesting that they are self-referential, as suspected by Ennio Simeon (1995: 64). Last but not least is a similar model that, when applied to non-narrative audiovisual texts, is unsuccessful in grasping audiovisual pathways.

Philip Tagg's work also deserves consideration in its search for a fusion of semiologically and empirically oriented psychological surveys. As highlighted by Sergio Miceli, his research is upheld by the utopian idea of 'a democratic circulation and appropriation of knowledge that on the one hand fascinates and encourages respect; on the other hand however, we must also consider the possibilities (probably unintended by the author) of its worrying demagogic consequences' (Miceli 2009: 560).[9] Similarly, Nicholas Cook's studies should be mentioned: he saw in the digital era a new democracy of listening and vision, thanks to the materials now available to the public.

Given the ease with which they sometimes treat various realms of audiovisual language, these types of approach are limited above all by the low consideration they reserve for historiography. The complexity of historical layering should on the contrary be kept in consideration during any kind of reflection. Going back as far as the days of silent film, these layers provide a fundamental key to understanding the diversity with which musical language has been received in different areas and contexts, such as Europe and America.

[9] Miceli refers to 'verbal–visual associations'; the results are the replies of the participants Tagg tested, often creating doubts in the world of musicology when referring to the opportunity of extrapolating and valuing statistically a common reaction that manifests itself in stereotypes.

The Aesthetics of Sound

During the same period other analytical research dealt with the aesthetics of sound. Approaches of this kind can be traced back to Edgard Varèse, who in 1940 had already introduced the term 'organized sound' as a factor of dramaturgical renewal of moving images, at the precise point where words reached their limits. Cinema, in turn, could be an effective way of liberating the potentiality of organized sound, thus giving life to a new dramaturgy in which sound would no longer be conceived as a separate entity, but rather as thematic material 'organized into a score standing on its own merit' (Varèse 1940: 205). For this reason, Varèse hoped that the composition of moving images could take place in a research laboratory where 'the composer, or *sound organizer*, and the electrical engineer work together' (1940: 205). His idea seems to prefigure the concept of 'audiovision', affirming that 'between this sound score and dramatic continuity, the relationship must be an intimate and cooperative connection; a liaison of unity, of form and of rhythm' (Varèse 1940: 205). Moreover, 'this weaving together of disparate sounds and visuals, elements which will make a film a unified whole, cannot be achieved by the device of an imitative repetition of the visual' (Varèse 1940: 205).

French research, including Pierre Schaeffer's work, also displayed great sensitivity and care both in facing problems inherent to the relationship between music and image and in giving them theoretical weight. Some aspects appear to be anachronistic: 'the public, who remembers the names of actors and probably of the director, does not remember the name of the musician' (Schaeffer 1946a: 47).[10] This assertion is reminiscent of other contemporary – and equally banal – statements pronounced by musicians like Ildebrando Pizzetti.[11] Equally, the models that inspire him strictly involve French cinema – one thinks of *Les Anges du péché* (1943) by Robert Bresson, proposed by Jean-Jacques Grunenwald as a privileged repository for the use of the leitmotif in cinema which was by now a widespread practice, especially in America. Nevertheless, his definition of *musique-matériau* and its theoretical elaboration – starting from experimental psychology and acoustic phenomena of masking in cinema – are very interesting. Schaeffer deserves to be taken into consideration because of his analysis of audiovisual phenomena from a psycho-perceptive perspective: on the concrete basis of appearance, rather than a deductive aesthetic vision.

The importance of Schaeffer's ideas is easily traceable in the poetic acoustics of some directors, above all Robert Bresson and Jacques Tati, and his skills greatly inspired the construction of the soundscape of their films. In *Antoine et Colette* (1962),

---

[10] See also Schaeffer (1946b; 1946c) and, among his other writings on music and cinema, Schaeffer (1960).

[11] Although he composed many music scores for cinema, at the end of his career Pizzetti declared that he did not in the least believe in film music and in the possibility that it could comment on images: 'What need is there for music? People go to the cinema to see good actors, be part of a story they are interested in' (Pizzetti 1964: 463).

François Truffaut affectionately portrayed, as if in a dedication, Schaeffer during a conference of Bernard Gavoty dedicated to him. Video art also owes much to his teachings, where Chion establishes – although on the basis of a misunderstanding[12] – an equation between *musique concrète* and electronic images. Robert Cahen, Schaffer's pupil, affirmed that his master taught him to edit sounds, to listen to them and to understand their contents once they had been decontextualized from their source.

Music 'in' Film

Leaving aside the contribution of other noteworthy scholars – such as Michel Fano (1970) – the leap from Schaeffer to his pupil Chion is inevitable and direct. During the 1980s Chion produced a renowned triptych – *La voix au cinéma* (1982), *Le son au cinéma* (1985) and *La toile trouée* (1988) – that later converged in *Audio-vision* (1994), still a cornerstone for scholars (see Chion 1982; 1985; 1988; 1994). On the basis of a global and non-hierarchical phenomenology of the acoustic universe, Chion faced the problem of music *within* film, as opposed to music *for* film:

> It will be evident that for us it is a matter of putting on the same level all of the music, whether original or not, *that appears in the film*, because what matters is its contribution *to cinema*. At the same time we intend to show that *film music* as an autonomous musical genre obeying new and specific criteria, *does not exist*. (Chion 1985: 104)

By mediating his master's results regarding the specificity of cinematographic language – for example, in the importance of the notion of 'acousmatic' as opposed to 'visualized sound' (Chion 1994: 71–5) – Chion understood how to attain a global conception of the audiovisual, which allowed him to consider the work of some (particularly French) directors and produced remarkable and interesting results. However, his analysis can be criticized for consciously ignoring history and its multiple layers. Often his analyses 'suffer' from prejudices that in part invalidate the generosity of his theoretical model, sometimes overly limited to French cinema and short-sighted. This model does not recognize the need to contextualize the audiovisual within the close-knit weaving of a system – the cinematographic one, in particular – which inevitably influences its internal acoustic components. Moreover, in Chion's theory on audiovisual relationships the vertical dimension is given greater consideration than the horizontal one, where the employment of noise, music, effects and voice assumes meaning thanks to their status as recorded sound.

[12] Chion (1999b: 217–18) commented that the musical component of cinema and video does not present substantial differences when considering audiovisual processes. Actually, this new universe, in which electronic art allows a continuous exchange of languages with related forms and methods, offers the possibility of a complete synthesis and new analytical instruments.

This gives life to a symbolic and communicative system that unfolds over time, on a horizontal level, as is the case, for example, in Tarkovsky's films, where the acoustic material does not always find a visual correspondence and produces a layering of sound similar to radio drama. This explains the obvious superficiality with which he examines the presence of music in Antonioni's films (Chion 1999a), or again his significant silences as to the function of music in his monograph dedicated to Tarkovsky (Chion 2007).

Reading Cinema in Musical Terms

I will now propose a hypothesis for a possible musical reading of 'auteur cinema', investigating not a film's soundscape, but rather its articulation. This reading is based on Arnold Hauser's precept that visual images can translate situations and experiences that previously could only be expressed through musical forms (see Hauser 1958: 481–518), without forgetting that Adorno also asked whether films could be created in the same way as musical compositions (see Müller Doohm 2003: 620). It is a reading, in short, that while maintaining and accentuating the differences between music and image, does not convey meaning and continuity to them, and that contrasts the idea of the innate musicality of cinema.

This is precisely what happens in Werner Herzog's cinema. During the editing of *Lebenszeichen* (1968) the director stated how much he owed to Indian music. In the final sequence – in particular, the tracking shot of the plain where one expects something to happen, and yet all we are left with is an empty plain and a strip of dust – the incongruence of the passing of time is reflected in the bouzouki's sweet melody. This stylistic affinity, evoked by Herzog himself, provokes a series of theoretical and methodological questions. The sequence shot, in this case, is connected to a single musical note, similar to an Indian mantra, held for an undefined lapse of time. This insistent and repetitive sound has a precise objective: creating an atmosphere of suspense and a feeling that something is just about to happen. The hypnotic tendency of the trail of dust animating the image is enhanced by the repetitive nature and circular structure of the music. Herzog favours this device, where the image appears to resolve itself. A similar procedure can also be found in Atom Egoyan's films, whose mosaic-like narrative structures strongly favour the use of flashback, thus creating similarities between the characters' experiences. The narrative emerges from the use of sound by applying musical passages of similar structure.

Insisting on the innate musicality of his cinema, Carmelo Bene states that the seventh art has not taught music the editing process, but the other way round. According to Bene, Monteverdi, Bach, Mozart and Verdi have revealed how music derives from processes of composition in which montage plays a fundamental role. Walter Murch as well, when speaking of Beethoven's music, spoke of cuts, fadings, long shots and close-ups. The editing of a film, in Bene's opinion, comes about not only on the post-production Moviola, but occurs with the movements of the camera capturing the images, according to a logic dictated by a well-defined rhythm. The camera becomes an instrument of rhythm, which gives life to paratactic editing – that is, without relations involving syntactic connections and contiguity (see Saba 2005). Seen in this way, *Salomè* (1972) is an extreme example that illustrates the possibility of creating 'music for the eye'. The edited fragments, without connections and with definite cuts, generate a discontinuous and whirling flux of shots, translating itself into music. But let us consider the finale of *Don Giovanni* (1971), where we witness a true apology of editing, inspired by immediate changes brought together in a continuous transformation of the cinematographic point of view (objective, subjective and false subjective), enveloping the image or folding it upon itself. In the false prologue, however, the jump cuts simulate a horizontal panorama throughout the different faces until the camera moves out of range: here the images complement Mozart's music, which dictates the rhythm of the sequence.

Camera, editing and actors' bodies form a base for 'musicality *sub specie* film'. In reversing Eisenstein's theory – somehow fulfilling the secret dream evident in *Neravnodusnaja priroda* – Bene achieves the idea of a film without linguistic mediation, which subverts traditional audiovisual norms and denies the cinematographic soundspace its traditional reference points, such as the recurrence of synchrony, synchresis, accompaniment and comment. His cinema does not use music, but is in itself music, like an uninterrupted acoustic flow. In the continuous movement of shapes and language running through his films, in which the images are captured by the voice, silence and the word, the becoming of images produces figures that release sound and demand listening. An example of such freedom from language reminds us of Rossini's operas – Bene's repeated reference to *L'italiana in Algeri* is no coincidence – in which music is surpassed by musicality. Bene's cinema undoubtedly tends towards this model.[13]

Cinema in the Form of Music

In equally complex ways, other directors have looked to music for inspiration when editing their films, identifying some musical forms as references. Alain Resnais spoke several times of the musical construction of his films: the editing is unleashed by an image that in turn produces other images 'that must be homogeneous with the first, like the elements of a music composition' (Renais, in Carta and Mesnil 1960: 935). Every moment of his filmography can be associated with a musical form. *Hiroshima mon amour* (1959) is close to the form of a quartet,[14] and in *L'amour à mort* (1984) Schoenberg's String Trio op. 45 seems to be part

---

[13] See the significant anthology of Bene's writings in Morreale (2011).

[14] 'I believe that if we analyse *Hiroshima* with a diagram drawn on graph paper, it would look like a quartet. Themes, variations starting from the first movement; then the repetitions and reprise …. The last movement of the film is a slow, bewildering movement. There is a decrescendo there' (Liandrat-Guigues and Leutrat 2006: 151).

of the film's concept. In both cases we are constantly invited to read his films in musical terms. However, the most important reference is *Muriel ou le temps d'un retour* (1963). Hans Werner Henze, who composed the music, commented that in this film, 'the montage of the sequences from one shot to another, the movement of the camera from one place to another were phenomena that seemed familiar, very close to my work as a composer' (Henze, in La Rochelle 1997: 18). At the same time, the score consists of a series of arias, instrumental excerpts and chord fragments. The 'arias' recur eight times and create a structural connection in the editing process, like punctuation for the film's sequential units. They also have a lyrical function, thanks to the particular resonance of Henze's music. While on the one hand instrumental music accompanies the words (in this case, the interventions recur nine times, often revealing what is concealed by the protagonists' speech), on the other it is presented autonomously, creating a tight network of thematic connections between each segment, without taking on specific movements. This structure transforms the film into a cantata, once again confirming Resnais's desire to use music differently, making it part of precise audiovisual plots, while also creating clear autonomous and self-sufficient pathways.

Ingmar Bergman's cinema also makes constant reference to musical forms. In his own words, *Viskningar och rop* (1973) is similar to a Mozart quartet, and in *Höstsonaten* (1978) the action unfolds in a way that can be expressed in musical terms. The strongest example, however, is *Saraband* (2003). The form evoked by the title is reflected in the film. Here the music, apart from a glimpse of a Bruckner symphony in Chapter Six, is always the Sarabande from Cello Suite no. 5 in C minor by Johann Sebastian Bach, which recurs eight times. Textual similarities are recognizable on a large scale: in the subdivision into chapters, corresponding to a similar subdivision of a musical composition into fragments, and in the single sequences where the structure of the dialogue recalls the structure of the music. The emphasis on pauses and breaths during the musical performance corresponds to silences and pauses in the events represented in the film; the complexity and harmonic instability of Bach's score are linked to the drama's characters.

In *Zerkalo* (1975) Tarkovsky – whose entire filmography lends itself to a musical reading – seems to use the rondo form as a reference for the episodic structure of his film, which emancipates itself from any residual narrative element. When reading accounts of the film's creation, it becomes evident how Tarkovsky rejected the rules of traditional storytelling, preferring to juxtapose sequences according to a musical process. This film intentionally frees itself from narrative snares and chooses to follow a stream of consciousness through memories, dreams and few glimpses of the present time. Therefore, the work's unity – the strategies through which the fragments are held together, considering the 'fragility' of the narrative voice – is determined by the systematic repetitions, in the visual dimension, of strongly symbolic elements, such as water, earth, fire, milk and wind: elements dear to the Russian director.

Tarkovsky has clarified this poetic construction in these terms:

> A film is closer than anything else to the musical structuring of the material. What matters here is not the logic of the flow of events, but the form in which such events change, the form in which they exist in the cinematographic material. When form is understood that way, the sequence of episodes, characters, events does not matter, what happens is the logic of musical events: the theme, anti-theme, exposition etc. The film *Mirror* is based on such a principle of organizing material. (Tarkovsky, in Yegorova 2007: 78, 199)

The film therefore assumes a musical shape, similar to a rondo. The notes written when the film was being made (Tarkovsky 1993) – in particular during the 16 or 18 versions of the overall montage of *Zerkalo* – reveal how the director applied his pivotal principles when composing the entire film, allowing us to perceive his entire poetics – a poetics inspired by music with which it directly and concretely confronts itself, avoiding any type of superficial suggestion. Tarkovsky, like the other above-mentioned directors, invites us to formulate theoretical ideas and analytical methods far from those carried out during the first decades of the century, thus giving us new perspectives for a deeper understanding of auteur film.

One Possible, and Partial, Conclusion

Nicola Piovani, one of the most highly acclaimed composers in Italian cinema, once said during an interview that 'there is no such thing as "film music"' (Piovani 2005: 19). This was his way of implying that every film requires its own specific universe of sound, and that it is not possible to pinpoint anything that could define film music in itself. Film music cannot in fact be set within precise boundaries because it lacks an ability to develop itself according to laws of its own, and is forced, on the contrary, both to depend on technological progress and to adapt itself to the needs of the director, the system of production and, at times, the audience's tastes. This is what our overview of a few moments of the last century of theoretical-aesthetic reflection on film music allows us to conclude, within a historical prospective that was in no way intended to have evolutionary overtones.

A concise presentation of these theoretical models is clearly useful for all those who wish to adapt themselves to well-defined schools and cinematographic genres. In order to discuss Bresson's cinema, Schaeffer's writings are extremely interesting, while Chion's theoretical model is useful for analysing Tati's and other directors' filmography, but less so for Antonioni's films. His categories are inadequate for the audiovisual ideas that the Italian director stressed, outwitting the 'audiovisual pact' that Chion theorized. Furthermore, Cano's network of categories can help us understand the functions of Peter Greenaway's film music. In any case, if a film needs its own music, it equally requires a suitable analytical model, which therefore cannot be given *a priori*. In order to scrutinize a film and its acoustic components, Werner Herzog grasped the need for a 'physical test', where theory and method are secondary to the fundamental necessity of dismantling every segment of the soundtrack during the long editing process.

This is why analysing film music and attempting to trace out a few theoretical coordinates necessarily involves adopting a variety of different approaches. Reflecting on the problem of music in the cinema of Pier Paolo Pasolini, one understands that the director had a strongly subjective conception of Bach's music, unlike other directors such as Bergman and Tarkovsky, who used the same compositions with radically different aims, or again Luchino Visconti, who turned to the traditional repertory of European opera and late nineteenth-century symphonic music with musicological insight that is rarely found in the world of cinema. An entirely different approach is necessary for any form of *cinéma verité*, which demands highly connoted mimetic procedures from music, or for film genres that on the contrary search for audiovisual synaesthesia (in this case, the composer's role must be considered alongside those of other professional figures, such as sound designers), or filmographies of directors that turn to music using filmic procedures, causing the sound montage to become the link between the two languages. A few fundamental points do, however, remain that must be kept in mind during any reflection, and these range from the historical awareness with which any work must be analysed to a knowledge of the preparation of the soundtrack, if only to avoid the approximations or trivialities that may come up during analysis and that stem from an inadequate knowledge of the sonorous materials that make up a film.

Translated by Jane North

References

Adorno, Theodor W. and Eisler, Hanns (1969) *Komposition für den Film*, Munich: Rogner & Bernhard.

Antonioni, Michelangelo (1994) *Fare un film è per me vivere. Scritti sul cinema,* Venice: Marsilio.

——— (2002) 'Il fatto e l'immagine', in *Il cinema di Michelangelo Antonioni*, ed. Carlo Di Carlo, Milan: Il Castoro.

Arnheim, Rudolf (1979) 'Asynohronismus', in *Kritiken und Aufsätze zum Film*, Frankfurt am Main: Fischer.

Balázs, Béla (1952) *Theory of the Film (Character and Growth of a New Art)*, trans. Edith Bone, London: Dennis Dobson.

Billard, Pierre (1994) 'L'idea mi viene attraverso le immagini', in Antonioni (1994), pp. 129–35.

Bloch, Ernst (1974) 'Über die Melodie im Kino', in *Zur Philosophie der Musik*, Frankfurt am Main: Suhrkamp.

Bresson, Robert (1975) *Notes suawr le cinématographe*, Paris: Gallimard.

Calabretto, Roberto (2010) *Lo schermo sonoro*, Venice: Marsilio.

Cano, Cristina and Cremonini, Giorgio (1990) *Cinema e musica. Il racconto per sovrapposizioni*, Bologna: Thema.

Carta Jean, and Mesnil, Michel (1960) 'Un cinéaste stoïcien. Interview d'Alain Resnais', *Esprit*, 28/285, pp. 934–45.

Chion, Michel (1982) *La voix au cinéma*, Paris: Editions de l'Etoile.

——— (1985) *Le son au cinéma*, Paris: Cahiers du Cinéma (Essais) and Editions de l'Etoile.

——— (1988) *La toile trouée*, Paris: Cahiers du Cinéma and Editions de l'Etoile.

——— (1994) *Audio-vision: Sound on Screen*, trans. Claudia Gorbman, New York: Columbia University Press.

——— (1997) *Andreï Tarkovski*, Paris: Cahiers du cinéma.

——— (1999a) 'Antonioni prosatore del suono', in *La sonorità del visibile. Immagini, suoni e musica nel cinema di Michelangelo Antonioni*, ed. Alberto Achilli, Alberto Boschi and Gianfranco Casadio, Ravenna: Longo.

——— (1999b) 'La question de la conception sonore en vidéo', in *L'art vidéo 1980–1999. Vingt ans du VideoArt Festival, Locarno. Recherches, théories, perspectives*, ed. Vittorio Fagone, Milan: Mazzotta.

——— (2007) *Andreï Tarkovski*, Paris: Cahiers du cinéma.

Cook, Nicholas (1998) *Analysing Musical Multimedia*, New York: Oxford University Press.

Erdmann, Hans, Becce, Giuseppe and Brav, Ludwig (1927) *Allgemeines Handbuch der Film-Musik*, Berlin: Schlesinger.

Fano, Michel (1970) *Musique et film*, in *La musique en projet*, Paris: Gallimard.

Gianoglio, Mario (1980) 'La Coltura Cinematografica' [29 December 1919], in *Tra una film e l'altra. Materiali sul cinema muto italiano 1907–1920*, Venice: Marsilio, p. 361.

Gorbman, Claudia (1987) *Unheard Melodies: Narrative Film Music*, London: British Film Institute.

Hacquard, Georges (1959) *La musique et le cinéma*, Paris: Bibliothèque Internationale de Musicologie and Presse Universitaire de France.

Hansen, Miriam Bratu (2012) *Cinema and Experience: Siegfried Kracauer, Walter Benjamin and Theodor W. Adorno*, Berkeley, CA: University of California Press.

Hauser, Arnold (1958) *Sozial-Geschichte der Kunst und Literatur*, vol. 2, Munich: C.H. Beck.

Kracauer, Siegfried (1964) *Theorie des Films: die Errettung der äusseren Wirklichkeit*, Frankfurt am Main: Suhrkamp.

La Rochelle, Réal (1997), 'Quand le dialogue devient chant: entretien avec Alain Resnais', *Positif*, 437–8, p. 18.

Liandrat-Guigues, Suzanne and Leutrat, Jean-Louis (2006) *Alain Resnais. Liaisons secrètes, accords vagabonds*, Paris: Cahiers du cinéma.

Lissa, Zofia (1965) *Ästhetik der Filmmusik*, Berlin: Henschelverlag.

London, Kurt (1936) *Film Music: A Summary of the Characteristic Features of Its History, Aesthetics, Technique, and Possible Developments*, London: Faber and Faber.

Luciani, Sebastiano Arturo (1920a) 'Il poema visivo come genere letterario', *Fortunio*, 5/5, p. 12.

——— (1920b) *Verso una nuova arte: il cinematografo*, Rome: Ausonia.
Manvell, Roger and Huntley, John (1957) *The Technique of Film Music*, London: Focal Press.
Mayer, Theodor Heinrich (2000) 'Begleitmusik', in *Menschen im Kino. Film und Literatur erzählen*, ed. Anne Paech and Joachim Paech, Stuttgart: Metzler.
Miceli, Sergio (1994) 'Analizzare la musica per film. Una riproposta della teoria dei livelli', *Rivista Musicale Italiana*, 29/2, pp. 517–44.
——— (2009) *Musica per film. Storia, Estetica, Analisi, Tipologie*, Lucca: LIM.
Mitry, Jean (1974) *Le cinéma experimental: histoire et perspectives*, Paris: Seghers.
Morreale, Emiliano (ed.) (2011) *Carmelo Bene. Contro il cinema*, Rome: Minimum fax.
Müller Doohm, Stefan (2003) *Adorno. Eine Biographie*, Frankfurt am Main: Suhrkamp.
Musil, Robert (1996) *The Man without Qualities*, vol. 1, trans. Sophie Wilkins, New York: Vintage.
Ondaatje, Michel (2004) *The Conversations: Walter Murch and the Art of Editing Film*, New York: Knopf.
Papini, Giovanni (1951) 'La filosofia del cinematografo', in *Storia del cinema muto italiano*, vol. 1, ed. Maria Adriana Prolo, Milan: Il Poligono.
Pasolini, Pier Paolo (1984) untitled notes, in *Morricone. La musica nel cinema di Pasolini*, LP, GM73001, Milan.
Piovani, Nicola (2005) *Concerto fotogramma*, Milan: Rizzoli.
Pizzetti, Ildebrando (1964) 'Ildebrando Pizzetti non è tenero con il cinema' (interview by Marina Magaldi), *Rivista del cinematografo*, 37/9–10, p. 463.
Sartre, Jean-Paul (1964) *The Words*, trans. Bernard Frechtman, New York: George Braziller.
Schaeffer, Pierre (1946a) 'L'élément non visuel au cinéma. 1: Analyse de la bande son', *La Revue du cinéma. Série nouvelle*, 1/1, pp. 45–8.
——— (1946b) 'L'élément non visuel au cinéma. 2: Conception de la musique', *La Revue du cinéma. Série nouvelle*, 1/2, pp. 62–5.
——— (1946c) 'L'élément non visuel au cinéma. 3: Psychologie du rapport vision-audition', *La Revue du cinéma. Série nouvelle*, 1/3, pp. 51–4.
——— (1960) 'Le Contrepoint du son et de l'image', *Les Cahiers du Cinéma*, 108, pp. 7–22.
Saba, Cosetta (2005) *Carmelo Bene*, Milan: il Castoro.
Simeon, Ennio (1995) *Per un pugno di note. Storia, teoria, estetica della musica per il cinema, la televisione e il video*, Milan: Rugginenti.
Tarkovsky, Andrei (1986) *Sculpting in Time: Reflections on the Cinema*, trans. Kitty Hunter-Blair, London: The Bodley Head, p. 162.
——— (1993) *Der Spiegel, Novelle, Arbeitstagebücher und Materialien zur Entstehung des Films*, trans. Kurt Baudisch and Ute Spengler, Berlin: Limes.
Varèse, Edgard (1940) 'Organized Sound for the Sound Film', *The Commonweal*, 33/13, pp. 204–5.
Yegorova, Tatiana (2007) *Edward Artemiev's Musical Universe*, Moscow: Vagrius.

Chapter 11
Seeing Sounds, Hearing Images: Listening Outside the Modernist Box

Nicholas Cook

Multimedia Old and New

'Complete darkness', the Bristol Proms website promised, 'Proper darkness. Darkness so dark you can't see your hand in front of your face. Technical, 100% blackout. Like velvet. Like chocolate. Like deep dark water. Pure darkness in which exquisite choral music and harmony glow like light.'[1] It was publicity for an upcoming concert by the Fitzhardinge Consort that inevitably included Gesualdo's *Tenebrae Responsoria*. Such concerts are the musical equivalent of the dining in the dark movement that promises 'a sensory experience that awakens the senses and allows us to completely re-evaluate our perception of taste and smell'.[2] But more than that, they are the perfect embodiment of the aesthetics of so-called pure music, as it might be traced from the middle of the nineteenth century – in Eduard Hanslick's (1986: 29) exclusion of everything except 'tonally moving forms' from the purview of music aesthetics – to the twentieth- and twenty-first-century practices of electroacoustic music. The concept of the 'extra-musical' is predicated on the exclusion of everything except sonorous content: music is defined as an exclusively auditory phenomenon. In this way, the act of listening is reduced, stripped to an aesthetically valorized core – whether this takes the form of the structural listening advocated by Felix Salzer (1952) and deconstructed by Rose Subotnik (1988), or the phenomenological reduction that underlies Pierre Schaeffer's (2006) theory of acousmatic music. And all this is represented as self-evident, just how music is.

This is always an indicator that ideology is at work, as are the contradictions that emerge if the idea of purely acoustic music is given a moment's thought. I said that the 'musical' excludes everything except sonorous content, but for music theory, 'content' subsists in what is notated, or can be extrapolated from notation. That means the 'musical' is not defined in terms of sound, but rather of a graphic – which is to say, a visual – practice; Salzer's structural listening might be described as listening in which the visual has been so deeply internalized that it doesn't have to

[1] http://www.bristololdvic.org.uk/bristolproms.html (accessed 26 July 2013, no longer accessible); the concert took place on 29 July 2013. An American equivalent is the 'Concerts in the Dark' series organized by The Blind Café, http://www.theblindcafe.com/concerts-in-the-dark/ (accessed 8 September 2015).

[2] *Dans Le Noir*, http://london.danslenoir.com/idea.en.html (accessed 30 June 2015).

be literally present. Equally paradoxical is the textual dimension of the 'musical'. When, in the nineteenth century, absolute instrumental music supplanted vocal music as the paradigmatic condition of music's existence, the words now excluded from the music instead surged up around it. Music was from now on accompanied by a wide range of paratexts, from programme notes and newspaper criticism to record sleeves and blogs. As Scott Burnham (1999: 194) has written, under this regime, 'music no longer in need of words now seems more than ever in need of words'. And the implication of such historical change is, of course, that the aesthetic principles inherent in the idea of purely acoustic music are not in fact self-evident or universally applicable. They are social constructs of limited chronological, geographical, and indeed generic applicability.

If the idea of universality is to be taken seriously, then the place to ground it is evolution, and more specifically animal responses to a potentially dangerous environment. As Eric Clarke said at the conference 'Musical Listening in the Age of Technological Reproducibility' on which this volume is based, animals don't care whether they see, hear, smell or feel danger. All they need to know is that there *is* danger. In other words, they respond to a multimodal environment without making distinctions between one mode and another. And within the domain of human conceptualization it is possible to speak of a historical shift from a multimodal paradigm to one based on the idea of separate sensory modes. Citing Jonathan Sterne and Jonathan Crary, Sarah Hibberd refers to 'the separation of the individual senses for scientific study, arising from the realization that the same stimulus could excite different effects in different senses: each sense was abstracted from the others as a unique and closed experiential domain' (2013: 251). She locates this development – the precondition for an aesthetics of purely acoustic music – in the 1820s and 1830s, and from then on the unity of the senses came to be seen as a problem to be solved, rather than simply a fact of life. A distant ancestor of today's multimedia theory is Wagner's conception of the 'fertilizing seed' – the synthesis of word and music as a union of opposed principles – and Wagner aimed in his music dramas to re-create what, under Nietzsche's influence, he saw as the undivided sensorium of ancient Greek drama (Fry 2015: 113). In this way, the new thinking turned multimodality into mythologized history and utopian aspiration.

The 1820s and 1830s were also a time when, as documented by James Johnson in his book *Listening in Paris* (1995), patterns of concert hall listening were shifting towards a new focus on the musical work as the product of genius, a transcendent and enduring entity that was embodied in the score and reproduced in performance. And this reduction of listening to an exclusive engagement with sonorous content defined in notational terms was followed by two major developments in material culture: the emergence in the second half of the nineteenth century of concert halls designed to focus each individual's attention on the stage – the comparison is with the theatre, in which boxes promoted social interaction within the audience – and then, in the twentieth century, that of sound recording. In either case, the effect was to repress the social dimension, transforming music into the subjective and essentially solitary experience that still-dominant streams of aesthetics represent it as. In this way, the scientific separation of individual sensory modes found its correlate in an aesthetic approach that construed music as a purely auditory phenomenon, grounded in notation and reinforced by technological developments that gave rise to new practices of listening.

But of course aesthetic ideals are never straightforward descriptions of actual practice. Even the aestheticians had trouble adhering to their own principles. In his highly influential treatise *On the Musically Beautiful*, Hanslick pronounced that 'the performer can deliver only what is already in the composition' (1986: 29), so construing performance as reproduction, but as a critic he praised Adelina Patti for breathing life into 'empty and ineffective' operatic melodies, adding that 'we do not go to hear the works themselves – all dull – but to hear Patti' (Hanslick 1963: 167). And as a medium of solitary engagement with the masterworks, the concert hall was always severely compromised. The point can be made if we measure the public concert against an iconic image of nineteenth-century listening, occasioned by Liszt's impromptu performance of the first movement from Beethoven's Moonlight Sonata in the playwright Ernst Legouvé's salon. This took place in 1837, and became famous through the accounts of it left by Berlioz and by Legouvé himself. The fire had burned low and the only lamp was extinguished. The accounts disagree as to whether or not this was at Liszt's request, but concur on the profound effect created by the combination of music and darkness: Katharine Ellis links it to the idea of 'the interpreter disappearing anonymously behind the greatness of the composer's artwork' (2005: 7), citing Berlioz's observation that – for once – Liszt refrained from embellishing the composer's score. The reality of concert hall experience, however, was more accurately evoked in a letter published in *The Gramophone* nearly a century later: the advantage of the new technology, the correspondent wrote, is that 'You can shut your eyes and imagine yourself at the Queen's Hall, but a Queen's Hall without rustling programmes or anyone discussing their servants or illnesses in a seat behind you' (Morgan 2010: 156).

The ideal of purely acoustic music, as embodied in Liszt's performance of the Moonlight Sonata – and echoed in the Fitzhardinge Consort's performance of the *Tenebrae Responsoria* – may then lie at the heart of long-established music aesthetics, but in reality such sensorially reduced experiences represent rare exceptions to the ubiquitous experiences of music that I shall refer to as the old and the new multimedia. By the new multimedia, of course, I mean the convergence between auditory and visual media that was already under way in the 1980s with music videos and MTV, but was massively reinforced by digital technology and mobile multimedia, resulting in what Fabian Holt calls '*the video turn* in music' (2011: 50). This development was driven by popular culture, but classical music has by no means been untouched by it: witness the sustained production of classical music videocassettes and DVDs ranging from reissues of Toscanini's television broadcasts from the 1950s to Nigel Kennedy's videos of Vivaldi's *Four Seasons* and Brahms's Violin Concerto. And in 2008 Philip Auslander (2008: 26) documented the extent to which the live performance of both instrumental music and opera had already been supplemented by live-feed video – a trend that has increased in both frequency and technical sophistication since that time. Again, the Bristol Proms provide an example: a concert by the pianist Jan Lisiecki at which images from multiple cameras were projected onto a screen behind the performer. The signals were also relayed to a separate auditorium, where they were digitally manipulated to create 'an augmented and experimental event'.[3]

Commentators such as Henry Jenkins (2006: 139) emphasize how the cultural practices driven by digital and in particular internet technology rehabilitate values of the folk culture that was displaced by twentieth-century mass media. In a similar way, the new multimedia represent a continuation by other means of the practices of the old multimedia, by which I mean quite simply the working together of sight and sound in concerts and other social contexts of musical consumption. The continuity is obvious when, playing Chopin, the touring virtuoso Grigory Sokolov's hand flies up after he attacks an accented note, matching the clipping of the sound: he is creating musical effects through visual as much as auditory means, and the principles governing the relationship between these modalities are the same as in music videos or such digital genres as video mashup.[4] The same might be said of Sokolov's habit of keeping his finger on a key and rotating it in order to create an effect of sustain that the piano, as a percussive instrument, cannot create through sound alone. Both practices can be traced back to the nineteenth century, and more than that, to Liszt (Cook 2013b: 330–31). Against the iconic image of Liszt's playing Beethoven in the dark, then, it is salutary to cite the observation by another contemporary, Robert Schumann, that Liszt must be seen as well as heard, 'for if Liszt played behind a screen a great deal of poetry would be lost' (1983: 156).

Schumann's remark has been quoted by Jane Davidson (1993: 103), whose own experimental studies show the extent to which listeners depend on visual cues in order to identify performers' expressive intentions. This is only one example of a substantial body of empirical studies showing that – as Richard Leppert puts it – 'music's visual-performative aspect is central to its meanings' (2014: 7); again, for Friedrich Platz and Reinhard Kopiez, 'the visual component is not a marginal phenomenon in music perception, but an important factor in the communication of meaning', and they add: 'This process of cross-modal integration exists for classical as well as pop and rock music' (2012: 75).[5] Such studies range from demonstrations of the kind of cross-modal perception illustrated by Sokolov's playing to confirmations of the role of visual perception in

---

[3] http://www.watershed.co.uk/whatson/4235/jan-lisiecki-from-every-angle/(accessed 26 July 2013, no longer accessible); the concert followed on the Fitzhardinge Consort's.

[4] For intermedial relationships in video mashup, see Cook (2013a), and for Sokolov, Cook (2013b), where a number of ideas referred to in this chapter are explored at greater length. A chapter in press (Cook forthcoming) – in some ways a companion piece to this one – offers a close study of gesture in Glenn Gould's performances of Webern's Piano Variations.

[5] Marilyn Boltz (2013), who quotes Platz and Kopiez, describes a representative selection of such studies.

communicating musical structure, but perhaps most suggestive is the evidence that what people see decisively influences their evaluations of what they hear. Jane Davidson and Daniela Coimbra (2001) found that expert judges in a music college setting responded directly to visually expressive features of classical vocal performance. And Jennifer Huang and Carol Krumhansl (2011) show that more active stage behaviour results in listeners at classical concerts – and especially novice listeners – rating what they hear more highly. Indeed, they conclude that 'non-musicians attending a concert ... may base their judgement more on what they see than what they hear' (Huang and Krumhansl 2011: 362). Given widespread concerns about the future of classical concerts, the neglect of the visual dimensions of performance that results from audio-only aesthetics is of more than academic importance.

How Sound Recordings Work

There is an elephant in the room. If the visual is so important a dimension of musical experience, how do we explain the fact that audio recordings were the dominant medium through which music was experienced during most of the twentieth century, not only in popular, but also in 'art' music? We might begin by putting this obvious and undeniable fact in context. 'While the number of households containing a gramophone and audio recordings increased dramatically in the 1920s and after World War II,' writes Philip Tagg, 'it was not until the 1980s that videocassettes started occupying significant shelf space in the average Western home .... That means several generations during which phonograms dominated the home entertainment market as storage and distribution medium' (2013: 18).

Putting it this way underlines the fact that the dominance of audio-only music – what Peter Kivy (1990: 6) glosses as 'sound music' – is not a permanent or necessary condition: it might equally well be described as a sixty-year hiatus separating the regimes of the old and the new multimedia. The point Tagg wants to make is that this coincided with the development of the core repertory of popular music studies, and he sees that as explaining the discipline's fixation on the audio dimension of a tradition that is now routinely consumed as multimedia. Whether or not that is an accurate representation of popular music studies, we have seen that still-influential streams of music aesthetics bear the impress of the audio-only listening practices that became normal only after the First World War. It is also important to note that, for early audiences, audio-only listening did not come naturally: it was an acquired skill. Mark Katz observes that 'Sightless listening was far from the "natural" activity we now take for granted' (2012: 16), and corroborates this through reference to contemporary commentaries, advertisements that showed ghostly performers around the gramophone, and devices invented by manufacturers in order to fill the perceived sensory gap. More recently, the same kind of problems have arisen when electroacoustic music is presented in concert.

People learned to listen to sound recordings, however, and we need to explain what made that possible. There is an obvious answer: recordings mobilize listeners' remembered experiences of the visual and more generally non-acoustic dimensions of performance. After all, everyone has sung, if only as a child, and many have played instruments, or at least experienced them in the multimodal circumstances of live performance, film or television. This answer is good as far as it goes, but it goes far enough only when extended to encompass the kinaesthetic and corporeal dimensions of experience that are cued by both the sound and sight of music. In the words of Rolf Inge Godøy, musical listening must be understood in terms of 'body-based cognitive schemata and categories emerging from massive experience of being and acting in the world' (2010: 108): music mobilizes the experiences of embodiment that are a fundamental dimension of everyday life, together with the networks of affective or emotional connotation with which they are linked. That is why – as Robert Hatten says – 'a kind of virtual gravitational field or vectoral space provides an analogue to the forces working on the human body in physical space, enabling the motivated opposition of downwards grief versus upwards elation' (2006: 3). In short, we hear with our bodies. And in this way, sound and sight mobilize experiences that are inherently multimodal, or perhaps it would be more accurate to say panmodal, or even premodal.

A concrete illustration is provided by conducting. In his study of the visual in music, Simon Shaw-Miller speaks of the rise of the conductor bringing about 'a new language of vision … in the gestures of flying arms and leaping bodily enactment, or in the smaller, subtle movement of a flick of the baton or the raising of an eyebrow' (2013: 106), while for Michael Broyles dance is 'something the twentieth-century conductor has made his own art form' (2004: 317). Stephen Cottrell takes it further, writing that: 'This dancer's body symbolically represents the tensions and resolutions of the music', and adding that 'each listener empathizes with the physical stresses of the conductor's dance' (2007: 90). In saying this, Cottrell is drawing on what the ethnomusicologist John Blacking called 'bodily empathy': in Blacking's words, '"Waves" of feeling are generated in the body and between bodies, … analogous to the ebb and flow of a piece of music …. [A] general pattern of interaction … is shaped from within the body and monitored by patterns of energy' (in Cottrell 2007: 82–3). Such waves of feeling, Cottrell adds, 'may transcend individual consciousness but contribute nonetheless to the individual and collective experience of the event' (2007: 89). This idea of the dynamic shaping of experience is nowadays most familiar in the form of what Daniel Stern (2010) calls 'vitality affects', and central to Stern's conception is that such affects are cross-modal: they may equally be induced or expressed through hearing, vision or other sensory modalities.

Abstract film and music video are full of parallel morphologies of sound and vision that shape experience in the way Stern describes. And for Daniel Albright this is one of the principal ways in which different art forms relate to one another, even when they are not time-based: 'Instead of the kinaesthetics of motion,' he writes, 'painting has images of the human body in various contortions' (he mentions German crucifixes and the painful poses of Degas's ballerinas), the point being that 'these images produce shadows of contraction in our muscles' (2014: 162).

This illustrates the role the corporeal plays in such experiences, as expressed in the radically embodied nature of musical listening, even when the source of the music is a CD or an audio download. The key point is that the corporeal – what I have elsewhere called the 'virtual body' of the music (Cook 2013b: 323) – is encoded within the sound, or to use a different vocabulary, the sound specifies the body. At piano recitals, the seats on the left fill up quicker than those on the right, but even at a Sokolov concert it is not such a disaster if they have all gone: you may not be able see his gestures, but you still map the music's energetic profile onto your arms and legs and feel it as your own movement. Your body resonates with the music's body. It is a perfect illustration of what Michel Chion calls transsensorial perception: 'When kinetic sensations organized into art are transmitted through a single sensory channel, through this single channel they can convey all the other senses at once' (1994: 137). And that, in a nutshell, is how sound recordings work.

It is for this reason that, as Zohar Eitan says, music 'does not require actual visual images to suggest space and motion – it produces its own' (2013: 181), and he continues: 'Music-related multimedia thus combine two different spatio-kinetic configurations: the implied space and motion evoked by musical parameters, and actual movement in the visually-perceived space on the stage, screen, or computer display.' Part of the pleasure induced by the old multimedia may lie in the changing relationships between these spaces, and there are other aspects of the listening experience – for example, the fascination with virtuosity – that emerge more readily from live performance than from a recording (at least for non-musicians). But this is not like the relationship between soundtrack and moving images in narrative film, where the absence of one medium may well render the other unintelligible. It is more like the difference between black-and-white and colour film.

And that opens up a telling parallel between film and music. Like audio-only listening, black-and-white film entails a loss of veridicality, a deficit in literal reproduction: for eyes habituated to colour film, there is a reduction of visual bandwidth that distances the diegesis from the everyday, lending it a ritualistic quality. In this way directors use black-and-white to create a particular kind of emotional intensification. Audio-only presentation can do the same: in the words of bluecollartweeter, the inaugural contributor to a forum called 'Do you listen to music in the dark?', 'listening late at night in a quiet, totally darkened room distills the listening experience to its core'.[6] And Eric Clarke offers an explanation:

> The emphasis on abstraction and ineffability, which are powerfully associated with the ideology of music's autonomy and absolutism, is given extra impetus when the music is itself abstracted from the physical and visual circumstances of its production, and when all possibilities for communication between performers and audience have been eliminated. (Clarke 2007: 50)

[6] bluecollartweeter, 'Do you listen to music in the dark?', 27 July 2013, *Steve Hoffman Forums*, http://forums.stevehoffman.tv/threads/do-you-listen-to-music-in-the-dark.324746/ (accessed 30 June 2015).

If the references to autonomy and absolutism resonate with Ellis's characterization of Liszt's playing in the dark, it is not a coincidence. What happened in 1837 was the expression of an aesthetic ideal whose time had not yet come. In a classic example of desire stimulating the means of its fulfilment, the idea of absolute music – the idea of multimodal experience communicated through sound alone – was realized only a hundred and fifty years later, when technology had created the possibility of listening to music on headphones in a darkened room. If music is a feast for the ears, then that is truly the equivalent of dining in the dark.

A Culture of the Imperative

I said that aesthetic ideals are never straightforward descriptions of actual practice. Simon Shaw-Miller observes that 'the harder music tries to hide the visual, the more effective sight becomes in showing itself, as always, surprisingly present' (2013: xiii), and audio-only listening has never been what the discourses surrounding it made it out to be. For one thing, as Carolyn Abbate has said, 'the experience of listening to a live performance solicits attention more for the performers and the event and far less for the work than is perhaps generally admitted' (2004: 512), and – unlike Abbate – I would say the same even of recorded music. Perhaps that explains why Hanslick forgot his own principles in the presence of Patti, unless we just put it down to the difference between the aesthetician on and off duty. But it goes beyond that. Whether in the concert hall or the audiophile's sitting room, listeners hear with the body, invest sounds with meanings that are equally 'musical' and 'extra-musical' – or rather, that do not acknowledge the distinction. That is simply how people listen to music, yet you would never guess it from the literature of music appreciation and aesthetics. Broyles (2004) makes the same argument. He invokes the conductor's dance to make the point that concerts 'always had a strong visual element', but then refers to the 'tacit complicity that audiences and performers share' concerning it: the visual dimension 'lurks shrouded under the assumption of a pure, abstract art' (Broyles 2004: 317). Embedded in the ideology of what Kivy calls 'music alone', then, is an element of misrepresentation, of living a lie that is propped up by the discourses surrounding the music.

This ideology has deep roots, a point that is now well established and so need not be dwelt on. It is sufficient to cite Platonic metaphysics, the idea of genius erected in the sixteenth century on classical foundations, biblical hermeneutics and the philological search for origins associated with nineteenth-century European nationalism – and that takes us up to the period when scientific thinking divided up the sensorium and the orthodoxies of music aesthetics came into being. Common to these intellectual roots is the idea of a world both ordered and authored, a text into which meaning has been inscribed; referring specifically to the sixteenth century, Michel Foucault observes that language 'has been set down in the world and forms a part of it' (1970: 35). In the same way, the ideology of music alone – and music theory, and copyright law – is built on the premise that meaning is deposited in the work by its composer, initiating a communicative chain that passes through the performer to its intended target, the listener.

But, as usual, things are less straightforward than they might appear. Often seen as one of the founding documents of musical autonomy, E.T.A. Hoffmann's essay 'Beethoven's Instrumental Music' (1998; first published in 1814) argues that performers must subjugate their own personality and direct their powers to realizing 'the wonderful enchanting pictures and apparitions that the composer has sealed into his work with magic power' (1998: 1,198). A seal is a stamp of authority, and Hoffmann's formulation suggests that meaning is inherent, inviolate, unaffected by subsequent interpretation. But here two issues arise. For one thing, Hoffmann's original term (*verschloss*) is not quite so definite in its connotations: other translations of this passage render it as 'enclosed' or 'concealed'. But more importantly, as Matthew Pritchard argues,[7] Hoffmann's writings are full of poetic imagery that draws on established traditions of commentary that he simply takes for granted, as for example in his general characterization of Beethoven's music near the beginning of the same essay: 'Burning flashes of light shoot through the deep night of this realm, and we become aware of giant shadows that surge back and forth' (1998: 1,194). There is no suggestion that Beethoven sealed those images into the work: the 'enchanting pictures and apparitions' to which Hoffmann refers are collaborations between composer and listener, and that is what gives Hoffmann's commentary its *raison d'être*. It also means that Eitan's claim that music produces its own images is not quite accurate. Music engenders percepts of space and motion even when you listen with closed eyes or in the dark, but the translation of those percepts into specific images is the work of listeners and critics.

It is because of this cultural dimension that one can speak of traditions in seeing sound. In 1861, for example, the piano pedagogue Adolph Kullak summarized interpretations of the Moonlight Sonata by Czerny, Ubilischeff, Liszt, Marx, Köhler, Elterlein, Weber and Cornelius, based on imagery that ranges from churchyards and Gothic cathedrals to moonlit visions of the protagonist's corpse-like face (Kullak 1893). Kullak goes out of his way to explain that these images are not integral to the music – the music does not depict a churchyard, for example – but rather are alternative ways of expressing the motional and emotional properties inherent in the music (1893: 327). And whereas Kullak is drawing on published commentaries and recommending them to pianists, it is evident that listeners invent parallel imagery of their own. The most famous illustration, at least in English, dates from 1910: the passage in Chapter 5 of E.M. Forster's *Howards End* that describes a concert at which Beethoven's Fifth Symphony is played. Helen Schlegel, one of the three half-German sisters around which the novel revolves, hears the music in terms that could easily have come out of one of Hoffmann's essays: she speaks of heroes and shipwrecks in the first movement, and 'a goblin walking quietly over the universe' in the third.

---

[7] In a book under preparation; my account of Hoffmann, and more generally of the relationship between Romanticism and modernism, reflects Pritchard's thinking.

In an essay I have already cited, Scott Burnham (1999: 205–7) demonstrates the sophisticated nature of Helen's hearing of the Scherzo, linking it not only to specific features of the music as an analyst might describe it, but also to broader interpretive issues such as the relationship between affirmation and doubt. But there is an important feature of this passage from *Howards End* that Burnham does not mention. Before the third movement begins, Helen tells her aunt to look out for the goblins, but her brother, Tibby, tells everyone they should look out for the transitional passage on the drum, and he raises his hand when it comes. Again, there is a point in the first movement when Helen smiles at her German cousin, but 'Frieda, listening to Classical Music, could not respond', while 'next to her was Aunt Juley, so British, and wanting to tap. How interesting that row of people was! What diverse influences had gone to the making!' In short, everybody is listening in their own way. It is like the alternative interpretations that Kullak recommends to his readers. And it is the idea that there can, and should, be alternatives that is crucial in this context.

Although they had older roots, ideas of authorship, genius, textuality and transcendence have a strongly nineteenth-century ring: we think of the orthodoxies of music aesthetics as nineteenth-century in origin. But there is one massive difference. The nineteenth century was above all an age of eclecticism. Vienna's Ringstrasse, where each major building is in a different historical style selected as appropriate to its particular function, is a particularly conspicuous example of a pattern replicated, if on a less grandiose scale, in many well-preserved nineteenth-century cityscapes. The contrast with modernist architecture could not be more striking. The original French edition of Le Corbusier's *Towards a New Architecture* (1946) was published in 1923, only thirteen years after *Howards End*, but separated from it by the First World War. It is a sustained diatribe at one level against the adoption of historical styles, but at a deeper level against any deviation from the central tenets of architectural modernism: that form follows function and that ornament is crime (phrases coined respectively by Louis Sullivan and Adolf Loos, but definitive of architectural modernism more generally). Corbusier's central claim is that architecture is a matter of ethics as much as of aesthetics, so that to build otherwise is not only an error of taste, but also an act of moral turpitude. The resonances with modernist composers are obvious enough: like Corbusier, Schoenberg attacked historical styles, redefined function (for Corbusier the cantilever, for Schoenberg the series), and saw composition as an ethical practice. A nineteenth-century culture of alternatives was transformed into a modernist culture of the imperative, a culture that did not recognize the validity or even the existence of alternatives. In short, you had to listen like Tibby, not Helen – and what Joseph Horowitz (1987: 223) calls the 'music appreciation industry' came into being to make sure you did.

Seen this way, ideas such as the 'musical' and 'purely auditory' acquire a gatekeeping value: they relegate to some ill-defined domain of entertainment any practice that cannot be directly related to a sonorous content now purged of historical reference. In the decades after 1945, when the new music became both the object of and an instrument for denazification, it is hardly excessive to speak of a policing of composition, in the sense that a modernist cartel largely controlled who got commissions, performances and broadcasts on the one hand, and jobs in conservatories and universities on the other. And while the hardcore modernism built on values of authorship and textuality began to implode after the 1960s, modernist ideologies maintain to the present day a remarkable grip over performance, where ethical values generally revolve round faithfulness to score, composer or historical context, in other words to what is sealed into the work – and by now Hoffmann's perhaps misleading image has become an entirely accurate representation of aesthetic ideology. Complaining about this orthodoxy, Daniel Leech-Wilkinson suggests that 'performers who dared to offer a radically different view would be slapped down by performance police (teachers, critics, bloggers) and spurned by potential employers (agents, conductors, ensembles, venue managers, record and radio producers)' (2012: para. 3.3). And he adds: 'Where is the incentive to innovate when maintaining traditions is the very focus of everyone's professional engagement with music?'

In the case of listening, of course, policing is harder. Mark Twain (2009) wrote of the audience at Bayreuth that: 'You detect no movement in the solid mass of heads and shoulders. You seem to sit with the dead in the gloom of a tomb. You know that they are being stirred to their profoundest depths' (because at the end 'the dead rise with one impulse and shake the building with their applause'). In the same way, I spoke of listeners hearing with the body and investing sounds with 'extra-musical' meanings, but – at least in the concert hall – they do so invisibly. And whereas Tibby disclosed the way he was listening by raising his hand at the transitional passage on the drum, there is no way you could tell that Helen was seeing goblins. Despite this, or perhaps because of it, the Western 'art' tradition has a history of attempting to discipline the act of listening. On the one hand are educational initiatives such as Salzer's structural listening and the music appreciation movement, which developed in tandem with the audio-only medium of radio: both claimed to be talking about the music itself, while in fact valorizing, and mandating, a particular kind of imagery drawn largely from physics and engineering (Pritchard 2013: 147). On the other hand are the circumstances of concert presentation: Alex Ross (2010) complains about 'the vaguely Edwardian costumes, the convention-centre lighting schemes, the aggressive affectlessness of the average professional musician'. All these reflect the values of a culture that valorizes sonorous content underpinned by notation to the exclusion of everything else, and so conceives performance as the reproduction of an existing, sealed-in meaning rather than an event that is creative in the sense of engendering new experiences.

But the particular focus of Ross's attention is what he calls the 'No Applause Rule': the prohibition of clapping between movements that audience members enforce on one another through glaring or even shushing, a practice that can be explained in aesthetic terms as expressing a sensitivity to – or at least an awareness that one is supposed to be sensitive to – the technical and emotional integrity of multi-movement works. In social terms, however, it is hard to imagine a practice better calculated to embarrass and alienate novice listeners – the same novice listeners who respond to active stage behaviour, and who represent tomorrow's classical audiences. It is little wonder that Edward Said speaks of 'the alienating social ritual of the concert' (1991: 3). But what is most revealing about this social practice is the way it has been taken by seasoned concert goers to be a self-evident tenet of good taste. In reality it is, of course, historical, and the history in question is surprisingly recent: Ross traces the first examples of the No Applause Rule to the early years of the twentieth century, and sees the 1920s as the time when it became established. That is the same decade that saw the rise of the music appreciation movement, and in which Le Corbusier published *Towards a New Architecture*. Modernism is an invented tradition in the sense that it represents itself as based on principles that not only extend back into the past, but are self-evident, timeless, universally valid. The audio-only listening predicated by the aestheticians is modernist listening.

Breaking the Seal

John Butt writes that 'music is crucially dependent on a creative element in the capacity to hear' (2010: 7). If modernist aesthetics, drawing selectively on nineteenth-century sources, was built on the idea of meaning being sealed into the work – if it boxed listening in – then the foundation of postmodern aesthetics is the idea that meaning is produced through interpretation, negotiated between multiple stakeholders, and in that sense a creative achievement. But it is not my purpose to equate listening outside the modernist box with postmodernism, a term that carries a paradoxical implication of historical progression: one might equally well call it premodern, given the nineteenth-century culture of eclecticism to which I referred. Perhaps it would be better to see modernist listening as Tagg sees the audio-only culture of the 1920s–80s, a 60-year hiatus during which the culture of classical music was dominated by a mode of listening predicated on pre-existing meaning defined through sensory reduction. It pre-dated and yet was most perfectly realized by the technology of audio-only recording: as I said, listening to recorded music could afford an unprecedented intensity of experience, creating a palpable sense of direct, unmediated identification with work and composer – the experience of communication, in Beethoven's words,[8] from heart to heart. Viewed from such a perspective, the concert might easily be seen as *The Gramophone*'s correspondent saw it: inferior substitute for the recording. It is remarkable that while, in contrast, critics and scholars of classical music continued to insist that real music meant live music, they mostly went on thinking about it in ways that devalued precisely those aspects in which concerts offer a distinctively different experience from recorded music: multimedia and sociality. And Holt's 'video turn' in music – which Broyles elevates into 'a revolution in music as profound as any that has happened in the last 400 years' (2004: 334) – has only exacerbated the problem of the concert in contemporary culture.

---

[8] From the autograph of the *Missa Solemnis*: 'From the heart – may it go straight to the heart'.

It might seem rather late in the day to be writing this. The implosion of hardcore modernist composition was followed by that of the music appreciation movement: teaching framed within the ideology of autonomy persists in institutions of higher education, but Broyles – who at one time taught music appreciation classes – speaks for many when he wonders, 'in disparaging "nonessential" imaging in the listening process, how many students we actually turned off classical music' (2004: 359). And while, as I said, the grip of modernism on performance has been longer-lived, cracks have appeared in its facade. Historically informed performance developed at around the same time modernist composition was breaking up, and demonstrated that there were different ways of playing music from the past, but without challenging the underlying ideas of faithfulness to score, composer and historical context. Such challenges are developing in the admittedly narrow zone where professional performance and academia overlap. Building on historically informed performance traditions but extending them to the point that the modernist conception of the text becomes subverted, the improvisatory approaches spearheaded by David Dolan seek to re-create performance practices that are premodern in terms not just of style, but of the values that underlie style: in a recent empirical study, 'Audience members rated the improvised performances more improvisatory in character, more innovative in approach, more emotionally engaging, more musically convincing, and more risk-taking than the non-improvised (regular) performance' (Dolan et al. 2013: 1). A more radical approach, because divorced from any claim of historical faithfulness, has been taken by Leech-Wilkinson and Mine Doğantan-Dack. The premise of their work is that 'scores can make convincing musical sense in radically different performances'[9] – for example, much slower or faster than normal. The point is not to establish the correct mode of performance, but to explore alternatives. The discourse of modernism is stood on its head.

But there is another musical practice that has probably done more than anything to condition our expectations of how music should sound, which for the most part operates below the radar of criticism and – until recently – academic analysis, and which remains to a quite startling degree in the grip of modernist ideology. I can make the point in terms of the frequently invoked parallel between the cinema and sound recording. Traditional film theory sees all elements of a film – images, dialogue, music and other soundtrack elements – as working together in order to project a narrative. This translates to a form of spectatorship that is oriented to narrative diegesis: we do not experience the patchwork of edited takes, often shot at different times and sometimes in different places, as such, but rather hear and see through them to the narrated events that we understand as unfolding over a period of hours, days, weeks or even years. And we see the film's meaning

[9] Daniel Leech-Wilkinson, Mine Doğantan-Dack and Diana Gilchrist, 'How Creative Can a Musical Practice Be?', presentation, University of London, 24 June 2013, http://music.sas.ac.uk/sites/default/files/files/How creative can a musical practice be.doc (accessed 30 June 2015).

as grounded in the diegesis. The same applies to classical record production. We hear through the patchwork of edited takes, often recorded at different times and sometimes in different places, to the continuous, real-time performance that forms the object of our experience – even when we know perfectly well that in reality no such performance ever took place. Although in a sound recording the time of the narration and that of the narrated event are the same, it is as much a matter of diegesis as in the cinema: the recording is a signifier, the performance is the signified. In other words, recordings represent music not through literal reproduction, but through complex, culturally constructed processes of semiosis.[10]

It follows from this that there is in sound recording as much scope for the generation of meaning through processes of mediation – in short, for creative production – as there is in film, where traditional Hollywood-style narrative films, French New Wave films and music videos represent quite different ways of bringing together images, dialogue and sounds. Ever since 1967, when the Beatles released *Sgt. Pepper*, popular music has exploited studio production techniques that frankly display their own artifice, so transforming phonography into a medium of overt creativity. The 1960s saw some comparable initiatives in classical recording, such as Decca's Phase 4 Stereo and John Culshaw's operatic recordings, while until his death in 1982 Glenn Gould was developing the techniques of what he called 'acoustic choreography' – involving, for example, the purposeful alternation of obviously different microphone placements – as part of an integrated interpretive practice that encompassed both performance and production. There are, however, virtually no subsequent examples of this kind of creative production in classical music,[11] and the reason lies in the still-dominant discourses of classical record production. Colin Symes (2004) uses the term 'keystone discourse' to identify the realist paradigm most famously articulated by Walter Legge: 'I want to make records which will sound in the public's home exactly like what they would hear in the best seat in an acoustically perfect hall' (Schwarzkopf 1982: 73). Regularly reiterated in advertisements for high-end audio equipment from the 1950s into the twenty-first century, the 'best seat in the house' slogan conceals the artifice inherent in all recording, instead conveying the idea that recordings should reproduce performances in the same sense that, within the discourses of musical modernism, performances reproduce works. To repeat Hoffmann's image, the priority in either case is to keep the seal intact, and with it the boundary between the 'musical' and the 'extra-musical'.

The paradox is that while the discourses of classical music have represented recordings as reproductions of live music and placed the use of creative production

---

[10] I develop this argument at greater length in Cook (2013b): ch. 11.

[11] A rare exception is *Remixing Modernism: Berg, Schoenberg, Bartók*, a double CD set released in 2010 by the pianist Stephen Emmerson and the studio engineer Paul Draper (Move Records MD 4431); this project explicitly aimed to develop Gould's approach in a digital context, and – significantly – was based in the academic context of the Queensland Conservatorium Research Centre.

techniques off limits, concerts effectively ape recordings. By this I mean more than the frequently observed tendency for live music to sound increasingly like recorded music (Cook 2013b). Beyond the conductor's dance – itself, as Broyles said, shrouded within a conspiracy of silence – the visual dimension is neglected or even repressed, on the grounds that it is a distraction from the real business of music: hence the dour clothes, the convention centre lighting and affectlessness of which Ross complained. Meanwhile, the No Applause Rule stands not only for the authoritarian ethos of modernism, but also for the devaluation of the social dimension of concert-going, in particular the transformation through music of individual listeners into a community of participants united by Blacking's shared waves of feeling. It is hardly surprising that in London and other major cities there has been a trend towards the relocation of music from purpose-built concert halls to galleries, pubs, clubs and other non-traditional venues. Yet the problem is not with the buildings, but with the social practices that take place within those buildings, and the thinking that informs them.

Throughout the English-speaking world there is talk about the crisis of classical music, as evidenced by its 'shrinking, graying, and overly pale-faced' audiences (the phrase is Lawrence Kramer's [1995: 4]), by the collapse of the classical recording industry, by the funding problems faced by opera houses and orchestras at a time of financial retrenchment, and by the difficulties faced by musicians in finding sensibly paid work. Yet as a crisis it is a strangely patchy one: on many measures, performance standards have never been higher, European and American conservatories are full of students from the developing economies of East Asia, and through digital media, Western 'art' music is heard by more people across the world than ever before. I suggest that what lies at the heart of the sense of crisis is the reductive conception of music as authored and notationally valorized sound into which meaning was long ago inscribed. It is a conception that turns listening into hard labour, and concerts into the 'alienating social ritual' of which Said complained. It explains why, despite an outpouring of talent and the funding going into orchestral outreach programmes, the culture of classical music still strikes so many as exclusive and obsolete. It is, in short, a crisis we literally talked ourselves into. Luckily, that also means it is a crisis we can talk ourselves out of.

References

Abbate, Carolyn (2004) 'Music – Drastic or Gnostic?', *Critical Inquiry*, 30, pp. 505–36.

Albright, Daniel (2014) *Panaesthetics: On the Unity and Diversity of the Arts*, New Haven, CT: Yale University Press.

Auslander, Philip (2008) *Liveness: Performance in a Mediatized Culture*, 2nd edn, London: Routledge.

Boltz, Marilyn (2013) 'Music Videos and Visual Influences on Music Perception and Appreciation: Should You Want Your MTV?', in *The Psychology of Music in Multimedia*, ed. Tan Siu-Lan, , Annabel Cohen, Scott Lipscomb and Roger Kendall, New York: Oxford University Press, pp. 213–30.

Broyles, Michael (2004) *Mavericks and Other Traditions in American Music*, New Haven, CT: Yale University Press.

Burnham, Scott (1999) 'How Music Matters: Poetic Content Revisited', in *Rethinking Music*, ed. Nicholas Cook and Mark Everist, New York: Oxford University Press, pp. 193–216.

Butt, John (2010) 'Do Musical Works Contain an Implied Listener? Towards a Theory of Musical Listening', *Journal of the Royal Musical Association*, 135, pp. 5–18.

Chion, Michel (1994) *Audio-vision: Sound on Screen*, trans. Claudia Gorbman, New York: Columbia University Press.

Clarke, Eric (2007) 'The Impact of Recording on Listening', *Twentieth-century Music*, 4, pp. 47–70.

Cook, Nicholas (2013a) 'Beyond Music: Mashup, Multimedia Mentality, and Intellectual Property', in *The Oxford Handbook of New Audiovisual Aesthetics*, ed. Claudia Gorbman, John Richardson and Carol Vernallis, New York: Oxford University Press, pp. 53–76.

——— (2013b) *Beyond the Score*, New York: Oxford University Press.

——— (forthcoming) 'Seeing Sound, Hearing the Body: Glenn Gould Plays Webern's Piano Variations', in *The Oxford Handbook of Music, Sound, and Image in the Fine Arts*, ed. Yael Kaduri, New York: Oxford University Press.

Cottrell, Stephen (2007) 'Music, Time, and Dance in Orchestral Performance: The Conductor as Shaman', *Twentieth-century Music*, 3, pp. 73–96.

Davidson, Jane (1993) 'Visual Perception of Performance Manner in the Movements of Solo Musicians', *Psychology of Music*, 21, pp. 103–13.

Davidson, Jane and Coimbra, Daniela (2001) 'Investigating Performance Evaluation by Assessors of Singers in a Music College Setting', *Musicae Scientiae*, 5, pp. 33–54.

Dolan, David, Sloboda, John, Jensen, Henrik Jeldtoft, Crüts, Björn and Feygelson, Eugene (2013) 'The Improvisatory Approach to Classical Music Performance: An Empirical Investigation into its Characteristics and Impact', *Music Performance Research*, 6, pp. 1–38, http://www.mpr-online.net/Issues/Volume%206%20%5B2013%5D/MPR0073.pdf (accessed 30 June 2015).

Eitan, Zohar (2013) 'How Pitch and Loudness Shape Musical Space and Motion', in *The Psychology of Music in Multimedia*, ed. Tan Siu-Lan, Annabel Cohen, Scott Lipscomb and Roger Kendall, New York: Oxford University Press, pp. 161–87.

Ellis, Katharine (2005) 'Liszt: The Romantic Artist', in *The Cambridge Companion to Liszt*, ed. Kenneth Hamilton, Cambridge: Cambridge University Press, pp. 1–13.

Forster, Edward Morgan (2008) *Howards End*, Project Gutenberg, http://www.gutenberg.org/files/2946/2946-h/2946-h.htm#link2HCH0003 (accessed 30 June 2015).

Foucault, Michel (1970) *The Order of Things: An Archaeology of the Human Sciences*, trans. anon., London: Tavistock Publications.

Fry, Katherine (2015) 'Katherine Fry, Nietzsche and Wagner: Music, Language, Decadence', PhD dissertation, King's College, London.

Godøy, Rolf Inge (2010) 'Gestural Affordances of Musical Sound', in *Musical Gestures: Sound, Movement, and Meaning*, ed. Rolf Inge Godøy and Marc Leman, New York: Routledge, pp. 103–25.

Hanslick, Eduard (1963) *Music Criticisms 1846–99*, ed. and trans. Henry Pleasants, Harmondsworth: Penguin Books.

——— (1986) *On the Musically Beautiful*, trans. Geoffrey Payzant, Indianapolis, IN: Hackett.

Hatten, Robert (2006) 'A Theory of Musical Gesture and its Application to Beethoven and Schubert', in *Music and Gesture*, ed. Anthony Gritten and Elaine King, Aldershot: Ashgate, pp. 1–23.

Hibberd, Sarah (2013) '*Le Naufrage de la Méduse* and operatic spectacle in 1830s Paris', *Nineteenth-century Music*, 36, pp. 248–63.

Hoffmann, E.T.A. (1998) 'Beethoven's Instrumental Music' [1814], trans. Oliver Strunk, in *Source Readings in Music History*, ed. Oliver Strunk, rev. Leo Treitler, New York: Norton, pp. 1,193–8.

Holt, Fabian (2011) 'Is Music Becoming More Visual? Online Video Content in the Music Industry', *Visual Studies*, 26, pp. 50–61.

Horowitz, Joseph (1987) *Understanding Toscanini: A Social History of American Concert Life*, Berkeley, CA: University of California Press.

Huang, Jennifer and Krumhansl, Carol (2011) 'What Does Seeing the Performer Add? It Depends on Musical Style, Amount of Stage Behavior, and Audience Expertise', *Musicae Scientiae*, 15, pp. 343–64.

Jenkins, Henry (2006) *Convergence Culture: Where Old and New Media Collide*, New York: New York University Press.

Johnson, James (1995) *Listening in Paris: A Cultural History*, Berkeley, CA: University of California Press.

Katz, Mark (2012) 'Sound Recording: Introduction', in *Music, Sound, and Technology in America: A Documentary History of Early Phonograph, Cinema, and Radio*, ed. Timothy Taylor, Mark Katz and Tony Grajeda, Durham, NC: Duke University Press, pp. 11–28.

Kivy, Peter (1990) *Music Alone: Philosophical Reflections on the Purely Musical Experience*, Ithaca, NY: Cornell University Press.

Kramer, Lawrence (1995) *Classical Music and Postmodern Knowledge*, Berkeley, CA: University of California Press.

Kullak, Adolph (1893) *The Aesthetics of Pianoforte-playing*, ed. Hans Bischoff, trans. T. Baker, New York: Schirmer.

Le Corbusier [Charles-Édouard Jeanneret-Gris] (1946) *Towards a New Architecture*, trans. Frederick Etchells, London: Architectural Press.

Leech-Wilkinson, Daniel (2012) 'Compositions, Scores, Performances, Meanings', *Music Theory Online*, 18/1, pp. 1–17, http://www.mtosmt.org/issues/mto.12.18.1/mto.12.18.1.leech-wilkinson.html (accessed 30 June 2015).

Leppert, Richard (2014) 'Seeing Music', in *The Routledge Companion to Music and Visual Culture*, ed. Tim Shepherd and Anne Leonard, New York: Routledge, pp. 7–12.

Morgan, Nick (2010) '"A New Pleasure": Listening to National Gramophonic Society Records, 1924–31', *Musicae Scientiae*, 14/2, pp. 139–64.

Platz, Friedrich and Kopiez, Reinhard (2012) 'When the Eye Listens: A Meta-analysis of How Audio-visual Presentation Enhances the Appreciation of Music Performance', *Music Perception*, 30, pp. 71–83.

Pritchard, Matthew (2013) '"A Heap of Broken Images"? Reviving Austro-German Debates over Musical Meaning, 1900–36', *Journal of the Royal Musical Association*, 138, pp. 129–74.

Ross, Alex (2010) 'Hold Your Applause: Inventing and Reinventing the Classical Concert', Royal Philharmonic Society Lecture, 8 March, http://alexrossmusic.typepad.com/files/rps_lecture_2010_alex-ross.pdf (accessed 30 June 2015).

Said, Edward (1991) *Musical Elaborations*, London: Chatto & Windus.

Salzer, Felix (1952) *Structural Listening: Tonal Coherence in Music*, New York: Charles Boni.

Schaeffer, Pierre (2006) 'Acousmatics', trans. Daniel Smith, in *Audio Culture: Readings in Modern Music*, ed. Christoph Cox and Daniel Warner, New York: Continuum, pp. 76–81.

Schumann, Robert (1983) *On Music and Musicians*, ed. Konrad Wolff, trans. Paul Rosenfeld, Berkeley, CA: University of California Press.

Schwarzkopf, Elisabeth (1982) *On and Off the Record: A Memoir of Walter Legge*, London: Faber and Faber.

Shaw-Miller, Simon (2013) *Eye hEar: The Visual in Music*, Farnham: Ashgate.

Stern, Daniel (2010) *Forms of Vitality: Exploring Dynamic Experience in Psychology, the Arts, Psychotherapy and Development*, Oxford: Oxford University Press.

Subotnik, Rose Rosengard (1988) 'Toward a Deconstruction of Structural Listening: A Critique of Schoenberg, Adorno, and Stravinsky', in *Explorations in Music, the Arts, and Ideas: Essays on Honor of Leonard B. Meyer*, ed. Eugene Narmour and Ruth Solie, Stuyvesant, NY: Pendragon, pp. 87–122.

Symes, Colin (2004) *Setting the Record Straight: A Material History of Classical Recording*, Middletown, CT: Wesleyan University Press.

Tagg, Philip (2013) 'Caught on the Back Foot: Epistemic Inertia and Invisible Music', keynote address, IASPM 16th Biennial Conference, Grahamstown, South Africa, 27 June 2011 with minor revisions 15 February 2013, http://www.tagg.org/articles/xpdfs/IASPM1106.pdf (accessed 30 June 2015).

Twain, Mark (2009) 'At the Shrine of St Wagner', in *What is Man? and Other Essays*, Project Gutenberg, http://www.gutenberg.org/files/70/70-h/70-h.htm#link2H_4_0009 (accessed 30 June 2015).

Chapter 12
The Transformation of Musical Listening: The Case of Electroacoustic Music[1]

Martin Laliberté

Introduction

The twentieth century brought significant changes in the aesthetic expectations of composers as well as listeners. The musical crises of 1900–1920, together with significant scientific and technological developments, transformed the composer's purely musical mental universe into a hybrid one, incorporating visual and sonic sensitivity. Arguably, the post-MTV digital era has heightened this transformation.

This chapter discusses the case of early (1942–54) and classical (1955–70) electroacoustic music of the Paris school. This music, while apparently based on Schaeffer's 1966 theories of 'acousmatic music' and 'reduced listening', is marked by a curious paradox: its thinking and sonic operational categories are clearly the result of a visual transformation. As we will see, words like 'grain', 'allure', 'profile', 'sound projector' and the frequent existence of graphic scores in musical sketches of acousmatic pieces testify to a new musical sensitivity 'contaminated' by the visual domain. I suggest that Schaeffer and his colleagues were 'listening with images'.

In order to shed light on this important development, several electroacoustic concepts are discussed, and many examples of visual influence are offered. The chapter draws on various reissues of Schaeffer's texts as well as recent findings from his personal archives in order to arrive at a new understanding. The transformation thus presented might also elucidate the surprising ease with which some examples of auteur cinema have employed electroacoustic music since the 1950s. A few cases of resurgent electroacoustic sensitivity in auteur cinema are presented to illustrate this point (Tati, Tarkovsky, Lynch).

[1] The author wishes to thank Dr Joyce Shintani for her help with the English version of this chapter, and the editors of this book for their precision.

Before Electroacoustic Music and Sound Cinema

A Time of Crises, Evolutions and Experiments

Electroacoustic music arrives at a defining moment in Western arts history. It is a time of many crises and converging factors, creating difficult problems, but also opening the door to many creative solutions (Figure 12.1).

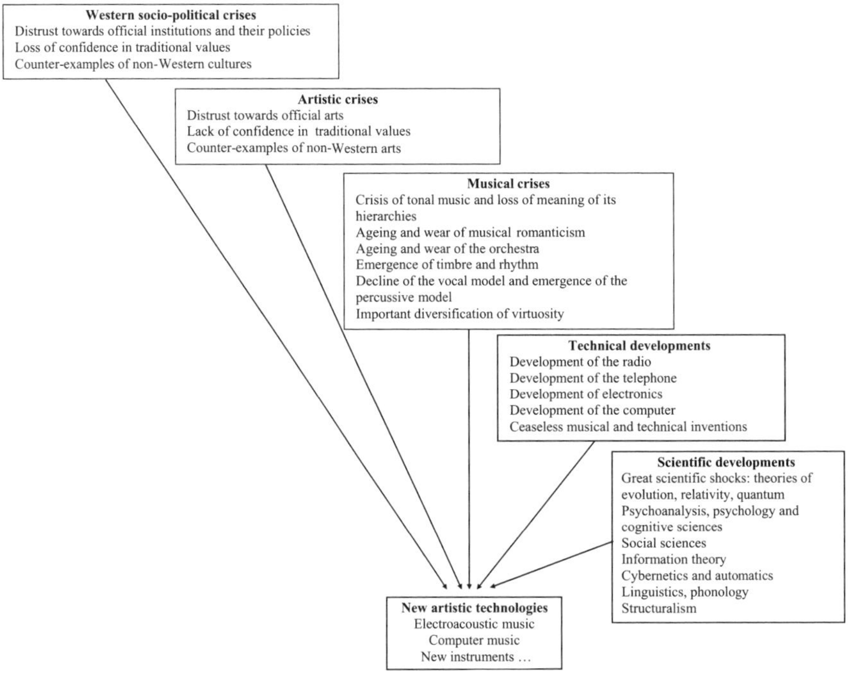

Figure 12.1 Converging crises around 1900

As Figure 12.1 tries to convey, music at the beginning of the twentieth century faced a series of converging crises in many areas, chief among them:

- social and political erosion;
- artistic erosion;
- musical erosion ('fatigue').

The musical crisis (the overuse and fatigue of its language, models, means and aesthetics) called for solutions, as one can gather from sources such as Arnold Schoenberg's writings. In tonal music, expressive chromaticism had reached a saturation point: no further note could be added to chords after the altered 13th with all its variants. Once the symphony reached Mahlerian proportions and the opera attained Wagnerian length, the development of musical form, too, reached a limit. More pertinently to our argument, the overuse of particular orchestral instruments created a need for new instruments capable of producing music adaptable to evolving tastes and aesthetics. In addition, deterioration of the traditional 'vocal' music model paved the way for the emergence of a 'percussive' model, as well as a renewed vocal model.[2] Edgard Varèse rejected bowed strings precisely for such reasons: these instruments were overused and possessed a sound too traditional for his aesthetics (Ouellette 1989: 64). He preferred winds and percussions, and hoped for new instruments.

A Graphical or Plastic Transformation

During the years 1900–1910 the musical crises caused a profound change in the composer's thinking. The ineluctable transformation of Western music was triggered by one of the 'solutions' to these crises. In order to replace the 'dead' system of tonal music with a strong and efficient way of organizing music, the mental landscape of the composer – and of the listener – had to become more graphic, more plastic.

A case in point is Schoenberg's evolution from traditional musical hierarchies towards a spatial sensitivity, clearly traceable in his writings. His demonstration advances as follows. Since all chromatic tones are to be found in every harmonic series, if one listens to the higher harmonics, the fundamental notion of dissonance is called into question, and equal temperament along with it:

> Efforts to make use of the more remote consonances (today called 'dissonances') as artistic means thus led necessarily to many an error, to many a detour. The way of history, as we can see it in that which has actually been selected by practice from the practicable dissonances, hardly leads here to a correct judgment of the real relations. That assertion is proved by the incomplete or unusual scales of many other peoples, who have, nevertheless, as much right as we to explain them by appeal to nature. Perhaps their tones are often even more natural than ours (that is, more exact, more correct, better); for the tempered system, which is only an expedient for overcoming the difficulties of the material, has indeed only a limited similarity to nature. That is perhaps an advantage, but hardly a mark of superiority. (Schoenberg 1978: 21)[3]

---

[2] For many developments of this proposal, see Laliberté (forthcoming).

[3] 'Das Bestreben, die fernerliegenden Konsonanzen (die man heute Dissonanzen nennt) als Kunstmittel anzuwenden, mußte also notwendigerweise zu manchem Irrtum, zu manchem Umweg führen. Der Weg der Geschichte, wie er sich kundgibt in dem, was an den gebräuchlichen Dissonanzen das Gebräuchliche ist, führt hier kaum zu einer richtigen Beurteilung der wirklichen Verhältnisse. Das beweisen die unvollständigen oder sonderbaren Tonreihen mancher Völker, die sich aber sicher auch auf die Natur berufen dürfen.

Therefore, since pitch and dissonance are thus now debatable, other musical dimensions can take the lead in renewing ways of composing music. Arguably, Schoenberg's famous 'emancipation of dissonance' resulted from the diminution of the role of the note or pitch in favour of other musical dimensions (Rosen 1979: 53–6). Thus, the old musical hierarchy was transformed:

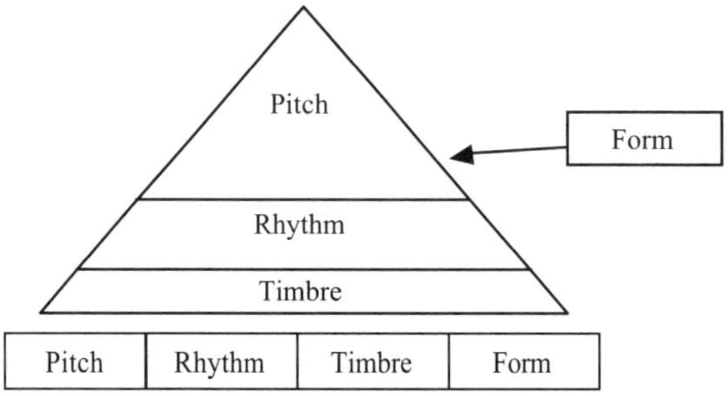

Figure 12.2 Equalization of musical dimensions

The musical dimensions are now 'democratic',[4] equal in importance, with one or the other dimension taking the lead for a while, such as timbre in *Klangfarbenmelodie*. Finally, at the end of his treatise Schoenberg renders musical dimensions in even more explicitly spatial terms (Figure 12.3):

> The distinction between tone color and pitch, as it is usually expressed, I cannot accept without reservations. I think the tone becomes perceptible by virtue of tone color, of which one dimension is pitch. Tone color is, thus, the main topic, pitch a subdivision. Pitch is nothing else but tone color measured in one direction. (Schoenberg 1978: 421)[5]

Vielleicht sogar sind ihre Töne oft natürlicher (das heißt: genauer, richtiger, besser) als unsere; denn das temperierte System, das nur ein Notbehelf zur Bewältigung der. Materialschwierigkeiten ist, hat ja nur in wenigem Ähnlichkeit mit der Natur. Was vielleicht ein Vorteil, aber kaum ein Vorzug ist' (Schoenberg 1922: 21).

[4] The political parallel is relevant at the time of the downfall of the Austrian Empire (Schoenberg 1951).

[5] 'Je ne puis admettre sans réserve la différence que l'on a coutume d'établir entre couleur sonore (timbre) et hauteur sonore. C'est en effet par sa couleur sonore – dont une dimension est la hauteur – que le son se signale. La couleur du son est donc le grand territoire dont une région est constituée par la hauteur du son. Cette dernière n'est rien d'autre que la couleur du son mesurée dans une direction' (Schoenberg 1983: 516). Interestingly, the French translation is closer to the German original in its use of a territorial metaphor, whereas the English translation uses a much more traditional figure of speech, that of direction, masking the important spatial aspect: 'Ich kann den Unterschied zwischen Klangfarbe und Klanghöhe, wie er gewöhnlich ausgedrückt wird, nicht so unbedingt zugeben. Ich finde, der Ton macht sich bemerkbar durch die Klangfarbe, deren eine Dimension die Klanghöhe ist.

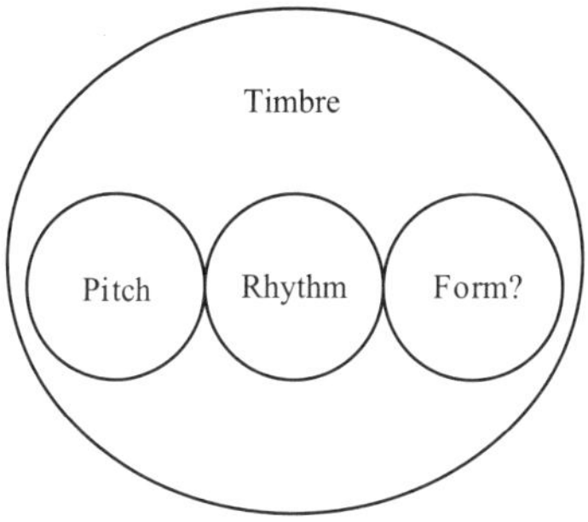

Figure 12.3 Musical territories

Schoenberg's equalization of the musical dimensions and his spatial or 'territorial' approach reveal a considerable evolution of the musical imagination. Schoenberg's thinking moves its focus away from the usual musical score towards an investigation of new concepts – in this case, a multi-layered 'map' of musical dimensions. Significantly, this evolution coincides chronologically with multidimensional mathematical approaches (the 'manifolds'[6]) in Albert Einstein's work. Moreover, Schoenberg's personal and artistic proximity to the Blaue Reiter group in the critical period 1910–20, as well as his personal experiments in painting[7] tend towards the deployment of colour and motion in space, rather than the representation of traditional figures and forms, confirming the mental transformation.[8]

Schoenberg was far from alone in this. A similar thought is observable in Debussy: 'I am more and more convinced that music is not, in its essence, a thing that can be put into a rigorous and traditional form. It is of colour and rhythmic time' (Debussy 1907, in Horodyski 1998: 223).[9] One could also evoke Igor Stravinsky, with his very developed rhythms[10] and timbres. Varèse is also quite clear on this kind of plastic transformation. As Horodyski (1998) and Ouellette (1989: 58) have pointed out, Varèse's imagination was marked by the emerging

Die Klangfarbe ist also das große Gebiet, ein Bezirk davon die Klanghöhe. Die Klanghöhe ist nichts anderes als Klangfarbe, gemessen in einer Richtung' (Schoenberg 1922: 506). This detail might some day contribute to a useful debate on the translations of Schoenberg's works.

6 Associated with Gauss and Riemann. See Claude Morlet, 'Variétés differentiables', in *Encyclopedia Universalis Online*, https://www-universalis--edu-com.fennec.u-pem.fr/encyclopedie/varietes-differentiables/ (accessed 2 July 2015).

7 The website of the Arnold Schoenberg Center is rich in details on this and many other topics: http://www.schoenberg.at/index.php?option=com_joomgallery&Itemid=339&lang=en (accessed 30 June 2015).

8 Before his return to a more traditional predominance of the pitch in the 12-tone system in the 1920s.

9 Our translation. Original: 'je me persuade, de plus en plus, que la musique n'est pas, par son essence, une chose qui puisse se couler dans une forme rigoureuse et traditionnelle. Elle est de couleurs et de temps rythmés.'

10 For more on this topic, see Laliberté (2007).

science of acoustics as well as by Schoenberg. It operates in a spatial world of at least two dimensions, where notes become points, melodies become curves, chords masses or blocks in opposition, and so on (Figure 12.4).

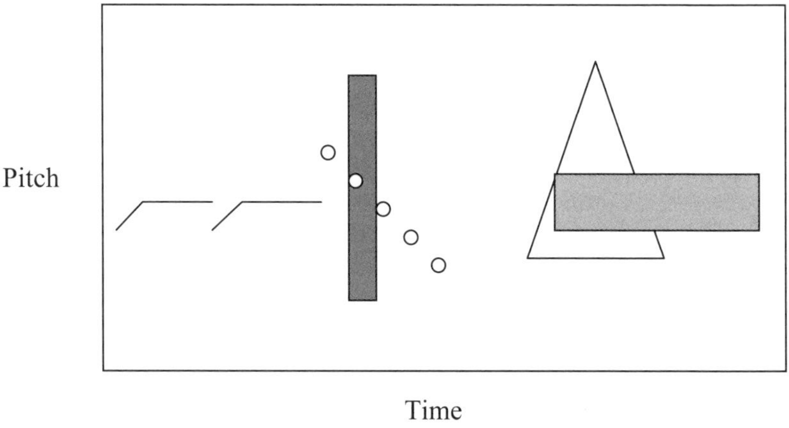

Figure 12.4 Varèse's 'mental map'?

Such representations become more frequent throughout the century, leading later to many electroacoustic graphical devices such as the UPIC (see Bello 2001) or the iPad.[11]

It is significant that electroacoustic music was born in this new graphical or plastic mental context. It will be a French complex artist and thinker who will take the crucial next step in this evolution.

Electroacoustic Music

Pierre Schaeffer: A Revealing Biography

Pierre Schaeffer (1910–95) is the main protagonist of the next stage in the evolution of music. Son of a violinist and a singer, himself a telecom engineer graduate from the Ecole Polytechnique (1929) and Supélec (1934), writer of novels, plays and essays, composer and music theoretician as well as pupil of Nadia Boulanger, Schaeffer had a lasting impact on contemporary music and sonic sensitivity. He spent his entire professional life at Radiodiffusion-Télévision Française (1935–75). He is best known for his invention of *musique concrète* in 1948, which evolved into electroacoustic music in the 1950s, and for founding the famous Paris studio Groupe de Recherches Musicales (GRM).

Why radio? Schaeffer answers:

[11] http://www.ipadmusicapps.ca (accessed 30 June 2015).

> But because radio was very amusing! It was the baroque daughter of an opera singer and of a postman, of the lyric theatre and the post-office. And it all came out of a lamp-box and a coal-microphone type 1929. And all that, of course, controlled by a bogeyman from rue de Rivoli to watch over everything. It fascinated me much more than being in the laboratory of a private enterprise. It's poetic, the waves, and public service is significant for those who have civic inspiration. (Schaeffer 1970: 29)[12]

Indeed, this multi-talented man chose radio as the field of research best suited for all his interests. It is the convergence of science, sound, music, literature, administration and politics.

The Far-reaching Impact of Microphone and Radio

The invention of *musique concrète* was not at all accidental, but rather the cumulative result of historical currents mentioned in the first section of this chapter. Pierre Schaeffer came to its invention gradually, but things accelerated during a research seminar on the artistic possibilities of radio in Beaune in 1943. Theatre director Jacques Copeau and Schaeffer, the group leaders, along with a few radio art enthusiasts, quickly came to the conclusion that the microphone could provoke a fundamental upheaval in the perception and transmission of meaning:

> The microphone, like the microscope and the camera, enlarges, exaggerates, emphasizes everything it picks up.
>
> … In front of the microphone, one must repress the habits of stage performance: gesturing – which is felt – abrupt attacks (that produce insecurity), brusque changes of tone (that ruin distinct perception).
>
> In all tones, one must sustain the voice because both facial mimicry and gestures lack to complete the meaning, to make intelligible by performance what is not clearly heard in the diction.
>
> … Interpretation in front of a mike is reading out loud.
>
> … Attitude in front of the mike is a purely interior attitude.
>
> The moderate tone, the discreet and intimate tone, in which the least inflection of the voice, the least nuance of sensitivity and even a person's little twitches are put in, so that the listener will believe, after some time, to know the

12 Our translation. Original: 'Mais parce que la radio, c'était très amusant! C'était la fille un peu baroque d'une chanteuse de l'Opéra et d'un facteur, des théâtres lyriques et des P.T.T. Tout ça sortait d'une boîte à lampes et d'un micro à charbon type 1929, et tout ça, bien entendu, étant contrôlé par un Père Fouettard délégué par la rue de Rivoli pour surveiller le tout. Ça me fascinait bien plus que de me retrouver dans le laboratoire d'une entreprise privée. C'est poétique, les ondes, et puis le service public, ce n'est pas rien pour qui a l'inspiration civique.' Note that the Ministry of Finance was then located on rue de Rivoli.

> character speaking better than if he had seen his face – this peculiar tone opens a considerable field to the art of the mike, its own and exclusive.
>
> … Deprived of the face, deprived of the authority of the gaze, deprived of hands and body, the voice that speaks is not disincarnate. On the contrary. It translates the being with extreme fidelity. It even translates it with indiscretion.
>
> … The voice with nothing in its heart nor in its head cannot be touching in a mike.
>
> … Radio, therefore, can be a school of sincerity. (Schaeffer 1977: 88–9)[13]

Pierre Schaeffer also realized that the recording of sounds and voices and their replay at will on a 'blind' apparatus (the radio with its speakers)[14] profoundly transformed the nature of listening, which became 'acousmatic', referring to Pythagoras' use of a curtain during his disciples' initiation. This acousmatic music was severed from its source and could be listened to at will, allowing concentration on sonic details and properties, on its inherent 'meaning', regardless of acoustic origin.

In 1944 Schaeffer conducted a series of further experiments for the radio play *La coquille à planètes*; he wrote the script and did most of the Foley work for it, but not the music. Thus, by 1948 the stage was set for a series of experiments for composing in a new style, perhaps even a new genre.[15] Thinking modestly at first that he was 'improving Foley', he discovered step by step an entirely new way of composing with sounds and noises. One can follow the daily account of these discoveries of the 'most general music possible'[16] (Schaeffer 1952).

---

[13] Our translation. Original: 'Le microphone, comme le microscope et comme la caméra, grossit, accuser, exagère tout ce qu'il saisit. / … Devant le microphone, il faut réprimer les habitudes du jeu scénique : la gesticulation – qui se sent – les attaques abruptes (qui produisent de l'insécurité), les brusques écarts de ton (qui nuisent à la perception distincte). / Dans tous les tons, il faut soutenir l'émission de la voix parce que ni la mimique du visage ni celle du geste ne sont là pour compléter le sens, pour rendre intelligible par le jeu ce qui n'est pas nettement audible pour la diction. / … L'interprétation devant le micro est une lecture. / … L'attitude devant le micro est une attitude purement intérieure. / Ce ton modéré, ce ton discret et tout intime où s'insèrent les moindres inflexions de la voix, les moindres nuances d'une sensibilité et jusqu'aux moindres tics d'une personne, si bien que l'auditeur croira, au bout d'un peu de temps, connaître le personnage qui lui parle mieux que s'il avait vu son visage, ce ton à lui seul ouvre un champ considérable à l'art du micro, un champ qui lui est propre, qui lui est exclusif. / … Privée de visage, privée de l'autorité du regard, privée de mains et de corps, la voix de celui qui parle n'est pas désincarnée. Au contraire. Elle traduit l'être avec une fidélité extrême. Elle le traduit même avec indiscrétion. / … La voix qui n'a rien dans le cœur ni rien dans la tête ne peut guère toucher au micro. / … La Radio pourrait donc être une école de sincérité.'

[14] Schaeffer (2010) talks about 'handicapped arts': the mute cinema and the blind radio.

[15] Ever since, there has been a lasting debate as to whether electroacoustic music is really music or an entirely new medium.

[16] In the sense that a generalized form of an equation (like y = a+bx) contains all the different forms of this equation.

Schaeffer was a man curious about his times, and he strove for a modern reconciliation of traditional poetry, literature, theatre and arts, as well as religious speculations, with the requirements of technocracy: science, hard facts, organization and big structures. To understand the impact of his work one must accept this strange hybridization, and not separate his different sides from one another. It took a curious man to hear and see in primitive radio technologies a tool for renewing music. The implications are far-reaching, as he develops in his *chef d'œuvre*, *Le traité des objets musicaux* (1966). After this initial step in 1948, as is well known, Schaeffer founded the Studio d'essais, the Groupe de Recherche de Musique Concrète, the Groupe de Recherche Musicale and even the Institut National de l'Audiovisuel, organizing and leading one of the main institutions of contemporary music. For these reasons, Schaeffer is rightly known as a radical acousmatic researcher.

But is the picture complete? Were Schaeffer and his team really 'blind'?

This chapter attempts to demonstrate a more nuanced view. Indeed, a detailed study of Schaeffer's writings reveals the graphic sensitivity outlined in its first section. As suggested, several of the words chosen by Schaeffer to describe sonic properties reveal a graphic or plastic/spatial sensitivity: *projector*, *grain*, *fringe*, *node*, *allure*, *channel*, *mass*, *calibre*, *site* and so on are all taken from the visual domain or are often associated with vision, either explicitly or in more subtle ways. For instance, 'mass' (Chion 2009) and its different 'calibres' and 'sites' generalize the former notion of 'pitch'; but mass and its nuances are obviously conceived in 2D pitch/intensity space, or even in 3D pitch/intensity/calibre space, as shown in Figure 12.5.

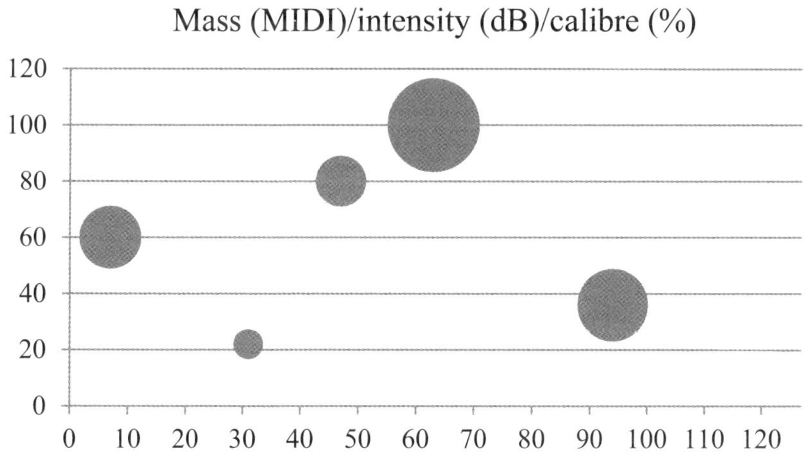

Figure 12.5 Mass, sites and calibre[17]

[17] For ease of representation, the pitch centre of the masses is represented by its equivalent usual MIDI number, despite the anachronism of this practice. Schaeffer was using a traditional scheme of note names and numbered octaves, which gives a similar linear pitch scale.

Similar discussions can take place about other key concepts, most of which exist within a multidimensional space of perceptive sound properties.

Thus, electroacoustic music possesses a significant spatial or visual part, despite its radical rejection of graphics as musical tool and its essential concentration on listening. One of Schaeffer's quandaries resided in the need to manipulate properly and, even more importantly, to think properly a new 'most general' music. In addition, since traditions concerning timbre were so limited, he had to invent a new vocabulary well before the generalization of acoustics or electronic musical instruments. At the time, almost nobody had heard of dynamic envelopes or recognized the difference between vibrato or tremolo, and most could not name different shades of noise nor even accept noises as having aesthetic potential. Schaeffer's literary sensitivity, his taste for multiple art forms and his understanding of music all came together in the invention of this new vocabulary. Sensations of all kinds – aural, but also visual or tactile – came into play.

The paradoxical importance of the visual for Schaeffer becomes less surprising if one remembers his personal interest in photography[18] and movies. This important citation from *In Search of a Concrete Music* is quite revealing in this respect:

> 22nd April. Once my initial joy is past, I ponder. I've already got quite a lot of problems with my turntables, because there is only one note per turntable. With a cinematographic flash-forward, Hollywood-style, I see myself surrounded by twelve dozen turntables, each with one note. Yet, it would be, as mathematicians would say, the *most general musical instrument possible*.
>
> Is it another blind alley, or am I in possession of a solution whose importance I can only guess at? (Schaeffer 2012: 15)

In this citation, famous for having the intuition of the sampler as early as 1948,[19] one notices the cinematic sensitivity joining the poetic and theatrical as well as the scientific – all those dimensions battling in Schaeffer's mind. Again, the terms 'grain', 'projector', 'profile', 'node' and 'fringe' come to mind. Not only are these words visual in general, but they are also cinematic or photographic in particular.[20] In a lesser-known proposition, Schaeffer even calls the speaker

[18] There were known photographers in his family, and there remains an interesting collection of art photographs in his personal archives held at the Institut Mémoires de l'édition contemporaine in the city of Caen.

[19] The American Harold Chamberlin had much the same idea the very same year, leading to his tape-based instrument the Chamberlin (as it was branded in the USA), and its derivative, the better-known Mellotron (as it was branded in the UK).

[20] 'Grain', 'node' and 'fringe' are also tactile. *Frange* (fringe) has been translated as 'white noise' elsewhere, which is clearer, but obscures the visual analogy to the fringe of a rug. Schaeffer often uses the term *frange* for broadband noise, preferring the concrete

a 'sonic screen' rather than a 'sound projector', thereby underscoring the cinematic analogy.

Indeed, the answers to these questions go back further than 1948. In the background preparation of the invention of *musique concrète*, Schaeffer wrote a most significant essay in 1942 called *Essai sur la radio et le cinéma*. In this early fascinating text he drafts many aspects of his later theories well before he conceived of a new kind of music or prepared *La coquille à Planètes*. In this essay Schaeffer promotes radio drama as a carefully crafted, new, mixed-media art form containing in this order: words, acting, music and sound effects. For him, because of the technological nature of the support, this art is much more closely related to cinema than to theatre or opera. For him, both constitute 'relay' or 'go-between' arts (*arts-relais*) sharing common traits. Among his sketches, one figure is particularly striking, reproduced in Figure 12.6 for ease of reading.

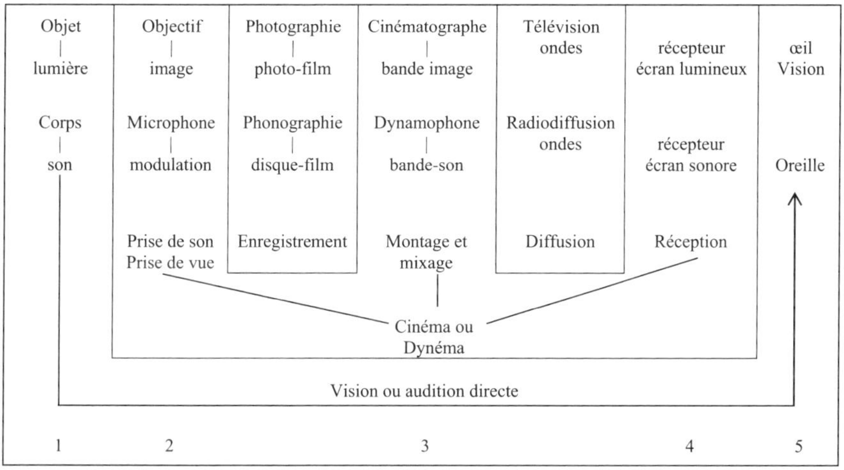

Figure 12.6 Relationship of a light object and sound body, left (1) to the eye and the ear, right (5), via the relays of cinema or 'dynéma' (2–4)[21]

Source: © Jacqueline Schaeffer © Editions Allia 2010, 2014. Reproduced by kind permission.

image of a disorderly fringe around a shawl or rug to the 'scientific' term that misses, in his view, the qualitative or perceptive point.

21 'Mise en rapport de l'objet lumineux et du corps sonore à gauche (1) avec l'œil et l'oreille à droite (5) par les relais du cinéma et du dynéma (2–4)'.

Taken from a newly reissued text (Schaeffer 2010), the sketch also constitutes the link between Schaeffer's literary practice and radio art. The 'dynéma' he proposes remained a constant image in the *musique concrète* group, eventually becoming the concept of 'cinéma pour l'oreille' ('cinema for the ear'), frequently evoked in electroacoustic music circles.[22] Very early, then, Schaeffer was contemplating a new art form akin to cinema and behaving like its visual counterpart. This analogy left many visual traces in later approaches. One can also notice that right from the start Schaeffer used a tabular method of communication,[23] well before his famous figures appeared in major books (Schaeffer 1952; 1966). In my view, this is also a clear expression of the post-Schoenberg/Varèse graphic way of thinking described above.

Other graphic tools involved in early Schaeffer confirm this paradigm. In his notebooks, sketches and early papers Schaeffer uses different kinds of notation. Indeed, it may come as a surprise to some more familiar with the 'militant' acousmatic attitude of the *musique concrète* school that Schaeffer used all kinds of notations throughout his career, and urged his team to develop and use them as well, music notation having proved too limited for his needs. In his perceptive paper on the analysis of electroacoustic music, François Delalande (2009) presents several examples of notation in use at the GRM (see Figure 12.7).

This sketch of an early version of the *Etudes concrètes*, mixing musical notation, drawings, rhythms and measures, is closely related to the well-known sketch of the *Etude aux chemins de fer* (1948). Both reveal a dominating spatial conception inherited from musical notation that is potentially multidimensional. Let us look at other examples by different members of his team. The example from 1952 by Monique Rollin shown in Figure 12.8 is still close to musical notation.

The *Etude violette*, being piano-based, can probably be transcribed more easily than other noise-based works; nonetheless, the transcription is not quite satisfactory, for it is too 'reductionist' – it does not have enough details as to the timbre. The example in Figure 12.9, despite having staves, is more abstract due to the 'criteria' related graphics, an attempt to symbolize crucial sonic phenomena.

Thirdly, let us look at an example of double notation, contemporary to Figure 12.9, including both the bathygrams and musical transcriptions (see Figure 12.10).

[22] Notice, for instance, the name of the well-known CD collection, edited by Metamkine.

[23] This may also be an inheritance from his engineering training at l'Ecole Polytechnique.

Figure 12.7 Schaeffer's sketch for a *symphonie de bruits* (1948)
Source: Reproduced by kind permission of Droz-HEM.

Figure 12.8 Monique Rollin's transcription (1952) of *Etude violette*
Source: Reproduced by kind permission of Droz-HEM.

Figure 12.9 Mireille Chamass's transcription of seven sound objects (1959)
Source: Reproduced by kind permission of Droz-HEM.

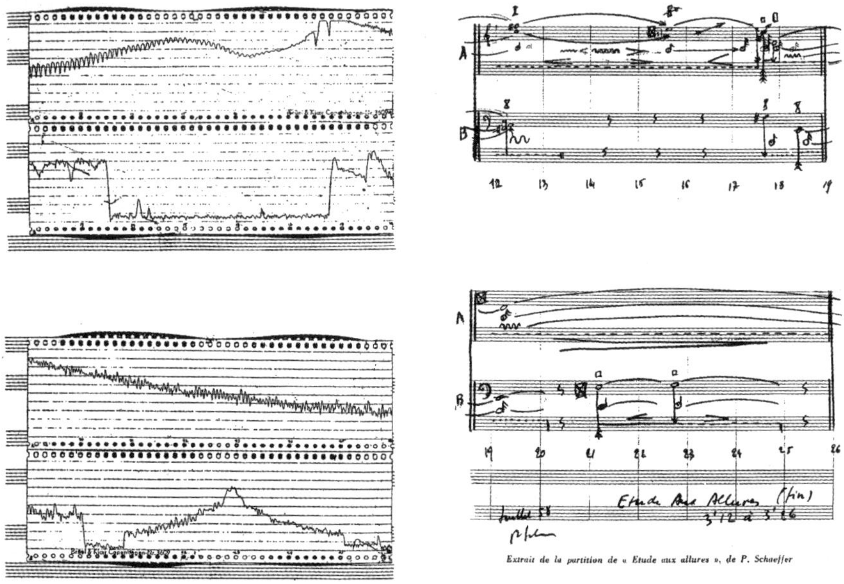

Figure 12.10 Schaeffer's transcription of *Etude aux allures* (1958)
Source: Reproduced by kind permission of Droz-HEM.

The objectively precise acoustic representation combined with notation of perceptive results makes this transcription more satisfactory; later visual tools will often retain such a dual approach. However, at the time, bathygrams and sonograms were costly and limited to short-duration fragments, so they did not become commonplace tools. Nevertheless, no matter how incomplete or dissatisfying the results – and Schaeffer's writings and teachings are very critical on these matters – Schaeffer and his group's graphic research remained constant. They were certainly listening to the sounds in great detail, but images were never far away.

Moreover, the images used at the GRM were a little peculiar, often complex in nature.[24] Let us look at some of Schaeffer's main figures in the final 1966 version. They can be deceptively simple. The scale of masses, for instance, seems clear at first glance (see Figure 12.11a).

[24] This is possibly a legacy of the esoteric practices that seduced Schaeffer for a while (Schaeffer 1970).

1. Pure sound
2. Tonic sound
3. Tonic group
4. Channelled
5. Nodal group
6. Nodal sound
7. White noise

Figure 12.11a Scale of masses
Source: Chion (2009).

Reading the texts more precisely, however, this scale can also be perceived with other symmetries: V-shaped or in espalier[25] (Figure 12.11b).

1. Pure sound	7. White noise
2. Tonic sound	6. Nodal sound
3. Tonic group	5. Nodal group
4. Channelled	

Figure 12.11b 'U' or 'V' symmetries

In fact, many of Schaeffer's graphics are similarly multi-level. An even richer case can be found in the famous *TARTYP* (Schaeffer 1977: 459; see Figure 12.12).

25 Reminiscent of the fruit trees of the north-east of France, where Schaeffer was born.

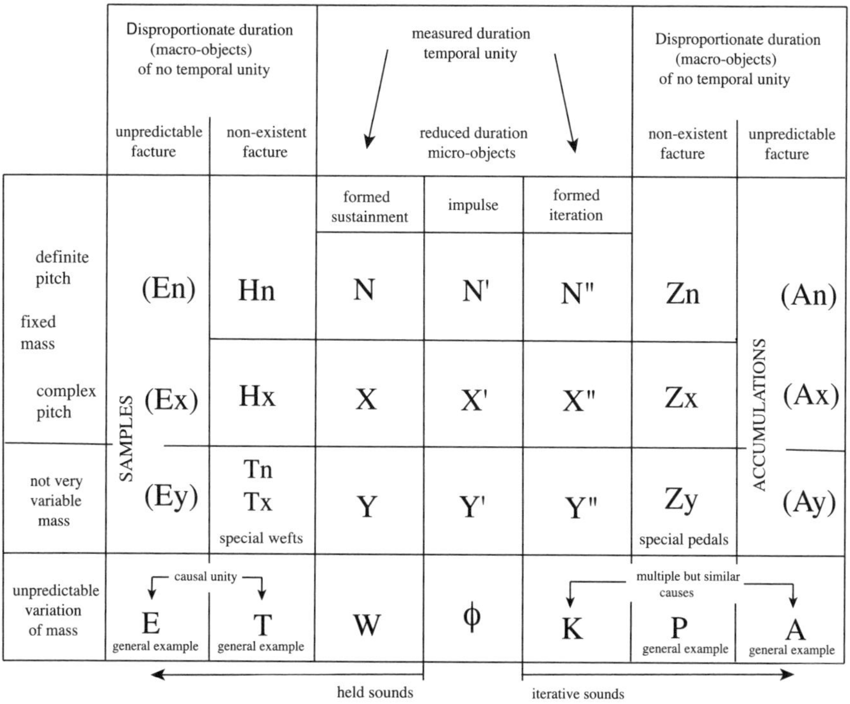

Figure 12.12 *TARTYP*

Source: © Jacqueline Schaeffer; translated by John Dack. Reproduced by kind permission.

Again we find a tabular and symbolic approach. But Figure 12.12 is extremely complex, showing three dimensions: variations of mass, duration and form. Looking more closely, one sees that it employs a radial symmetry with a centre (nine *balanced sounds*), a middle level (*redundant*, *homogeneous*, *wefts*, *pedals*) and extremes (*samples* and *accumulations*). Again, Figure 12.12 is really a multidimensional and dynamic analysis compressed into apparent 2D. The situation becomes even more complex if one takes into account the merging of the two extremes discussed by Schaeffer. The compressed 2D becomes a kind of cylinder within a timbre-space (see Figure 12.13).

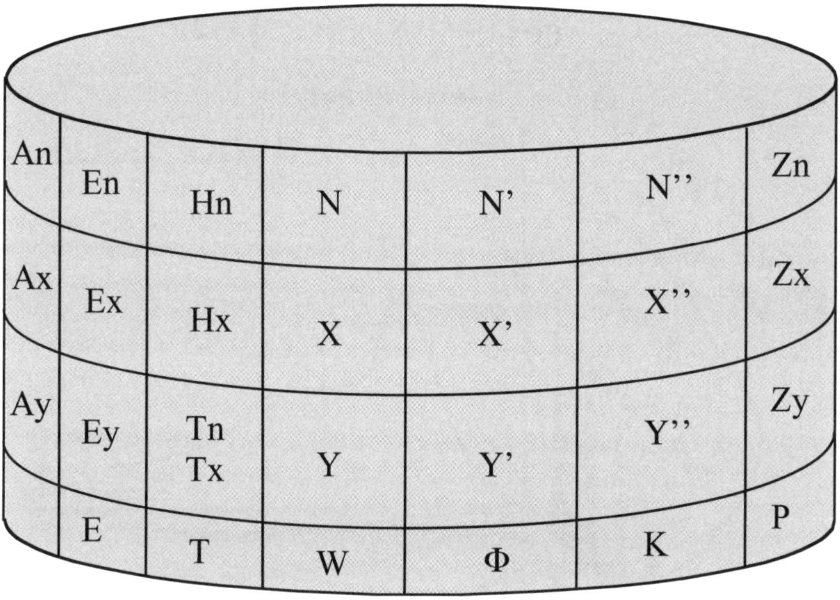

Figure 12.13 A cylinder in multidimensional timbre-space

In spite of this graphic complexity, the communication technologies in 1966 and, most likely, Schaeffer's own thinking at the time[26] excluded the topological complexities of 'n-dimensional' shapes. He kept to traditional 2D graphics.

Another example, the Moles–Schaeffer controversy of the late 1950s, led to the abandonment or at least diminished use of the acoustically inspired representation used then (Schaeffer 1952: 207; see Figure 12.14).

[26] One often finds in him a dual tendency towards extreme modernity and towards nostalgia for simpler times.

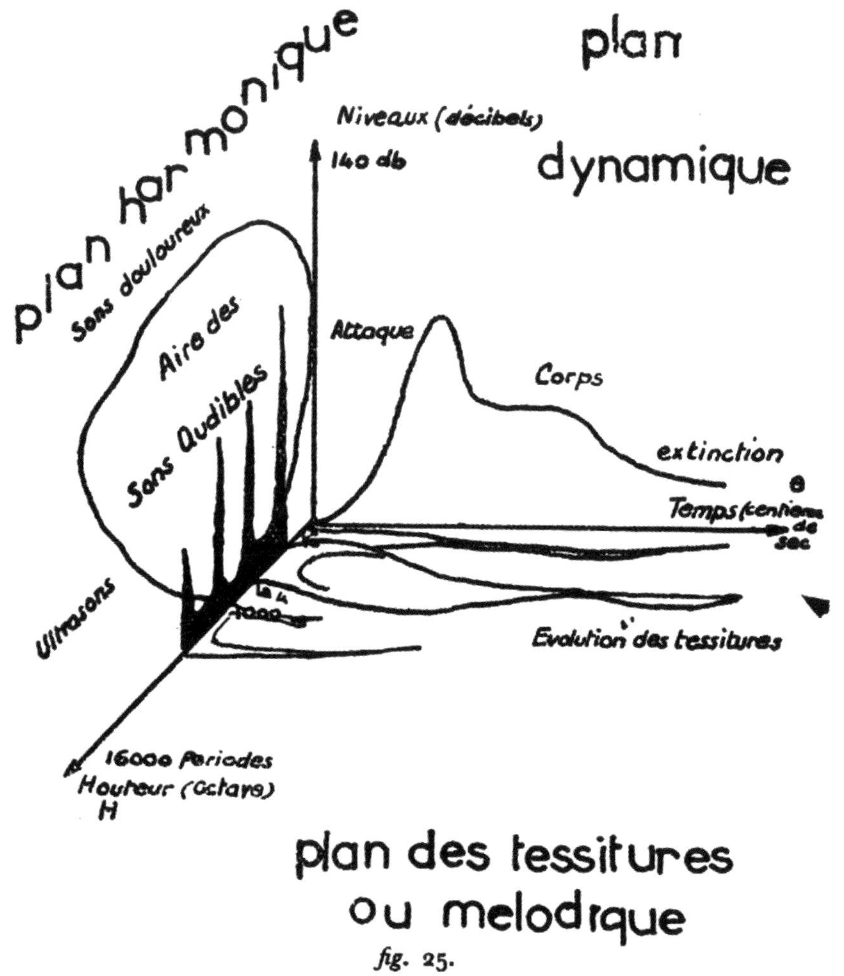

Figure 12.14 Implicit 3D space
Source: © Jacqueline Schaeffer. Reproduced by kind permission of the University of California Press.

Yet this 3D representation permeates all later approaches, thereby complicating further the situation by being both present and understated. The subliminal 3D space testifies the spatial evolution of contemporary musical thinking that Schaeffer included despite his reluctance.[27]

[27] I would argue that he was, along with Schoenberg, a 'reluctant Messiah', to borrow the term from Richard Bach (1977), or a 'sleepwalker', according to Arthur Koestler (1959) – never quite sure if he really wanted to go along with his avant-garde invention. I will shortly publish on this subject (Laliberté forthcoming).

Schaeffer's thinking is also dynamic, in the temporal sense. At a time when physicists still disregarded the unstable portion of sound, one of Schaeffer's major achievements was to attract attention to the attack and transition of a sound's 'dynamic profile': its dynamic envelope (Chion 2009: 174–8). This dynamic-temporal approach is even active in the simple-looking Figure 12.15).

4. COMPREHENDING – for me: signs – before me: values (meaning-language) Emergence of a sound continuum and *reference to*, *confrontation* with extra-sonorous notions	1. LISTENING – for me: indexes – before me; external events (agent-instrument) *Emission* of the sound	1 and 4: objective
3. HEARING – for me: qualified perceptions – before me: qualified sound object *Selection* of certain particular aspects of the sound	2. PERCEIVING – for me: crude perceptions, rough outlines of the object – before me: crude sound object *Reception* of the sound	2 and 3: subjective
3 and 4: abstract	1 and 2: concrete	

Figure 12.15 Four ways of listening: a cycle in time, 1–4

Drafted as early as 1942 (see Schaeffer 2010: 53, 61), the four types of listening form a cycle: usually 1–2–3–4. Schaeffer (1952: 35–6) also presents the interaction of abstract and concrete music as a cycle in time: (1) from abstract to concrete, and (2) from concrete to abstract. If space permitted, it would be intriguing to present here the four parts of morphologies, the *TARSOM* (Schaeffer 1977: 584–7). This elaborate figure shows complex and intricate multidimensional and temporal organizations, despite an apparent 7×9 grid.

In its place, let us pay attention to an animation film produced by François Delalande and Jacques Vidal for the GRM (*c.* 1970).[28] Here, one can understand just how important images were for the Paris group and how the subsequent Acousmographe was the crowning achievement of those attempts, as Delalande (2009) demonstrates. In spite of technical limitations in this animation film, different shapes are used to represent sounds and their properties according to a more or less Schaefferian analysis.[29] The representation derives from the musical score, being mass in function of time, and includes a representation of the dynamic envelopes and some references to timbre, although it does not yet scroll.[30] Instead, a pointer is used in synchronization with the music.

To conclude this section of the chapter, I stress that the surprising presence of visual aids for listening in the GRM's practices does not appear to contradict the group's founding principles. The use of visual aids does not diminish the true originality of this musical school: listening to sounds of all kinds with curiosity and concentration, reaching for ways to put them together to create satisfactory aural experiences. And conversely, such originality does not necessarily preclude a visual approach. I have shown many cases where the eye was involved as well as the ear to forge a characteristic manner of listening to and composing music. In the words of one of the GRM's main figures, François Bayle: 'Yes, of course, we used some visual tools, but always under the control of the ear. It would be a mistake to think that because of our concentration on listening we were blind. On the contrary.'[31] Like Schaeffer, Bayle's approach often presents visual aspects, despite his concentration on acousmatic music.

The persistence of the visual in electroacoustic practice can shed light on a complementary discussion related to this book.

Some Cases of Electroacoustic Resurgences in Auteur Cinema

A somewhat surprising fact of art history is the ease with which cinema integrated electroacoustic sensitivity, considering that film is a rather conservative medium concerning music. Could this be related to the half-hidden visual side of electroacoustic music? Let us discuss a few pertinent cases.

Electroacoustic thinking is an approach of a musician, but usually sound engineers are musicians as well. Gradually, electroacoustic sensitivity reached the cinema world and exerted an impact, almost automatically. This impact can be explained in part by the necessity for film directors and moviemakers to find new

28 *Partition animée:* étude *aux objets de Pierre Schaeffer, 4e mouvement, 1ere* écoute, Paris: INA-GRM. See http://fresques.ina.fr/artsonores/fiche-media/InaGrm00206/partition-animee-de-l-etude-aux-objets.html (accessed 30 June 2015).

29 Schaeffer himself was not a fundamentalist, and maintained a distance from analysis; he was instead pragmatic, seeking usefulness rather than perfection (Schaeffer 1998).

30 Versions of *Acousmographe* in the 1990s would include this feature.

31 François Bayle, personal oral communication, January 2013. Our translation.

ways to use sound in the reconstruction of reality. For certain avant-garde projects traditional music is not always appropriate, diverting attention from other aspects of the film or giving a romantic or overly 'produced' effect. Sound, ambient noise and soundscapes are used instead.

These two explanations converge towards a creative use of sound, where two major tendencies are evident:

1. a direct link between films and the electroacoustic community – quite a few soundtracks from 1950 onwards were composed by trained contemporary composers (Morricone, Fano, Constant, Artemiev) or were commissioned by directors with a high degree of musical sensitivity (Disney, Kubrick, Lynch, Godard, Visconti, Coppola, Lucas);
2. a more frequent indirect link – in a technical, 'mediological' (Tiffon 2005) and practical way, soundstages and cinema studios are true electroacoustic studios, often benefiting from ample budgets and the best technologies. They 'exude' electroacoustic music, even without even realizing it consciously.[32] As Marshall McLuhan (1964) has clearly shown, 'the medium is the message': a tool contains its own immanent properties that lead the user towards a certain way of doing things, and the listener of perceiving them. To paraphrase Molière's *Le Bourgeois Gentilhomme* (1670), several sound designers for film are doing electroacoustic music 'in spite of themselves'.

A Problematic Microphone

For better or worse, the camera and the microphone joined forces in the late 1920s. As the 1952 movie by Gene Kelly and Stanley Donen, *Singin' in the Rain*, lampoons, this marriage was not easy at first. Great creativity, artistic and technical, was necessary to overcome such problems as unwanted 'microgenic' sounds and noises, conflicting needs of recording (a quiet stage and proximity of the microphone to the source) and of filming (excluding the presence of the microphone from the frame and including a noisy camera on stage), and of an adapted acting different from traditional 'extroverted' theatre acting.[33] Once more, 'radio could therefore be a school of sincerity'. The opposition between stage acting and the Actors' Studio method also comes to mind. After 'moving' pictures, from 1930 onwards a new generation invented 'talking', 'sounding' or even 'singing' cinema; and it achieved spectacular success in the late 1940s, as the Kelly and Donen film celebrates, including superb technical broadcast quality. Hi-fi microphones and speakers have not improved all that much since the 1950s.

---

[32] I have proposed (Laliberté 2001, 2003) that pop music studios had the same evolution towards an electroacoustic sensitivity, whether explicit or unconscious.

[33] The famous scenes found on YouTube summarize it: 'Singin' in the Rain (3/8) Movie CLIP – The Sound Barrier (1952) HD', http://www.youtube.com/watch?v=OTFCctdiS04 and 'Singin' in the Rain (6/8) Movie CLIP - Out of Sync (1952) HD', http://www.youtube.com/watch?v=YMzV96LV6Cc (accessed 30 June 2015).

Auteur Cinema and Music

On the fringes of the movie industry, more demanding artists in auteur cinema also adopted the apparatus of moving and sounding images. In a few cases, sonic aspects take a singular place, recalling the primitive biological function of hearing: to inform the individual about what cannot be seen. Auteur cinema also rediscovered the function that music has served since Gregorian chant: to express what cannot be told. Finally, sound in auteur cinema took over the function of the old Greek chorus: to comment on and react to the action. This role had been fulfilled by music, notably with Wagner's *Leitmotiv*, and certainly cinema (along with television and multimedia) can be described as a new kind of *Gesamtkunstwerk*. It must be pointed out that film composers tend to be Wagnerian, whereas sound designers – the sons and daughters of Roy Disney or Spike Jones – often have a more modern – that is, more creative or even fully electroacoustic – approach. Let us illustrate this with a few examples.

Jacques Tati (1907–1982): Slapstick concrète

Jacques Tati, an important director for our discussion, created an original type of cinema in which humour and slapstick thinly disguise an anguished sensitivity towards modernization, seen as dehumanizing. In Tati's films things dominate man, and true communication has disappeared. This is especially the case in *Mon Oncle* (1958).[34] In their ultra-modern villa,[35] the Arpel family no longer communicate, speaking solely in empty advertising slogans: 'Tout communique', 'Comme c'est original.' They live in a mechanical and obsessive way, becoming the servants of their house and furniture – of the dolphin fountain, for instance. The 'uncle', who often visits his brother-in-law Mr Arpel, is a clumsy but charming man, never quite fitting in despite his good intentions, who introduces refreshing chaos into the household.[36]

Dialogue becomes almost impossible – one is reminded of Magritte. Sounds and noises, of people, things and places, often replace it. Tati uses a close microphone and unnatural amplification of sounds to bring sounds forward in the mix, literally constructing a study in expanded sounds similar to the Schaefferian approach. The amplified noises of Mrs Arpel's dress, the detailed and contrasting sounds of steps over various materials or the menacing machine sounds, either in the kitchen or in Mr Arpel's factory, are quite evident.

In *Trafic* (1971) chaos and noise dominate the French-style derisive road movie. At times it is a very attentive electroacoustic study. An interesting example is right

---

[34] One can find many clips on YouTube, such as: http://www.youtube.com/watch?v=gkvtE1AS6Qo [August 2013].

[35] Ironically, today this is seen as a great study in modern design.

[36] See 'Jaques Tati – Mon Oncle (Kitchen Scene)', *YouTube*, http://www.youtube.com/watch?v=LE9t98Gox60 (accessed 30 June 2015).

after the tumultuous car crash.[37] A red Volkswagen Beetle turns into a wild animal, 'quacking' like a duck and making savage 'grinding' noises, while a wheel 'runs away' and finally falls over with exaggerated metallic sounds. This is very close to early *musique concrète* aesthetics, where sounds metamorphose into surrealistic otherness, like the 'whale' or 'singing' squeaking doors of Pierre Henry's *Variations pour une porte et un soupir* (1963). Those studies in sounds could also be compared to Schaeffer's *Etudes de bruits* (1948), especially the metallic sound of the falling wheel near the beginning of the *Etude pathétique*.[38] Both creators share a distrust of modernity, as can be gathered from Schaeffer (1970) and from the movies of Tati. Incidentally, both men are from the same 'disillusioned' generation, born before the First World War and young adults on the eve of the Second World War.

Andrei Tarkovsky: Studies in matters or elements

Another case in point is Andrei Tarkovsky, director of only a few but highly regarded films in which sound, music and noise often replace missing or impossible dialogue. Tarkovsky's personal idiom is developed not in satire or comedy like Tati, but rather in visionary, poetic, even mystic films.

A striking feature of films such as *Stalker* (1979)[39] and *Solaris* (1979) is the director's taste for the elements, in the old Greek sense: water, air, fire, lava, stone, wood, grass and metal are deeply rooted, both in images and in sounds.[40] In *Stalker* the whole initiatory journey into the 'zone', where natural life has taken over the world from man, is a detailed study of textures, colours and sounds, akin to mature electroacoustic music. Those soundtracks approach the work of composers like François Bayle (*Tremblement de terre très doux*, 1978) or Bernard Parmegiani (*De natura sonorum*, 1975).

Solaris also puts forward technological sounds such as cars on a highway,[41] the sounds of the space station and so on. This creates a subtle comment on the state of mind of the cosmonaut and his apprehensions before his mission. Again, man seems small and menaced against such a sonic (and visual) ambience. Like the two compositions mentioned above, the soundtrack composed by Eduard Artemiev uses both recorded and synthesized sounds, thus being fully electroacoustic or even mixed-music rather than *musique concrète*.

This film is a late but fervent inheritor of the space race, seen from the USSR side, beginning with the science fiction literature of Stanislas Lem and his cohort,

---

37 See Jacques Tati, *Trafic* (1971), DVD, Studiocanal, 2015, in particular the 'rolling wheelcap' scene.

38 In fact, in both cases the sound of a turning and falling film box was used.

39 See 'Stalker (Сталкер) (1979) Trailer', *YouTube*, http://www.youtube.com/watch?v=GM_GOpfEQUw (accessed 30 June 2015).

40 'Stalker 1979', *YouTube*, http://www.youtube.com/watch?v=AoZvFD_e7Lo (accessed 30 June 2015).

41 'Solaris Full Highway Scene', *YouTube*, http://www.youtube.com/watch?v=rswYl7RLRNE (accessed 30 June 2015).

possibly the result of being 'red children'. This might be compared with successful US movies such as *The Right Stuff* or *Apollo 13*. Tarkovsky's particular fervour is evident in the 'apparition and levitation' scene at the end of the movie,[42] where the main character and the 'spirit' of his deceased wife float in the air, accompanied by an organ piece by Bach. To modernize the sound and give it distance, the composer doubles the organ with a vibraphone, lending a contemporary or jazzy tone.[43] Thus, the cosmonaut is presented as a kind of 'secular saint', surrounded in the space station by the best examples of European fine art. This also represents a kind of redemption of the main character (another signature of saints), confessed and blessed by the planet *Solaris*.

David Lynch and post-industrial individual anguish

Yet another example of electroacoustic sensitivity can be seen in David Lynch's film *Eraserhead* (1977). This dark and humorous movie is an interesting case of post-Space Age 'crash' – in drug parlance, the 'coming down' of the 1970s after the 'high' of the 1960s.

Henry's tribulations with his fiancée-turned-too-quickly-wife and their baby in sordid parts of Philadelphia, as he suffers from visions, hallucinations or even the real madness of the period, are constructed with few and empty words and foreground sounds, noises and music. For instance, in the mad first meal[44] with his soon-to-be family-in-law, we hear organic bubbling and disgusting noises, revealing Henry's embarrassment and anticipating the problematic result of his relationship: a baby, with its share of unavoidably physical and dirty aspects. The movie is often visually 'drenched' in liquids and dubious-looking matter, accompanied by disturbing sounds. The 'man in the planet' – either a *deus ex machina* or a demon plotting and torturing Henry – is accompanied by amplified sounds and menacing machine- or train-like noises[45] (perhaps those from Philadelphia's closing factories, struck at that time by economic crisis). On another level, the singing 'lady in the radiator'[46] is a complex chimera: a woman resembling Marilyn Monroe, with cheeks similar to testicles and who sings in a man's falsetto, becomes a good fairy or angel, apparently relieving Henry from his mad life.

The soundtrack is fascinating and well constructed, if one accepts noises as legitimate artistic sounds. Broken-down Philadelphia recalls the basic sounds recorded there by Varèse for his *Deserts* (1950–54), while the embarrassed silences of the family meal, the expressionist silent scream of Mary's mother and the organic

---

42 'Solaris by Andrej Tarkovskij - Levitation (Full Scene)', *YouTube*, http://www.youtube.com/watch?v=FcglyhUre4w (accessed 30 June 2015).

43 Something like *Jazz Sebastian Bach* by the Swingle Singers, a fusion classic of the 1960s.

44 See David Lynch, *Eraserhead* (1977), DVD, MK2, 2010, in particular the 'mad dinner' scene.

45 This appears close to Schaeffer in *Etudes aux chemins de fer* (1948).

46 See David Lynch, *Eraserhead* (1977), DVD, MK2, 2010, in particular the 'man in the planet' scene.

sounds recall early electroacoustic pieces like Luciano Berio's disturbing *Visage* (1961). Finally, the dark humour and deconstruction characterizing the movie in all its aspects are related to contemporary postmodern thinking. Berio again comes to mind, especially *Sinfonia* (1968), a landmark in deconstructive approach to music.

To Conclude: Listening with Images

After summarizing the growing importance of visual or spatial imagination on modern and contemporary music as a solution to post-Wagnerian tonal music crisis, this chapter studied the case of early electroacoustic music. Schaeffer and his school were presented by composers such as Schoenberg, Debussy, Stravinsky and Varèse as inheritors of the pioneer musical-spatial-visual shift of paradigm. From that perspective, all kinds of sounds are deployed and interact in a mental and perceptive multidimensional space of complementary musical properties.

Recent reissues, better translations of fundamental texts, direct discussions with the actors, and archive findings reveal a surprising and complex use of visual aids in radical acousmatic circles in the 1950s and 1960s, despite severe criticism and distrust. Schaeffer and his team listened with concentration and subtlety to sound, but they did so with visual assistance – 'always under the control of the ear', confirms Bayle. The key concepts (many of which stem from vision or touch rather than from hearing alone) and the tables, graphs and other visual aids were constructed and improved over the years leading to Schaeffer's fundamental texts of 1966–67, and then, after many more years of composition and research, to *Acousmonium*, the GRM's music analysis software.

The simultaneous presence of the visual dimension in electroacoustic practice may explain the success of electroacoustic music in cinema, both in practice and theory (Chion 2003). Many auteur films from the 1960s to the 1980s – Tati, Tarkovsky, Lynch – demonstrate clear electroacoustic sensitivity, as if the electroacoustic approach was naturally cinematographic.

In all of these ways, and with these ramifications, the Paris School was listening with images.

References

Bach, Richard (1977) *Illusions: The Adventures of a Reluctant Messiah*, New York: Dell.

Bello, Angelo, 'Notes on Composing with the UPIC System: The Equipment of Iannis Xenakis', in *Presences of Iannis Xenakis*, ed. Makis Solomos, Paris: CDMC, pp. 93–7.

Chion, Michel (2003) *Un art sonore, le cinéma, histoire, esthétique, poïetique*, Paris: Cahiers du cinéma.

——— (2009) *Guide to Sound Objects* [1983], trans. John Dack and Christine North, EARS. http://www.ears.dmu.ac.uk/spip.php?page=articleEars&id_article=3597 (accessed March 2013).

Delalande, François (2009) 'Pratiques et objectifs des transcriptions des musiques électroacoustiques', in *L'analyse musicale, une pratique et son histoire*, ed. Rémy Campos and Nicolas Donin, Geneva: Droz-HEM, pp. 131–53.

Horodyski, Timothée (1998) *Varèse: héritage et confluences (les masses sonores – l'espace du son – la spatialisation)*, Villeneuve-d'Ascq: Presses universitaires du Septentrion.

Koestler, Arthur (1959) *The Sleepwalkers: A History of Man's Changing Vision of the Universe*, New York: Macmillan.

Laliberté, Martin (2001) 'Problématique générale des outils dans l'histoire de l'électroacoustique', in *Du sonore au musical, 50 années de recherches concrètes (1948–1998)*, ed. Sylvie Dallet and Anne Veitl, Paris: l'Harmattan, pp. 33–53.

——— (2003) 'Anciennes et nouvelles technologies pour un jazz-rock actuel: Base #1 de Christophe Fellay', *De l'arsenic*, 5, pp. 106–71.

——— (2007) 'Vers une histoire des temps musicaux modernes: entre nuages dynamiques et pulsations obsessives', in *Les formes du temps, rythme histoire, temporalité, actes du Colloque International Temps, rythme et histoire, XVIIIe–XXe siècles*, ed. Paule Petitier and Gisèle Séginger, Strasbourg: Presses Universitaires de Strasbourg, pp. 385–98.

——— (forthcoming) *Modèles et archétypes de la musique contemporaine et ses instruments*, Paris: l'Harmattan.

McLuhan, Marshall (1964) *Understanding Media: the Extensions of Man*, New York: McGraw-Hill.

Ouellette, Fernand (1989) *Edgard Varèse*, Paris: Christian Bourgois.

Rosen, Charles (1979) *Schoenberg*, Paris: Les éditions de Minuit.

Schaeffer, Pierre (1952) À la *recherche de la musique concrète*, Paris: Seuil.

——— (1966) *Le traité des objets musicaux*, Paris: Seuil.

——— (1970) *L'avenir à reculons*, Brussels: Casterman.

——— (1977) *Le traité des objets musicaux*, 2nd edn, Paris: Seuil.

——— (1998) *Solfège de l'objet sonore* [1967], reissue, Paris: INA-GRM, three CDs with booklet.

——— (2010) *Essai sur la radio et le cinéma. Esthétique et technique des arts-relais* [1942], critical edn by Sophie Brunet and Carlos Palombini, Paris: Allia.

——— (2012) *In Search of a Concrete Music* [1952], trans. John Dack and Christine North, Berkeley, CA: University of California Press.

Schoenberg, Arnold (1922) *Harmonielehre* [1911], Vienna: Universal Edition.

——— (1951) *Style and Idea*, ed. Leonard Stein, London: Faber and Faber.

——— (1978) *Theory of Harmony*, trans. Roy E. Carter, Los Angeles, CA: University of California Press.

——— (1983) *Traité d'harmonie*, trans. Gérard Gubisch, Paris: Lattès.

Tiffon, Vincent (2005) 'Pour une médiologie musicale: une étude critique des interactions entre innovations techniques et inventions musicales contemporaines', habilitation à diriger des recherches, Université de Lille 3.

PART IV
Recordings and the New Aura

Chapter 13
Neo-auratic Encoding: Phenomenological Framework and Operational Patterns[1]

Vincenzo Caporaletti

A notable idea expressed by French philosopher Gilles Deleuze about the history of philosophy, which 'rather than repeating what a philosopher says, has to say what he must have taken for granted, what he didn't say but is nonetheless present in what he did say' (1997: 136), reminds us of Nicholas Cook's striking inspiration concerning music history. Cook has in fact suggested, in the wake of Richard Dawkins's (1995) biological model (whereby humans are the carriers of biological dynamics at the genetic level), that 'historical process would reside not in musical works … but in what lies between them: the continuously changing … patterns of conception which brought those works into being' (Cook 1998: 72). Now, we can see these 'patterns of conception', through the perspective of analytical philosophy (formulated by Willard Van Orman Quine, Donald Davidson and others),[2] as 'conceptual schemes' – the way we structure and schematize reality, or how a paradigm of reality is patterned.

This chapter, which focuses on the ontological status of rock, jazz and pop (both live and recorded), will deal precisely with the relations between paradigms or conceptual schemes in the musical dimension, their limits, and the feasibility of finding new ones apart from those which can be found in scientifically oriented literature. It will also attempt an answer to the question raised by Nicholas Cook: 'whether we should think of jazz, rock and pop as all part of the same tradition, as "classical" music, or whether they should really be thought of as separate traditions' (1998: 58); in addition, it proposes a new perspective on the aesthetic identity of alternative versions of the same work in multiple recordings.

Dyadic versus Oralistic Conceptual Schemes

One central paradigm through which musical phenomena are interpreted is what I call the *dyadic* conceptual scheme. It allows us to see the musical work as a polarity, a dyad between composition and interpretation, between the unchanging

1 I wish to express my sincere thanks to Laurie Schwartz, whose meticulous work in translating this chapter assumed the character of an extremely stimulating intellectual discussion which has influenced its present form.

2 See Quine (1980; 2013) and Davidson (1984).

text found in the score and any given performance: the aesthetic image of the work lies exactly within this magnetic tension. This attitude, deriving from the specific ontology of musical works in the Western written tradition (see Ingarden 1986), is well known, and I won't dwell on it.

It is interesting instead to note how this conceptual scheme is at the root of some famous formalizations of Western musical experience. Leaving aside Nelson Goodman's (1968) philosophical framework, these include, for instance, Lydia Goehr's (1995–6) dichotomy between the 'perfect performance of music' (work-oriented) and the 'perfect musical performance' (performance-centred). This model has been applied to the aesthetics of recording, for example in Handy Hamilton (2003), where the 'aesthetics of perfection' focuses on shaping a work of art through editing techniques in the recording process, while the 'aesthetics of imperfection' would tend to preserve the freshness of performance, refusing any 'optimizing' or 'compensating' action (Caporaletti 2007a).

But still, our starting point is the textual ontology of popular music. Here an important musicological theory holds – rightly, I believe – that if we linger inside a 'dyadic conceptual scheme' – 'surfing' between the notions of composition and performance, intrinsic to classical music – we cannot solve the problem of text in so-called popular music.[3] It follows – and here, I believe, less rightly – that in those repertoires of recorded music, an 'opus' cannot exist; what we have instead is a performative tradition, of which the recorded text is only a snapshot.[4]

This attitude derives, in my opinion, from the application of another conceptual scheme to recorded artefacts – which I call *oralistic* – that emerged in the ethnomusicological and anthropological tradition of studies of oral cultures. In those cultures, in fact, the concept of 'opus', as theorized by late-modern aesthetics (Kantian, Baumgartnerian), does not exist, nor does the Western concept of authorship, which is established by the coexistence of an author and an objectified artistic text. In the following pages, we will see how this condition relates to the textual ontology of oral cultures in which performative text, singing and dance – Bruno Nettl's 'units of musical thought' (2005: 117) – are configured inside a tradition which did not originate from, nor develop through a crystallization into, notationally codified or recorded texts, but rather through short-lived, transient

---

3 Nicholas Cook is an authoritative exponent of this position. With regard to the identity of the work in popular music, for instance, he says: 'We have here a continuum of creative acts which cannot be mapped onto the binary oppositions of work and performance, composition and interpretation' (Cook 1995: 436).

4 See Cook again: 'Read for its variety rather than its unity, a song like "Whole Lotta Love" is not so much a work as a performance tradition, within which we might distinguish two levels of variance: routine or gradual change from one occasion of performance to another, taking place within some kind of invariant framework, and catastrophic change, such as when Led Zeppelin reworked Willie Dixon's original. And in such a context, traditional notions of authorship and authority clearly need rethinking' (1995: 436).

and evanescent performances. This is the sense in which we can talk about an 'interpretative tradition', and not about 'opuses'.

As a consequence, we will see how musical processes, and in particular, rock, jazz and pop texts, are interpreted through these two competing conceptual schemes: dyadic and oralistic. This dyadic/oralistic super-scheme is characterized by a *binary fallacy*; in order to interpret the nature of recorded works of rock and jazz music, another conceptual scheme is required, which I will call *audiotactile*. In the audiotactile conceptual scheme, the notions of text and opus are reconfigured, and the matter of textual authority is rephrased.

The Audiotactile Conceptual Scheme

This is not the place for a detailed presentation or critical debate on the theory of audiotactile formativity (see Caporaletti 2000; 2005), of which I will only present a few specific applications. However, it is necessary to take a step back in time.

In the mid-1970s I began studying (first as a musician, then as a musicologist) the 'mysterious' motor sensory energy which in jazz culture is known as 'swing' and/or 'groove' (see also Caporaletti 2014). The only thing I am certain about, after years of research, is that interpreting swing and groove through Western rhythmic-metric categories leads to irreconcilable aporias. Swing and groove, in their micro-structural aspects, cannot be represented in 'traditional' musicological discourse, nor can they be concretely performed if we do not free ourselves from the cognitive system laid out by Western music theory and its technological by-product, musical notation, acquiring full awareness of its ideological implications from the perspective of a critical musicology.[5]

This happens for many reasons, including the irreversibility of the cognitive structures (Michel Imberty's *schèmes d'ordre*) implemented during improvisational processes (but also to control performance), and these are different from the reversible cognitive structures active during composition. Imberty relates these psycho-cognitive aspects to generic musical experiences, but I think they shed some light on how 'audiotactile' perceptional experiences can be described. We can assert as a matter of fact that the effect of *schèmes d'ordre* is fundamentally extraneous to the experience of (written) composition of the classical/romantic/modernist traditions (and to its aesthetic image), and that audiotactile formativity

[5] Beginning with Prögler (1995), on the basis of intuitions put forward by Charles Keil in the 1960s (see Keil 1994), a different orientation in studies on swing and groove appeared, using information technology to integrate metric-rhythmic categorizations. See also the notion of *entrainment* in London (2012), and the research presented in Fink (2001), Danielsen (2006) and others. For a detailed reconstruction of the critical debate on swing and groove in the USA and in Europe from the late nineteenth century until the present, see Caporaletti (2014): 1–184.

actually implies the use of both schemes.[6] Let us now examine the make-up of these various psycho-cognitive schemes.

> *Schèmes d'ordre* [order schemes] form the set of intuitions that a subject has of temporal series without being aware of the elements that make up these series. These are, therefore, intuitions which are motor-sensory or representational in nature, whose contents cannot be separated from the ordered sequences themselves. … *Schèmes de relation d'ordre* [order relationship schemes] organize the logic of the series within a period of time independent of the events that it contains. Each event, each note or chord, for example, has its position defined in relationship to other events, that is to say through a syntax. (Imberty 2003: 103)

Let us look at an example of how these schemes act with respect to musical cognition. *Schèmes de relation d'ordre* are responsible for our cognition of structural elements (notes, chords, scales, metres and so on). These entities are 'cognitively reversible', in that temporality plays no role in their cognitive constitution (they do not vary over time: a C is a C now, and it will be ten seconds from now). The important thing, in our context, is the fact that this particular cognitive scheme selects and forms a system of discrete units that can produce superordinate structures by means of various combinatorial rules. This is of the utmost importance in the structuring processes brought into play, for instance, by historically defined forms of tonality, or again in the organization of melodic linearity and the voice leading that ensues from it. A problem arises, however, when one attempts to formalize sonorous phenomena identifiable with extra-codified nebulas,[7] such as the sensorimotor energy of groove, that can be neither conceptualized nor performed – at the micro-structural level – by way of a syntactical combination of *discrete units* (quavers, semiquavers and so on, which, if anything, act on groove's macro-structural level), and that depend instead on the activation of global, non-segmented gestalt-like *textual units*, which in turn are the result of a bodily interface that continues to unfold over the flow of time (see Caporaletti 2014: 185ff.). Here, while dealing with a musicological representation, one must refer to the specifically corporeal 'rationality' discussed by Merleau-Ponty (1962), and not to Descartes's mathematical-deterministic *ratio* that presided over the development of modern music theory and that cannot account for an intentional relation, via systematics and rules, with this type of phenomenon. Groove, for example, beyond its macro-structural quality based on repetitive rhythms and metres, is produced above all in a micro-dimension of time, articulating a rhythmic

[6] In crude terms, the 12-note series used by Arnold Schoenberg in op. 25 does not imply a specific motor quality and an élan vital in its metric-rhythmic configuration, whereas the aesthetic sense of the ride cymbal played by the jazz drummer Elvin Jones is a kinetic-corporeal experience that can be fully perceived by the listener, since he/she feels it with as much physicality as the performer (see Keil 1994).

[7] For the notion of *extra-coding*, see Eco (1976): 136.

formula with stylized inflections that lie in the vicinity of 10–20 milliseconds, as the result of sonorous gestures and a musician's synaesthetic and psychophysical inclinations. It can thus be performed and perceived only during the temporal course of music, and not set out beforehand in written composition. One can only experience and produce these qualities through other types of cognitive activity, which in turn react to a context that progresses over time.

Schèmes d'ordre are none other than the psycho-cognitive foundations of those processual formal factors highly relevant to the repertories that I referred to previously (swing, groove, *laykārī* in Hindustani music, *repriz* or *lokans* in the Isle of Guadeloupe, *balanço* in Afro-Brazilian music, *ombak* in gamelan music and so on).[8] Our conceptual scheme, when we realize these *schèmes d'ordre*, is generated by the particular construction of reality set up by our sensory faculties through the psycho-corporeal medium, which reformulates and reconfigures the 'theory-laden' aspect of Western music theory. In keeping with a cognitive-anthropological perspective, I have named this cognitive psycho-corporeal medium the *audiotactile principle* (ATP).

Audiotactile music theory is based on the mediological[9] element of a general framework of research on sensorial and cognitive outcomes induced by the means (media) through which culture is produced and communicated.[10] The formative and communicational function of the medium is intended as a constituent of the perceptive and cognitive arrangements, in line with the outcomes of contemporary epistemology, well delineated by Norwood Russell Hanson: 'Observation of *x* is shaped by prior knowledge of *x*. Another influence on observations rests in the language or notation used to express what we know, and without which there would be little we could recognize as knowledge' (1975: 19). Applying this perspective – according to which a theoretical model or a communication channel is hypostasized, predetermining the

---

8 For an in-depth discussion of this topic, particularly through the experience and perception of Darius Milhaud, who discovered these sensory motor phenomena in Brazil in 1917, see Caporaletti (2012).

9 Thus, seizing upon the methodological requisites posed again by Bruno Nettl: 'Do oral and aural transmission and oral creation affect the forms of pieces and repertories? No doubt they must, but we have no theory to explain just how' (2005: 296). And with specific reference to the effects of phonographic recording on forms and repertoires: '… the field has not developed much by way of a generalized theory' (Nettl 2005: 292).

10 With respect to the theoretical framework to which we refer (particularly the Toronto School of Marshall McLuhan, Derrick De Kerkhove and Harold Innis, but also the mediology of Regis Debray, and with reference to the 'mediality' of language and of symbolic systems in general, Wittgenstein, Whorf and others, Heidegger included), the specific conception of the formative/communicative medium plays a decisive role as a conceptual supporting model, and is not considered neutral for the purpose of message configuration and reception. As a consequence, prominence is given to the dynamic function which epistemic principles carry out in the structuring of the constructs themselves, as well as on the reconfiguration of the perceptive structure and on the conceptual pattern of whoever produces or receives them.

very synthesis of the data according to its own epistemic working logic – to music, the psycho-corporeal function, as the medium influencing and guiding perceptive and cognitive outcomes, is identified as the *audiotactile principle*. We define the homologous one carried out by the operating system of standard Western musical notation and conceived by Western musical theory, as the *visual* function.[11]

This cognitive/perceptive function of predetermination is promoted by the medium according to the guidelines of its specific 'operating system', the working logic of its intrinsic internal 'programme'. For instance, the visual logic of notation can, in the first place, be considered as promoting, on a phenomenological level, a 'technique of fragmentation' of the sonic landscape and a consequent generative-combinatorial compositional strategy which controls the immanent mechanistic quality of the Western theoretical system as pointed out by Adorno: 'the rational and mechanical principle that pervades the entire history of Western music' (1998: 305). But it can also be represented by the epistemological principles inherent in the written medium, of lineality, sequentiality, segmentation of experience, uniform repeatability, inside an abstract and mathematized order.[12] The coherence of motific integration and the rules of voice leading in a polyphonic context, or the structuring of numerical relations of learned harmony, are merely the more evident epiphenomena of these deep epistemic structures.

Conversely, the notion of autographicity plays a key role within the context of the audiotactile conceptual scheme.[13] As everyone knows, Nelson Goodman links the autographic quality to visual arts, where the 'hand' of the artist has a great importance in the definition of the identity of a work of art, and thus a copy of the *Mona Lisa* becomes a forgery. However, he considers music an allographic art (the copy of the score of Beethoven's Fifth Symphony is not a forgery, and there is a notation that sets the work up for performance). This perspective, of course, only holds if we consider written Western music (where the process of musical reproduction of a

[11] Mediological functions identified by notational visuality and by the ATP are to be intended, on the anthropological level, as the foundation of cultural cycles, with respect to the pre-eminence and pervasiveness imposed by their operational logic on the cognitive processes in a given era or cultural context (that is, for European art music of the common practice and the contemporary repertories of jazz, rock, popular, and world music).

[12] The quantitative reduction of the holistic qualities of sound reality fostered some elements as creatively feasible and expunged others which, instead, are free to exist inside a cognitive audiotactile order. For instance, the possibility of creating a formal plexus endowed with meaning and relevance in the domain of 'good rhythmic organization' (in the sense of the *Gestalt* theory) and based on the energetic modulation of temporal micro-entities which in ATP-based music is known as 'swing' or 'groove' in jazz or *laykārī* in Hindustani music, is compromised in the very 'musical conceivability' of European tonal music (see Caporaletti 2005).

[13] I adopt a concept expressed by Nelson Goodman in *Languages of Art* (1968), albeit in a new sense. Besides, Goodman pointed out other specifications in the allographic/autographic dichotomy (such as singular/plural, single-stage/double-stage), even though we will only consider the basic notions of his categorizations.

written text presumes a distinction between composer and performer), but it is not valid for audiotactile music such as jazz, rock and pop, in which the score undergoes a 'mediological subsumption' by the ATP, with the primacy of gesture over text. In this case, I propose a reversal of Goodman's theory with relation to the effect of the ATP in musical formativity which is made explicit in musical autographicity.

From this perspective, the history of the production of the sign that objectifies the compositional/creative idea – for audiotactile music, the realization of the material/sub-syntactical values of sound in their phenomenological actuality, crystallized later by the phonographic recording – is a decisive factor. In Goodman's terms:

> What distinguishes an allographic work is that identification of an object or event as an instance of the work depends not at all upon how or when or by whom that object or event was produced. (Goodman 1984: 140)
>
> … Let us speak of a work of art as *autographic* if and only if the distinction between original and forgery of it is significant; or better, if and only if the most exact duplication of it does not thereby count as genuine. (Goodman 1968: 113)

These instructions suit jazz and rock perfectly, because in practice the 'who', 'where' and 'when' of a certain recording determine an 'opus' (for the time being). As for the issue of forgery, I have discovered and published a case of forgery related to a version of Charlie Parker's 'A Night in Tunisia', a 'fake' published as an original in the collected works of that author edited by the label Philology (see Caporaletti 2007b). And this holds true both for genres which are more artist-centred, like jazz and rock, and for those which are more centred on the producer or the sound engineering, like pop music:[14] the idiosyncratic configuration that is taken on by the sonic signature at the sub-syntactical level is a pertinent trait.

These ideas outline a new perspective that can help us to interpret certain culturally meaningful phenomena in the aesthetics of those musical genres where audiotactile formativity comes into play. An implementation of the audiotactile conceptual scheme gives rise to culture-specific autographic values in two distinct dimensions: in the micro-structure or micro-timing with the sub-syntactical features of phenomena such as swing, groove, participatory discrepancies (Keil 1994), sound projection, drive and so on, and in the macro-structure with improvisational processes.

The Identity of the Audiotactile Text: Neo-auratic Encoding

These ideas also foreshadow an alternative representation of text in jazz, rock and pop, in view of the audiotactile conceptual scheme. Here, *the autographic*

[14] On the concept of producer-centred production, see Blake (2009). On engineer-centred production, see Zak (2009).

text is inscribed neo-auratically into the audio(visual) process of phono-fixation.[15] But what do we mean by 'neo-auratically'?[16] In the phenomenology of music based on the audiotactile formative medium, the text 'processing' carried out by the phonographic recording (whether the text is a performance of a pre-composed/written plan – with an 'open' encoding – or has an exclusively performative nature) plays a crucial role. A definitive textual status derives from this phono-fixation, acting similarly to the notational crystallization typical of 'written' composition in the individualized authorship of the Western art music tradition[17] (even though firmly attached to the audiotactile performative dimension). The possibility of using the phonographic recording medium as a creative tool gives rise, in audiotactile music, to consequences of a cognitive nature: these in fact also exist as a conceptual scheme in performances which are not recorded, as a cultural possibility informing the performers' cognitive system. Such cognitive behaviour is reflected upon the aesthetic image of audiotactile music as a distinctive feature, in contrast to the music of traditional/oral cultures, which are analogous under the profile of audiotactile formativity.

The repertoires of oral traditions, also based on the formative mediation of the ATP, did not originate or develop historically through the formative medium of phonographic recording, which intersects with them only *a posteriori*, as an ethnomusicological document. Instead, from its initial musical conceptualization up to its phenomenological manifestations, audiotactile music (including so-called urban popular traditions) is permeated by the formative/cognitive influence of the phonographic recording medium. I have traced back the theoretical component to the notion of 'neo-auratic encoding' (NAE), differing from the idea of the loss of aura for the artwork in the era of mechanical reproducibility, as theorized in 1936 by Walter Benjamin.

If it is unquestionable, indeed, that mechanical reproducibility forces us to renounce the *hic et nunc* of the work, it is also true that the ATP finds in the phonographic recording the means for a fixation of significant indexes of processual/phenomenal qualities, thus building a new model of 'auraticity' through technological means for these musical formations. Such objectified textualization, rescuing musical form from the evanescence which is ontological in oral cultures,

[15] We will see how the magnetic tape medium has played a particular role in segmenting the semantic field of the 'recording'. It is therefore incorrect to place the magnetic tape medium in the same category as the phonographic medium, identifying a 'magnetic tape and vinyl' phase in the periodization of the history of recorded music, as David Patmore (2009: 120) does by drawing on Cyril Ehrlich's classification. In this case, there is some confusion between the technological medium and the primary and secondary level of NAE (see below).

[16] For a more extensive discussion on the notion of NAE, see Caporaletti (2005): 121–34 and Caporaletti (2004).

[17] By 'Western art music tradition', I mean the age of the *werktreues Ideal* (the German *Fassung letzter Hand*), between the mid-nineteenth and mid-twentieth centuries.

has a relevant mediological effect. The technology of sound crystallization renders audiotactile music available to the categories of late-modern aesthetics – creative originality, autonomy of the work, 'disinterested' reception, personal artistic consciousness, mobility of the norm – thus cancelling *de facto* the opposition between 'low' and 'high' culture. Therefore, the technological 'inscription' of the ATP, that is to say, its phonographic fixation connected to the processes of NAE – or the 'inherent' possibility of such crystallization as a conceptual scheme, which also shapes artistic awareness in non-recorded performances – circumscribes the phenomenological and cognitive area, in which the instances of audiotactile music are projected. In the information-/electronic-centred culture of technological globalization, oral traditions are disappearing for good and are acquiring the features of audiotactile music.

On the basis of an anthropology of the text, we can determine an ontological difference between the practices of oral tradition, where the text, even though produced through the cognitive mediation of the ATP, is evanescent and coincides with the very moment of the performance, and on the other hand audiotactile music, where the text mediated by the ATP is crystallized by NAE in a stable and objective form.

A prophetic phrase by Luciano Berio regarding this matter clarifies this perspective:

> If Walter Benjamin were still among us, he would have nothing to worry about, he could set his mind at rest: the same means that contribute to the reproducibility of the work, and hence to the crisis of its authority, its authenticity, its 'aura', may perhaps be the very means that contribute in the future to a different definition of its authority, its authenticity, its 'aura'. (Berio 2006: 66)

Neo-auratic encoding – not to be confused with the material aspect of sound recording, in so far as it is, rather, the cognitive and mediological effect of the recording medium – is a factor which contributes to the articulation of the taxonomy of musical experiences within the perspective of a textual anthropology.

The Triadic Model and NAE Operating Patterns

In my triadic model, the three different conceptual schemes identify three distinct operative implementations of neo-auratic encoding, which are important for the definition of the semantic field of sound recording experiences: optimizing/compensative (dyadic scheme), documentary (oralistic scheme) and creative (audiotactile) (see Table 13.1). The phenomenological function of the textual objectivation in NAE shows well-defined stylistic materializations or operational patterns depending on the conception – the ideological model – that lies in the background.

Table 13.1 The triadic model and NAE operating patterns – synchronic perspective

Conceptual scheme	**Phenomenology**	**Textual identity**	**NAE operating patterns**
Dyadic (European written tradition)	Allographic	Dialectic tension between score and performance	Optimizing/ compensating
Oralistic (oral musical traditions)	Autographic evanescent	Performance is the only manifestation of the text	Documentary ethnographic
Audiotactile (jazz, rock, pop, world music)	Autographic	The audio (video) recording is the text	Creative

Precisely because of the absence of a text fixed through objectivation via the traditional (written) process of music production and communication, an oralistic view of the musical event generally implies a resistance to phono-fixation, especially in the de-contextualized recording studio.[18] An *a posteriori* ethnographic documentary approach, aiming to provide a 'neutral' representation of performance, can be contemplated in this particular oralistic conceptual scheme. Alas, this is but an illusory position, as it implies the transparency and ineffectuality of the recording medium. Furthermore, this theoretical position, particularly for jazz or rock artists, considers musicians as exponents of a traditional culture, with a shared patrimony of cultural heritage in which creation is not configured authorially (or, better, in which there is no authorial attribution, whether owing to a communal creative process[19] or due to a loss of authorial memory).[20]

[18] This was manifest in the behaviour of many musicians, especially in the early stages of sound recording technology, in the friction between oral and audiotactile cultures. For a discussion on the socio-psychological disruptions caused by NAE within the oral culture of New Orleans musicians when the first recordings by the Original Dixieland 'Jass' Band appeared, see Caporaletti (2011: 74ff).

[19] The notion of anonymous communal creation is a legacy of the Romantic tradition of the Grimm brothers and Ludwig Uhland. The disposition to creative variation was then taken up and supported in the context of ethnomusicology with the concept of *Variation-trieb* by Constantin Brăiloiu (1984). This structuralistic viewpoint seems to correspond to the systemic, ahistoric impersonality of his representation of creativity in traditional cultures. For the notion of Phillips Barry's 'communal re-creation', see Barry (1910; 1933). For an innovative perspective on the authorial dimensions in oral cultures, see Nattiez (1993) and Cavanagh (1982).

[20] The present discussion is not concerned with the aspect of authoriality as it pertains to traditional cultures, since it is not relevant to the theoretical model presented here. As a matter of fact, the possibility or impossibility of encoding a 'musical conceptualization unit' (*both* authorial or anonymous) – that is to say, the feasibility of a practical fixation in

Each and every NAE transforms oralistic texts into audiotactile ones, bestowing upon them an objectified status, in contrast to oralistic phenomenology. This aspect pertains both to discographical production and to the attitude of radio broadcasting during the first half of the twentieth century, for which a recorded broadcast was considered 'faked' and unfair.[21]

In the dyadic and audiotactile conceptual schemes, however, we have a real textual objectification, via score and phono-fixation. This produces a deep awareness of neo-auratic work-oriented implications, which are carried out in original creativity, aesthetic autonomy, mobility of the aesthetic norm and 'disinterested' contemplation (in the Kantian sense of non-functional fruition) on the part of the audience, and artistic self-awareness on the part of the musician. This produces two different kinds of behaviour: one is aimed at performative optimization, the other at developing an aesthetic that is intrinsically 'anti-realistic' or 'creative', shaping new timbral-phonic worlds centred on technological values similar to electroacoustic music: in fact, sound dimensions did not previously have a correspondence in the traditional ecological dimensions of a live performance. The first historical examples of the creative sound sphere in pop music are Les Paul's experiments with multi-track recording in 1948, the use of reverberation in the Sun Records by Jack Clement and Sam Phillips in the 1950s, Phil Spector's 'wall of sound' and the contemporaneous work of Joe Meek in the UK in the 1960s, Frank Zappa's xenochrony, and the use of multi-tracking in general ever since The Beatles (even if this technique itself includes the two aesthetics).

The performative optimization and the compensatory attitude of neo-auratic phenomenology (the improvement of performance and the reduction and correction of errors through editing) are particularly affected by the dyadic conceptual scheme of 'composition/performance': the performance guarantees the ontological status of creative objectivation as an implicit counterpart of a written and self-sufficient work. It is clear that Adorno's *Reproduktion* function (interpretation) is aimed at a perfectibility of score instantiation, which would eliminate idiosyncratic and erratic performative inaccuracies, casting itself in a sphere of ideal correspondence with the numinous and definitive quality of the creative idea sedimented through writing. Here, the uniqueness and individuality of the written text demands a structural homology, an ideal uniqueness of the performative possibility (which is, of course, a utopian point that is never truly reached). In the operational sphere, this is manifested through a compensative attitude exercised by the editing and selection of repeated takes.

---

a form other than pure performance (which is itself volatile and ephemeral) – is a pertinent and decisive factor for various anthropological structures within a perspective of textual anthropology.

21 'Perhaps the biggest difference between today's radio and radio before 1945 was that back then it was considered unethical to play records on the air. It was thought that by playing a record you were trying to fool people into believing a performance was live when it really was not …' (see Covach 2006: 20).

The third model, the audiotactile, is fully in keeping with the epistemic principles hingeing on the notion of NAE, and with audiotactile autographic specificity: there is a homology between the conceptual scheme, practices and processed materials. For this reason, sound recording imposes self-established determinants, thus revealing an audiotactile anthropological-cognitive model that incorporates autographic values during the act of composing (and in its concomitant performative realizations). It is not surprising that these cognitive attitudes are intrinsic to the mediological factor of textual fixation that NAE shares with notated written text.

The Primary and Secondary Perspectives of NAE

What we have just outlined is but a systemic representation of a triadic model of conceptual schemes. In order to fully grasp these dynamics, it is important to move from a synchronic representation to a diachronic, historical one. There has been an implicit awareness of a 'catastrophic' gap (as René Thom and Erik Zeeman would term it) in the history of popular music of the twentieth century. Both Allen Forte and Alec Wilder, in their books on American popular song, acknowledge the chronological conclusion of a historical phase in 1950.[22]

In order to understand how technological innovation and aesthetic criteria interact with one another, we must address some issues related to the parameter of temporal integrity of the recorded phenomenon/sound event, which is how the relationship between NAE and ontological time has historically evolved. As we know, the availability of sound recording introduced the possibility of rendering sound 'objective', causing it to become phenomenologically relevant in an 'ontology of objectuality', in Molino's (1998) words. But this process has another important consequence: the possibility of reversing ontological time, given the temporal reversibility of the process of recording, which can be achieved simply by replaying the event. We can define this process, using the semiotic categories of Nattiez (1975) and Molino, as the *subversion of diachronic integrity in the aesthesic phase*.

This first phenomenological level, which I call the *primary NAE* in reference to the anthropological innovation of the objectified textualization of the sound artefact, encompasses the following aesthetic effects: valorization of creative originality, aesthetic autonomy, identitary artistic assumption and fruition, mobility of the aesthetic norm, and *Wirkungsgeschichte*.

With magnetic tape, however, there is a *subversion of the diachronic integrity of the sound event in the poietic phase*, which produces some interesting effects. I call this condition the *secondary NAE*. These phenomenological dimensions interact with the conceptual scheme in the representation and creation of sound (see Table 13.2).

[22] See Wilder (1972): xxxv–xxxvi ('By 1950 ... a long era in popular music was drawing to a close') and Forte (1995): 3–4 ('The year 1950 ... marked the closing of the career of many of the major songwriters and lyricists of the Golden Era').

Table 13.2 Subversion of diachronic integrity in the poietic and aesthesic phases with two anthropological shifts

Pre-1950	Primary NAE	Subversion of diachronic integrity in the aesthesic phase
Post-1950	Secondary NAE	Subversion of diachronic integrity *also* in the poietic phase

Text as Score and Performance

In the first half of the twentieth century, for obvious historical-sociological reasons, the dyadic conceptual scheme was the prevailing one, and it 'processed' the primary NAE. In contrast to pure performance, the sound recording became distinct, especially with regard to the aesthesic polarity of the temporal reversibility of a given event – the possibility of replaying a piece multiple times. The piece itself remained diachronically intact over time. In fact, because of historical and technological contingencies, there was no artistically valid way to interfere with the internal diachronicity of a musical performance[23] (the 'set time' in terms of the taxonomy of performative temporalities by Schechner 2003: 6–8). The musical performance offered itself to technological processing as an intangible and self-sufficient performative factor.[24]

In this sense, with regard to acoustic and electronic recording during the first half of the twentieth century, we can speak of the *reproducibility* of a given performance, in line with the traditional dyadic conceptual scheme, wherein performance guarantees the ontological identity of the artwork. From the point of view of the operating models of NAE, the documentary function of a given performance therefore prevails, both for the music of the written tradition (allographic) and for the autographic practices of jazz. In this latter case, we have a *dystonic condition*, in which audiotactile practices were cognitively processed by the persistent dyadic conceptual scheme: this was also active in radio broadcasting, which rejected the 'fakeness' of recording in favour of an ethic of live performance mediatized by the radiophonic medium.

Recording as Text

This situation underwent a change when magnetic tape technology, introduced shortly after the end of the Second World War, offered the possibility to interfere

23 The technique of recording disc-to-disc led to crackling noises.

24 In a top-down view, the reciprocal can also be valid: namely, the dyadic conceptual scheme discouraged the search for devices that would subvert diachronic integrity in the poietic phase, given the devaluation of the aesthetic potentiality of this practice, brought about by the dyadic cognitive model.

with the internal diachronicity of a sound event, borrowing the already well-established technique and aesthetic of montage from cinematographic art. In this case, the recorded artefact moved away from the ecological dimension of the performance; an audiotactile conceptual scheme began to control the audiotactile practices of rock, also transforming the image of jazz (with the crucial passage through jazz-rock) and introducing a radical modification in the perception of the Western art music tradition.

A homology was established *de facto* between the *type* of conceptual scheme and the *phenomenology* of the practices. Therefore, if in past times a dyadic conceptual scheme also formalized practices which were not intrinsically connatural with it, whether they were audiotactile jazz improvisation practices or Tin Pan Alley songs, now an audiotactile conceptual scheme imposed the autographic quality during the very act of composing audiotactile texts – which induced Leiber and Stoller, two of the Brill Building's most famous songwriters, to say: 'we write records' (see Covach 2006: 20).

From the point of view of the NAE operational model, by privileging its consubstantial values, the autographic quality in the poietic phase directed the configuration of the recorded text/composition towards a *xenochronic* regime (in Frank Zappa's terms), with a subversion of the internal diachronicity through the editing process and through the use of multi-track devices and/or overdubbing. In this way, different *dynamic vectors* (in Imberty's terms) were incorporated into the very act of composing (not only in performance/improvisation, as was the case with pre-war jazz). Thus, the phenomenological scenario of the rock tradition took shape: here is the true sense of Miles Davis's transition to jazz-rock, which is to be understood not in terms of pure rhythmic grooves, but in light of a transformation of the dyadic conception of NAE (still at work in his famous second quintet in the 1960s) into an audiotactile one (also subverting the diachronic integrity of the sound event in the poietic phase with overdubs and tape splices).

Formal features deriving from corporeal interaction (which cannot be controlled cognitively) and *a priori*, personalized idiosyncratic aspects (which cannot be predetermined) come into play in the (recorded) composition of popular music, in the creation of a song (and not only during interpretation). This feature was not present in the dyadic composition of Tin Pan Alley's songs. This personalization also spread to other variables of the text, in search for an original 'sound signature' and for ways of structuring the sonic landscape consubstantial with audiotactile autography.

On the other hand, because of the allographic quality of the 'classical' repertoire, the all-encompassing audiotactile conception of the text as recording imposed an aesthetic in which factors which optimize and/or compensate the performance ended up forming the leading criterion. We can then consider the first part of the twentieth century as the 'age of technical reproducibility', and starting from the second, the 'age of technical producibility' of the audiotactile and autographic work of musical art (see Figure 13.1).

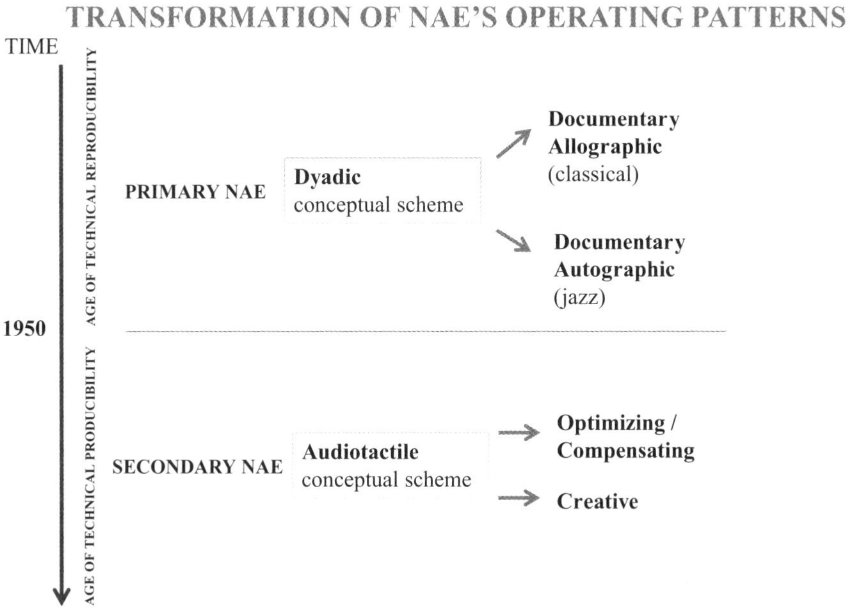

Figure 13.1 NAE operating patterns – diachronic perspective

Further Applications of the Theoretical Model

I believe that this theoretical model resolves some problematic issues and offers a key to rephrase some assumptions in the literature. With regard to secondary NAE, in the words of Carl Belz:

> rock has existed primarily on records. In this, the music is rather different from jazz and traditional folk music *to which it is related*. Although jazz and other types of folk music exist on records, they did not originate in that medium. For the most part, they *originated and developed* through live performances. Rock, it seems to me, has generally done the opposite. Records were the music's initial medium. (Belz 1972: viii; italics added)

Belz, after noticing the common phenomenological affiliation of rock, jazz and folk (but without specifying the *kind* of phenomenology, based on the ATP), rightly considers the genetic aspect and the development of jazz and folk traditions as relevant factors in their relationships with recording technology. Regarding jazz, however, the issue must be reformulated as a function of the *terminus ab quo* (the nineteenth century or the 1910s?), the starting point for the tradition. Initially, it was oral, therefore folk; from 1917 (or even before, depending upon different interpretations) onwards, it became part of the history of recording. At any rate, the main point is that pre-Second World War jazz is an expression of the primary NAE, and rock is an expression of the secondary NAE.

With respect to the metamorphosis of the conceptual scheme (described as moving from dyadic to audiotactile), Robynn Stilwell agrees on placing the border around 1950: 'with the arrival of the 45 rpm single and the 33 1/3 rpm album … sheet music and even live performance receded as the definition of a piece of music; according to Rebee Garofalo, 1952 was the first year in which record sales outstripped sheet music in sales revenue' (2004: 428).

However, there is some confusion between the levels of neo-auratic operativity. Stilwell's perspective is correct in terms of the conceptual scheme ('sheet music and even live performance receded as the *definition* of a piece of music'), but she misses the relevance of temporal reversibility (or subversion of chronological integrity) during the poietic phase, possible thanks to the first technological device, the magnetic recording. The change in the conceptual scheme cannot be ascribed to the diffusion of 33 r.p.m. or 45 r.p.m. discs or to the 'increased exposure of recordings on radio and television': this mistakes cause for effect, for these sociological phenomena must be explained.

Let us consider the position of Glenn Gould, who in 'The Prospects of Recordings' (1984) announced the imminent death of the 'habit of concert-going and concert-giving', and declared the LP to be the modern embodiment of music, predicting that tomorrow's people would ridicule the idea that 'the concert is the axis upon which the world of music revolves'. We must not confuse Gould's position with ours. His vision is inspired by a McLuhanism that is perhaps a bit too mechanistic: in fact, it is focused on detecting macroscopic and palingenetic effects of changes 'in pace or scale or pattern' (McLuhan 1994: 24) brought about by electronic technology, hence the envisioned obsolescence of concert life (a prediction that really never happened). Gould refers to the LP overlooking the sense of transformation of the secondary NAE afforded by the recording on magnetic tape: when he speaks of 'recording', he does not distinguish the *storage* medium of musical information in and of itself from the *internal logic*, the operating system of the storage, which concerns the primary or secondary quality of NAE (even though, in practice, he had a positive relationship with editing). The problem with Gould's position and his search for a 'definitive' recording is that it approaches the secondary NAE from the point of view of the written and allographic tradition, disregarding the sense of audiotactile formativity and of the neo-auratic encoding of the ATP: its innovative consequences in terms of form and aesthetic values in fact forestalled the predicted end of concert life.

Ultimately, the present theoretical model can help to clarify crucial aesthetic questions about multiple recordings (in the studio or live) of the same audiotactile opus/song. Their audiotactile nature itself places jazz, rock, pop, so-called world beat and so on ontologically outside the Western written music tradition. One issue in particular has yet to be defined: if the recording is the text, what is the original audiotactile text in the case of multiple recorded versions of the same piece? Now that we have the autographic nature of the audiotactile text fresh in our minds, we can see how the autographic art of painting has already answered this issue. The Rouen Cathedral series by the French painter Claude Monet captures the cathedral's façade under different light conditions. Monet made more than thirty of these paintings between 1892 and 1893, and reworked them in his studio in 1894: nobody would ever consider the various representations of the cathedral as different instances of the same 'opus'.

We must absolutely recognize the relevance of the first studio version, especially in rock music, where there is an evident intentional projection of the 'formal wish' in setting up the sonic landscape, in the equalization, and in the textural and dynamic balance. However – and this is an unquestioned criterion in jazz due to its improvisational character – it must be acknowledged that every recorded live performance represents a separate 'opus' which must be aesthetically evaluated and analysed in relation to other instances of the same piece. This goes for both studio versions and live performances.

In recorded replicas of a given audiotactile piece, both remixes and live, the reference class set up by the notational dyadic ideology – based on a syntagmatic string of melodic-harmonic/rhythmic-metric syntax – recedes in favour of a proliferation of contextual *language* phenomena; these are linked to the idiosyncratic vitality of performative expressivity or technological reformulation of the sonic signature, neo-auratically encoded. Thus, drawing a comparison with linguistics, the significant distinctiveness does not lie in traits discernible on the phonematic level, but in suprasegmental factors like those that occur in tonal languages. In this sense, all of the multiple versions of a given piece are actually different 'works' because, under the textual profile, they exhibit different compositional features that are aesthetically and culturally relevant.

Translated by Laurie Schwartz

References

Adorno, Theodor W. (1998) 'Vers une musique informelle', in *Quasi una fantasia: Essays on Modern Music*, London: Verso.

Barry, Phillips (1910) 'The Origins of Folk Melodies', *Journal of American Folklore*, 23, pp. 440–45.

——— (1933) 'Communal Re-creation', *Bulletin of the Folk Song Society of the Northeast*, 5, pp. 5–6.

Belz, Carl (1972) *The Story of Rock*, 2nd edn, New York: Oxford University Press.

Benjamin, Walter (1936) 'Das Kunstwerk im Zeitalter seiner technischen Reproduzierbarkeit', in *Gesammelte Schriften*, vol. 1, Frankfurt am Main: Suhrkamp.

Berio, Luciano (2006) *Remembering the Future*, Cambridge, MA: Harvard University Press.

Blake, Andrew (2009) 'Recording Practices and the Role of Producer', in Cook et al. (2009), pp. 36–53.

Brăiloiu, Constantin (1984) *Problems of Ethnomusicology*, Cambridge: Cambridge University Press.

Caporaletti, Vincenzo (2000) *La definizione dello swing: i fondamenti estetici del jazz e delle musiche audiotattili*, Teramo: Ideasuoni.

——— (2004) 'Musica audiotattile e musica di tradizione orale', *Musica Theorica Spectrum*, 7, pp. 2–19.

——— (2005) *I processi improvvisativi nella musica. Un approccio globale*, Lucca: LIM.

——— (2007a) 'Codifica neoauratica e post-produzione: alcuni effetti sul jazz', in *Il suono registrato*, ed. Paolo Russo and Alessandro Rigolli, Turin: EdT, pp. 127–41.

——— (2007b) 'Miniature audiotattili. I *break* di Charlie Parker nelle 24 incisioni di *Night in Tunisia*', *Acoustical Arts and Artifacts: Technology, Aesthetics, Communication*, 3, pp. 97–111.

——— (2011) *Jelly Roll Morton, the 'Old Quadrille' and 'Tiger Rag': A Historiographic Revision*, Lucca: LIM.

——— (2012) 'Milhaud, *Le bœuf sur le toit* e o paradigma audiotátil', in *O boi no telhado. Darius Milhaud e a música brasileira no modernismo francés*, ed. Manoel Aranha Corrêa do Lago, São Paulo: Instituto Moreira Salles, pp. 229–88.

——— (2014) *Swing e Groove. Sui fondamenti estetici delle musiche audiotattili*, Lucca: LIM.

Cavanagh, Beverly (1982) *Music of the Netsilik Eskimo: A Study of Stability and Change*, 2 vols, Ottawa: National Museums of Canada.

Cook, Nicholas (1995) 'Music Theory and the Postmodern Muse: An Afterword', in *Concert Music, Rock and Jazz since 1945: Essays and Analytical Studies*, ed. Elizabeth W. Marvin and, Richard Hermann, Rochester, NY: Rochester University Press, pp. 422–39.

——— (1998) *Music: A Very Short Introduction*, Oxford: Oxford University Press.

———, Clarke, Eric, Leech-Wilkinson, Daniel and Rink, John (eds) (2009) *The Cambridge Companion to Recorded Music*, Cambridge: Cambridge University Press.

Covach, John (2006) *What's that Sound? An Introduction to Rock and Its History*, New York: Norton.

Danielsen, Anne (2006) *Presence and Pleasure: The Funk Grooves of James Brown and Parliament*, Middleton, CT: Wesleyan University Press.

Deleuze, Gilles (1997) *Negotiations 1972–1990*, New York: Columbia University Press.

Davidson, Donald (1984) *Inquiries into Truth and Interpretation*, Oxford: Oxford University Press.

Dawkins, Richard (1995) *River Out of Eden: A Darwinian View of Life*, London: Phoenix.

Eco, Umberto (1976) *A Theory of Semiotics*, Bloomington, IN: Indiana University Press.

Fink, Robert (2011) 'Goal-directed Soul? Analyzing Rhythmic Teleology in African American Popular Music', *Journal of the American Musicological Society*, 64/1, pp. 179–238.

Forte, Allen (1995) *The American Popular Ballad of the Golden Era, 1924–1950: A Study in Musical Design*, Princeton, NJ: Princeton University Press.

Goehr, Lydia (1995–96) 'The Perfect Performance of Music and the Perfect Musical Performance', *New Formations*, 27, pp. 1–22.

Goodman, Nelson (1968) *Languages of Art: An Approach to a Theory of Symbols*, Indianapolis, IN: Bobbs-Merrill.

——— (1984) *On Mind and Other Matters*, Cambridge, MA: Harvard University Press.

Gould, Glenn (1984) 'The Prospects of Recording', in *The Glenn Gould Reader*, ed. Tim Page, New York: A. Knopf, pp. 331–53.

Hamilton, Handy (2003) 'The Art of Recording and the Aesthetics of Perfection', *British Journal of Aesthetics*, 43/4, pp. 345–62.

Hanson, Norwood Russell (1975) *Patterns of Discovery* [1958], Cambridge: Cambridge University Press.

Imberty, Michel (2003) 'Langage, musique et cognition: quelques remarques sur l'évolution nécessaire des problématiques psychologiques des vingt dernières années', *Circuit: musiques contemporaines*, 13/2, pp. 93–110.

Ingarden, Roman (1986) *The Work of Music and the Problem of Its Identity*, trans. A. Czerniawski, ed. J.G. Harrell, Berkeley, CA: University of California Press.

Keil, Charles (1994) 'Motion and Feeling through Music', in *Music Grooves*, ed. Charles Keil and Steven Feld, Chicago, IL: University of Chicago Press, pp. 53–76.

London, Justin (2012) *Hearing in Time: Psychological Aspects of Musical Meter*, 2nd edn, Oxford: Oxford University Press.

McLuhan, Marshall (1994) *Understanding Media: The Extensions of Man*, Cambridge, MA: MIT Press.

Merleau-Ponty, Maurice (1962) *Phenomenology of Perception*, trans. Colin Smith, London: Routledge & Kegan Paul.

Molino, Jean (1998) 'Expérience et connaissance de la musique à l'âge des neurosciences', in *Le temps et la forme*, ed. Etienne Darbellay, Geneva: DROZ, pp. 253–280.

Nattiez, Jean-Jacques (1975) *Fondements d'une sémiologie de la musique*, Paris: Union Générale d'Edition.

——— (1993) *Le combat de Chronos et d'Orphée*, Paris: Christian Bourgois.

Nettl, Bruno (2005) *The Study of Ethnomusicology: Thirty-one Issues and Concepts*, Urbana, IL: University of Illinois Press.

Patmore, David (2009) 'Selling Sounds: Recordings and the Record Business', in Cook et al. (2009), pp. 120–39.

Prögler, J.A. (1995) 'Searching for Swing: Participatory Discrepancies in the Jazz Rhythm Section', *Ethnomusicology*, 39, pp. 21–54.

Quine, Willard Van Orman (1980) *From a Logical Point of View: Nine Logico-philosophical Essays*, 2nd rev. edn, Cambridge, MA: Harvard University Press.
——— (2013) *Word and Object* [1960], Cambridge, MA: MIT Press.
Schechner, Richard (2003) *Performance Theory*, (rev. and expanded edn, London: Routledge.
Stilwell, Robynn (2004) 'Music of the Youth Revolution: Rock through the 1960s', in Cook et al. (2009), pp. 418–52.
Wilder, Alec (1972) *American Popular Songs: The Great Innovators, 1900–1950*, Oxford: Oxford University Press.
Zak, Albin (2009) 'Getting Sounds: The Art of Sound Engineering', in: Cook et al. (2009), pp. 63–76.

Chapter 14

'If a Song Could Get Me You': Analysis and the (Pop) Listener's Perspective[1]

Dietrich Helms

My project of a functional pragmatic approach towards the analysis of music from a listener's perspective did not start from theory, it started from analysis, or to be more precise, from pondering possible ways to cope with problems of analysing popular music (Helms 2002). It is concerned not so much with discussing semiotics in music, but with finding ways to approach analytically a music that is performed and recorded rather than written down in a score, a music that has to be watched and listened to, and not read.

Every analysis has to consider four aspects:

1. the object that is to be described as a whole made up of parts;
2. the material it is supposed to be made of, or rather its smallest possible units;
3. the method that is used to describe it;
4. the issue that is to be studied or the question that is to be answered.

In a nutshell, a traditional musicological analysis would deal with a piece of music from the canon of classical – or better, art – music as objectified in a score. It would define notes (representing pitches of varying duration) as the smallest possible unit;[2] and it would – with the help, for example, of Schenkerian theory – aim to describe the form that is created by a composer in arranging the medium: the notes. Some analyses would venture further and discuss meaning that is supposed to be encoded into the piece by its composer.

None of the four corners of my quadrangle of analysis should be taken for granted: if one is changed, all the others may change too. If we change our object of study from a piece of music objectified in a score to a piece of music represented by the same symbol, the words that make up its title, but objectified by a CD, not only will the material of the carrier of the information change from paper to plastic, but our idea of the material that is stored on this carrier will also

---

[1] The first half of this chapter draws on a group of older articles of mine that have been published in German. They contain a more extensive discussion of what I can only summarize here.

[2] For a long time musicology has defined music as *Tonkunst*; Stefan Kunze observes: 'Die Töne sind die Elemente der Musik' ('Notes/pitches are the elements of music') (1998: 179).

change: a sound recording is not made up of notes as the smallest unit; its medium is sound.[3] There are various ways to define sound. I will not go into this problem here, but even if pitch may play a role in a definition of sound, it is obvious that functional or degree theory offer no sufficient method to describe it satisfyingly. Sound as a medium is produced by musicians, not by a composer. An analysis that aims to describe the form of recorded sound therefore has to consider the form of the performance by a group of musicians, rather than the notes written by a composer. Likewise even the meaning of 'meaning' has to be redefined, as it is no longer a 'message' encoded with the help of notes into a score by a composer, but something that is expressed with the help of sound by a musician.

The principle of the interdependency of the corners of my analytical quadrangle applies to all music; it becomes a problem, however, if you leave the secure ground of the paradigms of traditional musical analysis of music as notes in a score and venture to analyse popular music. Described as a communication system, popular music as recorded music produced by musicians is very different from art music as written music produced by composers which has been the main focus of musicological analysis by now.

First of all, in popular music there are no scores. In most cases, a pop song is created by making, not by writing, music. The quality of a piece of art music that is considered by music theory to lie in the originality of the formation of notes does not apply to popular music. Its melodies are simple; rhythm, harmony and the form resulting from these parameters are highly standardized. An analysis of a mainstream pop song with the traditional tools of music theory inevitably leads to one result: a demonstration of the song's triteness – at least compared to the music for whose analysis the tools were developed: art music.[4] The quality of a mainstream pop hit can only to a small extent be understood by analysing a lead sheet; it mainly lies in recorded performance: its sonic as well as its visual aspects, the latter, for example, in music videos, promotional pictures or CD artwork.

The concept of the author in popular music differs from that of traditional art music. The invention of the concept of the note as the smallest unit of music (from the eleventh century onwards written as a *punctum* in a stave and named with a letter in spoken language) resulted in the emergence of a new communication system featuring the then new roles of a composer communicating with the help of a score with his/her interpreters.[5] Notation as a medium was not developed to store music as such, but to pass on instructions to musicians of how an author,

[3] This is not to deny that a sound recording may be translated or re-translated into notes, but in transcribing a recording into a score, we have to be aware that we are not only changing the material aspect of the medium, but also the informational value.

[4] German music pedagogues of the 1960s used analysis of popular music to demonstrate to their pupils its inferiority – with the hope that they would leave beat music and turn to classical compositions (see Helms 2002: 91f.).

[5] I am using the term 'interpreter', not 'performer' or 'musician', to suggest that those who make aural music from a score and musicologists analysing and interpreting a score

later called composer, wanted them to act to make music. With the invention of methods to record sound, however, a communication system became possible that could do without the role of a composer, and indeed, we speak of listening to Simon Rattle's recording of Stravinsky's *Sacre du printemps*, but nobody would speak of listening to a recording of Rod Temperton's 'Thriller' sung by Michael Jackson. Although the song is frequently covered, it is Michael Jackson who is being covered, not Temperton. Popular music, as I understand it, can be described as a communication system that is based on the roles of musicians and listeners. A recording, be it an MP3 file or a music video, stores the results of the activities of musicians making music, and it is the originality, individuality and skill of these activities encoded in the medium of sound that makes up the quality of a recording.

As an objectification of a musician's work, the recording has a similar effect to a score: whereas the activities of an author (making music or composing) are dependent on time and not repeatable, the recording and the score are objects, symbols for the activities of their authors, which are thought of as independent of time and repeatable (Helms 2003: 207–9, see also Katz 2010: 4). Comparable to a score that symbolizes the musical work, the *Werk*, of a composer, the recording may be described as the 'opus perfectum et absolutum' (Listenius) of a musician, assumed to be complete and final for all time. However, there are differences: the score is only an imperfect representation of the process of the composer's activities; like all symbols, it needs an interpreter, someone who translates the symbol into actions again – these actions may be the playing of an instrument, but also a verbal reconstruction (or narration) of the thoughts and ideas of the composer when writing the score. The sound recording, for example on a CD, also needs a translation of an object that symbolizes human actions into these actions. This process of interpretation, however, is executed by a machine; the problem of translating symbols into actions again is solved for us by the CD player or a program on our MP3 player, and although every machine solves the problem differently, we do not consider this a problem of the music, but a problem of the technique. The CD suggests that it is a repeatable recording of a single event of music making (Helms 2003: 207). We all know that this is fiction: single tracks may be recorded at different times in different studios, and it is not a performance but post-production processes (including the shooting of a music video) that give a song its space and context. We do, however, accept this fiction – it sounds so temptingly 'real', it has a 'high fidelity'.

A recording as such does not automatically raise questions of interpretation as a score does – if it should do, we may easily solve it by buying a new 'interpreter' – for example, a CD player. The fact that recording has made a direct comparison of several realizations of a score easily possible has accelerated the development of performance studies in musicology. However, the issues raised by recordings of 'composed music' are still problems produced by the interpretation of scores,

have a similar position in the communication system. Both are communicating directly with a composer (via a score).

and not by recordings. To call performers 'informants, consultants, or co-researchers' (as Cook [2014: 49] does, although his approach is by far more elaborate than my quotation suggests) reveals that the musicological interpreter of recorded 'composed' music still considers him/herself an interpreter working from the same position as the musicians.[6] The score is still the basis, the *tertium comparationis*, the unchanging text that allows us to compare two different interpretations of allegedly the same thing.

Popular music is different: in 1950s rock'n'roll we see the changeover from composed and notated 'light music' to recorded popular music without score as the basis of its production. In 1954 Jesse Stone, a.k.a. Charles E. Calhoun, wrote 'Shake, Rattle and Roll' and recorded it early that year with blues singer Big Joe Turner and a band of studio musicians. In June the same year Bill Haley and His Comets produced their version of the song, and in 1956 a third version sung by Elvis Presley was released. All three versions were hits in their days, although today Haley's is the best-remembered. Although the song was written for Turner and its composer contributed to his recording, it feels wrong to speak of Haley's and Presley's versions as covers – as secondary performances that refer to an original one, or as interpretations of a composition. They are originals in their own right. The fact that we have three versions of an identical status is not due to the authority of the composer, as is the case with a Beethoven sonata played by three famous pianists. On the contrary, Stone's position as author of a *tertium comparationis* is rather weak – only experts knew then and remember today his name. Turner, Haley and Presley are not interpreting a composition, they are using Stone's lyrics, the contours of his melodic line that consists to a great extent of a few rhythmically repeated notes, and the unoriginal harmonic formula of a 12-bar blues to turn something rather conventional into three highly original recordings.

The fact that the song is known by the names of its singers and not by its composer shows how musicians took over ownership of a song from composers. That all three versions could exist independently and side by side was only possible because the three singers performed in different musical genres (Turner was a blues shouter, Haley coined rock'n'roll with his performance) or highly individual singing styles (Elvis's notorious 'boogiefication' [Middleton 1990: 18–21] and his rock'n'roll sound with country roots). To conclude: the 'original' in popular music is not rooted in the notes, but in the performance (including the use of recording technology); rock'n'roll – and all popular music afterwards – is not a compositional, but a '*performance* style' (Gracyk 1996: 6).

Since the 1960s parallel releases of the same song by different performers have become increasingly uncommon. Musicians and their production teams try to coin originals. Song and performance style have become a unit. If a song is played by another performer, it is considered to be a cover, which is not regarded as a second

---

[6] Although, for the first time in history, music scholars are accepting the help and competence of musicians and finally bridging the gap between 'musicus' and 'cantor' that has been in existence since antiquity.

interpretation of equal status, but rather comparable to an arrangement of a score by someone other than the composer, only it doesn't change the notes, but rather the performance style (Helms 2003: 208).

To sum up: the introduction of the sound recording (emphasized some time later by sound film) resulted in the emergence of a new communication system, which in its purest form can be studied in recorded popular music. It has redefined the roles of the agents in music communication, of both musicians and listeners, and brought a new medium to our attention that I suggest calling 'sound' – not as a physical, but as a communicational quality, a code that is used to communicate the difference of individual performances and performers (Helms 2003). The history of sound as a medium began with the increasing awareness of the individuality of performers: for example, with the castratos and sopranos of Baroque opera, the virtuosi of nineteenth-century instrumental music and the singers of the late nineteenth-century English music hall. The gramophone record brought forth the first global performing stars, such as Caruso (for the effects of the gramophone, see Katz 2010). With the introduction of the tape recorder in music production after the Second World War, post-production became possible. Compiling, mixing, equalizing and the possibility to add sound effects like reverberation and echo after the musicians had done their work enormously increased the means to produce individuality, complexity and the effect of a performance, and at the same time it further decreased the need for complexity and individuality in musical parameters that can be written down in a score.

For popular music studies, the standardization of these parameters raises the question: What is the material we should analyse (see Helms 2002)? If hundreds of pop hits have the same I-V-vi-IV harmonic structure[7] and a simple $\frac{4}{4}$ ostinato beat, a traditional analysis of voice leading and harmony only reveals the perhaps least important qualities of a song. In German musicology, scholars discussed the need to redefine the 'material' that should be analysed in the early 1970s (Rauhe 1972); however, the development of analytical tools to describe performance has only recently begun (to name only a few recent publications: Everett 2008; Moore 2012; Tagg 2013; von Appen et al. 2015). Unlike the reader of a score, who has only one medium (notes) – or in the case of vocal music, two media (notes and language) – to cope with, the listener is making sense of music with the help of many more code systems. Just imagine the wealth of information there is in a singing voice (see Frith 1998: 183–202): you can hear words, a melody, emotions, gender, a body, a nationality, social status and sometimes even a political persuasion – for example, in the characteristic vocal style of German fascist rock bands of the 1990s and 2000s. Instrumentation, instrumental sounds and playing techniques likewise contain a wealth of information, as does the mix of a recording, like the special arrangement of voices and instruments in the 'sound box' (Moore 2012: 29–44). A musicologist analysing a performance soon reaches the limitations of

7 As the music comedians Axis of Awesome demonstrate impressively in '4 Chords', http://www.youtube.com/watch?v=oOlDewpCfZQ (accessed 30 June 2015).

his/her competence: performance analysis also has to study visual information as the 'signifying body' (Cook 2014: 288–307): clothes, gestures, ways of dancing, concert venues, stage decorations, lights, camera positions and so on. Moreover, it has to discuss all other elements that are supposed to create meaning, or better, to make sense to a listener witnessing a performance; there is a difference in where a new song is launched: on radio or TV (on which show and on which station?), in the latest blockbuster movie, in a fashionable club or on YouTube; there is meaning in the cover of a CD and a poster advertising a new release.

All the parameters or code systems I have hinted at create form: sound, such as the contrast between choral and soloistic arrangements, is important for the difference between chorus and verse, but also for the virtual social context that is created in the recording; the mix creates a virtual space in which the listener is immersed when he/she perceives a song; a movement is part of a choreography; a spotlight part of a lighting concept; a dress or a performance venue are part of the image of a musician .... A thorough analysis of a pop song considering all the parameters I have mentioned, extending the text to what in traditional terminology would have been regarded as context, may thus easily fill 500 pages and a two-volume publication (see, for example, Rappe 2010).

Facing the mass of information that is the outcome of a formal analysis of music in performance – a pop song, and the great variety and sometimes incoherence of data we may collect – a simple question may arise: Why? I am not suggesting that formal analysis of popular music is a waste of time; what I want to make clear is that with changes in the communication system we venture to describe, the material we have to analyse changes, and consequently we should reconsider the issues of our research. Form is important for interpreters of scores, who need to know how to transform notes into what is considered to be the thing as such: the sound of music. For readers of scores it is important, since the medium invites formal analysis as being independent of time. However, if the communication is stored on a medium that needs no interpretation by human beings, but only by machines, to become the thing as such, and if music making is no longer considered to be the interpretation of something that was written down by an absent third party (the composer), but a creative act in its own right, some issues lose their urgency and others gain importance. In popular music much more communication is about the personality of the musicians than about the musical features of their songs. This should be no surprise when we consider what has been said about the characteristics of the medium by now. Obviously, in different communication systems emphasis is laid on different functions of communication. A score is a much more 'intellectual' medium than a recording, which has a more direct bodily appeal. It seems more natural to think about a score than to dance to it (although musicians are supposed to translate notes into bodily movements by pressing keys or plucking strings and so on). To follow a recording as a consciously analysing 'expert' listener (as was Adorno's [1997: 182] ideal of listening to art music) takes a great effort and is definitely highly demanding, as first of all you have to overcome the reactions of your body and its tendencies to indulge in wordless dream worlds.

Listeners have different demands of music than interpreters of scores. It is true, some enjoy thinking about what they are hearing, but many listen to music to dance or to dream to it, to stimulate themselves, to modify their mood, or to demonstrate that they are part of a social group. They choose music according to its effects. Music satisfies all these demands.

What I want to make clear is that there are more functions of music than being an object of art, of ingeniously formed material, and transporting a meaning. Centuries of work on the interpretation of texts, or in our case scores, have focused scholars' attention too much on these two objectives. The change of perspective from the scholar as an interpreter of scores to the scholar as a listener broadens the view. What Simon Frith writes about popular music may be said about all music perceived from a listener's perspective: 'The question is not what does it mean but what can I do with it' (1998: 13). A song or a symphony do not necessarily have to have a meaning to make sense to a listener. Much music that we hardly know because it doesn't appear in our history books was and is written to fulfil other functions than the existence of a piece of art: to make its audience dance, to make them feel happy or sad, to get them marching, or even something so simple as to attract their attention.

One of the implicit and sometimes explicit consequences of traditional methods of analysis has been the justification of a hierarchy of music: on the highest point of our Gradus ad Parnassum we find compositions which are so complex and innovative that interpreters write books about them that prove their ingenuity; these pieces are high art. On the other side of our stair – in the basement, so to speak – we have performances that are so simple that they make millions of people dance or feel happy. This kind of music is called popular, subcultural, trivial, and considered to be of low quality. Both, however, should be considered as masterworks which perfectly fulfil the respective functions they were intended for. There would be no need for hierarchical thinking if analysis considered form and meaning as two functions of music among others. This is especially true for music seen from a listener's perspective. In a concert, only very few listeners can perceive the qualities that make a Beethoven symphony a piece of art. Few people have an idea of the sonata form and can perceive the composer's play with formal conventions. They listen to it as they listen to a pop song: unconsciously, emotionally, associatively, bodily, enjoying the powerful beginning of the fifths and the romantic lyricism of the sixths. If we find methods to analyse music with the aim of discussing its functions, we will be able to write about a symphony of the classical period and a 1970s disco dance hit on the same level, acknowledging the different qualities that help them to fulfil the functions they are expected to have as of equal status. We may then also bridge the gap between the canon that is acclaimed by musicologists and the repertoire that is successful in the concert hall. We may find ways to explain why Beethoven is a success with both, whereas Sibelius is only successful in the concert hall (Helms 2014). We may compare all kinds of music according to their functions.

Sociology, psychology and economics have been studying the social, emotional and economic functionalization of music for years. However, they analyse social, psychological and economical phenomena, not music. Their ideas of the functions of music are, for example, group building, individuation, emotional stimulation or profit maximization. I am neither aiming at such an idea of functions nor at the other extreme: a description of functions immanent in music, as can be found in Hans Keller's approach of wordless functional analysis (see Keller 1994; 2001). I am looking for a way in between, a way that allows us to connect a song's immanent structure and its extra-musical functionalization. This way lies in a description of the functions of communication.

In his article 'Linguistics and Poetics' linguist Roman Jakobson (1960) offers a model of six functions of verbal communication that I find highly stimulating. The model has already been described by musicologists (Schneider 1980: 197; Monelle 1992: 17–19; Tarasti 2012: 124–7), and single functions are frequently quoted, with (Feld and Fox 1994: 27) or without (Tagg and Clarida: 644) reference to Jakobson. Usually Jakobson is discussed in theoretical studies of music semiotics. Schneider (1980: 198) uses it to introduce his readers to the more complex ideas of the equivalence of principles of selection and combination (see also Gruhn 2004: 81f., 143–6) and to link it to Nicolas Ruwet's ideas of a semiotic analysis of music. As I said at the beginning of this chapter, my interest is analysis, not semiotics. I will therefore spare us a long-winded theoretical discussion and use Jakobson's functions – without their theoretical background – simply as categories for my analysis.

Jakobson's basic idea is very simple. Starting from an older model by Karl Bühler (1982: 28f.), Jakobson (1960: 353–7) differentiates six functions of language. Each of these functions is connected to one of the constitutive factors of a speech act: we have the two sides of the communication circle, the *addresser* and the *addressee*, the *context* to which a speech act might refer, the *message* as a selection from a certain code in a certain form, the *code*, the repertoire of signs, which constitute the message, and finally the *channel*, or in Jakobson's terms, the *contact* between addresser and addressee.

A speech act can inform the recipient about each of these constitutive factors. And each of these factors has a particular function: a speech act, Jakobson writes, that refers to things and facts outside the conversation has a *referential* function. It may also appeal to the addressee to do something, and therefore have a *conative* function. In many cases it expresses the condition the addresser is in, and therefore has an *emotive* function. These three functions had already been described by Bühler in 1934. What was new in Jakobson's approach of 1960 were the following three functions.

According to Jakobson, a speech act may also contain signs that signal the beginning and the end of a conversation and which help to secure the contact between both sides. Jakobson calls this function *phatic*. A fifth function of speech acts is called *metalingual*. This function helps to ensure that the recipient understands the message as intended by the addresser. In language, the paraphrase of a difficult word may have a metalingual function. Finally, speech acts can also have a *poetic* function. I understand this poetic function as signs that bring the form of a speech act to the addressee's attention. Jakobson sets out his model in two illustrations which I have merged into one (see Figure 14.1).

Referential function → Context
Emotive function → Addresser Phatic function → Contact Conative function → Addressee
Poetic function → Message
Metalingual function → Code

Figure 14.1 Functions of language and what they refer to
Source: Jakobson (1960): 353, 357.

Strictly speaking, the three new functions that distinguish Jakobson's system from Bühler's organon model are already contained in the latter. His phatic function is in a way conative, or appellative, as Bühler terms it: both communicants are appealing reciprocally to each other to pay attention, to take up and to sustain communication. The same is true for Jakobson's metalingual and poetic functions: they refer to things that exist in the context of a communication act. To communicate metalingually about the meaning of a sign or poetically about the beautiful form of a communication act means changing from object language to meta-language (communication about communication); that means referring to code systems or aesthetic ideas of beauty that are part of the context of the actual communication. Unlike Bühler's rather global model, Jakobson's system was set up as a kind of poetics – it was constructed to describe communication in the context of art, where communication about code and form is highly important. The poetic function helps to include the concept of an autonomous work of art as an act of communication that only refers to itself, and not to things and ideas in its contexts. This produces some logical difficulties in Jakobson's system, as we shall see later in this chapter, but it is of great help in describing and differentiating the functions of communication in music.

A second advantage of Jakobson's model is the fact that it can be applied perfectly not only to language, but to any medium (this distinguishes it from Austin's and Searle's speech act theories, which can be applied only to language). It is therefore ideal for the description of multimedia communication acts, like a musical performance that uses sound, rhythm and language, as well as visual symbolic systems, like bodily gestures, stage decorations, clothes and musical instruments.

To discuss the potential of Jakobson's model for analysis, it seems advisable to apply it to the practical example of a single recorded performance. As my interest here is to demonstrate the usefulness of Jakobson's six functions of communication acts as objectives of the analysis of a performance, I will not go into too much detail about the song. I will consider the performance as a whole – not only the fiction of a performance that I can listen to on CD, but also the fiction of a performance that I can watch on video. Listening to music is hardly ever a single-channel perception. The brain wants to see what it hears, and if it can't see a source for the sound it hears, it will make it up in its imagination; this is why recorded music needs images. The music video is merely a consequence of this urge to visualize sound. Videos are not only a marketing tool, but an integral part of the song.[8]

My example 'If a Song Could Get Me You'[9] was a great hit for Norwegian singer Marit Larsen in 2008 and 2009, especially in Scandinavia and German-speaking countries, but it also charted in the large markets of the Philippines and Brazil. The song demonstrates wonderfully the dilemma of popular music analysis and the problems of performance analysis. If we apply the established tools of traditional musicology, we won't get very far: the song has a standard verse-chorus form, with a bridge after the second repetition of the chorus. The harmonic pattern is nothing that would excite a music theorist. The verse has a standard I–vi–V–V7 progression; the chorus, with a I–(V)–vi–(I)–IV–I–ii–V progression, is slightly more complex than the average mainstream hit. Only the sequence in the bridge is of particular interest. The first half of the melody of the verse is a sequence of three descending fourths, the first four notes of which are well known as a typical motif symbolizing bells. A brief look at the lyrics will show that the tools we have learned at school to interpret poetry hardly apply in this case. The rhymes are imperfect or simply non-existent, there are no metaphors, no symbols, no images. It is all very straight, no hidden meaning. The Wikipedia article sums up the whole content in two sentences: 'The song deals with a broken relationship. The singer would do everything and try every song to get her boyfriend back.'[10] From the perspective of art music, the song is trite, a commercial product for a mass audience, no challenge for analysis. However, the song was and still is popular with millions of people – not because they are stupid and dull, as Adorno might have presumed, but because it functions exactly the way it is supposed to.

Referential Function

In traditional analytical approaches, signs with a referential function are central in establishing a meaning. Exploring how far 'music alone' (Kivy 1996) can refer to things outside the composition would make for a controversial and long discussion that would be far too detailed in this context. In his discussion of Jakobson's system of functions, Raymond Monelle (1992: 18f.) repeats the doubts of generations of musicologists adhering to autonomy aesthetics that music can

8 Readers who wish to know more and who are curious to know how well the model works in the case of notated music should read two articles in which I have analysed Lady Gaga's 'Pokerface' (Helms 2015) and Jean Sibelius's *Finlandia* (Helms 2014) in much greater detail than my example here.

9 In my analysis I refer to the video clip of 'If a Song Could Get Me You' that can be viewed at Marit Larsen's website, http://www.maritlarsen.de (accessed 30 June 2015). For copyright reasons I won't quote the lyrics in full, but they can easily be found on the Internet.

10 'If a Song Could Get Me You (Song)', *Wikipedia*, http://en.wikipedia.org/wiki/If_A_Song_Could_Get_Me_You_%28song%29 (accessed 30 June 2015).

have a referential function. This may be true if we implicitly define music as notes written on a score and argue from the perspective of an interpreter in an imagined conversation with a composer. However, as scholars who analyse performed music, from the perspective of a listener in communication with musicians, we can hardly ignore the context of perception as interpreters of scores tend to do. We even have problems defining the limits between musical performance and context. The sound of a performance refers to its context: physically, to a certain location (the concert hall or a virtual room audible in the recording); to other songs (for the many associations only a few seconds of music may have, see Tagg 1979); to the bodies of performers; to certain instruments and so on; psychologically, it is highly suggestive, and it refers to things and ideas in the individual listener's memory – for example, to associations of situations in which he/she has heard the song before (such as the phenomenon of 'our song', symbolizing a treasured memory shared by two lovers). Analysing music in performance means 'analysing musical multimedia' (Cook 1998) – that is, an incredibly more complex sign system than a score. The objectification of a performance, the sound recording, shows how important reference is: what in a live performance might be (but should not be) disposed of as context becomes an integral part of the song in the process of recording; post-production is the art of creating a virtual space and virtual performing bodies. Performed music is never 'alone'.

For many performances in popular music genres, the communication of a coherent meaning, a string of signs that sums up to a 'message' that is intersubjectively valid, is of minor importance. In mainstream popular music, the performers rather send out hundreds of references, hoping that a few will catch the audience's attention and inspire their individual imagination. A song is successful not if many people agree on a meaning, but if every single listener can adapt it individually to his/her life and experiences. This can be explained by the structure of the communication system of recorded music. While in direct face-to-face communication both sides of the communication circle permanently check their counterpart's reactions for signs of understanding and if necessary correct their partner, in communication via a sound recording the musicians have hardly any chance of controlling the way their listeners understand the song. The only feedback they get (apart from journalistic criticism) consist of chart positions and sales figures. A pop song is therefore no ideal medium to change the world. The most important aim for the producer of a pop song is to make sure that it helps to construct an individual identity (the branding of the product, so to speak) and that as many people as possible can do something with the song[11] – whatever that may be, as long as they buy the record and pay attention to the broadcast. In many mainstream pop songs, we can therefore show that their producers amass stereotyped images rather than developing a logical, coherent argumentation that results in a clearly discernible meaning. However, they make sure that the imagery

[11] Elsewhere, I have described popular music as a social system that works on the basis of two antagonistic principles: individuation and proliferation (Helms 2008).

they use is linked by a semantic field, often combining metaphors from two differing or even conflicting fields (see my analysis of Lady Gaga's 'Pokerface' in Helms 2015).

Many references in 'If a Song Could Get Me You' can be assigned to two semantic fields: the little teenage girl and the singer-songwriter.[12] In the lyrics one may find the little girl not so much in the words, but in the insecurity and indecision expressed by the excessive use of the auxiliary verb 'could'. The melody of the verse, sequencing downwards in fourths in a skipping rhythm, has a somewhat childlike attitude. The voice itself very strongly reminds me of the singing of a teenager: it has on the one hand a high, nasal, childish sound, but on the other hand includes certain flirtatious elements in the performance. The video abounds with references to the teenage girl: the short skirts, the angel costume, the way the performer moves, the way she chews her fingernails and so on.

The singer-songwriter and proficient musician is also clearly represented in all parameters of the performance; in the recording we hear many acoustic instruments: an acoustic guitar, a slightly out-of-tune bar piano (or is it a child's toy piano?), a grand piano and a mandolin. In the video we can see Larsen playing most of these instruments herself, assuming the performance style of a singer-songwriter. In the music of the bridge we can hear the rapid scale passages in octaves, which are a cliché of nineteenth-century virtuoso piano music. The harmonies are slightly richer than is standard in mainstream pop. In the lyrics she mentions all the musical genres she can, or at least could, perform – waltz, rock'n'roll, blues – and she says that she could sing 'high or low'. Listeners acquainted with pop history may notice references to the titles of Stuart Hamblen's 1954 country hit 'This Ole House' (which charted in 1981 as a cover by Shakin' Stevens), Dionne Warwick's 'A House is Not a Home' and the song 'Jupiter (Swallow the Moon)' sung by the American singer-songwriter Jewel. Experts in music video history will also recognize the reference to one of the first music videos of a singer-songwriter: in a performance of 'Subterranean Homesick Blues', Bob Dylan's first top-40 hit, the singer can be seen holding up signs repeating the words of the text at the moment they are sung.

The reference function of Marit Larsen's song has two aims. One is to help the listener to adapt the song to his/her own circumstances, experiences and knowledge with the help of signs that have a highly associative effect. At the same time the quotations appeal to specialist knowledge, and may be used by listeners to show off their experience. The second aim of the referential signs in this particular performance is to inform the listener about the identity of the performer, as many signs with a referential function can be connected to the singer. In interviews and press releases, Marit Larson is described as a multi-instrumentalist and singer-songwriter, and as we have seen, the song helps to support this image. Signs that inform the listener about the performer, however, have a second function: they are

[12] This combination of semantic fields had already been extremely successful in 1982 with Nicole's European Song Contest-winning 'Ein bißchen Frieden'. A less harmless variant of this combination can be found in the image of Björk.

emotive. As Jakobson (1960: 353) makes clear, most communication acts have several functions simultaneously.

Emotive Functions

The emotive function refers to the addresser. In Jakobson's words, it aims at 'a direct expression of the speaker's attitude toward what he is speaking about' (1960: 354). I suggest extending Jakobson's definition. A communication act can say more about the addresser than his/her 'attitude'. In the sound of a voice, we not only hear attitudes like irony or emotions like anger. It is a common experience, for example on the telephone, that we more or less unconsciously associate with the voice of an unknown and unseen person a certain personality, and even form a picture of his/her looks. We speak of someone having a beautiful voice, and are disappointed if the person's appearance doesn't live up to the promises of that voice. I suggest that communication acts not only inform the recipient about attitude, but also about the identity of the addresser. Therefore, I would prefer the term 'self-revelation', introduced by the German psychologist Friedemann Schulz von Thun (1989: ch. II.1). For the sake of coherence, however, I will stick to the term 'emotive'. It is important to mark the difference from the word 'emotional': when we speak of an emotional piece of music, we mean that we feel moved by it – we refer to ourselves as addressees of a communication act. 'Emotive', however, refers to the addresser. An emotive sign in a communication can refer to a real emotion in the addresser, but it can also be feigned (Jakobson 1960: 354), like an actor or a singer who performs an emotion he/she doesn't really feel.

In music, the emotive function in communication is important to mark the ownership of a song or a composition. Gaining an idea of the personal style of a composer takes a lot of experience and know-how. The identity of a performer, however, is something that may very easily be perceived, as he/she embodies the performance. For composers, as for performers, it is important to be identifiable; however, for pop musicians it is absolutely crucial, as their products have to reach a mass market. Therefore, great efforts are made to produce an original and singular fictional image. A song will only proliferate if it offers some information that its listeners didn't know before. Moreover, emotive signs are decisive for the authenticity of a performance. An audience will perceive a performance as authentic if its immanent emotive signs (that make up the performing persona) agree with what they know of the performer outside the song (for the terms 'persona' and 'performer', see Moore 2012: 180f.; for a discussion of authenticity, see von Appen 2013 and Moore 2012: 260).

The music video that was made to introduce the persona called 'Marit Larsen' to the public is one long self-revelation: there is not a single second in the video that does *not* show the singer. The same is true of the text: in 38 lines we have 27 repetitions of the word 'I' – many of them at the beginning of a line – and 11 occurrences of the words 'me' and 'my'. Although she expresses her wish to have her lover back, the persona is definitely not too desperate, as she sings her song with a smiling voice and she can be seen smiling all the time in the video. The voice and her gestures in the performance suggest that she is rather in a flirtatious mood. The lyrics don't reveal any emotions except in the last verse, where the lyrical 'I' mentions her love and fears – without really expressing them. However, every single auxiliary verb she uses is in the subjunctive mode: 'I could', 'I would', 'I should'. Rather than expressing the vainness of all actions to get the lover back, they reveal a certain irony, because she doesn't make clear what she will actually do. This ironic attitude can also be found in the exaggerations of the video: the angel costume; the construction of 12 megaphones in a row; her heavy metal guitar playing; sliding over the stage, not on her knees, but on a board with wheels. Every now and then one can see the performer change the stage decorations, moving a ladder about, pushing the piano to its place, rolling out plastic foil. The camera, which zooms in and out but never changes its position in the room, supports the impression that we are watching a play on a theatrical stage. The performer makes clear that she is only acting.

Phatic Function

The phatic function, I suppose, is one of the most important functions for performers in popular as well as art music. Signs with a phatic function help to keep up the contact between the two sides of communication; they secure attention and signal the beginning and the end of a contact. For a listener without a university degree in music theory, it may be difficult to analyse the form of a piece of instrumental music while listening to the music. Therefore, the attention of listeners has to be secured with the help of *phatic signs* – signs that make a performance interesting. The beginning of Beethoven's Fifth Symphony or the 'Dies irae' of Verdi's *Requiem* are wonderful examples for such a phatic function in art music. My analysis of Sibelius's *Finlandia* (Helms 2014) shows how composers build phatic elements into their scores to help musicians keep their audience's attention.

In the concert hall or on a sound recording, musicians are not in a position to control whether their audience understand them correctly – all they can control is attention. Musicians on stage know precisely whether or not they are fascinating their audience, and they react accordingly; performers who produce sound recordings control attention via charts, airplay or sales. Therefore, for a musician, attention is an aim that is much more important than being understood correctly. Jakobson mentions the example of small talk as purely phatic verbal communication. In a way, performances (of all kinds of music) can be compared to small talk: there is no need to transfer meaning as long as one side can be sure of the other's attention. (Of course, I am not suggesting that a performer or a listener doesn't produce meaning; however, it isn't necessary for the continuance of communication.)

Our video starts without music. One can see a close-up of the performer with downcast eyes. After a second, she seeks eye contact with the observer to signal that what comes now is addressed to him/her. At this very moment, the music starts. Throughout the film the performer is always seeking eye contact – often in a flirtatious manner. (This is obviously a sign that also has an emotive function, as it expresses sympathy with the addressee.)

There are dozens of phatic signs in the visual performance (such as Larsen waving a sign or opening her blouse to present a gingerbread heart). I will concentrate on mentioning a few in the music: the so-called 'hook' at the beginning of a song in popular music is of extreme importance in attracting listeners' attention and for the branding of the song. In 'If a Song Could Get Me You', the initial hook is made up of the individual sound of the performer's voice, the individual instrumental sound of the first chord that blends a guitar arpeggio and a piano chord, and finally, the appealing or calling quality of the first bright vocal sound [aɪ] combined with a descending fourth in the melody.

A pop song has to imprint itself on its audience's memory. This is why repetition is so important. However, if repeated too often, the elements of a song lose interest for the listener. This is why a musical bridge after two repetitions of the chorus is a standard phatic element in mainstream pop. This is also why every repetition of a verse has some small elements that vary the sound and help to attract the listener's attention. The second and third verse in our example have different guitar and mandolin riffs.

The sound of the song contains more elements that maintain contact: the distance between addresser and addressee as encoded in the studio mix, or to be precise, in the virtual distance between the voice and the listener. As a camera positions the observer in relation to the action on the screen, the microphone positions the listener in relation to the musician(s) (Zagorski-Thomas 2013: 138f.). In our example we have two instances of great closeness: at the beginning and in the third verse (directly after the bridge), Marit Larsen sings in a very low voice: you can hear her breathing, the sound of the voice has many high frequencies, there is no added reverb. This very intimate relation between the listener and the performer changes in the chorus. There, the performer's voice is doubled, she sings in a loud voice, and reverb is added to create a larger space and a distance between addresser and addressee.

Conative Function

In many pop songs, choruses have a strong conative function – they appeal to the addressee to do something. To induce the audience to sing along, the sound gets broader and fills the whole width of the panorama, the voice is virtually distancing itself from the listener (moves from a you-and-I position to a we-position, so to speak), and it is multiplied or supported by a chorus of additional singers. Vocalises may also induce the audience to sing along. 'If a Song Could Get Me You' has few conative signs in the music. The chorus is a moment of relief: a large room filled with sound is opening up, all instruments join in, the suspense produced in the verse is gone, but neither is it a chorus to sing along with (it has too much text, there is no choir and there are no vocalises), nor is the rhythm strong enough to make a listener want to dance to the song. The lyrics of the song have a few conative lines: 'believe me', and repeatedly, 'tell me'. Especially conspicuous is the 'Just look at me' at the end of the bridge, as it is sung while the instruments pause. The function of these phrases, however, is more phatic – attracting attention – than truly conative. The listeners know that they cannot answer to a voice that comes out of a loudspeaker. The same is true for the written messages in the video: 'believe me' written on the sail of her ship, 'come back' on a sign formed of light bulbs and 'help!' on a sheet of paper she is holding up. The clearest invitations to do something are the flirtatious looks of the performer, which have a function somewhere in the middle of emotive, phatic and conative. They show the observer 'I'm in a flirtatious mood', help to attract and to fix his/her attention and invite him/her to get into contact – to look for more information from and about the performer.

The experienced observer knows that movies are fiction – that they tell stories which are interesting to watch, but which do not refer and appeal to him/her as such; they have no self-reference (Luhmann 1996: 24–44). Music videos, however, differ from movies as their aesthetics allow actors to look directly into the camera; they may address their audience (seemingly) directly. Performance videos that show the actors making music still have – some more, some less – traces of the documentary character of a live concert, where the musicians may address the audience directly. The music video as a genre is situated somewhere between movies, which usually produce no self-reference in the audience, and commercials, which address them directly and appeal to them to do something, namely to buy the product. If there is an appeal in 'If a Song Could Get Me You', it is: 'Enjoy me, love me, buy me!'

Poetic and Metalingual Functions

As mentioned above, the poetic and metalingual functions of communication cause problems in Jakobson's model. Other than the four functions I have dealt with up to now, they can only be perceived if they provoke a change in the mode of communication, a switch from object to meta-communication. A sentence only has a poetic function when it causes the observer to think or inquire about its form. Jakobson uses the example of someone speaking of 'horrible Harry', and her partner asking: 'Why horrible?' 'Why not dreadful, terrible …?' (1960: 357). The girl in the example answers that horrible fits Harry better. We see that the conversation about what Harry has done or said is interrupted, and what follows is a discussion about the aesthetics of everyday language. The same applies to the metalingual function. Metalingual communication is used to ensure understanding. If I don't understand a word my partner has said, I have to interrupt conversation and ask: 'What was her name?' or 'What does "objectivation" mean?' The same is true with communication between performers and listeners. If I play the violin in a string quartet and I notice, as a listener to the music we make, that my part doesn't fit with what the viola is playing, I interrupt the rehearsal and we discuss who is wrong or how to make it better. The listener to a piece of orchestral music may suddenly be stirred up from contemplation and wonder whether the irritating sounds he/she perceives are caused by intonation problems of the hornist or part of the composition. If he/she decides that the composer is to blame, he/she may feel stimulated to think about poetical aspects of the piece: its form or its meaning. If the listener is a critic, he/she may mention the wrong notes, if he/she is a musicologist, he/she may quote the phrase as a sign for the composer's ingenuity in playing with the audience's expectations. My examples should be proof enough that Monelle's (1992: 19) doubts about the possibility of a metalingual function in music are not at all justified. Music in performance has all the communicative functions language has.[13] As the metalingual function is not unique to language, I suggest speaking of a *metacommunicational function*.

In performed music, the switch from object to metacommunication is more conspicuous than in language as it is accompanied with a switch in the whole communication system. A listener who wonders about a certain phrase of music stops to communicate with the musicians. He/she is no longer involved in the music, he/she doesn't follow the sound any longer, but starts to think or to speak about his/her irritations – which means that he/she switches the medium from sound to language.[14] In a concert situation, listeners are unable to get up and ask the musicians; they either have to discuss the problem with their neighbours, or with themselves in their minds. The performers have lost their attention, and them as partners in communication.

My interpretation of Jakobson's poetic and metalingual or metacommunicational functions has consequences for our idea of a functional analysis. An analysis of the poetic function of a piece of music is not identical with a formal analysis. It looks for those elements in a performance that are suited to inducing thoughts about form, just as an analysis of the metacommunicational function shows up those moments in a song that may endanger understanding.

Art music may be supposed to provoke its audience to think – although not all listeners go to concerts with the expectation of getting something to think about. For popular music, however, a listener who thinks about a song while the music is playing is a proof that the song doesn't work the way it should. You don't

[13] And even written music has a metacommunicative function. Editors of critical editions of music have to discuss the right 'understanding' when they find a 'wrong' note in their source.

[14] Language, I suppose, is the only medium that may be used for metacommunication. It is hard to imagine that there might be music about music. Therefore, Monelle (1992: 19) is right to criticize the effectiveness of Hans Keller's wordless functional analyses (Keller 1994; 2001), which make sense only because they refer to a long tradition of verbal interpretation.

want to wonder about the music while you dance or dream or do your homework. If you love to be in the music, you will possibly hate being thrown out of it by a phrase your subconscious has no explanation for, which therefore alarms your consciousness. Mainstream popular music definitely doesn't want the audience to ask questions while the music is playing. In genres of popular music that have no ambition to be arty, the producers do everything to make sure that all thinking is postponed to the time after the song has ended. Provocation is useful, but it should provoke attention, not thought. As mentioned before, attention is the gospel of performance, and the high art, the virtuosity, of a performer lies in arresting his/her audience's attention. In a mainstream song like 'If a Song Could Get Me You', we may therefore expect many elements with a phatic function, but none with a poetic or metacommunicational function.

There is, however, one moment in the lyrics of this song that might have such a metacommunicational function. Right in the first verse, Larsen sings three lines that begin with 'I could try', and each time she swallows the fourth word in the line. The many versions of the lyrics on the Internet document this lack of clarity of pronunciation: 'I could try you/it with a waltz; I could try you/a/– rock and roll; I could try it/you with the blues' (I hear 'with *a* blues'). One might speculate whether this ambiguity is deliberate. Many songs in popular music have moments like this, and their fans discuss passionately which version might be the right one (see my analysis of 'Pokerface' in Helms 2015). Unclear pronunciation won't endanger communication. A listener to a pop song doesn't expect to understand every word on first hearing, and in our case he/she does perceive at least something that makes sense, although 'to try it' versus 'to try you' makes quite a difference. The problem emerges only if you try to follow the lyrics word by word – a situation that in popular music usually occurs not on the first, but rather the second or third hearing. By then, the song has already 'got' the listener. He or she is hooked and wants to know more. Ambiguities like this may help to keep interest up even when the song is already familiar and has lost its novelty – they function as metacommunicational only in hindsight.

'If a Song Could Get Me You' also has an element that might have a poetic function. It is placed at the very end of the song, I suppose on purpose: the song ends not on the tonic, but on the dominant D major, and the melody finishes on the leading tone F♯. This may induce a question about the code, like 'Oops, has the DJ cut off the last chord?' It may, however, also raise a question about why the performer has used this open ending. What does she want to express by using this formal means? The broken-off ending is another smart means to keep the listener absorbed even beyond the end of the piece. He/she is invited to think about it – but only when the music is over.

Looking back on this analysis, we may now sum up and categorize the song. Its function is not so much to appeal to the listeners to join in, to dance or to sing along with it. It has quite a few elements that refer to the semantic field of 'artiness', but these elements are only used to support the image of a singer-songwriter, and not to provoke the listener to think on a meta-level of communication. Moreover, they are counterbalanced by references to the 'little girl'. The ironic attitude in the lyrics and in the video bridges both spheres, of the artist and of the girl: anyone who cares to think about the music video may wonder whether the 'little girl' is meant to be the immanent persona of the song, or only a role that the persona is playing, a protagonist (Moore 2012: 181) performing onstage; this interpretation might imply a certain artfulness. If, however, Marit Larsen were a singer-songwriter in the tradition of Bob Dylan, who is quoted in the music video, one would have expected more elements with a poetic function in the song. The song is more entertaining than thought-provoking. It is designed to attract the listener's attention and to instil the song into the audience's memories. It is not made for dancing, but for (easy) listening.

In the music video, Marit Larsen acts in brightly coloured dresses against a black and white background. This is highly symbolic for the whole song, which focuses all the audience's attention on the performer. The performance is a document of a fictitious self-revelation. It is an ideal first hit for a newcomer,[15] as it firmly establishes the image of the performer.

Conclusion

To sum up the use of Roman Jakobson's categories of the functions of communication acts for musicology: the analysis of music from a listener's perspective has to cope with an enormous wealth of information. Jakobson's categories help to filter and to organize it. An analysis of performed music, an analysis from the perspective of a listener, has to reconsider the traditional issues of music theory. To write of form and meaning in the face of a multimedia communication system deals only with a small part of a much larger whole. In fact, Jakobson's model shows that the meaning of 'meaning' is a misty amalgam of the referential, poetical and emotive functions. It may help to differentiate what meaning actually is. A functional analysis will not reveal the meaning of a piece of music, but it may show which elements in the performance, or indeed in the score, make an observer feel that there is something called 'a meaning' in it.

The great advantage of a functional approach to music analysis lies in its integrative effect: it may formulate an aim for analysis that integrates the findings of a description of multimedia communication acts. Analyses of performances tend to have problems making clear what a D major chord has in common with a blue skirt. Functional analyses of communication acts are helpful in integrating the analysis of visual and acoustic media.

---

15 Or rather, an experienced artist who tries to succeed with a radical change of image. Before her success with 'If a Song Could Get Me You', Marit Larsen, then with curly blonde hair, had been successful as one half of the pop duo M2M, with minor hits like 'Don't Say You Love Me'.

The functional approach also may help to bridge the gap between music analysis and music psychology and sociology by helping to identify elements in the music, or rather in the performance, which may be linked with the music's effects on the listener. Some pieces of music may induce their audience to think about meaning and form; others may make them want to dance. Some songs arrest a listener's attention although he/she utterly dislikes them; others produce a wonderful feeling of unity in all who hear them. A functional analysis can help to explain which elements in the music may be causing these effects. It may explain how music actually 'works'. For a long time, scholarship has regarded popular music as a phenomenon that is interesting for psychology and sociology, but too banal to reward any serious music analysis. Only recently have musicologists begun to discuss popular music *as music*. A music theory that takes popular music seriously should not only ask, 'What is its form?' and 'What does it mean?' If we follow Simon Frith and turn his sociological question 'What can I do with it?' into a musicological question, we might come up with new guiding question for analysis – 'What is in the song that makes me do the things with it that I do?' – or from a psychological perspective: 'What is in the song that makes me feel about it the way I do?' The answers to these questions may not only interest the inhabitants of musicological ivory towers, but also the fans of popular music.

Finally, the functional approach bridges the gap between traditional music analysis and popular music analysis, as it may be applied to all kinds of communication acts and all kinds of music. It annihilates the hierarchy of high and low that traditional analysis has established. A song doesn't have to have meaning or a high degree of formal complexity to be worthy of analysis. 'Art music' is only one result of the working of functional elements in a communication act. It has the same status as a communication act that works wonderfully as 'dance music'. The functional analysis of the one can be as complex and rewarding as the other.

References

Adorno, Theodor W. (1997) 'Typen musikalischen Verhaltens', in *Einleitung in die Musiksoziologie*, ed. Rolf Tiedemann, *Gesammelte Schriften 14*, Frankfurt am Main: Suhrkamp, pp. 178–98.

Bühler, Karl (1982) *Sprachtheorie. Die Darstellungsfunktion der Sprache* [1934], New York: Gustav Fischer.

Cook, Nicholas (1998) *Analysing Musical Multimedia*, Oxford: Oxford University Press.

——— (2014) *Beyond the Score: Music as Performance*. New York: Oxford University Press.

Everett, Walt (2009) *The Foundations of Rock: From 'Blue Suede Shoes' to 'Suite: Judy Blue Eyes'*, Oxford: Oxford University Press.

Feld, Steven and Fox, Aaron A. (1994) 'Music and Language', *Annual Review of Anthropology*, 23, pp. 25–53.

Frith, Simon (1998) *Performing Rites: Evaluating Popular Music*, Oxford: Oxford University Press.

Gracyk, Theodore (1996) *Rhythm and Noise: An Aesthetics of Rock*, Durham, NC: Duke University Press.

Gruhn, Wilfried (2004) *Wahrnehmen und Verstehen. Untersuchungen zum Verstehensbegriff in der Musik*, Wilhelmshaven: Noetzel.

Helms, Dietrich (2002) 'Musikwissenschaftliche Analyse populärer Musik?', in*Musikwissenschaft und populäre Musik. Versuch einer Bestandsaufnahme*, ed. Helmut Rösing, Albrecht Schneider and Martin Pfleiderer, Frankfurt am Main: Peter Lang, pp. 91–103.

——— (2003) 'Auf der Suche nach einem neuen Paradigma: Vom System Ton zum System Sound', in *Pop Sounds. Klangtexturen in der Pop- und Rockmusik*, ed. Thomas Phelps and Ralf von Appen, Bielefeld: transcript, pp. 197–228.

——— (2008) 'What's the Difference? Populäre Musik im System des Pop', in *PopMusicology*, ed. Christian Bielefeldt, Udo Dahmen and Rolf Grossmann, Bielefeld: transcript, pp. 75–93.

——— (2014) '"Von Interesse ist die Wirkung". Musikalische Pragmatik und notierte Musik, z.B. Sibelius' "Finlandia"', in *'Ich sehe was, was du nichts hörst.' Etüden und Paraphrasen zur musikalischen Analyse*, ed. Stefan Hanheide and Dietrich Helms, Osnabrück: epOs.

——— (2015) 'Pragmatic Pokerface: Lady Gaga's Song and Roman Jakobson's Six Functions of Communication', in von Appen et al. (2015), pp. 73–96.

Jakobson, Roman (1960) 'Closing Statement: Linguistics and Poetics', in *Style in Language*, ed. Thomas Sebeok, Cambridge, MA: MIT Press, pp. 350–77.

Katz, Mark (2010) *Capturing Sound: How Technology has Changed Music*, Berkeley, CA: University of California Press.

Keller, Hans (1994) 'The Musical Analysis of Music [On Functional Analysis]' in *Hans Keller. Essays on Music*, ed. Christopher Wintle, Cambridge: Cambridge University Press, pp. 126–8.

——— (2001) *Functional Analysis: The Unity of Contrasting Themes. Complete Edition of the Analytical Sores*, ed. Gerold W. Gruber, Frankfurt am Main: Peter Lang.

Kivy, Peter (1996) *Music Alone: Philosophical Reflections on the Purely Musical Experience*, Ithaca, NY: Cornell University Press.

Kunze, Stefan (1998) 'Die Bedeutung der Semiotik für die Musik', in *Stefan Kunze. De musica. Ausgewählte Aufsätze und Vorträge*, ed. Rudolf Bockholt and Erika Kunze, Tutzing: Hans Schneider, pp. 177–88.

Luhmann, Niklas (1996) *Die Realität der Massenmedien*, Opladen: Westdeutscher Verlag.

Middleton, Richard (1990) *Studying Popular Music*, Milton Keynes: Open University Press.

Monelle, Raymond (1992) *Linguistics and Semiotics in Music*, London: Routledge.

Moore, Allan F. (2012) *Song Means: Analysing and Interpreting Recorded Popular Song*, Farnham: Ashgate.

Rappe, Michael (2010) *Under Construction. Kontextbezogene Analyse afroamerikanischer Popmusik*, 2 vols, Cologne: Dohr.
Rauhe, Hermann (1972) 'Der Musikmarkt', in *Musik und Musikunterricht in der Gesamtschule*, ed. Helmut Segler, Weinheim: Beltz, pp. 125–62.
Schneider, Reinhard (1980) *Semiotik der Musik. Darstellung und Kritik*, Munich: Fink.
Schulz von Thun, Friedemann (1989) *Miteinander reden 2. Stile, Werte und Persönlichkeitsentwicklung. Differentielle Psychologie der Kommunikation*, Reinbek: Rowohlt.
Tagg, Philip (1979) *Kojak – 50 Seconds of Television Music: Toward the Analysis of Affect in Popular Music*, Gothenburg: Skrifter fran Musikvetenskapliga institutionen.
——— (2013) *Music's Meanings: A Modern Musicology for Non-musos,* New York: Mass Media Music Scholars' Press.
——— and Clarida, Bob (2003) *Ten Little Title Tunes: Towards a Musicology of the Mass Media*, New York: Mass Media Music Scholars' Press.
Tarasti, Eero (2012) *Semiotics of Classical Music: How Mozart, Brahms and Wagner Talk to Us,* Berlin and Boston, MA: De Gruyter and Mouton.
von Appen, Ralf (2013) 'Schein oder Nicht-Schein? Zur Inszenierung von Authentizität auf der Bühne', in *Ware Inszenierungen. Performance, Vermarktung und Authentizität in der populären Musik*, ed. Dietrich Helms and Thomas Phelps, Bielefeld: transcript, pp. 41–70.
———, Doehring, André, Helms, Dietrich and Moore, Allan F. (eds) (2015) *Song Interpretation in 21st-century Pop Music*, Farnham: Ashgate.
Zagorski-Thomas, Simon (2013) 'Musical Meaning and the Musicology of Record Production', in *Black Box Pop. Analysen populärer Musik*, ed. Dietrich Helms and Thomas Phelps, Bielefeld: transcript, pp. 135–48.

Chapter 15
The Persistence of Analogue

Mark Katz

Consider a small wooden box. Rectangular and stained dark brown, it measures about seven inches long by four inches high and wide. One end is open, offering a view of a thin sheet of wood descending in a gentle arc from the top rear to the bottom front; imagine a miniature ski jump. Only one other feature is worth noting – a thin slot on the top rear of the box. Not coincidentally, the aperture is exactly the same dimensions as the bottom of an Apple iPhone 4, *circa* 2011.

The box is, and was designed to be, an acoustic loudspeaker. Set the iPhone (as music player) in the slot and press play, and the sound is transformed. The transistor radio tinniness of its unamplified operation is gone. Instead, a pleasantly pinched though certainly not timid sound emanates from the box, one that might conjure the experience of listening to an antique wind-up phonograph, minus the surface noise of a spinning record. The incongruity of this scene is fascinating. Hard, sleek glass and metal versus porous, full-grained wood. Cold versus warm. Inorganic versus organic. Digital versus analogue.

At this point, we must ask a question: Why? Why connect a gleaming, state-of-the-art digital device to a homely wooden box? What's the point? In a sense, the incongruity is the point. The purpose of a wooden iPhone speaker is to recapture, in some small way, what has been lost in the digital age. A description of one of these speakers – the Mini Koo, by Koostik – articulates this point:

> In today's modern world, you hear a lot of lamenting about how 'plugged in' we are. Music seems like a more human escape, right? But somehow when it's digitally processed and coming at you from an electronically amplified, digitized player and speaker, music can feel just as plugged in as everything else.
>
> Of course, our modern world is digital. So, how do we dial our music back without sacrificing sound? Unless you're prepared to hire a string quartet on retainer, you're still going to need the services of your digital player, which also requires a speaker. But check this out: the Koostik's mini koo amplifies the volume output of your iPhone and is made entirely of wood – no wires. It uses the natural acoustics of American black walnut wood to fill your room with tunes. It's like an entirely modern old-school wooden instrument.

> If you're tired of all the wires on your desk, give a mini koo a try. It's nature's little amplifier.[1]

The rhetoric in this statement is clear. A wooden iPhone speaker helps us be just a little less plugged in, just a little closer to nature in this modern digital world. But also notice that the wooden iPhone speaker does not represent a rejection of the digital. In fact, its very existence depends on digital technologies. After all, without an iPhone, the Mini Koo is a just a piece of wood.

I use the example of the wooden iPhone speaker to illustrate the persistence of analogue in a digital world. Analogue is supposed to be dead, long ago swept into obscurity by digital technologies. But it never did quite die, and in fact the past decade has seen the resurgence of analogue technologies and media, such as vinyl records, cassette tapes and the like. Why the comeback? The rising popularity of vinyl records and other analogue technologies is often attributed to their anti-digital qualities: their supposed warmth of sound versus the cold sterility of digital, or the appealing material and visual qualities of analogue formats versus the insubstantiality of the zeroes and ones of MP3s. This may be part of the story, but it's not even the most important part. Rather, the persistence of analogue derives less from its resistance to digital than its symbiotic relationship with digital. When it comes to analogue and digital, it's not a matter of either/or, but one of both/and.

In order to explore this relationship I offer two case studies: one that focuses on listeners, and one on performers (in the figure of the DJ), and both of which revolve around vinyl records. The vinyl record is just one example of an analogue sound technology, but it is talismanic and totemic; more than perhaps any other artefact, it represents, and it is freighted with, analogue values and ideals. The broader purpose of these case studies, and this chapter in general, is to explore the intersections of music, technology and culture, and to understand culture as a crucial force that shapes our musical engagement with technology.

Before proceeding, it is worth taking a moment to consider the differences between analogue and digital. A technology is analogue if it stores or represents data (sound, for example) in continuous patterns. A record groove, which under magnification appears as a sinuous canyon, is an analogue means of reproducing sound; the collection of twists and crags in a particular vinyl canyon are analogous to the ever-changing sounds captured on that record. A technology is digital if it

---

[1] Samantha Green, 'Mini Koo: Nature's Wooden Amphitheater for Your iPhone', *Red Envelope*, 13 November 2012, http://www.redenvelope.com/blog/mini-koo-natures-wooden-amphitheater-for-iphone (accessed 25 January 2013; currently unavailable). Koostik offers other speaker models as well, and is only one of many small companies or individuals that make wooden iPhone speakers. Craft sites like Etsy carry a wide range of iPhone docking stations made of wood from a variety of sources, including driftwood: see https://www.etsy.com/search?q=iphone%20wood%20speaker%20docking%20station. Other examples include a speaker created out of a length of bamboo, and another that affixes small Victrola-like horns to wooden bases.

represents data in the form of discrete values, for example, the 0s and 1s of binary code. MP3s and CDs represent sound as collections of these two digits. According to this standard definition, some very old music technologies could be considered digital. Dating from the nineteenth century and earlier, player pianos, music boxes, barrel organs and other forms of mechanical musical instruments used holes in paper rolls or discs, or pins on cylinders or barrels, to trigger sound. The presence of a hole or pin in a particular position activated a specific pitch; the absence of such a perforation or protrusion left the pitch unactivated, silent. These holes and pins encoded sound as discrete, binary, on/off values, and by all rights should be considered digital. In the popular imagination, analogue and digital map onto the categories of old and new, and by extension suggest antique or modern sounds; in reality, the distinction is less clear.[2] In fact, there is no such thing as digital sound. When we hear sound we experience fluctuations in air pressure that propagate from the source of that sound in the form of waves. Waves are analogue. When we listen to a CD we are thus hearing analogue sound, even if that sound was originally encoded in digital form before being converted into analogue form. That conversion is necessary for the sake of our ears, which can hear waves, but not digits.

If all sound is analogue, what are we talking about when we compare the sound of analogue and digital media? It turns out that we are mostly talking about noise. All sound systems generate noise – that is, sounds that are not part of the signal (for example, music) that the system was intended to capture and reproduce. A diamond-tipped stylus gliding through a vinyl groove generates a wash of white noise, more or less noticeable depending on the quality of the equipment, the condition of the needle and the record, and the amount of dust on the record. Digital systems also create noise, the consequence of tiny timing errors in the mechanism that samples (represents in binary code) the sound of, say, Franz Schubert's *Der Doppelgänger* or Radiohead's 'Paranoid Android' tens of thousands of times per second. This type of error, called jitter, introduces extraneous frequencies that can distort the sound of the music. Both analogue and digital noise arise from technological limitations or defects; the difference lies in how they are perceived. The preference for analogue over digital is really a preference for analogue noise over digital noise.[3] Aden Evens speculates that this preference suggests that analogue noise detracts less from, and is more compatible with, music:

---

[2] Along these lines, David Suisman has argued against 'the narrative of the development of sound recording that proceeds linearly from analogue to digital, from sound-based to data-based' (2010: 17).

[3] There is more to the perception of the differences between the sound of analogue and digital systems than the quality of the noise they generate; frequency range and other factors are significant as well. It is sometimes argued that because the methods used to digitize sound waves ignore certain frequencies – ones that lie beyond the threshold of human hearing or would be masked by other sounds in a recording – the end result is always aurally impoverished because such frequencies, even if not directly perceptible, can shape the quality of those sounds that are perceptible.

'Perhaps the "noise of analogue" meshes better with much music than does "the noise of digital"' (2005: 23).[4]

In fact, the most profound differences between analogue and digital – that is, the differences that seem to matter most to users of these technologies – have little to do with sound at all. Rather, as will become clear in the following two case studies, it is the differences in the physical and symbolic aspects of analogue and digital that matter the most, both for how they are valued and how they enjoy a largely peaceful coexistence.

Case Study 1: Listening to Vinyl

A while back, I called my father to wish him a happy 78th birthday, and while we were on the phone we ended up chatting about records. He expressed surprise when I told him that people were still buying and listening to vinyl discs. 'I have no interest in listening to vinyl records,' he told me. 'Why?' I asked. 'Because I remember them,' he explained. 'What a pain in the ass they were. I'd rather listen to a CD.'

My father could hardly believe that anyone still bothers with vinyl, but in fact sales of vinyl record have soared in recent years. Every year since 2006, global record sales in the USA have increased by at least 20 per cent, according to conservative estimates. Sales may actually be severely under-reported, given that many new records are sold without bar codes, and thus are not registered in any statistical way. And this only accounts for new records; it's reasonable to assume that sales of second-hand records are increasing as well.[5]

What could account for this newfound love of this old technology? I would suggest that listeners have been drawn to vinyl records in recent years for three main reasons: for the supposed superiority of their sound, for the multimodal experience, and out of technostalgia.

First, there is the sound quality. Some who listen to vinyl records ardently believe that the sound of pristine vinyl on a high-end turntable is superior to anything that could be produced digitally. Certainly, a song played on good vinyl will sound fuller and richer than if it were played as a low-bit rate digital file. But high-quality digital files can sound excellent, and even if they sound somewhat different from records, it is difficult to maintain that the sound of one is demonstrably better than the other. At a certain point, comparisons between analogue and digital formats become irreducibly subjective. When listeners are drawn to vinyl because of its sound,

---

[4] My discussion of analogue versus digital noise is indebted to Evens.

[5] Sales of vinyl records have increased consistently and significantly since 2006. In the context of overall music sales, however, vinyl records still account for less than about 3 per cent of the market. For a discussion of the surge in and under-reporting of vinyl sales, see Allan Kozinn, 'Weaned on CDs, They're Reaching for Vinyl', *New York Times*, 9 June 2013, http://www.nytimes.com/2013/06/10/arts/music/vinyl-records-are-making-a-comeback.html (accessed 30 June 2015).

it is because of the distinctive qualities that make it different from, but not necessarily better than, digital. Ironically, and as suggested above, what is most distinctive about the sound of vinyl – and what many listeners value – is the by-product of an inherent defect: the near inescapability of surface noise created by the contact of stylus against vinyl.

A second reason why listeners are drawn to vinyl records is that it engages senses other than hearing, primarily sight and touch, and perhaps even smell. Consider the experience of playing a record in the early twentieth century:

> before ever setting needle to groove, the operator of the phonograph … encountered one of the most remarkable characteristics of recorded sound: its tangibility. Taking the disc out of its paper sleeve, he held the frozen sound in his hands, felt the heft of the thick shellac, saw the play of light on the disc's lined surface. (Katz 2010: 12)

In the years before records were ubiquitous, listeners marvelled at these qualities – at least until they became a household item and remembered more for, as my father described it, being a pain in the ass. Those now embracing vinyl, then, share much in common with their forebears from more than a century ago. They are experiencing records (though now in vinyl, rather than shellac form) for the first time, and they are marvelling at the tangibility of sound.

I saw a demonstration of this sense of wonder in a course I taught to first-year university students. Early in the semester I asked the students how many had ever played a record. Only one or two out of 20 had.[6] Intent on rectifying this poor showing, I organized a spontaneous field trip to my office down the hall, where I kept several turntables. I demonstrated the proper record playing technique, then had them form lines, each student taking a turn with a turntable. These students – for whom the most advanced digital devices are commonplace – were wide-eyed with wonder. What struck them the most was the tactile immediacy of their encounter with vinyl. For students whose interactions with recorded sound were largely limited to the clicking of a mouse or the tapping of a touchscreen, the experience of holding a record, placing it over a spindle and gently (and often not so gently) lowering the stylus into a groove gave them an intimate sense of connection with sound recording that they had never known. Analogue records and digital sound files both offer electronically mediated forms of listening to music; but as this story illustrates, there are many gradations of mediation when it comes to recorded sound, and for many listeners the analogue offers the more immediate experience.

In the multimodal experience of the vinyl record, the sense of sight plays an important role as well. Many music lovers who grew up in the 1970s and before have fond memories of listening to a record soon after purchasing it –

[6] This occurred in 2011. I have continued to poll students in subsequent semesters, and have seen a steady increase in the numbers of students who have had close encounters with vinyl records.

an experience that would engage the eyes as much as the ears. Listening to a record, especially a new one, was often accompanied by attentive contemplation of the cover art and close reading of the text inside. As records shrank into CDs and then evaporated into MP3s, the visual experience of listening changed, diminished in the eyes of many. With the resurgence of vinyl, many listeners are discovering or rediscovering the attendant visual pleasures of listening to vinyl. In marketing vinyl releases, record labels often tout the visuality of the album and include additional artwork. Go into a record shop nowadays and notice the stickers placed prominently on new albums, proclaiming 'INCLUDES A GIANT FOLD-OUT POSTER' or '10 High Quality Photos' or 'Remastered audio with restored artwork'. Some people who buy records in fact do so almost exclusively for their visual qualities, often purchasing them from antique shops or thrift stores for their kitschy or retro covers. There's now a brisk sale of 12 inch by 12 inch frames made exclusively for mounting LPs.

Tied up with, but distinct from, the sensory appeal of vinyl – whether for its sound quality, its tactility or its visual pleasures – is a particular sense of nostalgia that records trigger in many users. This nostalgia has been described as *technostalgia*, a term that has gained currency in various fields of scholarship over the past fifteen years, and refers to a longing for the technologies of past eras.[7] This longing can either be for the technologies of one's own past, or for a technological past that one never experienced; in either case, the technological past is remembered or imagined to be in some way more authentic, immediate or satisfying than the technological present. The vinyl or shellac record is a powerful agent of technostalgia, acting as a metaphor or synecdoche, invoking or standing in for what is presumed to be a simpler, less fraught time. This sense of the past is activated, I would suggest, through visual, aural or tactile experiences with records. Simply looking at a black, grooved disc can have the same effect as the sight of an antique telephone or car, and conjure an entire culture and era now lost to us.

The physical ritual of playing a record – a much more involved process than clicking a mouse or pressing a button – can also connect us to the past. So too can the surface noise of a needle playing dusty vinyl act as a technostalgic trigger. Vinyl's multimodal evocation of memory, whether these memories are real or constructed, is an important part of its current appeal. I look at technostalgia in the same way Trevor Pinch and David Reinecke do. As they explain: 'Technostalgia is more than a [desired] return to an ideal past, but rather an attempt to mediate between past and present to achieve a particular sound and feel' (Pinch and Reinecke 2009: 153).

This mediation between past and present is crucial for understanding the persistence of analogue. New vinyl records sold today very often come with download codes for digital versions of the music. It is now common to see stickers affixed to these releases stating, in all capital letters, 'FREE MP3 DOWNLOAD

---

[7] For more on technostalgia, see Eley (2011), Gill (1997), Pinch and Reinecke (2009) and Taylor (2001): 96–114.

OF THE ENTIRE ALBUM', or similar inducements. Indeed they are inducements, for they offer consumers the best of both worlds: the authenticity and immediacy of vinyl, and the ease and convenience of the MP3. Although it is a rather extravagant example, the 2013 reissue of hundreds of tracks from Paramount, the early twentieth-century popular music label, points to the increasingly common technostalgic strategy of mediating between past and present. The box set included six newly pressed LPs, a portable computer drive (holding MP3 versions of the songs) disguised as an antique phonograph cabinet key, reproductions of vintage Paramount advertisements, and more, all housed in what is described as a 'handcrafted quarter-sawn oak cabinet with lush sage velvet upholstery and custom-forged metal hardware'.[8] Musician Jack White, whose Third Man record label (motto: 'Your turntable's not dead') released the set, explained the distinctive packaging: 'I wanted to make it as appealing as possible to somebody in a physical, tactile way, all of that, the smell, everything, so as to lead you into the incredible stories that are contained in the music.'[9] After purchasing these records (or any release that combines analogue and digital), one can sit at home listening to the vinyl while contemplating its spinning grooves, or one can download the album to a digital player and take it out for a jog. I would argue that for many consumers considering whether or not to buy an LP, it is the digital option that clinches the deal; the MP3 thus helps, not hurts, vinyl sales. Put another way, the persistence of analogue depends in part on the existence of digital.

Case Study 2: DJs and Digital Vinyl

My second case study considers the relationship between DJs and vinyl records. In particular, I will focus on a technology used by DJs called a *digital vinyl system*. To introduce digital vinyl, I want to go back to 2002, when the still-new technology was introduced at a hip-hop DJ battle I attended in New York City.[10]

'Like it or not, this is the future!' The speaker, a representative from the DJ equipment manufacturer Stanton, stood sweating under the stage lights at the B.B. King Blues Club, where the competition was held. He was trying to woo the palpably hostile crowd with his company's new product.[11] The product was called

---

[8] See Third Man, 'Paramount Records Wonder-Cabinet', *Third Man Records*, 24 September 2013, http://thirdmanrecords.com/news/view/paramount-records-wonder-cabinet (accessed 30 June 2015).

[9] Quoted in Larry Rother, 'A Menagerie of Music Lives in a Box: Jack White Explores History of Paramount Records', *New York Times*, 25 October 2013, http://www.nytimes.com/2013/10/27/arts/music/jack-white-explores-history-of-paramount-records.html (accessed 30 June 2015).

[10] Parts of this section draw on Katz (2012), ch. 8, 'Falling Barriers, 2002–2011'.

[11] Unidentified speaker, 5 June 2002, New York City. The event was the 2002 DMC regional battle held at the B.B. King Blues Club and Grill in Manhattan.

Final Scratch, a system that connected laptops to turntables, allowing DJs to play digital sound files by manipulating vinyl records. Standing next to the Stanton rep was DJ B-Side, who had gamely been trying to demonstrate the new technology. Hecklers rained abuse on the pair; some started chanting, 'We want vinyl! We want vinyl!' Never mind that *Final Scratch* did use vinyl; the mere presence of a computer plugged into the traditional analogue system of two turntables and a mixer was offensive to many. After B-Side and the Stanton rep beat a hasty retreat, the competition resumed, with not a computer in sight.

Many hip-hop DJs resisted digital technology at the time, back in 2002, but in the end the Stanton representative was right: this technology was the future. It wasn't love at first sight, as the story about DJ B-Side demonstrates. Nevertheless, countless DJs who got their start in the vinyl age are using digital vinyl systems and rave about them unashamedly. This enthusiasm has come out over and again in my interviews with veteran DJs. 'Thank God [for it],' Steve Dee testified. 'It has saved my life,' gushed Cash Money. Even Afrika Bambaataa, one of the founders of hip-hop told me simply, 'I love it.'[12]

What exactly is this miraculous technology that has some of the most revered DJs swooning for its charms? To understand how a digital vinyl system (DVS) works, I'll use the popular *Serato Scratch Live* system as an example, but most of what I say here can be generalized to other products as well.[13]

Serato Scratch Live consists of two vinyl records, the proprietary *Serato* software, and a small black metal box that acts as an interface between the turntables and computer.[14] At first glance the *Serato* records seem like any other, but they are in fact what are called 'control records'. Encoded with digital time stamps that map onto the MP3s on the DJ's computer, these records simply emit a long, high-pitched sine wave known as a control signal when played on a turntable not connected to a laptop. When played on *Serato*-enabled turntables, however, that long *beeeep* is replaced by a sound file on the computer, which can now be controlled by manipulating the control records. In order for this to happen, the control record conveys three basic bits of information to the software: record speed, record direction (backward or forward) and the position of the needle on the record. This information, in turn, tells the computer how to change the sound of the digital file when the DJ manipulates the record. Scratch or mix a phrase, and you hear just what you would expect if you were using a regular record.

[12] Afrika Bambaataa, telephone interview with the author, 19 July 2011.

[13] In 2013 Serato replaced *Scratch Live* with a new system called *Serato DJ*. At the time of writing it is too early to address the use and impact of the new system. It is, however, similar enough to the old system that the general points made here about *Scratch Live* are likely to apply to the newer system.

[14] The interface can also be built directly into a mixer, the piece of electronic equipment that controls the sound from the turntables (the mixer usually sits between the two turntables) and connects them to the sound system.

The software, as crucial as the control records, is represented by a computer screen filled with an array of coloured symbols, scrolling and rotating graphics, and columns of song information (see Figure 15.1). Functionally, the screen is split into an upper and lower half. The lower simply displays track information taken from the laptop's music library, and is used to locate and select songs to be played. The top half of the screen is where the action is. The two white circles – 'virtual decks', they're called – represent the songs playing on turntables one and two, and indicate beats per minute, the length of the song and the current position in the song. Most eye-catching about the *Serato* screen are the colourful waveform displays that sit in between the virtual decks. The waveform displays provide the DJ with a great deal of information. The different colours indicate frequency, and even bass and snare sounds are colour-coded, making it easy to line up drum hits and match tempos. The *Serato* screen offers an abundance of information to DJs. Some, especially those who learned their craft before the days of the DVS, barely look at their laptops; others get lost in their screens, their faces taking on a blank expression – a look common enough to have its own (derisive) moniker: 'Serato Face' (White 2013).

Figure 15.1 *Serato Scratch Live* software screenshot
Source: Serato INC LP 2015.

A DVS is, as its name suggests, a digital technology, but analogue simulation is its *raison d'être*. The control records, though encoded with digital time stamps that map onto the MP3s on the DJ's computer, simulate the traditional analogue vinyl record. Serato and other DVS manufacturers even encourage a traditional analogue vinylphilia among DJs by making the control discs a collector's item, offering them in a wide variety of colours and patterns, usually in limited quantities.[15] The virtual decks and the waveforms offer analogues to the revolving record and the groove density of traditional vinyl, though both offer more information than the original analogue could provide. As with the recent releases of vinyl records that come with download codes (or USB drives), the appeal of the DVS is its digital–analogue hybridity. It is this hybridity that, as I'll explain, makes the DVS a more popular option for hip-hop DJs than a purely digital alternative which might seem to offer as much or more in terms of functionality and convenience.

Over the course of the past decade, the digital vinyl system has become a staple in the world of the hip-hop DJ. Go to a club, a house party or an outdoor jam, and more likely that not, if you see a set of turntables, you'll see it tethered to a laptop. What's especially noteworthy about this development is that DVS is, at least in the hip-hop world, considerably more successful than another digital alternative to the traditional analogue turntable technology: the *CD turntable*. CD turntables, which allow DJs to manipulate CDs through a plastic, simulated record platter known as a jog wheel, came onto the market at about the same time as DVS. Like DVS, the CD turntable allows DJs to do many things that can be done with purely analogue turntables, as well as many things that can't be done on turntables at all.

Despite the many capabilities of the CD turntable, many hip-hop DJs reject the technology. So why is it that two digital forms of DJing – one that uses a CD player and one that uses a laptop computer – are treated so differently by hip-hop DJs? The answer is simple: vinyl. In short, DVS allows DJs to keep what they love about vinyl – its feel, look and authenticity – and avoid what they don't love about it – its weight, cost and inconvenience.

The feel of the CD turntable is markedly different from that of a traditional turntable. Most crucially, the jog wheel just doesn't have the immediacy and tactility of vinyl. As DJ Maseo, longtime DJ and member of the group De La Soul, explained: 'I like the feeling of that wax. Licking my fingers so I can get that grip on the record, spin it back and cut it up.' 'Vinyl is the essence of DJing,' he maintained; he identified its absence as the CD turntable's 'main flaw'.[16]

There are crucial ideological objections to CD players as well. The absence of vinyl is a serious problem for many hip-hop DJs, but not just because they miss its feel. Vinyl is a precious substance in hip-hop. It is authentic, it is elemental, it is fundamental. Vinyl was present at and largely responsible for the birth of hip-hop. There is more than just music inscribed in those black discs; vinyl carries with it the whole history, the DNA, of hip-hop. Some DJs even see the decision to use vinyl as an ethical choice. For example, in a Facebook post from 2012, a veteran turntablist and battle champion DJ characterized the use of CD turntables as an act of infidelity. 'If You Ever see Me On A pair Of CDJ's [CD turntables] I Give

15 A Facebook group, Serato Control Vinyl Collectors' Group, had over 2,400 members as of late 2013. See: https://www.facebook.com/groups/SeratoControlVinylCollectors/ (accessed 30 June 2015).

16 DJ Maseo, telephone interview with the author, 17 November 2011.

You All the green Light To Slap the Shit Out of Me On the Spot!, if you catch Me Cheating On These.'[17] And by 'These', he was referring to traditional turntables.

Back in 2002 I asked the world champion turntablist (and now producer) A-Trak what he thought about digital DJing, at the time still a new development:

> I definitely think that vinyl is fundamental to turntablism, but these new technologies can be good tools or good additions to what we do. For a while I wasn't even paying attention to any of them, but now with the Pioneer CDJ [CD turntable] and especially with Final Scratch and this new version called Serato Scratch (which is being developed right now) you can't help but want to try it out and see how you can integrate it into what you do. But what you do as a turntablist stays essentially rooted in vinyl.[18]

A-Trak identifies two different forces here – technology and culture – which, although not necessarily in opposition, exert distinct pressures on DJs. When A-Trak says of the digital technologies, 'You can't help but want to try it out,' he seems irresistibly drawn to these new tools, curious about how their features might expand his musicianship. But his first and final sentences reveal what is, for him and many of his colleagues, an even stronger force. And that is vinyl, which stands in for hip-hop DJ culture. At that point in his career A-Trak hadn't made his choice between CDJ and DVS. He chose the latter, and when he did, his sense of DJ culture was a decisive factor. Faced with a choice between two digital systems, A-Trak (and countless other hip-hop DJs) favoured the one that valorizes vinyl, that symbol of an analogue age in music.

Conclusion: Technocultural Choice and the Analogue–Digital 'Divide'

A-Trak's words illustrate what I call *technocultural choice*, a concept that I believe helps us understand the persistence of analogue in a digital age. The process of deciding what technologies to use and how to use them, and indeed our whole relationship with technology, is driven by more than features, design and cost. Technology, neither invisible nor deterministic, exists in a state of constant interplay with cultural and subcultural forces, all of them shaping how we engage with music. In the case of vinyl-loving listeners, it is not so much the real or perceived sonic superiority of the medium that drives their choice. They are drawn to vinyl because it allows them to engage with music in a particular way, one that feels to them more immediate and immersive, and thus perhaps more authentic and meaningful. Such an attitude towards vinyl is necessarily embedded within the cultural values of the listener. Perhaps vinyl evokes nostalgia for a lost age, signifies a rejection of rampant disposability and instant gratification, announces

---

17 DJ Cheese, post to the Facebook group '1200s and Vinyl DJs Only', 2 May 2012.

18 DJ A-Trak, e-mail message to the author, 26 August 2002.

its owner's hipness or connoisseurship, or some combination of these and other attitudes. For hip-hop DJs, the widespread adoption of DVS is only partly about the differences in user interface. The decision is also tied up with notions of history, authenticity and legitimacy. In every case, the choice of vinyl reveals a good deal about the values of its users. This is what I mean by technocultural choice.

To make a final point, the story of analogue's persistence is not one of resistance to, but rather coexistence with, digital technology. We speak of a digital age, as if digital has completely supplanted analogue.[19] Yet digital is simply a means of representing data in discrete values; digital audio technologies are mute until the 0s and 1s can be converted in sonorous, analogue waves. Analogue technologies once existed, and thrived, without digital assistance; their current popularity, however, owes a great deal to their association with digital. Digital depends on analogue; analogue depends on digital. Think of it as a May/December romance. Analogue turntables and vinyl records gain new life from their connection with digital technologies, while the older technologies bring a sense of history and credibility to the relationship. It may be a codependent relationship, but as it turns out, this tale of analogue and digital is a love story.

References

Buckley, Jake (2011) 'Believing in the (Analogico-)digital', *Culture Machine*, 12, pp. 1–15.

Davis, John D. (2007) 'Going Analog: Vinylphiles and the Consumption of the "Obsolete" Vinyl Record', in *Residual Media*, ed. Charles R. Acland, Minneapolis, MN: University of Minnesota Press, pp. 222–36.

Eley, Craig (2011) 'Technostalgia and the Resurgence of Cassette Culture', in *The Politics of Post-9/11 Music: Sound, Trauma, and the Music Industry in the Time of Terror*, ed. Joseph P. Fisher and Brian Flota, Farnham: Ashgate, pp. 43–54.

Evens, Aden (2005) *Sound Ideas: Music, Machines, and Experience*, Minneapolis, MN: University of Minnesota Press.

Gill, Pat (1997) 'Technostalgia: Making the Future Past Perfect', *Camera Obscura*, 14, pp. 161–79.

Katz, Mark (2010) *Capturing Sound: How Technology Has Changed Music*, 2nd edn, Berkeley, CA: University of California Press.

——— (2012) *Groove Music: The Art and Culture of the Hip-hop DJ*, New York: Oxford University Press.

Massumi, Brian (2002) *Parables for the Virtual: Movement, Affect, Sensation*, Durham, NC: Duke University Press.

[19] Cultural theorists and philosophers have problematized the commonplace notion that analogue and digital are somehow mutually exclusive. See, for example, Massumi (2002): 133–43 ('On the Superiority of the Analog'), and Buckley (2011).

Osborne, Richard (2012) *Vinyl: A History of the Analogue Record*, Farnham: Ashgate.

Pinch, Trevor and Reinecke, David (2009) 'Technostalgia: How Old Gear Lives on in New Music', in *Sound Souvenirs: Audio Technologies, Memory, and Cultural Practices*, ed. Karin Bijsterveld and José van Dijck, Amsterdam: Amsterdam University Press, pp. 152–68.

Suisman, David (2010) 'Sound, Knowledge, and the "Immanence of Human Failure": Rethinking Musical Mechanization through the Phonograph, the Player-piano, and the Piano', *Social Text*, 28/1, pp. 13–34.

Taylor, Timothy D. (2001) *Strange Sounds: Music, Technology, and Culture*, New York: Routledge.

PART V
Composing and Performing with Electronic Means

Chapter 16
Semiconducting: Making Music after the Transistor[1]

Nicolas Collins

Introduction

At some point in the late 1980s the composer Ron Kuivila proclaimed: 'We have to make computer music that sounds like electronic music.'[2] This might appear a mere semantic distinction. At that time, the average listener would dismiss any music produced with electronic technology – be it a Moog or Macintosh – as 'boops and beeps'. But Kuivila presciently drew attention to a looming fork in the musical road: boops and beeps were splitting into boops and bits. Over the coming decades, as the computer evolved into an unimaginably powerful and versatile musical tool, this distinction would exert a subtle but significant influence on music.

Kuivila and I had met in 1973 at Wesleyan University, where we both were undergraduates studying with Alvin Lucier. Under the guidance of mentors such as David Tudor and David Behrman, we began building circuits in the early 1970s, and finished out the decade programming pre-Apple microcomputers like the Kim 1. The music that emerged from our shambolic arrays of unreliable homemade circuits fit well into the experimental aesthetic that pervaded the times (the fact that we were bad engineers probably made our music better by the standards of our community). Nonetheless, we saw great potential in those crude early personal computers, and many of us welcomed the chance to hang up the soldering iron and start programming.[3]

---

[1] This chapter is adapted from a lecture first presented at the 'Technology and Aesthetics Symposium', NOTAM (Norwegian Centre for Technology in Music and the Arts), Oslo, 26–27 May 2011, revised for presentation at the conference 'Musical Listening in the Age of Technological Reproducibility. Giovanni Morelli in Memoriam', Venice, 22–24 March 2013. The author gratefully acknowledges NOTAM's support for his research.

[2] Private conversation, New York City, exact date unknown.

[3] Although this potential was clear to our small band of binary pioneers, the notion was so inconceivable to the early developers of personal computers that Apple trademarked its name with the specific limitation that its machines would never be used for musical applications, lest it infringe on The Beatles' semi-dormant company of the same name – a decision that would lead to extended litigation after the introduction of the iPod and *iTunes*. This was despite the fact that the very first non-diagnostic software

The Ataris, Amigas and Apples that we adopted in the course of the 1980s were vastly easier to program than our first machines, but they still lacked the speed and processor power needed to generate complex sound directly. Most computer music composers of the day hitched their machines to MIDI synthesizers, but even the vaunted Yamaha DX7 was no match for the irrational weirdness of a table strewn with Tudor's idiosyncratic circuits arrayed in unstable feedback matrices. One bottleneck lay in MIDI's crudely quantized data format, which had been optimized for triggering equal-tempered notes, and was ill suited for complex, continuous changes in sound textures. On a more profound level, MIDI 'exploded' the musical instrument, separating sound (synthesizer) from gesture (keyboard, drum pads or other controller) – we gained a Lego-like flexibility to build novel instruments, but we severed the tight feedback between body and sound that existed in most traditional, pre-MIDI instruments and we lost a certain degree of touch and nuance.[4]

Now, MIDI no longer stands between code and sound: any laptop has the power to generate directly a reasonable simulation of almost any electronic sound – or at least to play back a sample of it. But I'm not sure that Kuivila's goal has yet been met. I can still hear a difference between hardware and software. Why?

After all, most music today that employs any kind of electronic technology depends on a combination of hardware and software resources. Although crafted and/or recorded in code, digital music reaches our ears through a chain of transistors, mechanical devices, speakers and earphones. 'Circuit benders' who open and modify electronic toys in pursuit of new sounds often espouse a distinctly anti-computer aesthetic, but the vast majority of the toys they hack in fact consist of embedded microcontrollers playing back audio samples – one gizmo is distinguished from another not by its visible hardware, but by the program hidden in ROM. Still, whereas a strict hardware/software dialectic can't hold water for very long, arrays of semiconductors and lines of code are imbued with

---

written and demonstrated at the Homebrew Computer Club in Menlo Park, California in 1975 was a music program by Steve Dompier, an event attended by a young Steve Jobs. See 'Homebrew Computer Club', *Convivial Tools Database*, http://www.convivialtools.net/index.php?title=Homebrew_Computer_Club (accessed 30 June 2015).

4 For more on the implications of MIDI's separation of sound from gesture, see Collins (1998). One magnificent exception to the gesture/sound disconnect that MIDI inflicted on most computer music composers was Tim Perkis's 'Mouseguitar' project of 1987, which displayed much of the tactile nuance of Tudor-esque circuitry. In Perkis's words: 'When I switched to the FM synth (Yamaha TX81Z), there weren't any keydowns involved; it was all one "note" .... The beauty of that synth – and why I still use it! – is that its failure modes are quite beautiful, and that live patch editing [can] go on while a voice is sounding without predictable and annoying glitches. The barrage of sysex data – including simulated front panel button-presses, for some sound modifications that were only accessible that way – went on without cease throughout the performance. The minute I started playing the display said "midi buffer full" and it stayed that way until I stopped' (email from Tim Perkis, 18 July 2006).

various distinctive traits that combine to determine the essential 'hardware-ness' or 'software-ness' of any particular chunk of modern technology.

Some of these traits are reflected directly in sound – with sufficient attention or guidance, one can often hear the difference between sounds produced by a hardware-dominated system versus those crafted largely in software. Others influence working habits – how we compose with a certain technology, or how we interact with it in performance; sometimes this influence is obvious, but at other times it can be so subtle as to verge on unconscious suggestion. Many of these domain-specific characteristics can be ignored or repressed to some degree, just like a short person can nevertheless play basketball, but they nonetheless affect the likelihood of one choosing a particular device for a specific application, and inevitably exert an influence on the resulting music.

I want to draw attention to some distinctive differences between hardware and software tools as applied to music composition and performance. I am not particularly interested in any absolute qualities inherent in the technology, but in the ways certain technological characteristics influence how we think and work, and the ways in which the historic persistence of those influences can predispose an artist to favour specific tools for specific tasks. My observations are based on several decades of personal experience: in my own activity as a composer and performer, and in my familiarity with the music of my mentors and peers, as observed and discussed with them since my student days. I acknowledge that my perspective comes from a fringe of musical culture, and I contribute these remarks in the interest of fostering discussion, rather than to prove a specific thesis.

I should qualify some of the terms I will be using. When I speak of 'hardware' I mean not only electronic circuitry, but also mechanical and electromechanical devices from traditional acoustic instruments to electric guitars. By 'software', I'm designating computer code as we know it today, whether running on a personal computer or embedded in a dedicated microcontroller or digital signal processor (DSP). I use the words 'infinite' and 'random' not in their scientific sense, but rather as one might in casual conversation, to mean 'a hell of a lot' (the former) and 'really unpredictable' (the latter).

The Traits

Here are what I see as the most significant features distinguishing software from hardware in terms of their apparent (or at least perceived) suitability for specific musical tasks, and their often-unremarked influence on musical processes:

- Traditional acoustic instruments are three-dimensional objects, radiating sound in every direction, filling the volume of architectural space like syrup spreading over a waffle. Electronic circuits are much flatter, essentially two-dimensional. Software is inherently linear, every program a one-dimensional string of code. In an out-take from his 1976 interview with Robert Ashley for Ashley's *Music with Roots in the Aether*, Alvin Lucier justified his lack of interest in the hardware of electronic music with the statement, 'sound is three-dimensional, but circuits are flat'.[5] At the time Lucier was deeply engaged with sound's behaviour in acoustic space, and he regarded the 'flatness' of circuitry as a fundamental weakness in the work of composers in thrall to homemade circuitry, as was quite prevalent at the time. As a playing field, a circuit may never be able to embody the topographic richness of standing waves in a room, but at least a two-dimensional array of electronic components on a fibreglass board allows for the simultaneous, parallel activity of multiple strands of electron flow, and the resulting sounds often approach the polyphonic density of traditional music in three-dimensional space. In software, most action is sequential, and all sounds queue up through a linear pipeline for digital-to-analogue conversion. With sufficient processor speed and the right programming environment, one can create the impression of simultaneity, but this is usually an illusion – much like a Bach flute sonata weaving a monophonic line of melody into contrapuntal chords.[6] Given the ludicrous speed of modern computers, this distinction might seem academic – modern software does an excellent job of simulating simultaneity. Moreover, 'processor farms' and certain DSP systems do allow true simultaneous execution of multiple software routines. But these latter technologies are far from commonplace in music circles, and like writing prose, the act of writing code (even for parallel processors) invariably nudges the programmer in the direction of sequential thinking. This linear methodology can affect the essential character of work produced in software.

- Hardware occupies the physical world, and is appropriately constrained in its behaviour by various natural and universal mechanical and electrical laws and limits. Software is ethereal – its constraints are artificial, different for every language, the result of linguistic design rather than pre-existing physical laws. When selecting a potentiometer for inclusion in a circuit, a designer has a finite number of options in terms of maximum resistance, curve of resistive change (linear or logarithmic), number of degrees of rotation, length of its slider and so on, and these characteristics are fixed at the point of manufacture. When implementing a potentiometer in software, all these parameters are infinitely

[5] This quote is drawn from my memory of working as a technical assistant on the recording session, and has been confirmed by one other colleague present at the time. This version of the interview was not used in the final video series or transcribed in the book, but Lucier has made similar observations in subsequent interviews.

[6] This limitation in software was a major factor motivating Kuivila to develop, with David Anderson, the programming language Formula, whose strength lay in its accurate control of the timing and synchronization of parallel musical events – taking linear code a little closer to planar. See David P. Anderson and Ron Kuivila, *FORMULA Version 3.4 Reference Manual*, May 1991, http://www.eecs.berkeley.edu/Pubs/TechRpts/1991/5643.html (accessed 30 June 2015).

variable, and can be replaced with the click of a mouse. Hardware has edges; software is a *tabula rasa* wrapped around a torus.

- As a result of its physicality, hardware – especially mechanical devices – often displays non-linear adjacencies similar to state-changes in the natural world (think of the transition of water to ice or vapour). Pick a note on a guitar, then slowly raise your fretting finger until the smooth decay is abruptly choked off by a burst of enharmonic buzzing as the string clatters against the fret. In the physical domain of the guitar, these two sounds – the familiar plucked string and its noisy dying skronk – are immediately adjacent to one another, separated by the slightest movement of a finger. Either sound can be simulated in software, but each requires a wholly different block of code: no single variable in the venerable Karplus and Strong 'plucked string algorithm' (1983) can be nudged by a single bit to produce a similar death rattle; this kind of adjacency must be programmed at a higher level, and does not typically exist in the natural order of a programming language. Generally speaking, adjacency in software remains very linear, while the world of hardware abounds with abrupt transitions. A break point in a hardware instrument – fret buzz on a guitar, the unpredictable squeal of the STEIM Cracklebox[7] – can be painstakingly avoided or joyously exploited, but is always lurking in the background – a risk, an essential property of the instrument.
- Most software is inherently binary: it either works correctly or fails catastrophically, and when corrupted code crashes, the result is usually silence. Hardware performs along on a continuum that stretches from the optimum behaviour intended by its designers to irreversible, smoky failure; circuitry – especially analogue circuitry – usually produces sound even as it veers toward breakdown. Overdriving an amplifier to distort a guitar, feeding back between a microphone and a speaker to play a room's resonant frequencies, 'starving' the power supply voltage in an electronic toy to produce erratic behaviour – these 'misuses' of circuitry generate sonic artefacts that can be analysed and modelled in software, but the risky processes themselves (saturation, feedback, under-voltage) are very difficult to transfer intact from the domain of hardware to that of software while preserving functionality in the code.[8] Writing software favours Boolean thinking – self-destructive code remains the purview of hackers who craft worms and Trojan horses for the specific purpose of crashing or corrupting computers.
- Software is deterministic, while all hardware is indeterminate to some degree. Once debugged, code runs the same every time. Hardware is notoriously unrepeatable: consider re-creating a patch on an analogue

[7] See 'Cracklebox', *Studio for STEIM*, http://steim.org/product/cracklebox/ (accessed 30 June 2015).

[8] This comparison echoes the familiar 'digital versus analogue' distinction, but I prefer to focus on the difference between software and hardware because even digital hardware can be made to sing outside its 'normal' mode of operation.

synthesizer, restoring mixdown settings on a pre-automation mixer, or even tuning a guitar. The British computer scientist John Bowers once observed that he had never managed to write a 'random' computer program that would run, but that he could make 'random' component substitutions and connections in a circuit with a high certainty of a sonic outcome (a classic technique of circuit bending).[9]

- Hardware is unique, software is a multiple. Hardware is constrained in its 'thinginess' by number: whether handcrafted or mass-produced, each iteration of a hardware device requires a measurable investment of time and materials. Software's lack of physical constraint gives it tremendous powers of duplication and dissemination. Lines of code can be cloned with a simple Ctrl/Cmd-C and Ctrl/Cmd-V: building 76 oscillators into a software instrument takes barely more time than one, and no more resources beyond the computer platform and development software needed for the first. In software, there is no distinction between an original and a copy: MP3 audio files, PDFs of scores and runtime versions of music programs can be downloaded and shared thousands of times without any deterioration or loss of the matrix – any copy is as good as the master. If a piano is a typical example of traditional musical hardware, the pre-digital equivalent of the software multiple would lie somewhere between a printed score (easily and accurately reproduced and distributed, but at a quantifiable – if modest – unit cost) and the folk song (freely shared by oral tradition, but more likely to be transformed in its transmission). Way too many words have already been written on the significance of this trait of software – of its impact on the character and profitability of publishing as it was understood before the advent of the World Wide Web; I will simply point out that if all information wants to be free, that freedom has been attained by software, but is still beyond the reach of hardware. (I should add that software's multiplicity is accompanied by virtual weightlessness, while hardware is still heavy, as every touring musician knows too well.)
- Software accepts infinite undos, and is eminently tweakable. But once the solder cools, hardware resists change. I have long maintained that the young circuit-building composers of the 1970s switched to programming by the end of that decade because, for all the headaches induced by writing lines of machine language on calculator-sized keypads, it was still easier to debug code than to de-solder chips. Software invites endless updates, whereas hardware begs you to close the box and never open it again. Software is good for composing and editing, for keeping things in a state of flux; hardware is good for making reasonably stable, playable instruments that you can return to with a sense of familiarity (even if they have to be tuned). The natural outcome of software's malleability has been the extension of the programming process from the private and invisible pre-concert preparation

[9] Private conversation, Norwich, England, January 2004.

of a composition to an active element of the actual performance – as witnessed in the rise of 'live coding' culture practised by devotees of the SuperCollider[10] and ChucK[11] programming languages, for example. Live circuit-building has been a fringe activity at best: David Tudor finishing circuits in the pit while Merce Cunningham danced overhead, the group Loud Objects soldering PIC microcontroller chips on top of an overhead projector, and live coding versus live circuit-building in ongoing competition between the younger Nick Collins (UK) and the author for the Nic(k) Collins Cup.[12]

- On the other hand, once a program is burned into ROM and its source code is no longer accessible, software flips into an inviolable state. At this point, re-soldering, for all its unpleasantness, remains the only option for effecting change. Circuit benders hack digital toys not by rewriting the code (typically sealed under a malevolent beauty-mark of black epoxy), but by messing about with traces and components on the circuit board. A hardware hack is always lurking as a last resort, like a shim bar when you lock your keys in the car.
- Thanks to computer memory, software can work with time. The transition from analogue circuitry to programmable microcomputers gave composers a new tool that combined characteristics of instrument, score and performer: memory allows software to play back pre-recorded sounds (an instrument), script a sequence of events in time (a score) and make decisions built on past experience (a performer). Before computers, electronic circuitry was used primarily in an instrumental capacity – to produce sounds immediately.[13] It took software-driven microcomputers to fuse this trio of resources into a new paradigm for music creation.
- Given the sheer speed of modern personal computers and software's quasi-infinite power of duplication (see above), software has a distinct edge over hardware in the density of musical texture it can produce: a circuit is to code as a solo violin is to the full orchestra. But at extremes of its behaviour, hardware

[10] See 'SuperCollider', *GitHub*, http://supercollider.github.io/ (accessed 30 June 2015).

[11] See 'ChucK: Strongly-timed, Concurrent, and On-the-fly Music Programming Language', http://chuck.cs.princeton.edu/ (accessed 30 June 2015).

[12] See Nic Collins, 'The History Of The Nic(k) Collins Cup', http://www.nicolascollins.com/collinscup.htm (accessed 30 June 2015).

[13] Beginning in the late 1960s, a handful of artist-engineers designed and built pre-computer circuits that embodied some degree of performer-like decision-making: Gordon Mumma's 'Cybersonic Consoles' (1960s–70s), which as far as I can figure out were some kind of analogue computers; my own multi-player instruments built from CMOS logic chips in emulation of Christian Wolff's 'co-ordination' notation (1978). The final stages of development of David Behrman's 'Homemade Synthesizer' included a primitive sequencer that varied pre-scored chord sequences in response to pitches played by a cellist ('Cello With Melody Driven Electronics', 1975) presaging Behrman's subsequent interactive work with computers. And digital delays begot a whole school of post-Terry Riley canonical performance based on looping and sustaining sounds from a performance's immediate past into its ongoing present.

can exhibit a degree of complexity that still seems beyond the power of software to simulate effectively: the initial tug of rosined bow hair on the string of the violin; the unstable squeal of wet fingers on a radio's circuit board; the supply voltage collapsing in a cheap electronic keyboard. Hardware still does a better job of giving voice to the irrational, the chaotic, the unstable.

- Software is imbued with an ineffable sense of now – it is the technology of the present, and we are forever downloading and updating to keep it current. Hardware is yesterday, the tools that were supplanted by software. Vinyl records, patchcord synthesizers and tape recorders have been replaced by MP3 files, software samplers and *Pro Tools*. In the ears and minds of most users this is an improvement – software does the job 'better' than its hardware antecedents. Before any given tool is replaced by a superior device, qualities that don't serve its main purpose can be seen as weaknesses, defects or failures: the ticks and pops of vinyl records, oscillators drifting out of tune, tape hiss and distortion. But when a technology is no longer relied upon for its original purpose, these same qualities can become interesting in and of themselves. The return to 'outmoded' hardware is not always a question of nostalgia, but often an indication that the scales have dropped from our ears.

Hybrids

There are three areas of software/hardware crossover that deserve mention here: (1) interfaces for connecting computers (and, more pointedly, their resident software) to external hardware devices; (2) software applications designed to emulate hardware devices, and (3) the emergence of affordable rapid prototyping technology.

The most ubiquitous of the hardware interfaces today is the Arduino, a small, inexpensive microcontroller designed by Massimo Banzi and David Cuartielles in 2005.[14] The Arduino and its brethren and ancestors[15] facilitate the connection of a computer to input and output devices, such as tactile sensors and motors. Such an interface can imbue a computer program with some of the characteristics we associate with hardware, but there always remains a MIDI-tinged sense of mediation (a result of the conversion between the analogue and the digital domains) that makes performing with these hybrid instruments slightly hazier than with a purely hardware device – think of manipulating a robotic arm with a joystick, or hugging an infant in an incubator while wearing rubber gloves.

[14] See http://www.arduino.cc/ (accessed 30 June 2015). Close to 500,000 Arduinos had been sold as of early 2013.

[15] Most notably the STEIM SensorLab (see 'Legacy Products', *Studio for STEIM*, http://steim.org/product/discontinued-products/ [accessed 30 June 2015]) and the Infusion Systems I-Cube (see http://infusionsystems.com/catalog/index.php and http://www.xspasm.com/x/sfu/vmi/ISEA95.html [accessed 30 June 2015]), more expensive MIDI-based interfaces produced in the 1990s.

The past decade has also seen a proliferation of software emulations of hardware devices, from smartphone apps that simulate vintage analogue synthesizers to *iMovie* filters that make your HD video recording look like scratchy Super 8 film. The market forces behind this development (nostalgia, digital fatigue and so on) lie outside of the scope of this chapter, but it is important to note here that these emulations succeed by focusing on those aspects of a hardware device most easily approximated in the software domain: the virtual Moog synthesizer models the sound of analogue oscillators and filters, but doesn't try to approximate the glitch of a dirty pot or the pop of inserting a patch cord; the video effect alters the colour balance and superimposes algorithmically generated scratches, but does not let you misapply the splicing tape or spill acid on the emulsion.

Although at the time of writing affordable 3D printers and rapid prototyping devices remain the purview of the serious DIY practitioner, there is no question that these technologies will enter the marketplace in the near future. When they do, the barrier between freely distributable software and tactile hardware objects will become quite permeable. A look through the Etsy website[16] reveals how independent entrepreneurs have already employed this technology to extend the publishing notion of 'print on demand' to something close to 'wish on demand'.

Conclusion

I came of age as a musician during the era of the 'composer–performer': the Sonic Arts Union, David Tudor, Terry Riley, LaMonte Young, Pauline Oliveros, Steve Reich, Philip Glass. Sometimes this dual role was a matter of simple expediency (established orchestras and ensembles wouldn't touch the music of these young mavericks at the time), but more often it was a desire to retain direct, personal control that led to a flowering of composer-led ensembles that resembled rock bands more than orchestras. Fifty years on, the computer – with its above-mentioned power to fuse three principle components of music production – has emerged as the natural tool for this style of working.

But another factor driving composers to become performers was the spirit of improvisation. The generation of artists listed above may have been trained in a rigorous classical tradition, but by the late 1960s it was no longer possible to ignore the musical world outside the gates of academe or beyond the doors of the European concert hall. What was then known as 'World Music' was reaching American and European ears through a trickle of records and concerts. Progressive jazz was in full flower. Pop was inescapable. And composers of my age – the following generation – had no need to reject an older tradition to strike out in a new direction: Indian music, Miles Davis, The Beatles, John Cage, Charles Ives and Monteverdi were all laid out in front of us like a buffet, and we could heap our plates with whatever pleased us, regardless of how odd the juxtapositions might seem.

16 http://www.etsy.com.

Improvisation was an essential ingredient, and we sought technology that expanded the horizons of improvisation and performance, just as we experimented with new techniques and tools for composition.

It is in the area of performance that I feel hardware – with its tactile, sometimes unruly properties – still holds the upper hand. This testifies not to any failure of software to make good on its perceived promise of making everything better in our lives, but to a pragmatic affirmation of the sometimes messy but inarguably fascinating irrationality of human beings: sometimes we need the imperfection of things.

References

Collins, Nicolas (1998) 'Ubiquitous Electronics – Technology and Live Performance 1966–1996', *Leonardo Music Journal*, 8, pp. 27–32.

Karplus, Keven and Strong, Alex (1983) 'Digital Synthesis of Plucked String and Drum Timbres', *Computer Music Journal*, 7/2, pp. 43–55.

Chapter 17
'Live is Dead?': Some Remarks about Live Electronics Practice and Listening

Angela Ida De Benedictis

Here we offer some considerations on performing practice with live electronics, in a deliberately 'open' format in which the discussion can be rather erratic. Actually, this is a theoretical 'reflection in progress' that requires a fundamental premise and has some inevitable limitations. One of the limitations lies in the decision to focus above all on European art music produced since the early 1980s, determining both the examples and the treatment.[1] The premise derives from the realization that for many of the producers and/or sound engineers I have consulted during the research, and indeed for a number of composers, live electronics simply *no longer exists* (hence the provocation implicit in the title). Many performers,[2] whether on the basis of their practical experience or for aesthetical or poetical reasons, now call into question a category which – with the new technologies and means for synthesizing and processing sound – has taken on new practical and conceptual meanings and which can now be analysed in a historical and theoretical perspective.

Today 'live electronics' is used as a *passe-partout* term that may refer to equipment, a set of technological instruments or a performing practice. Composers themselves may consider it a creative medium or a performing medium, depending on whether it is seen as a 'linguistic' requisite (in order to broaden audio horizons), an 'operative' requisite (involving a more profound interaction between author, performer and machine) or simply a 'technological' requisite.

---

[1] Hence the decision to exclude from this chapter the first period of live electronics which nonetheless saw masterpieces such as *Mikrophonie* (*I* and *II*) and *Mantra* by Stockhausen (on this early period, see Haller 1996). During the convention, another limitation came to light in all its complexity: although we were speaking about 'listening', no musical examples were presented referring to the musical production discussed. Its deferred reproduction would have involved an irreparable short-circuit between the typology of sound discussed and the listening conditions that were available in the conference room, *a posteriori*, using pre-recorded examples. I shall come back later to this complex issue concerning the reproduction of music with live electronics.

[2] It should be noted that in live performance, the 'performer' often coincides with the 'composer'.

In the complex and heterogeneous universe of electroacoustic music, the term 'live electronics' implies a clear opposition between real-time and non-real-time. By definition, all music is 'live' at the moment of listening and performance, even when it is played back on tape. But in this case what is 'live' is not the music, but the electronics: the standard meaning of live electronics is the processing, elaboration and control of the sound in real time during a concert,[3] giving the acoustic event the 'vital energy' of a performance.[4]

However, since the 1980s the use, and indeed definitions, of live electronics have become so extended and diversified as to make impossible a single, unequivocal, all-embracing definition.[5] Today, for example, speaking of music that is transformed in real time, we are beginning to distinguish between 'live electronics', 'live computer music' and 'non-digital live electronic music'.[6] Moreover, live electronics is increasingly used in an interactive way to generate other forms of artistic expression, ranging from installations to multimedia works, theatre to motion capture, and so on. But even if we remain in the commonly accepted semantic sphere, there is general consensus as to the existence of two main phases of live electronics: the 'historical' phase (in the 1980s and 1990s), characterized by a limited and virtually standard technology (Harmonizer, Halaphon, delays, filters and so on), and the more recent phase, in Europe referring to centres like the Institut de Recherche et Coordination Acoustique/Musique, universities or private studios, characterized by a hybridization of live electronics with computer music, where 'real-time' applies to the transformation of certain parameters (such as dynamics), whereas other audio dimensions are pre-recorded.[7] In both these macro-phases, every work realized using live electronics may be seen as a more or less convincing and successful response to questions touching three fundamental aspects (all of which have specific implications for listening):

---

3 I include also the elaboration of sounds which have been processed or recorded in real time (and reused during the performance, whether transformed or identical).

4 In some cases, the vital energy of the sound transformed in real time is compounded by the vital energy of a *creative* and/or *improvisational* threshold achieved during the performance by composer/performers.

5 See, among others, the definitions of live electronics in Emmerson (2007): xv–xvi, 104, *passim*; Emmerson (2012): 152–5; Frisius (2011): 251–71; Cremaschi and Giomi (2005b): 7; Haller (2000): 213, and in general, Haller (1995); and Montague (1991): 85.

6 See Jordà (2007): 89. Jordà makes a further distinction between 'computer-based realtime music system' (which includes live electronics) and 'non-digital live electronic music'. Among the most recent experimentations, we can recall the improvisation groups for laptop ensembles, which also imply new notational solutions (see Lee and Freeman 2013).

7 The German composer and sound engineer Andreas Breitscheid (2009) has called these two phases 'reactive' (1980s and 1990s) and 'interactive' (from the 1990s to the present) (typescript kindly made available to me by the author). See also Stroppa (1999), esp. 47. In the terminology of Nicolas Collins (Chapter 16 in this volume), the two phases could be divided up into 'hardware' and 'software'.

1. spatial projection of the sound;
2. 'interpretation' of sounds modified electronically in real time;
3. interaction between composer, performer and technology.

A fourth fundamental aspect concerns the particular modality of transmission and notation of these musical works, which I shall come back to later.

Given the jungle of existing definitions and applications, it would hardly be meaningful or useful to present an overview of the individual replies given by composers and musicologists to the question: 'What is live electronics?' Instead, starting from an analysis of the applications made since the 1980s, it will be more productive to discuss some issues implicit in the use of live electronics in music – a 'hyperinstrument' able to control 'a large number of relations', whose action 'begins at the design stage, continues at the moment of performance and culminates in the listener's imagination' (Cremaschi and Giomi 2005b: 13).

Live electronics implies a process of interpenetration between composition, sound production technique (during the performance), transformation technique and listening process. In analysing this complex system, it is important to dwell on the difference between events in real time (typical of live electronics) and non-real-time events. This is particularly appropriate because – at least in the early days of live electronics – the composers doing the groundwork for this experimentation (Nono, Berio, Boulez and Stockhausen, among others) were the same ones who in previous years conducted experiments with tape recording and/or in radiophonic studios. The term 'live', as we have suggested, indicates a watershed between music produced and composed in the studio (studio electronics) and music realized and electronically transformed in real time during performance (regardless of whether the modified event is performed live or is pre-recorded, instrumental or synthetic). In the first case, in the studio, the electronic technology plays the role of a 'compositional instrument' (which generates or transforms material fixed prior to the performance); in the second case, it seems to play the role of a 'performing instrument' (the machine transforms an audio element and, as we shall see below, 'depends' on this).

At the same time, this distinction implies (1) a performing equivalence and (2) a creative difference:

1. whether it is deferred or live, it is still 'music for loudspeakers', and in both cases it presupposes a new, conscious use of space as well as various typologies of listening;
2. but in live electronics, the space becomes a structural and *creative* component of the work, an element which is modified artificially and elaborated 'musically' on the basis of specific artistic requirements.

The loudspeakers no longer serve (only) to project sounds, but 'participate' in the work's definition as sound sources for discrete events projected in space: their position corresponds to that of an instrumentalist, or group of instruments,[8] in a spatial arena (whether artificial or virtual) constructed *ex novo* for each new event. At the creative level, precisely on account of the changes the composer can introduce in successive interpretations in every new space, with respect to composition in studio,[9] the emphasis moves from *listening by doing*, typical of tape composition, to *doing by listening*, which characterizes live electronics.

We can identify one further oscillation – in terms of both practice and theory – *vis-à-vis* 'non-real-time music' in the concept of the *synchronization* of events, which is fundamental in any use of electronics in the studio. In compositions using live electronics, the emphasis seems to be rather on the *de-synchronization* and flexibility of and between events, as well as on being able to control and vary in real time the sound parameters which are harder to determine and quantify – timbre and dynamics. Thus, on one hand the live capturing and processing involves different sound components which – to use a term dear to Luigi Nono – have to *con-fuse* together (see Vidolin 1996: 42–7); on the other hand, in listening (above all on account of the spatial projection), the individual lines that make up this mobile and articulated intermingling can be perceived as stratified and directional, rather than as *con-fusion*. From this perspective, and from a strictly conceptual standpoint, live electronics seems to stand as an unmistakable evolution of a 'serial' approach, as the triumph of a vision of the various parameters that is synthetic and interactive, rather than compartmentalized and hierarchical. In live electronics, in fact, each parameter of the sound can influence and modify the next, or be influenced by it in its turn: with the Harmonizer, for example, timbre can become rhythm; with the Halaphon, tempo becomes movement; and again harmony becomes tempo, and everything becomes dynamics.[10] To cite Tristan Murail (1980: 78), in live electronics sound is no longer seen as the sum of various parameters, but as a 'force field' in which each 'force' undergoes its own evolution.

Compared to composition in the studio (whether analogue or digital) and computer music, in live electronics there is a true schism between two sound states: the 'composed' and the 'interpreted'. To these two categories, outlined by

---

8 On 'loudspeakers as instruments', see also Emmerson (2007): 149–69.

9 Whether for tape/analogic or digital/informatic.

10 In this respect, what Luigi Nono said in 1981 about the use of live electronics in *Das atmende Klarsein* is also of interest: 'not only the transformed sound, as sole perceptive phenomenon, or the sound elaborated and fixed on tape, but also the "live-natural" sound of the chorus and bass flute and, *at the same instant* and not in the temporal or visual succession, its becoming other, its germinating both as compositional spectrum and as spatial dynamic' (Nono 1981).

Marco Stroppa (1999: 54),[11] I would add a third one: the 'processed' state (surely processing and interpretation are two different levels in the performing practice of live electronics). It is in the dialectic between these three different perspectives on the state of the sound material that the use of live electronics reveals all its innovative potential, and at the same time its limits (and ambiguities). In traditional music, just as in tape music or computer music, the composed sound coincides with the interpreted sound (regardless of the media used in capturing the sound and the various performing practices). In live electronics, on the other hand, there is a scission among the three states, which in the most extreme cases can actually change the status of the work: the level of what is 'composed' – fixed in the score, when this exists, as in the patches, in the programs and algorithms regulating the sound transformation[12] – is the equivalent not of the *Werk*, but of the stage immediately preceding the audio 'definition' of the work itself (its 'rendering in sound'), which is realized only in the performance. The work is realized and completed only at the moment of performance and listening, and its interpretation using electronics in real time bestows on it an additional layer which cannot be analysed, transcribed or reiterated.[13]

In saying this, I am well aware that every work, in all traditions, is 'completed' only in performance and listening, and that, in the case of written traditions, a sign devoid of sound is unheeded. But it is precisely this awareness that makes the new type of dissociation which, in performances of music using live electronics, is created between eye and ear even more evident. Precisely on account of the dialectics between action and transformation typical of live performance, what is stated in scores or programs (and duly realized by acoustic or electronic instruments) does not correspond to what is heard, to the sound of those same instruments modified by live electronics technology.[14] On one hand, what is fixed in the score is a skeleton which will not be heard as such; and on the other, what is fixed in the patches, the algorithms or the electronic score describes a process, not the audio event (Figures 17.1–3). In the first case, the eye is betrayed by a fictitious coincidence between sign and sound, whereas in the second, by the impossibility of representing the event using signs.

---

11 See also Stroppa's handout 'Assistance à la diffusion et à l'interpretation: une application potentielle pour la nouvelle station de travail IRCAM' (December 1988): 3; copy consulted at the Paul Sacher Stiftung, Basle.

12 Or also the pre-recorded samples in the most hybrid cases.

13 In some cases, the importance of listening is mimed in the performative act itself: in some of Nono's projects, such as *Découvrir la subversion: hommage à Edmond Jabès* or *Post – Prae – Ludium n. 3 Baab-arr*, which understandably remained unfinished (or impossible to finish), the soloist had to move around the platform or among the audience, playing and almost 'following' the transformed sound projected over the loudspeakers, allowing him/herself to be guided by listening (see also Vidolin 1996: 44).

14 This dissociation between eye and ear proper to the performative act is quite distinct from the associative process of sight-listening typical of the perceptive act (discussed below, pp. 313–14).

This dissociation is also reflected during performance: the action of the Harmonizer, of spatialization, and of a performer's filtering of the sound has immediate effects on the perception of the event, so that the performative action and the aural response (listening) do not coincide. The consequences of this 'dissociative revolution' also influence the speculative field of analysis, which can no longer take only the physical score as its starting point (as in traditional music), or just the sound (as in concrete or electronic music): it has to work on the awkward combination of score and sound (fixed *donnée* and interpreted *donnée*). This leads to a dual problem: not only is the concept of 'reading' and 'listening' to the score abundantly superseded and called into question (What are we reading? What are we listening to?), but one might also ask: *What are* the 'objects' to be analysed: do they refer to the 'skeleton' event or the defined 'body' of sound?[15]

The answers provided to date have been as numerous and diverse as the analyses carried out on music with live electronics. But whether one focuses on the project (the skeleton), the 'nude' structure (the score) or the 'clothed' object (the audio realization), each analysis is legitimate and at the same time limited and misleading. One possible solution could be to reshape the investigative methods so that analysis of the work becomes analysis of the performance (or of the performed work).

In works with live electronics – and this has not changed since the 1980s – there are contemporary 'processual' dimensions corresponding to two different musical practices: the realization of the instrumental part is often linked to the written tradition, while the part of live electronics is often conditioned (even when defined using algorithms) by a practice quite close to oral performance. The performance itself is the result of a hybridization involving the audio materialization of a defined 'object' – regardless of the degree to which it is merely outlined, indeterminate or closed – and a processuality typical of the creative context of *doing*:

> The interpretative practice becomes a fundamental aspect of the life of a work once any stable medium (such as the score or tape) becomes absolutely insufficient to reproduce, in itself, its complexity. The audio image of music with live electronics ... cannot exist without the performers, whose role is further renewed with respect to tradition. (Cremaschi and Giomi 2005b: 8–9)

It is also for this reason, and in view of the ongoing development of technology, that today it is becoming more and more difficult to establish boundaries between *performance* (performance of an event that can be reproduced) and *electronic-*

---

[15] Each experience of listening with live electronics is in fact inherently artificial and conditioned by specific external (local) and internal (psycho-acoustic) conditions. The same doubt concerns the 'philological' enquiries or issues, which have to be re-discussed and redefined on each new occasion: the project for the work is one thing, its performability and mobility another.

based installation (an event, often unique, whose focuses on the listener/viewer): the electronic transformation of live sound is increasingly used as one of the ingredients in the realization of unique and non repeatable events,[16] or for concept-works which are mutant and never the same twice over.[17] Thus, a performance using live electronics is a 'live' musical process, also because it is always potentially influenced by physiological, acoustic and spatial components (and also by the psychological interaction between performers and composer) which often rule out a precise notation.

Scholars, performers and in many cases also composers have discussed much about the difficulty, or indeed impossibility, of notating music with live electronics. In fact, the topic touches on what is perhaps the most problematic issue concerning this musical practice: its transmissibility (in the spheres of publishing, performance and recording).[18] In the existing scores – I am thinking of both the 'historical' specimens, which are invariably lacking in one respect or another, and the more recent editions or re-editions (Figures 17.4 and 17.5) – the data that can be more or less established, relating to the transposition, selection and control of the sound, are always notated together with other relative data that are relative (and may even be totally lacking), such as the dynamics, temporal functions and sound localization.[19] However, it would be a mistake to see this as a limit: right from the first applications (and one is bound to think of Luigi Nono), it was clear that this type of sound world *could not* (by its very nature) have a specific notation, but was destined to remain empirical and delivered in a series of performances which were always potentially new and/or renewable (not so much 'work in progress' as 'progress in the work').

Above all, in the first phase of live technology (in the 1980s and 1990s), such an awareness led to true interaction between the work and the composer, and in a certain sense this *appeared* to take music back to a pre-transcriptive age (prior

---

16 In order to 'relive' the work in a similar fashion, one should have turned to a video recording of the event, which would betray *tout court* the aural dimension implicit in the work.

17 It should be noted that in these cases the problem of reproducibility is not related to the notation (the algorithm exists and is to be applied in all the various performances), but to the *hic et nunc* nature of the performed sound event.

18 When recording works with live electronics on CD, studio simulations are often used (which may in fact be preferable to a recording of the original event performed live). This, for example, is the case of the edition of *Orfeo cantando tolse* by Adriano Guarnieri, where the live electronics are replaced by a stereophonic simulation of the sound spatialization (see Vidolin 2005: 91, note); and also of the recordings on disc of *NoaNoa* for flute and live electronics by Kaija Saariaho.

19 When it exists, the electronic score (above all in 'historic' works using live electronics) is often the last element to be completed in the graphic elaboration (but not in the creative process). Many decisions are taken or revised during the rehearsals immediately preceding the first performance. Again, in the parts relating to the electronics one has to distinguish between general (fixed) and local (changeable) indications, the latter referring to the performance spaces.

to musical notation, or at any rate to the early stages of its development). I wish to emphasize the word 'appeared', because what is lacking is not the notation: even if not complete, notation is at least present in the form of annotations, notes, a project, a program or whatever, or else it is latent in the performing indications provided by the composer in a whole range of forms. Rather, what is lacking is a shared code which could make that type of annotation perfectly decipherable or inductively reproducible.[20] It is not unusual for the sign to incorporate data that are 'said but not set down', which may be lost or become even more vague as the technology develops and changes.[21] In fact, some composers (Berio, Nono, Boulez and Stockhausen, among others) came to rely on a 'group' performing practice which allowed the performers – who were almost always the same – to interpret scores beyond what was actually notated. In some cases, the score itself became the upshot of the experimentation carried out with the performers.[22] All this meant not only that the composer often became a performer of him/herself (together with a trusted team of performers and sound engineers), but also – even more radically – that any 'detachment' between the composer, his/her work and his/her usual performers becomes impossible. In the Western tradition of art music, this detachment can in fact only be mediated and realized in notation (by which I mean the fixing of the sound on whatever medium – paper, digital, mnemonic or other).

In this respect, the positions of Nono and Stroppa, similar and yet opposing, are emblematic.[23] For Nono, experimentation with live electronics made more and more evident the impossibility of fixing on paper the sound reality (he had already come up against this limitation during the 1960s and 1970s). But this 'notatory impotence', and the consequent state of approximation in which Nono left his scores involving live electronics in the 1980s, did not worry him particularly: as he said, it was not so important whether a work outlived him or not (Nono 1987: 423). For him, the interest in creation lay 'in the moment of working, of study, in the

[20] Nono, for example, in the period he spent working at the Experimental Studio in Freiburg, kept notes of every single experiment performed with the machines (see Haller 1995, vol. 2: 119–20, 154). At the rehearsal stage he set down almost everything on paper (albeit often in a personal semiography), ensuring that each experiment was reproducible. In the case of impossible scores like the first edition of *Guai ai gelidi mostri* (see Figure 17.4), it is not the annotation that is lacking, but precisely a cognitive practice of decodification, making the work practically illegible.

[21] Above all for the scores now considered 'historic' there is a sort of oxymoron: the more advanced the technology, the greater the 'undefined' element in the score.

[22] As Vidolin recalls: 'Nono himself was at the console and gave indications to his collaborators during the work's actual performance, but these were rarely noted down, above all on account of the difficulty of transcribing them' (1996: 47). This is one reason why Nono's scores with live electronics often feature the names not of the instruments, but of the performers ('Ciro', 'Roberto', 'Rudi').

[23] It should be noted that these two examples are cited as extreme cases which nonetheless reveal two tendencies that are readily recognizable in composition with live electronics.

errors that are made and from which we discover fantastic things. Afterwards, the interest is bound up with the possibilities of still being able to change something. And then you have to abandon everything, even in a rather brutal fashion' (Nono 1987: 424), to go on to new compositions. Although this statement – like whatever has been placed on record by composers – has to be filtered and interpreted with due precaution, we can nonetheless recognize a significant awareness. Nono knew that the pursuit of a 'mobile' sound, achieved using live electronics, imposed an indissoluble bond between his presence and the realization, the performance act and indeed the life of the work itself. When it existed, the notation became a 'hypothesis', and the first versions of some works – for example, *Das atmende Klarsein*, *Guai ai gelidi mostri* or *Omaggio a Kurtág* – have to be seen as trials for the ultimate verification, often cast in new versions (or editions), which in turn are also potentially 'verifiable' and 'subject to other performances' in contexts with a different resonance and different spaces.[24]

We can see the same awareness in Marco Stroppa, although he was very keen to ensure that his works should be performed in the future. As early as 1988 he declared that there are three implicit reasons for the 'need' to find a system of notation for electronics. The main reason reflects:

> my wish to separate myself from a finished work as soon as possible, to give it a life that is independent of my physical presence, and to ensure that, however complex it is, this score can be understood and performed by anyone willing to devote enough time and concentration to the task. (Stroppa 1991: 488)[25]

This led to a very critical stance – which he developed as time went on – regarding live electronics, and the desire to establish *a priori* the 'potential for interpretation' of his sound material according to a *fichier de sons*, moving on from live electronics first to computer music and then to 'chamber electronics' (based on a technology of synchronic languages) which celebrated the 'reliability' of deferred sound, while renewing it: 'This potential must be defined in advance by the composer

---

24 In his unending pursuit of new sound spaces, Nono always changed the sound projection and spatialization at each performance, so that each indication in the score in this respect has to be taken as 'relative'. Nothing is dogmatic, whether the indication of the sound's movement or delays or feedback, and above all not the arrangement and orientation of the loudspeakers. See (in Haller 1995, vol. 2: 151, 152–4) the account of five different performances of *Guai ai gelidi mostri*, in Paris in 1985, in IRCAM's *Espace de projection*, each time with a different exploitation of the space. We can note in passing the proliferation and extension in this context of the term 'version': with the practice of live electronics, this term becomes ambiguous, its meaning oscillating between 'structural' variations (pertaining to the creative process) and 'local' variations (pertaining to the performative process).

25 The second need derives from the wish to provide the performer (in this case, the pianist in *Traiettoria ... deviata*) a means for 'synchronizing' the instrumental and electronic parts.

according to his own creative will and the nature of the material. This leaves the performer free to explore this field of potentialities' (Stroppa 1988: 3).

In his careful critique of live electronics, Stroppa further argued that not only is it unlikely to have real 'scores' for productions involving live electronics, but that even the concept of 'repertory' proves to be impossible (Stroppa 1999: 54). The same conclusion is reached in a recent book devoted to the analysis of music using live electronics, where it is said that this production: 'raises major issues … on account of its determination to exist outside a tradition or a stable, universally recognized practice able to mediate between the composers' ideas and the audience' (Cremaschi and Giomi 2005b: 9). However, the problem risks becoming tautological: one must take care not to apply to this production terms which are perhaps (at least conceptually) unrelated to it. By definition, music with live electronics lies *outside* a tradition on account of the technology it adopts. In fact, the radical development and continuous renewal of the technologies – which is matched by their sudden demise – makes it impossible for:

1. any program or machine to become 'tradition';
2. any performing or prescriptive procedure to become 'a stable practice';
3. any form of listening to become consolidated or 'universally recognized'.

If they did, we would be in the presence of a contradiction in terms, with *live* being transformed into *frozen-live* and the concept of 'tradition' immediately mutating into 'archaeology'.

In practice, the revolution (more conceptual than practical) that live electronics has introduced into the music world has been to restore to the performing event (in art music) a genuine aura of 'unrepeatability', or rather, an 'immanence of sound' which has nothing to do with a 'return to orality'.[26]

In using the term 'revolution', one may wonder – except for a few rare cases – whether such a revolution has ever actually taken place, and whether, in the extraordinary panorama of works with live electronics, the use of technology can really be seen as 'structural' or as a 'vital' component of the work. If one runs down even a partial list of these works (as found, for example in the online catalogues of music publishers, including Ricordi, Schott and Suvini Zerboni, or the programmes of recent music festivals), there is a clear separation between works devised to exploit live electronics – composed starting from the idea of transforming the sound, so that the technology is structural and the electronics serves to convey the author's creative intentions – and works composed regardless of the modifications of the sound made subsequently in real time. The first group

[26] The reference is to the theses set out by Walter Ong (1982). From this point of view, the use of live electronics overturns Benjamin's premise and makes the reproducibility of a sound event impossible.

of works includes compositions which many sound engineers I have consulted for this research refer to as 'real live': virtually Luigi Nono's output of the 1980s, certain works by Berio (*Ofaním* and *Altra voce*), works like Marco Stroppa's *Spirali*, and again some compositions by Tristan Murail, Adriano Guarnieri and so on. The second group is much larger, extending to names such as Pierre Boulez[27] and Salvatore Sciarrino. This progressive loss of a 'structural sense' for live electronics emerges above all in the most recent production of art music, where often the transformations in real time are merely accessory, providing a 'colouring' of spatialization or delay.[28] The affirmation of this second attitude to live electronics reveals (or is the consequence of) various issues – which may include purely economic or pragmatic considerations (such as a restricted number of rehearsals or the time available for research)[29] – and is often an indicator of a generational change. For the first who experimented with live electronics, its use represented an answer to a compositional or aesthetical problem. These were composers who – for the most part – were *not* familiar with the machinery, but had a clear idea of the sound they wanted; they put themselves entirely in the hands of 'intermediaries' and specialized collaborators able to assist them in the various phases of creation and performance. Today, the use of live electronics is often the prerogative of musicians who themselves experiment with and prepare patches and algorithms; they are proficient with the technology, and their compositions apparently provide responses to the technology rather than to questions of poetics.[30] They often establish the computer score and define its implementation, the synthesis algorithms, the language of computer notation, the performance environment and so on. What was once the task of a team made up of several professional figures (in addition to the composer and the instrumentalists, the hardware designer, computer analyst, programmer, sound technician and sound engineer) is nowadays increasingly taken care of by the composer him/herself.

---

27 Apart from compositions like *Répons* (1981–5), where live electronics almost exclusively achieves a spatial projection of the strands of sound (see the visualization of the spatialization project for the six instruments published in Boulez and Gerzso 1988: 26–7), for Boulez one could speak of 'structural electronics' only for *...explosante-fixe...* (1991–3).

28 Among the various accounts gathered during my research, I must mention particularly the private conversations I had with Francesco Giomi (13 March 2013), Marco Stroppa (6 March 2013), Alvise Vidolin (9 March 2013) and Andreas Breitscheid (4 June 2009). See also Stroppa (1999): 52.

29 Except for rare and important exceptions, it is no coincidence that the 'structural' use of live electronics came to be increasingly associated with a reduction in the equipment used and to favour chamber ensemble or solo forces as opposed to orchestral or operatic forces.

30 In this parabola towards works viewed as 'technological experiments', there has also been a mutation in the figure of the sound assistant or technician, less and less used by composers.

Up to now, I have tried to use the word 'interaction' sparingly. I am convinced that, above all when speaking of the performing sphere, one should revise the common perception of the interaction between performer and electronic technology, which too often conjures up a sort of mythical aura surrounding the practice of electroacoustics in real time.

There is no doubt that live electronics exerts an influence, starting from a 'live' musical process, on a musical form that may be more or less 'free' or fluid. In the same way, there can be no doubt that the instrumentation associated with live electronics allows us to produce new sounds or, to quote Nicolas Collins, to induce 'new approaches to organising the sonic world' (2007: 38). Nor is there any doubt that the apparatus of live electronics is not merely a technical medium, but constitutes a set of 'generative' instruments which extend indefinitely the acoustic reality ('liveness') of musical phenomena.

The doubts concern whether or not one can speak of live electronics as a 'performance instrument',[31] even when this vision is extended to real-time applications of computer music (like the UPIC [Unité Polyagogique Informatique CEMAMu] in Xenakis).

Let us go back to the distinction between the 'reactive' and 'interactive' dimensions of live electronics.[32] Actually, live electronics represents a gregarious instrument, and I think it is misleading to speak of a real 'interaction' between instruments and electronics. In musical productions using live electronics, there is a *principal sound event* (natural, when produced live by performers; synthetic, if produced by machinery) which in any case becomes the 'generator of a series of *derived events* yielded by the electronic treatment' (Vidolin 1996: 42; my italics). The system responds to a 'pilot sound' which, in purely theoretical and conceptual terms, paradoxically endorses the priority of the onstage event (whether instrumental, vocal or synthetic) over the transformations of the live electronics: if the performers of the pilot sound fall silent, the live electronics is also silent.

From the capturing via a microphone, used either as a 'microscope'[33] or as 'the magnification of the work's minimal, acoustic, musical aspects',[34] to the spatialization of the same events transformed and projected according to ever-changing sound trajectories, the reality of a 're-active' condition for live electronics ('pre-active' for the live performer) remains an immutable constant. But it is more problematic to speak of a truly 'inter-active' condition between the

[31] I borrow the expression from Pierre Bernard (1991): 47–57.

[32] See note 7 above.

[33] This metaphor recurs in several composers, including Berio, Nono, Stockhausen and Stroppa.

[34] Luciano Berio, interview for the television programme *Superquark* (Milan, Teatro alla Scala, 17 September 1999), RAI-Radiotelevisione Italiana (I wish to thank Francesco Giomi for bringing this interview to my attention).

actors of the principal and derived sound events.[35] Certainly, electronics responds to the acoustic event, but the contrary is practically impossible. If one is going to speak of 'interaction' or of the instrumentalist's response to the electronics, surely it is true to say that music for instruments and tape is actually more interactive (*Kontakte* by Stockhausen, ... *sofferte onde serene* ... by Luigi Nono, *Musica su due dimensioni* by Maderna, to give a few examples).

Lastly, we can ask whether it is true, as is often claimed, that true 'interaction' in live electronics takes place between performers and audience in the act of listening. This question reveals a further paradox produced by music using live electronics, once hailed as the 'triumph of listening', but which in reality has endorsed a subtle but inevitable shift of focus, in terms of performance perception, from the ear to the eye.

During performances with live electronics, the presence of the performers onstage is fundamental, just as they have to perform sounds produced by an instrument (which may also be the voice or a computer) that is recognized as such by the community of listeners. A performer hidden from the audience's sight or the presence on stage of no more than a mixing board cannot make a performance with live electronics seem 'live'.[36] With live electronics, the visual aspect, which is already predominant in a concert situation, takes on a greater (and certainly not lesser) importance than the aural aspect. If we have to speak of 'interaction' in this music, it may perhaps be what, thanks to the electronics, is achieved in the audiovisual perception of an event in which sound and environment are projected into a 'third perceptive dimension' where the frontality of sight combines with the poly-directionality of listening.

We can find proof of the fact that live electronics alone is not enough to 'revolutionize' the act of listening if we think of listening with one's eyes closed (often invoked by composers).[37] In fact, this bears out the arguments of those who claim that the era and traditional concept of live electronics belong to the past: when concert-goers can listen but not see, it is practically impossible to establish the difference between a sound event that has been transformed and projected into space in real time, and one that has been pre-transformed and is broadcast over loudspeakers using specific spatial strategies (just as it is often impossible to identify the nature or origin of the sound event in a recording of music with live electronics). And whenever, in asserting the status of 'pure' listening, attempts have been made to get rid of at least part of the visual apparatus associated with electronics, the consequences and repercussions have had an even more dramatic effect on the alleged 'interactive' sphere, or on that 'interpenetration' of acoustic and electronic instruments that is traditionally exalted in live performance.

---

35 'Interaction is not interpretation, since the latter, if it ideally implies the former, is a much subtler and more complex phenomenon' (Stroppa 1999: 52).

36 On the importance of the 'body' in electronic music, see also Peters et al. (2012).

37 See also Emmerson 2007: 168–9.

In this respect, one of the performances of *Ofaním* by Luciano Berio – a work that involved massive and complex use of electronics[38] – may well represent an extreme case. It took place at the Opéra Bastille, Paris in 1992, five years prior to the work's definitive version (1997). Alvise Vidolin, the sound engineer who worked since the 1980s alongside many composers including Nono, Berio and Sciarrino, recalls for that performance:

> Berio did not want the electronics to be visible in the auditorium (unlike Nono and [the staff of the studio in] Freiburg, who actually displayed it on stage, with the control board at the centre of the stalls). … When we did *Ofaním* in Paris at the Opéra Bastille (1992) we were behind the stage, in a separate room, and couldn't see anything of what was happening in the auditorium; we only had two little loudspeakers as monitors. During the rehearsals there was someone in the auditorium … who gave us indications concerning the levels over a radio. And what's more, the performance of the electronic part was anything but plain sailing. There were delays with feedback that had to be calibrated in real time according to the voices and the soloists. The fact that we couldn't hear what was going on in the auditorium made our task almost impossible. It's rather as if you made a pianist play with his ears blocked up: even if he managed to play the right keys, the result is bound to be disappointing precisely because musical performance depends on listening to what you are playing (all the more so in collective music making). Preventing a performer from hearing the sounds he is making and relating them to those of the others makes musical nonsense.[39]

In addition to the transmission of music, to making (performing) music, and to the concept of 'interaction' between humans, electronic technology and listening, there are other issues associated with live electronics which I have only alluded to, or completely passed over. For example: the collective dimension of the activity; the current function of the sound engineer – a figure who, over time and with the evolution of technology, has undergone a radical change, if not completely disappeared; or again the restrictions imposed by concert organizers who, with limited budgets and no time for rehearsals, have put an end to any real experimentation with live electronics. In postponing these issues for another occasion,

[38] See Giomi et al. (2003), who also give diagrams of the arrangement of the loudspeakers and the sound spatialization in *Ofaním*.

[39] Alvise Vidolin, email to the author, 12 March 2013 (quoted by kind permission). Vidolin goes on: 'Paris was not the only case: at the Philharmonie in Berlin (1993) we were up in the gods, hidden behind a curtain … [while] at the Lingotto in Torino (1997) we were behind the stage …. For *Outis* things were a bit better (we were in the royal box), even if for some parts Berio had us determining the orchestral sound levels working "in the dark" on the pre-editing mixer which was in a room separated from the royal box.'

I wish to end with one final provocation that calls into question the very paradox that was my starting point ('live is dead?').

Whether alive or dead, in fact, it is undeniable that, from the 1980s onwards, live electronics brought about a fundamental change in musical experience, shifting the focus from compositional problems (central to its immediate progenitor, music for tape) to problems of performance, listening and reproducibility of the event. However, we can recognize in this change the squaring of a circle which – starting with Schönberg and Varèse and continuing through 12-tone music, serialism, electronic music to live electronics and all their derivations – surrounds the (overblown) universe of *timbre*, illuminating it with a new light so that, conceptually and aesthetically, this 'revolution' too can be seen in the perspective of an imperceptible and fragmentary continuity …

Translated by Mark Weir

References

Bernard, Pierre (1991) 'The UPIC as a Performance Instrument', *Contemporary Music Review*, 6/1, pp. 47–57.

Boulez, Pierre and Gerzso, Andrew (1988) 'Computers in music', *Scientific American*, 258/4, pp. 26–32.

Breitscheid, Andreas (2009) 'Live electronics e tecniche digitali: nuove forme di collaborazione dietro la produzione del suono', paper presented at the conference 'Scolpire il suono', Casa della Musica, Parma, 4 June.

Collins, Nick and d'Escriván, Julio (eds) (2007) *The Cambridge Companion to Electronic Music*, Cambridge: Cambridge University Press.

Collins, Nicolas (2007) 'Live Electronic Music', in Collins and d'Escriván (2007), pp. 38–54.

Cremaschi, Andrea and Giomi, Francesco (eds) (2005a) *Il suono trasparente: analisi di opere con live electronics*, Lucca: LIM.

Cremaschi, Andrea and Giomi, Francesco (2005b) 'Introduzione', in Cremaschi and Giomi (2005a), pp. 7–13.

De Benedictis, Angela Ida and Rizzardi, Veniero (eds) (2001) *Luigi Nono. Scritti e colloqui*, 2 vols, Milan: Ricordi.

Emmerson, Simon (2007) *Living Electronic Music*, Aldershot: Ashgate.

——— (2012) 'Live Electronic Music or Living Electronic Music?', in Peters et al. (2012), pp. 152–62.

Frisius, Rudolf (2011) 'Elektronik – Live? Paradoxen in der Musikentwicklung des 20. Jahrhunderts: Das Problem der Live-Elektronik als "Unanswered Question"' [1997], in *Die Innovation bleibt immer auf einem Fleck. Die Donaueschinger Musiktage und ihr Metier. Begleitende Texte zum Festival*, ed. Armin Köhler, Mainz: Schott, pp. 251–71.

Giomi, Francesco, Meacci, Damiano and Schwoon, Kilian (2003) 'Live Electronics in Luciano Berio's Music', *Computer Music Journal*, 27/2, pp. 30–46.

Haller, Hans Peter (1995) *Das Experimentalstudio der Heinrich-Strobel-Stiftung des Südwestfunks Freiburg 1971–1989: die Erforschung der elektronischen Klangumformung und ihre Geschichte*, 2 vols, Baden-Baden: Nomos.

——— (1996) 'Live-Elektronik', in *Von Kreinichstein zur Gegenwart. 50 Jahre Darmstädter Ferienkurse*, Stuttgart: Daco Verlag, pp. 450–57.

——— (2000) 'La tecnica del "live electronic" allo Studio sperimentale di Friburgo', in *Luigi Nono e il suono elettronico*, Milan: Edizioni del Teatro alla Scala, pp. 213–17.

Jordà, Sergi (2007) 'Interactivity and Live Computer Music', in Collins and d'Escriván (2007), pp. 89–125.

Lee, Sang Won and Freeman, Jason (2013) 'Real-time Music Notation in Mixed Laptop-acoustic Ensembles', *Computer Music Journal*, 37/4, pp. 24–36.

Montague, Stephen (1991) 'Live Electronics – Introduction', *Contemporary Music Review*, 6/1, pp. 85–8.

Murail, Tristan (1980) 'La révolution des sons complexes', in *XVIII Ferienkurse '80*, ed. E. Thomas, Mainz: Schott, pp. 77–92.

Nono, Luigi (1981) 'Das atmende Klarsein', in De Benedictis and Rizzardi (2001), vol. 1, p. 487.

——— (1987) 'Intervista di Philippe Albèra', in De Benedictis and Rizzardi (2001), vol. 2, pp. 415–29.

Ong, Walter (1982) *Orality and Literacy: The Tecnologizing of the Word*, London: Methuen.

Peters, Deniz, Eckel, Gerhard and Dorschel, Andreas (eds) (2012) *Bodily Expression in Electronic Music: Perspectives on Reclaimed Performativity*, New York: Routledge.

Stroppa, Marco (1991) 'Un orchestre synthétique: Remarques sur une notation personnelle' [1988], in *Le timbre: métaphore pour la composition*, ed. J.-B. Barrière, Paris: Christian Bourgois and IRCAM, pp. 485–538.

——— (1999) 'Live Electronics or … Live Music? Towards a Critique of Interaction', *Contemporary Music Review*, 18/3, pp. 41–77.

Vidolin, Alvise (1996) 'Il suono mobile', in *Con Luigi Nono*, ed. R. Doati, Milan and Venice: Ricordi and La Biennale, pp. 42–7.

——— (2005) 'Percorsi sonori di un teatro immaginario. Da *Noms des airs* a *Lohengrin II*', in Cremaschi and Giomi (2005a), pp. 89–109.

Figure 17.1 Luciano Berio, *Altra voce* (for alto flute, mezzo-soprano and live electronics): exemplification of bars 29–33 of *Altra voce* by Luciano Berio, reproduced at the top as established in the printed edition (Universal Edition) and at the bottom in their probable audio rendering according to the transpositions obtained by applying the algorithms for the Harmonizer

Source: Giomi et al. (2003): 35. Luciano Berio, *Altra voce* | für Altflöte, Mezzosopran und live electronics. © Copyright 1999 by Universal Edition AG, Wien/UE, 35958. Reproduced by kind permission.

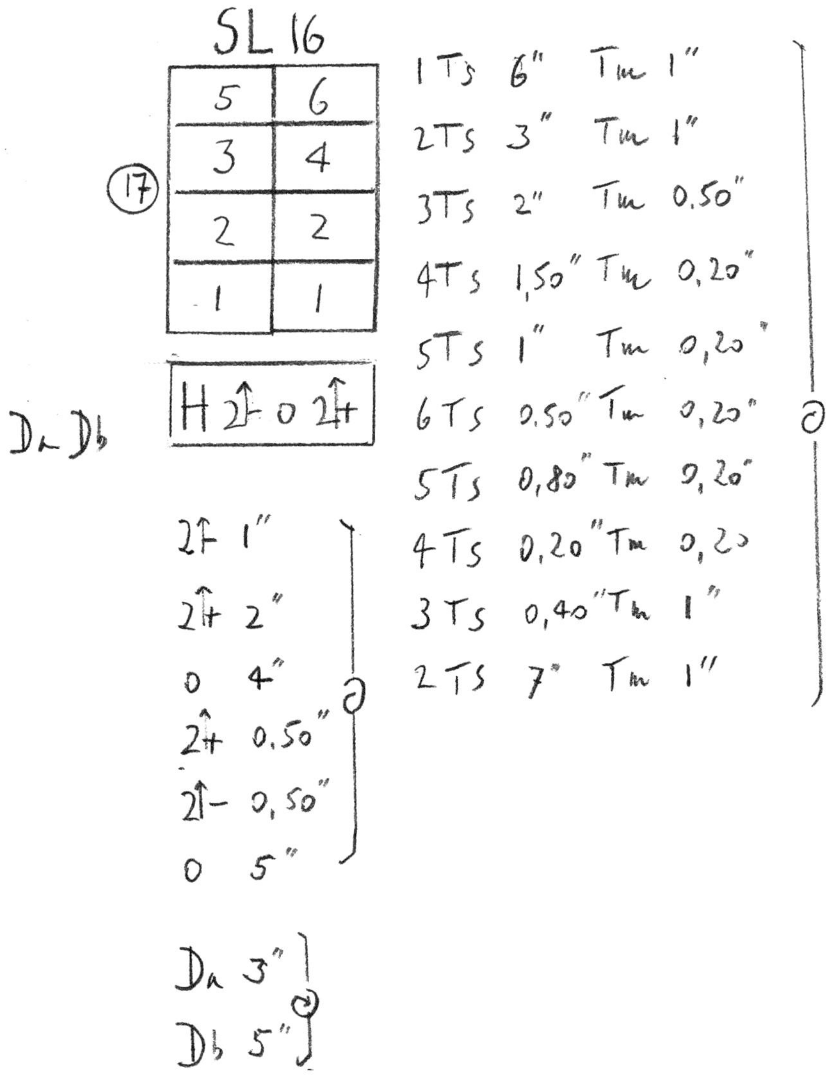

Figure 17.2 Luciano Berio, *Ofaním* (for two children's choirs, two instrumental groups, female voice and live electronics, 1988–97), autograph manuscript of *Cue 16*, solo clarinet (part IV)

Source: Basle, Paul Sacher Stiftung, Luciano Berio Collection. Reproduced by kind permission.

Cue 19

Harmonizer: H 2-↓, 0, 2-↑, 4↑

interval	duration
-100	0.3
0	0.2
100	0.4
500	0.6
-100	0.5
0	0.3
500	0.6
100	0.5
500	0.3
0	0.3

Spatialization:

4	5
3	3
1	2

location	t_s	t_m
1	0.5	0
2	0.4	0
3	0.3	0
4	0.8	0
5	0.8	0

Cue 20

Play sample: PS 7

Spatialization:

3	3
2	2
1	1

location	t_s	t_m
1	0.3	0
2	0.3	0.
3	0.3	0

Cue 21

Harmonizer: H 2-↑, 0, 2+↓

interval	duration	
100		R
0		
-200		
	0.25	R
	0.35	
	0.5	

N.B. Random permutations of the given harmonization intervals and durations.

Spatialization:

4	5
3	3
1	2

location	t_s	t_m
1	0.25	0
2	0.25	0
3	0.25	0
4	0.25	0
5	0.25	0

Cue 22

Harmonizer: H 2-↑, 0, 2-↓, 2-↑

interval	duration
100	3
0	1
-100	2
0	1.5
200	2.5
0	0.8

Spatialization:

3	4
3	4
1	2

Figure 17.3 Luciano Berio, *Altra voce* (for alto flute, mezzo-soprano and live electronics), *Technical Manual* provided with the new edition (2013), p. 10

Source: Luciano Berio, *Altra voce* | für Altflöte, Mezzosopran und live electronics. © Copyright 1999 by Universal Edition AG, Wien/UE, 35958. Reproduced by kind permission.

Figure 17.4 Luigi Nono, *Guai ai gelidi mostri* for two contralti, flute, clarinet, tuba, viola, cello, double bass and live electronics (1983), first edition (autograph of Luigi Nono)

Source: Copyright © 1983 by Casa Ricordi. Reproduced by kind permission of Hal Leonard MGB, Italy.

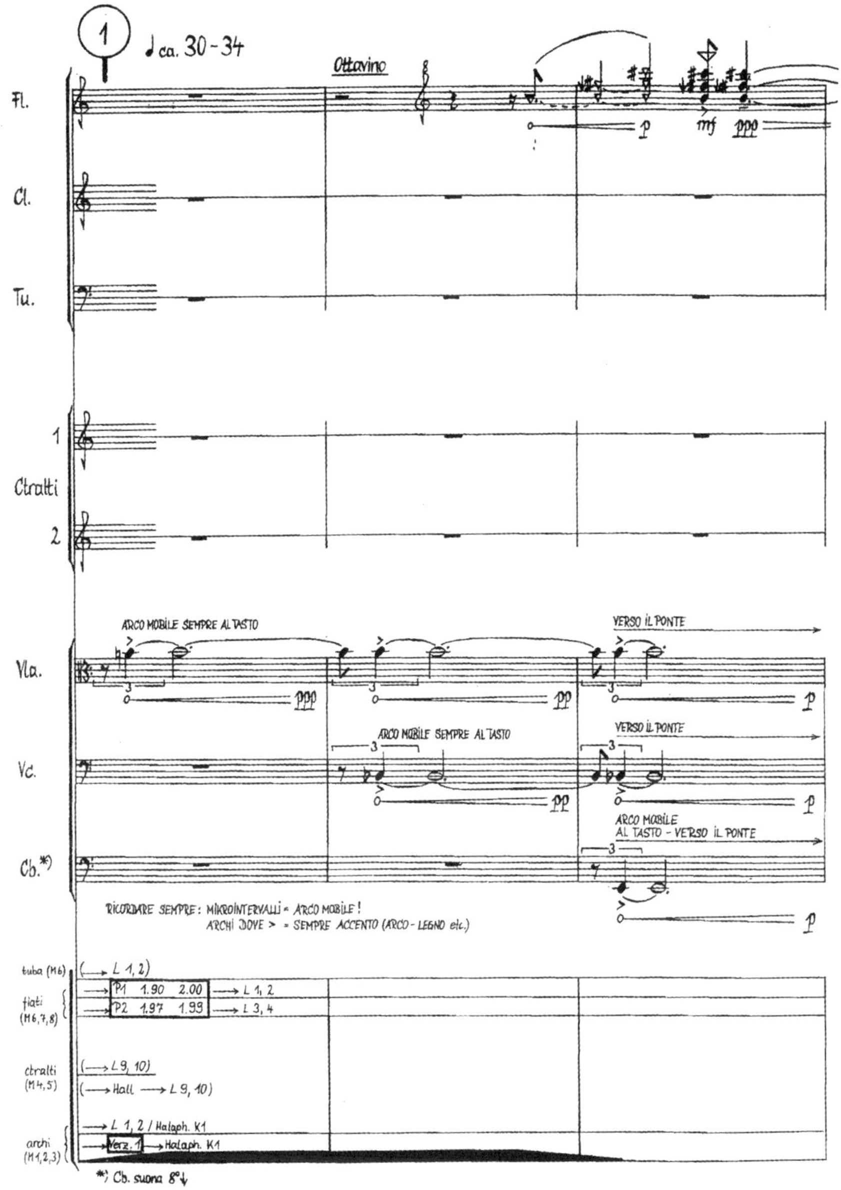

Figure 17.5 Luigi Nono, *Guai ai gelidi mostri* for two contralti, flute, clarinet, tuba, viola, cello, double bass and live electronics (1983/88), second edition (autograph of the copyist Roland Breitenfeld)

Source: Copyright © 1992 by Casa Ricordi; reproduced by kind permission of Hal Leonard MGB, Italy.

Chapter 18
Sonic Imprints: Instrumental Resynthesis in Contemporary Composition

Nicolas Donin

The Reproducibility Mix of Twenty-first-century Composers

The rise of digital technologies in music since the 1980s has obviously impacted listening, archiving and sharing in many ways, but how transformational has it been in the realm of composition? Once fierce, analogue resistance to the digital has almost vanished among musicians (or mutated into technostalgia), seemingly paving the way for an all-digital musical era; yet is far from being clear how comprehensively the hegemony of computer (or computer-like) devices affected compositional practices. Some composers would fiercely denounce the copy/paste temptation which comes with the use of music software, whereas others would argue that critical-mindedness is not more strongly needed when it comes to technologies than it used to be towards any other matter or ideology (Rea 2008). Some musical subcultures straightforwardly stem from the digital (such as live coding music performance), whereas others – such as contemporary concert music – enduringly position themselves as being essentially unbound by the intense technological drive of our times: composers should be free to define software applications as mere tools determined by their musical thinking, or merely not use them.

Not every contemporary composer would therefore subscribe to the following claim by composer/improviser/turntablist/sound artist Matthew Wright. Responding to a query from Keith Potter, author of *Four Minimalists: La Monte Young, Terry Riley, Steve Reich, Philip Glass* (Cambridge University Press, 2002), Wright wrote: '[Today,] our four musical minimalists are the keys Ctrl (Windows), Command (Apple), C and V' (Potter 2013: 800). The most basic keyboard shortcuts of our personal computers – 'copy' and 'paste' – may well be more often needed in music composition than, say, in the creative process of writers. But should we consider these few keys as the quintessential alphabet of current music making (be it in minimalist aesthetics or elsewhere)? Beyond its provocative and ironic tone, Wright's sentence suggests to me that crucial compositional operations long associated with the act of score writing have now been implemented in computer programs and enjoy transparent accessibility via specific user interfaces. According to this narrative, musical writing would have been absorbed by musical coding, in a final move away from the traditional craftsmanship of notation as a medium of invention, henceforth letting gesture and orality take over the very nature of compositional practice.

But, as far as I know, contemporary composers generally haven't given up writing. Nor do they like to automatically replace former technologies with newer ones. Indeed, their current medium of invention may well be described as a complex entanglement of historical and technical layers, including the following: pencil-and-eraser-based score writing habits, computer-aided composition/sampling/typing software, music instruments of all kinds, Beethoven-like sketchbooks and/or Xenakis-like graph paper, analogue devices for the recording and diffusion of sound, and so on. Among the several kinds of musical reproducibility at stake, not all pertain to twentieth-century paradigms. For reproducibility was a touchstone of musical ontology well before the modern technologies of sound reproduction – since the times when the transmission of music started to rely upon notation (coupled with mnemonic devices). Just consider Theodor W. Adorno's unfinished essay on music reproduction, drafted over the course of the 1930s, 1940s and 1950s (Adorno 2001). While he was elaborating his *Reproduktionstheorie* during the boom in music recording technologies and the emergence of the 'culture industry' (as he and Horkheimer coined it), Adorno almost excluded technical reproducibility of sound from his scope.[1] As paradoxical as it may sound today, he conceived resolutely of *instrumental performance*, not recording, as being the means of music reproduction *par excellence* – as if the ongoing development of music recording was not to have any consequence on his very object of study. Or this should be construed another way: perhaps the effectiveness of this new technology lays precisely in the opening up for the first time of a retrospective definition of music based on its notational reproducibility.

It is thus worth distinguishing among at least three main types of reproducibility in our current situation: *notational*, *analogue* and *digital*. These should not be understood as purely technical categories, into which any device present in a composer's workshop could be unambiguously sorted, but as deep-rooted paradigms that shape tools as well as ways of thinking and acting over various time spans. In that sense, not only is analogue reproducibility present in the twenty-first century through those devices still in use in some studios and home studios, but its influence is pervasive even after essential analogue technologies have been absorbed by the digital, notably in the form of a so-called 'metaphor' which orients most user interface software design.[2] Since the notational, the analogue and the digital are so deeply interrelated, various concepts of what music is *made of* coexist in the very material infrastructure of contemporary composers'

[1] As he focused on the relationship of performance and text, as well as expression and notation, Adorno willingly discussed Walter Benjamin's theories of language and translation, but would not refer to *The Work of Art in the Age of its Technical Reproducibility*, even *en passant*.

[2] Paradigmatic of this trend is *Reason*, a computer program developed by Propellerhead Software which emulates a rack of hardware synthesizers, samplers, sequencers and mixers, all of which enjoy a realistic visual rendering, adorned by a no less realistic representation of cables and connections on the back of the equipment rack.

workshops. These concepts compete, co-operate or simply alternate in the course of the compositional process. Contemporary compositional practice deals with a multi-layered substratum that allows the musician to perform various kinds of 'remediations' (Bolter and Grusin 1999), not *of* a work or body of works, but *within* a work: a notational element played by an instrument can be recorded and processed as an audio file; the content of an audio file can be analysed and transformed digitally, or conversely, manually transcribed onto a score; a graphic idea can be transposed into sound or structure, and so forth.

Construed that way, 'composition' encompasses more than its traditional meaning. It is not only about putting together successive or simultaneous bits of music according to rules and taste (may the reader excuse this minimalist attempt at a commonsense definition of composition), but now includes as well the navigation between different 'reproducibilities' through operations of translation such as transcription, transcoding or transformation (Sanio and Scheib 2004). Developing musical material no longer implies the exclusively two-dimensional plane in which derivation and variation techniques take place, but has to deal with a third, perpendicular dimension, as it were: those inner trans-mutations of musical material, from sound to note to structure in any order. Such ductility can prove highly stimulating for composers over the course of their creative processes, and allows them to explore unexpected aspects of their musical material, as has been analysed in detail in Philippe Leroux's *Voi(rex)* (2002) (Donin and Theureau 2007). In some particular cases, exploring that 'third dimension' of trans-mutations can also define the intrinsic concept of the entire work, as in Peter Ablinger's pieces from the *Quadraturen* series (1995–2004), where an initial sound is analysed and re-composed in another setting:

> *Quadraturen* ('Squarings') is a cycle of installation-, electroacoustic-, and concert-pieces, or *one work* that appears in one instance as symphony orchestra, in another as sound installation, and in the next as a computer-controlled player piano.
>
> (1) The first step is always an acoustic photograph ('phonograph'). This can be a recording of anything: speech, street noise, music.
>
> (2) Time and frequency of the chosen 'phonograph' are dissolved into a grid of small 'squares' whose format may be, for example, 1 second (time) to 1 second (interval).
>
> (3) The resulting grid is the score, which is then to be reproduced in different media: on traditional instruments, computer controlled piano, or in white noise.
>
> The reproduction of 'phonographs' by instruments can be compared to photo-realist painting, or-what describes the technical aspect of the 'Quadraturen' more precisely-with techniques in the graphic arts that use grids to transform photos into prints.[3]

[3] Peter Ablinger, 'Quadraturen', 21 August 2006, http://ablinger.mur.at/docu11.html (accessed 30 June 2015).

Ablinger's reference to visual artists is certainly not innocent. He argued elsewhere: 'I am a painter, who works with compositional means, with music instruments, loudspeakers, the sound, the listening' (Ablinger 2004). *Quadraturen* emphasizes his conception of art as a procedural transfer from one portion of reality onto a perceptual proposition, and raises the issue of musicality: if much of the procedure can be formally described as a chain of predefined operations, where are compositional decisions located?

As it happens, a visual artist, namely Pierre Huyghe, made this point in a manner both minimalist and bold in his *Silence Score* as early as 1997[4] – and no musician to date has been more straightforward in raising this issue. Huyghe applied a sound-to-note transcription procedure to a recording of John Cage's *4'33"*. All the cracks and pops of Cage's (recorded) silence were automatically converted into a MIDI file, and then presented as an edited score in musical notation. The final work consists of four pages of printed music displaying apparently randomized pitches and (short) durations in the middle of long rests. The melodic absurdity of the resulting score echoes the aesthetic absurdity of Huyghe's hypothetical project (transcribing silence), which at the same time failed (inasmuch as notes emerged throughout the process) and succeeded (in that the initial sound recording has been replaced by a perfectly silent, visual object). As in many of his works, Huyghe here achieved the goal 'to translate an experience without representing it' (Baker 2004: 92).

In so doing, he was also providing musicians with a powerful minimalistic implementation of the kind of transcoding procedure that they were to use more and more, year after year, thanks to the increasing accessibility of computer-assisted composition and sound processing software.

Instrumental Resynthesis: From Spectral Music to Musical Spectres

To be fair, neither Pierre Huyghe nor his musical contemporaries invented that particular procedure. It can be traced back at least to Tristan Murail, Gérard Grisey and other musicians, all of whom, in the 1970s, grew more and more interested in the derivation of new compositional techniques out of audio effects and technologies.

Grisey coined the term 'instrumental synthesis' for the orchestration of a single sound, based on the acoustic analysis of its frequency content over time. Actually, this technique is scarcely present in Grisey's works. At the same time, it exemplifies strikingly what the spectralist approach to objective properties of sound is about, and this may explain why the concept was so influential in the discourse surrounding spectral music. Whereas Scelsi, for example, explored the holistic character of sound by empirically varying a single 'note' on his ondiola, Grisey drew significant aspects of his compositional technique from findings in acoustic science.

4 For a reproduction of the whole 'score', see Lavigne (2013: 52; the folios are not presented in the right order: 1, 4, 3, 2).

His journey from a Stockhausenesque theorization of the spectrum of harmonic sounds (*c.* 1972), to the art of deriving material from the sonogram of an instrumental sound (from *Modulations* [1976–77] onward), has been thoroughly described (by Féron 2011) based on the composer's working documents. Féron challenges the well-established notion that the whole *Espaces acoustiques* cycle refers to the sonographic analysis of a certain recording of a trombone's e, and shows instead how much the first instances of 'instrumental synthesis' in *Dérives* (1973–4) and *Périodes* (1974) relied upon Grisey's reading of Emile Leipp's and Fritz Winckel's writings on musical acoustics.

A concern for combination and coherence, much more than a drive towards mimesis and 'phonorealism', oriented Grisey's evolution. Composers of the so-called 'second generation' of spectral music took another step towards the derivation of compositional techniques from acoustic objects and properties. They searched for more ductile 'models' than those promoted by their elders: second-degree models, non-acoustic models, or conversely, more complex acoustic models. A paradigmatic example of this evolution is a work by Joshua Fineberg appropriately called *Paradigms*:

> I began to wonder if … a work could derive its timbres not from a sound, but from an ensemble recreating a sound. I recorded several passages of instrumental music that normally would have, themselves, served as music but here they were to become my new models. The recordings of these sounds and processes were then analyzed; not, however, in the ordinary manner (analysis techniques generally aim to produce as complete an analysis, in every detail, as possible; the goal being a technique that would permit an exact re-synthesis of the original). Instead, I sought to extract the essence of the color, sound and motion not of these passages in their abstract existence, but of their realization. To find a model in which each individual instrument playing in a precise way is fused together in one global timbre. This global timbre then, once understood, could serve as my new model, to be re-interpreted, re-evaluated and again transformed into a new musical structure: *Paradigms*. (Fineberg 1994)

Fineberg explicitly refers to 're-synthesis' (spelt without a hyphen in this chapter), a technical process used in the science of acoustics: given the physical analysis of a recorded audio signal, one may be able to synthesize another audio signal based on the information retrieved from the initial one. If the analytical model employed is strong enough, the synthesized sound will resemble the first one – or at least it will share all of the significant features that the analytical model aimed to retain.[5] Although resynthesis may be no more than a validation procedure within

[5] The *ElectroAcoustic Resource Site* gives the following definition: 'Resynthesis Techniques concern the modification of existing recorded or synthesised sounds, generally through the application of a computing algorithm to some form of computer representation of the sound. Frequently Resynthesis Techniques will involve the creation of a new

the domain of audio signal processing, and for this reason it is not a core scientific concept alongside analysis and synthesis techniques, it has much more significance as a musical notion. It has been regularly used by researchers in sound and music computing with artistic applications in view, for whom the distinction between synthesis 'from scratch' as opposed to synthesis based on the consistent result of a given sound analysis algorithm matters a great deal. As Diemo Schwarz puts it:

> Musical sound synthesis allows the creation of new sounds, either from scratch, or by changing an existing sound (this is usually called resynthesis). In both cases, the parameters of the synthesis model used have to be specified. In synthesis from scratch they are completely given by the user. In resynthesis, the parameters obtained by analysing an existing sound are modified. (Schwarz 2004: 1)

The principle of resynthesis is relevant in musicology, too, although its practitioners do not necessarily label it as such. *Computer Music Journal* once presented a panel of contributions to the 'Reconstruction of *Stria*' (31 March 2007). Based on the original programming instructions as well as the composer's memories and technical guidance, young musicologists were able to track all the information needed to synthesize John Chowning's 1977 masterwork anew, and ended up producing two different versions of it (corresponding to two different reconstructive methods). Putting aside the interesting ontological and aesthetic issues raised by such production of cultural clones, this research helped to point out various philological obscurities, tacit technical procedures, undocumented sources and forgotten memories that probably would have never surfaced had musicologists been satisfied with more casual ways of dealing with the piece. This attempt with *Stria* thus touches upon a general stake that goes well beyond electroacoustic and computer music: the validation of an analytical model through generation. A structuralist view of music analysis would claim that a successful analytical approach to a given composition consists of breaking it up consistently into elementary bricks and rules of assembly, then making the analyst able not only to rebuild the piece, but to generate a set of pieces obeying the same principles and bearing a strong family resemblance to the initial one. As in acoustic resynthesis, the degree to which one is able to match the detail of the original piece is a measure of success here.

According to this first discussion of the concept, resynthesis unavoidably introduces difference within reproduction. In some cases, resynthesis is aimed at identity; difference is thus viewed as a mark of imperfection that has to be analysed and fixed over the course of an iterative process. In some other cases, it is aimed at generating difference within family resemblance, then opening up a large range of possibilities, from tight imitation to deep alteration of original material that can itself be displayed, or not. (The most radical option along these

---

"output" sound based on the desired signal processing applied to the original "input" sound' ('Synthesis and Resynthesis Techniques', *Glossary*, *EARS: ElectroAcoustic Resource Site*, http://www.ears.dmu.ac.uk/ [accessed 30 June 2015]).

lines might be the one Johannes Schöllhorn took with his *berstend-starr* [1990], a tonality-friendly 'realization' of Boulez's 1971 'matrix' for *...explosante-fixe...*; see Schöllhorn 2000).

In the forthcoming pages I will restrictively refer to 'resynthesis' as the use of audio signal analysis techniques (usually a Fast Fourier Transform [FFT] algorithm, though they can also feature descriptor-based segmentation and classification) as a springboard for composition based on pre-existing sounds. The output may be a score in which instruments 're-create' the initial sound (usually by addition of individual sounds along a canvas derived from the result of FFT), and/or an electroacoustic re-creation of it (for example, through corpus-based [granular] concatenative synthesis – see Figures 18.2a and 18.2b below). Characterizations of resynthesis that go beyond this rather technical sense, though not pivotal to the works discussed in this chapter, still play a role in that they shape a web of context of meanings and connotations that frames the narrower definition and sheds light upon its implicit artistic consequences.

Let us return to our previous examples with this discussion of resynthesis in mind. Whereas Fineberg's procedure for *Paradigms* fully embodies instrumental resynthesis as has been previously defined, Grisey's seminal 'instrumental synthesis' did not itself pertain to resynthesis until it was applied to a particular recorded sound established as a target. And what about Huyghe's *Silence Score*? It is a mere transcription, yet it could lead to resynthesis were it used as the starting point for a particular instrumentation (or any acoustic realization of the score). According to this scenario, the disembodied score signed and displayed by Huyghe would be further revised and arranged in order to match performance requirements, then having the whole concept of the piece disintegrated exactly when silence and score would pour into sound and music.

The previous remarks help to point out that automated transcription is only separated from resynthesis by one step, but not a negligible one: the final return of the abstracted to the world of sound. This step allows the process of abstraction to become audible on its own right. The listener cannot distinguish the original stuff from the model that conveys it: he/she perceives both at once. The mere noticeability of resynthesized material in the musical work from a listener's perspective depends on two independent qualities that are blended together as a result of the creative process: the salience of the seminal sound, and the efficiency of the analysis and transcription techniques employed. For the composer, mastering these two leverages is the key to a fine-tuned final rendering balancing identity (of the pre-existing sound) and parameters (of the models). It is not surprising, therefore, that the pioneers in musical resynthesis tapped into very recognizable sound samples as they experimented with novel tools and uncertain procedures for transforming them; they secured identity over parameters. The very first use of instrumental resynthesis I am aware of, François-Bernard Mâche's *Le son d'une voix* (1964), is indeed at the opposite pole of the 'parameters over identity' option symbolized by Fineberg's subtle concept of instruments playing a computer-assisted transcription of their playing. Mâche recorded himself reading an extract of Eluard's *Poésie ininterrompue II* and closely studied a spectrographic representation of the resulting sounds (see Figures 18.1a and 18.1b). Whereas a repertoire of percussion gestures seemed appropriate to translating consonants, vowels were rendered by assigning to various instruments specific pitch and length derived from the information available in the sonogram. Far from aiming at a stable set of musical 'phonemes' in which one given vowel would have been automatically translated into one given instrumental sound or aggregate, Mâche was interested in the 'real content of speech', notably the 'unfolding of spectral content in time' (1991: 245), which in fact is ever-changing since every utterance of a same phoneme by a single speaker slightly differs from the other, depending on the phonemes surrounding it, as well as several contextual peculiarities of talk and recording (1991: 246). A detailed discussion of the transcription process (Assayag and Bloch 1997) showed that Mâche, once he had established his principle of sonogram-based transcription, felt free to approximate values (for example, all pitches are in a semi-tempered scale) and explore various compositional possibilities opened up by this ductile transcription procedure. Neither the transcription nor its instrumentation obeyed a rigid, unifying rule. Crucial compositional decisions occurred at each local step within an overarching pre-determined process.

A handful of composers echoed Mâche's efforts towards instrumental resynthesis of speech. Clarence Barlow independently developed a technique of Additive Synthesis through Musical Instruments which 'creates a polyphonic note score in which all pitches at any given time are upper partials of a (not necessarily explicitly played) melody, acoustically coalescing to project the melody' (Barlow 1998: 184). 'Synthrumentation', as he later coined it, was first devised for the simulation of speech by the string section of the chamber ensemble for *Im Januar am Nil* (1981–4). With the assistance of the Institute for Phonetics of Cologne University, Barlow selected 'a set of sentences in the German language excluding all phonemes containing noise spectra such as plosives and fricatives' (Barlow 1998: 184), and proceeded in a similar way to Mâche. He refined this technique in 1989 with an orchestral piece entitled *Orchideæ Ordinariæ or the Twelfth Root of Truth*, which afforded more accuracy in the translation of the spectral content into aggregates. Significant (and documented) undertakings designed along similar guidelines include passages of Thomas Hummel's *Nicanor* (1996–97) for orchestra,[6] Claudy Malherbe's *Locus* (1997) for real voice and virtual voices (see Malherbe 2008) and Jonathan Harvey's *Speakings* (2008) for orchestra (see Nouno et al. 2009). All of these, though they do not belong to spectralism in the strictest sense, are certainly indebted to spectral aesthetics when coping with the spectral content of a particular recording of human voice as a material for score writing. In channelling unmistakably vocal qualities from sound to score, these works more or less straightforwardly achieve the auditory illusion of 'making the orchestra speak' (Nouno et al. 2009). They confront listeners with a ghostly voice suddenly emerging from the orchestral texture: a reign of musical spectres more than spectral music.

---

[6] Thomas Hummel, 'Über Nicanor', January 1997, http://www.thomashummel.net/english/main1_english_Publikationen.htm (accessed 6 January 2013; no longer available).

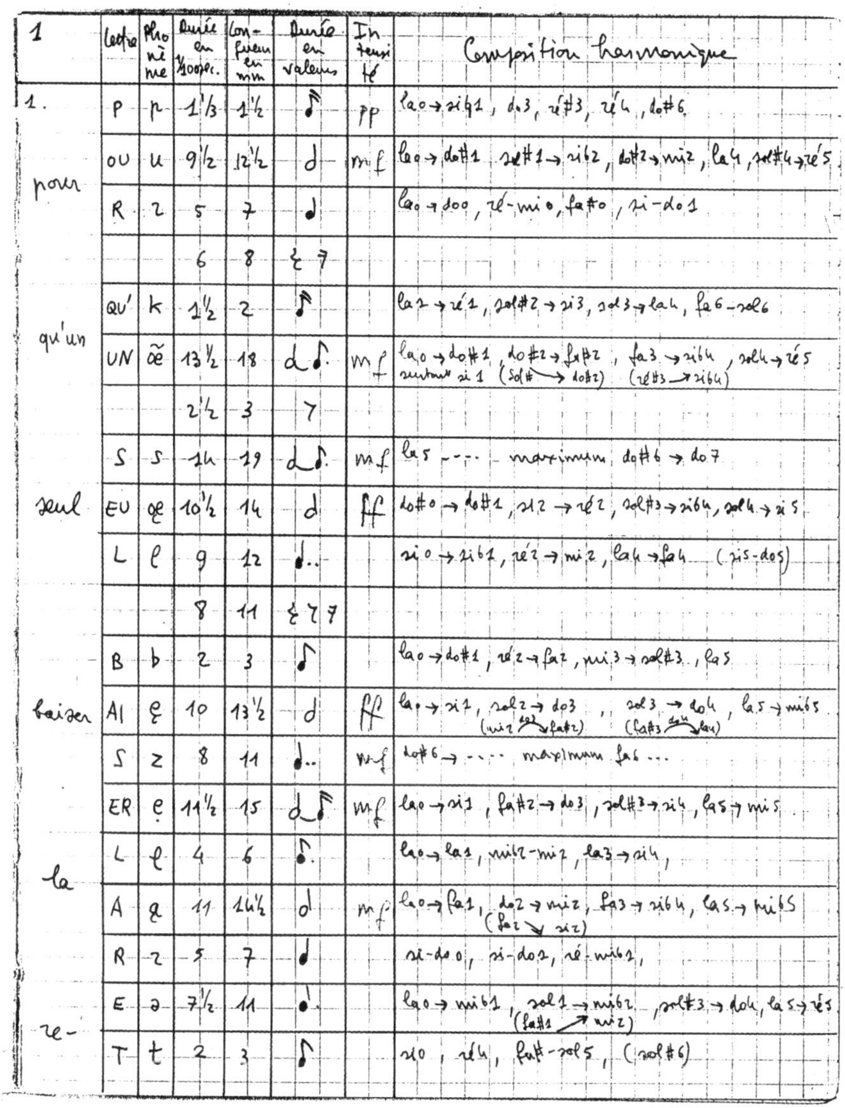

Figure 18.1a François-Bernard Mâche, sonogram for *Le Son d'une voix*
Source: Assayag and Bloch (1997). Reproduced courtesy of François-Bernard Mâche.

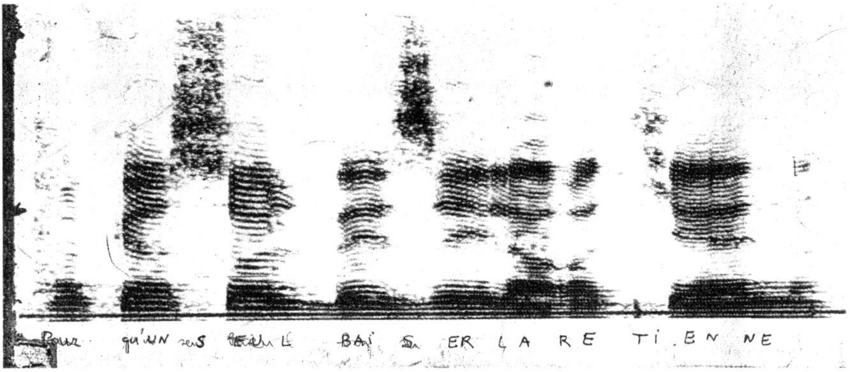

Figure 18.1b François-Bernard Mâche, transcription chart for *Le Son d'une voix*[7]
Source: Assayag and Bloch (1997). Reproduced courtesy of François-Bernard Mâche.

From Mâche to Barlow to the 2000s, however, computer-assisted composition changed radically. As is clear from previous examples, resynthesis was technically and compositionally designed in the world of analogue reproducibility; it cost pioneers a lot of time and effort.[8] Nowadays, the same kind of compositional chain can quite easily be processed as part of the daily business of sound and music software users. In particular, the Institut de Recherche et Coordination Acoustique/Musique's *OpenMusic* and Michael Kateley Klingbeil's *SPEAR* afford fine analysis, editing and synthesis facilities (Klingbeil 2009). Computer-aided orchestration software helps the composer to assess different options for the subsequent instrumentation phase (for a short description of these tools and their musical significance, see O'Callaghan 2012: 6–7, 9–12). Various alternatives to and combinations of these tools are investigated. In a series of works starting with *Beside Oneself* for viola and live electronics (2008), Aaron Einbond used *CataRT*, a software tool for corpus-based concatenative synthesis,[9] either as a means to surround sonic events with their real-time granular resynthesis or to generate descriptor-based analytical data that could be imported and computed in *OpenMusic* (Einbond et al. 2009; see Figures 18.2a and 18.2b).

[7] See Assayag and Bloch (1997) for additional samples of the original sonogram, transcription chart and score. The author wishes to thank Georges Bloch for having gracefully provided access to his own copies of these documents.

[8] Barlow once noticed that his 'synthrumentation' of voice for *Im Januar am Nil* was 'an almost peripheral aspect which, however, cost me most of the time. I think eighty percent of my time went on this orchestrational aspect of the piece [which corresponds to the] first three minutes [of the piece]' (Kaske 1985: 27).

[9] The principle of audio resynthesis using *CataRT* is as follows: 'A sound or phrase is taken as the audio score, from which a certain set of descriptors is used to constitute the synthesis target. We then resynthesise with these descriptors, e.g. the pitch, amplitude, and timbre characteristics, using units from the database' (Schwarz 2004: 159).

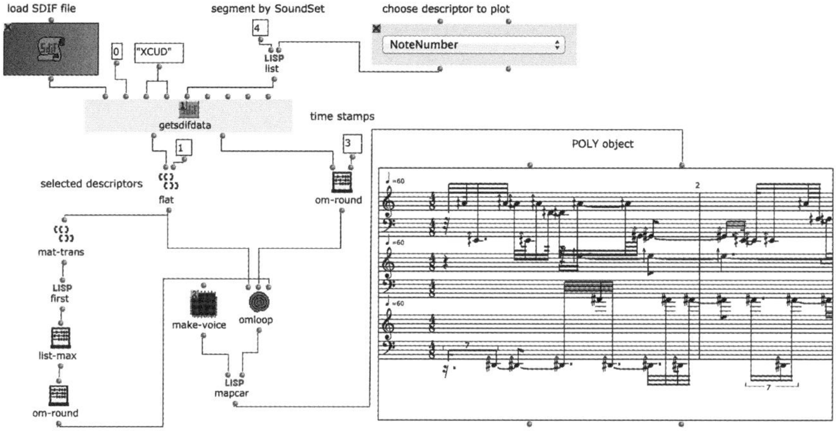

Figure 18.2a Aaron Einbond, *OpenMusic* patch for *What the blind see* (interactive sound installation, 2008; chamber music piece, 2009). Timbral features of a commercial field recording of rain analysed with *CataRT* are converted into symbolic data with the help of *OpenMusic*[10]

Source: Reproduced courtesy of Aaron Einbond.

The increasing use of this kind of technique by composers over the two last decades reveals the gradual transition of musical material from analogue to digital reproducibility: the more powerful and user-friendly computer-assisted composition tools become, the more variable in length and nature samples become. In the twenty-first century, virtually any sound is susceptible to being resynthesized and becoming creatively ghost-incorporated into the final musical work.

[10] Here is the composer's comment on this figure: '[This screenshot] shows an *OM* patch to transcribe a score with the *poly* object, which can then be exported in ETF format and subjectively-edited in *Finale*' (Einbond et al. 2009: 226).

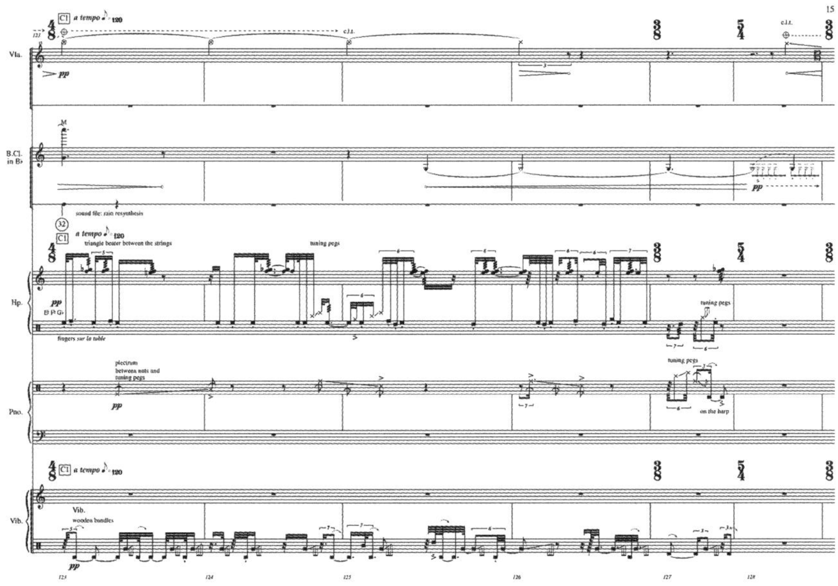

Figure 18.2b Aaron Einbond, *What the blind see* (2009), for seven instruments and live electronics, p. 15. The rain excerpt in Figure 18.2a corresponds to bars 123–7 in harp, piano and percussion, as well as a sound file triggered by the clarinettist

Referentiality: Lost in Translation?

In a sense, not all sounds are equal under resynthesis, though. Obviously, some sounds are more or less well-suited to analysis, transcription and instrumentation. Some are still easily recognizable once in their resynthetic guise, while others lose essential features that used to define their identity. As O'Callaghan (2012) puts it, there is a distinction to be made here between sound referents pertaining to the world of music instruments, and 'extra-musical' sound referents. Only the second class of sound referents may be recognized by the audience 'from purely aural information' – assuming that the transcription process ensured 'high acoustic-similarity' and an appropriate musical context was set (O'Callaghan 2012: 4). On the contrary, spectralist 'instrumental synthesis' of natively instrumental sound stays within the world of musical sound and does not enable the imitation or representation of the pre-existing sonic object to be grasped by the listener (if this had ever been the point in the context of spectralism). O'Callaghan's inquiry, indeed, focuses upon the potential of resynthesis to refresh musical imitation: 'the ability to use recordings of the environment and 'found sounds' as materials may afford a referential, narrative or mimetic discourse familiar to other artistic disciplines, but rare in the history of music' (O'Callaghan 2012: 1). As a composer, he is interested 'in the preservation of semantic information through the transcription process' as well as 'what *changes* as a result and *why*' (O'Callaghan 2012: 2). But this is not necessarily a shared concern among resynthesis practitioners. They range from (modernist) enemies of imitation and semantics to those who, like Ablinger or O'Callaghan, vow to translate objects of the world into their music without any fear of falling outside the agreed boundaries of 'music', or at least 'composition'.

Referentiality is crucial as well to what I previously called the 'ghostly' character of instrumentally resynthesized sounds. One must be the ghost *of* somebody (or something). Well, not all resynthesized sounds are mimicking such vibrant testimonies of humankind as people's voices, and whatever the sound referent is, the illusion may not be perfect enough for the listener to catch the reference. So, if not ghosts, resynthesized sounds at least evoke some unusual – and at times unsettling – sort of contact between the *concrète* and the abstract (to put it in Schaefferian terms), the living and the artificial, or even nature and culture. A 'live' sonic event happened to be recorded, then analysed; this process of reification culminated in its being written down onto a fixed score; and now it radiates again, from afar, so to speak, as soon as musicians perform the score.

Here a useful parallel is to be drawn with the interaction of dead and living sounds through recording technologies pointedly discussed by Stanyek and Piekut (2010) with respect to popular music. Stanyek and Piekut theorize on the 'technologies of the intermudane' – the variety of unstable arrangements that shape the dialectics of deadness and liveness in recorded music, involving the following: humans and non-humans, technologies and bodies, booth and stage, studio and scene, and so on. Their narrative is built around a discussion of Natalie Cole's 'duet' with Nat King Cole, *Unforgettable* (1991), a subtle mix of 1961 and 1991 recordings (and not only recordings: people, situations, rights management issues and so forth). This is only one of a long list of 'posthumous duets' of great singers that, for the authors, eloquently exemplifies the 'mutually effective co-labouring' of living and dead in late capitalism (Stanyek and Piekut 2010: 14). For instance, the technological substratum of this interpenetration lies in overdubbing and multitrack recording practices, which allow a fine matching of significant features of the respective contributions of dead and living agents (including singers, musicians, sound engineers, microphones, studio installations and machines). Stanyek and Piekut place this cluster of technologies at the heart of an unprecedented transgression of the well-established segregation of the dead from the living in modern Europe. One could easily transfer their analysis of the coexistence of deadness and liveness in popular music to so-called learned music, in replacing the studio recording practices they highlighted with resynthesis-related practices of sound re-engineering. Such translation would not be without adaptation and discussion, however. First, resynthesis is certainly a more discrete phenomenon within contemporary classical music than transhistorical multitrack sound engineering is within popular music. Moreover, it would be fair to admit that true 'co-labouring' doesn't really happen in resynthesis: the dead surfaces within the living, as it were, more than it is put at work by/with it.

On the other hand, Stanyek and Piekut's point can help us to highlight a no less significant difference between popular and classical contemporary music. In posthumous duets, the referent must be obvious. The fine work of sound engineers and producers aims at giving a perfect illusion of immediacy: the listener must be able to both identify the unique aura of the 'dead' voice from the first seconds, and be subjugated by the paradoxical feeling of compresence and attunement conveyed by the duet. In Western art music, most composers would tend to consider the referent inessential to musical meaning: the piece's musical qualities must be fully satisfying even if the referential dimension is missed. The aura of the original sound may fade or vanish due to the loss of the reference, anyway some 'subcutaneous' trace of it will last and effectively shape the passage in a specific way, just as some timbral quality of Einbond's rain sample (see Figures 18.2a and 18.2b) was successfully conveyed into the final score without being capable of (nor intended to) evoking rain in an unprepared listener. According to this point of view, the referent is secondary, subliminal – it is consumed in and by the writing, reduced to a quintessential flavour, emancipated from the disturbing boldness of conventional meaning.

A likely emanation from the discourse of absolute music, the previous approach is not without internal contradiction as it combines dedication to the complex processing of meaningful units with a proclaimed indifference to their distinctive perceptibility and effectivity in the final output. In a rare ethnographical inquiry into the cosmopolite tribe of classical contemporary composers, Yara El-Ghadban highlighted the multiple layers of meaning two young composers were coping with as they composed – and thus publicly introduced – their work in an international course called the VIIIe Forum International des Compositeurs (Amsterdam, 2006): here a top-level musical ensemble (the Montreal-based Nouvel Ensemble Moderne) was to play their music, and eminent senior composers were to award prizes to some of the candidates (see El-Ghadban 2009). At one point, the ethnographer focused on the creative process of Ezequiel Menalled's *El Sistema* (2006), one of the contenders:

> His piece is based on a recording of himself reading [Eduardo] Galeano's text. The recording was analyzed with the help of a sonogram and a sound synthesizer. An enormous amount of musical material was extracted from the recording with the help of a computer. … The first variation is a harmonic elaboration on the tones and rhythms of Menalled's reading voice, which he uses as basic musical material: he does not use the words themselves but only the sound material they produce. (El-Ghabdan 2009: 144–5)

Still more than in Mâche or Harvey's cases, one might wonder what remains of an unmistakably vocal signature when the quintessential 'signature' becomes strongly separated from the 'voice'. Menalled's resynthesis raised eyebrows for another reason, however. The content of the text, a funny story unambiguously serving a sound criticism of contemporary society, happened to be neither conveyed in the 'first variation' nor in the subsequent variations based upon computer-assisted-extracted material from the initial recording:

> Menalled's strategy begged a question from the audience during his analysis conference: why codify the text in such a manner that the audience would probably not be able to understand the message simply by listening to the music? In response, Menalled underlined the importance of artistic intentionality and of the aesthetic experience in composing and listening to music as opposed to using music to transmit Galeano's message. (El-Ghabdan 2009: 145–6)

For Menalled, the political message of the text had to remain encrypted, so that the reception of the piece could be positive even if the listener disagreed with the politics.

While some composers focus on referentiality and others definitely avoid it, a third option is available: playing at the borders of sound and sense. This border can be reached simply by the fact that resynthesis nears (and sometimes achieves) auditory illusion. In the case of Barlow's *Im Januar am Nil*, instrumental resynthesis of speech by strings was not really recognizable, but repeated listening and text content awareness allowed the composer to perceive the illusion at some point:

> I have heard the computer synthesis of the first three minutes very many times; and recently while presenting a string ensemble performance of the piece I was suddenly able to hear speech at the beginning. … I knew where to look for the proper phonemes and I now heard them, much to my own surprise. (Barlow, in Kaske 1985: 27)

Having sound get to the verge of sense can also be the main aim of the compositional design, as in Ablinger's following claim: 'Actually however, my main concern is not the literal reproduction itself but precisely this border-zone between abstract musical structure and the sudden shift into recognition – the relationship between musical qualities and "phonorealism": the observation of "reality" via "music".'[11]

It could well be that resynthesis practitioners, far from enrolling *pro* or *contra* referentiality, are interested in those *liminal* effects that blur our comfortable distinctions between reality and illusion, sound and sense, music and non-music.

Music and the Aesthetics of Imprint

One may wonder why resynthesis is becoming widespread in compositional practice nowadays. Is this a mechanical consequence of a technological state of the art? I suspect that it is not only that. Resynthesis, as it instantiates a paradigm

---

[11] Peter Ablinger, 'Quadraturen', 21 August 2006, http://ablinger.mur.at/docu11.html (accessed 30 June 2015).

of imprint within the ethereal realm of sound, newly introduces into music a feature ever present in other arts.

In a fascinating book related to an exhibition he co-curated (*L'Empreinte*, Centre Georges Pompidou, 1997), Georges Didi-Huberman (2008) discusses the ubiquity of imprint, a basic technical operation characterized by its 'open-ended heuristics', throughout history. Imprint, Didi-Huberman writes, is anachronistic: it defines the older as well as the nearest artistic achievements of humankind – from early prehistory towards contemporary art through Rodin and Duchamp. There is some troubling immediacy in the imprint, or casting, or moulding, compared to any 'normal' work of art based on imitation. Moreover, imprint/casting/moulding allow multiple reproductions of the original object, which points towards a pre-Benjaminian dialectics between the aura of the work and its technical reproducibility. Imprint generates art works (among other possibilities), and at the same time it short-circuits the most basic mediations of artistic craftsmanship. Imprint challenges and undermines the essential concepts that have been shaping fine arts for centuries: figuration, representation, mimesis. This is why imprint has always been perceived as the 'dark side' of art (and of art history), as Didi-Huberman (2008: 92–171 and elsewhere) brilliantly demonstrates based on aesthetic and critical discourse since the Renaissance.

Music has a long history of mimesis, too, from Baroque rhetoric and word painting to programme music to post-Second World War art/science confluences. Unlike art history, however, no equivalent of the 'imprint paradigm' has been identified in opposition to the figural tradition over recent centuries. Should resynthesis in turn be subsumed into the category of mimesis? The answer is not obvious. Yes, inasmuch as it uses today's technologies to do the same kind of things that were done in earlier times – translating the particular shape of a given sonic event into a musical context. No, as it does so by directly imprinting the whole acoustic structure of a sound object onto a medium of inscription. Yes again, as this operation is never purely objective, and calls for the musician's ear and sensibility to (1) interpret the raw output of acoustic analysis as a function of algorithm parameters themselves set, and (2) more or less depart from it when coming to the final compositional phase. And no again (and finally): as a paradoxical and liminal phenomenon, resynthesis is definitely closer to haunting, possession, illusion or ventriloquism than to imitation. When we hear an uncertain rain or a shadowy voice, some pre-existing sound appears to be at once present and not fully audible. Resynthesis goes well beyond (or short of) mimetic practices such as bird imitation, speech-like melodies or madrigalism, where what is meant is plainly present in the listener's recognition without leak or loss. Hence a rather different genealogy: resynthesis might be seen as a 'hardcore', technologically instrumented instance of ancestral practices such as transcription, arrangement and borrowing. This proximity is perceptible in many places among a vast body of contemporary scores explicitly based upon great works of the past that are rewritten, altered or expanded. I cannot listen to Gérard Pesson's *Nebenstück* for clarinet and string quartet (1998), an arrangement of Brahms's Fourth Ballade for piano (op. 10), without thinking that its noise-oriented 'filtering', meant to reflect the author's idiosyncratic listening and process of remembering, also pertains to some kind of handcrafted resynthesis. The 'algorithm' of *Nebenstück*, metaphorically speaking, would include both awareness of electroacoustic filtering, and nostalgia of the time and places where the essential infrastructure of music reproducibility resided in human and instrumental bodies.

It is hard, then, to decide whether the compositional technique of resynthesis is a flickering, epiphenomenal aspect of current music, or a deep trend underlying a significant part of today's musical invention. Resynthesis, in the strictest sense, is rarely used as a pivotal, explicit concept of an entire piece, but it is indeed a pervasive (albeit discrete) gesture within current compositional practice – not to mention the larger field of arrangement, re-writing, realizations and so forth. Building a true musical aesthetics of imprint would require in-depth analytical discussion of all previously mentioned works and approaches, as well as a more accurate delineation of the various species of resynthesis. Such musical aesthetics of imprint should also define what its borders and in-between zones with other concepts are – starting with mimesis. After all, 'resynthesis' in a general sense might well encompass, if not mimesis per se, at least various kinds of translations of speech patterns into instrumental idioms, like those found in the multi-threaded 'intonationist' trend that Jacques Amblard detected in Pascal Dusapin, as well as his ancestors (Leoš Janáček) and contemporaries (Steve Reich), all involved in the instrumental imitation of national/individual ways of speaking a particular language (Amblard 2002). In this chapter, I have deliberately limited myself to a subset of this web of meanings. As narrow as this focus may be, it sheds light on far more general features of the techn(olog)ical infrastructure of composition today, including the following: the intertwining of distinctive reproducibilities, the ductility of computer-assisted composition, the new mediations of the concrete and the abstract, the blurring of referentiality, and the paradoxes of haunted sonorities in a world of immediacy.

References

Ablinger, Peter (2004) 'METAPHERN (Wenn die Klänge die Klänge wären)', in Sanio and Scheib (2004), pp. 425–75.

Adorno, Theodor W. (2001) *Zu einer Theorie der Musikalischen Reproduktion: Aufzeichnungen, ein Entwurf und zwei Schemata*, ed. Henri Lonitz, Frankfurt am Main: Suhrkamp.

Amblard, Jacques (2002) *Pascal Dusapin: l'intonation ou le secret*, Paris: Musica Falsa.

Assayag, Gérard and Bloch, Georges (1997) 'Quantification et création musicale', in *Les modèles dans l'art: Musique, peinture, cinéma*, ed. Marta Grabocz, Strasbourg: Presses Universitaires de Strasbourg, pp. 127–56.

Baker, George (2004) 'An Interview with Pierre Huyghe', *October*, 110, pp. 80–106.

Barlow, Clarence (1998) 'On the Spectral Analysis of Speech for Subsequent Resynthesis by Acoustic Instruments', *Forum Phoneticum*, 66, pp. 183–90.

Bolter, Jay David and Grusin, Richard (1999) *Remediation: Understanding New Media*, Boston, MA: MIT Press.

Didi-Huberman, Georges (2008) *La ressemblance par contact. Archéologie, anachronisme et modernité de l'empreinte*, Paris: Minuit.

Donin, Nicolas and Theureau, Jacques (2007) 'Theoretical and Methodological Issues Related to Long Term Creative Cognition: The Case of Musical Composition', *Cognition, Technology & Work*, 9/4, pp. 233–51.

Einbond, Aaron, Schwarz, Diemo and Bresson, Jean (2009) 'Corpus-based Transcription as an Approach to the Compositional Control of Timbre', in *Proceedings of the International Computer Music Conference (ICMC 2009), Montreal, Canada, August 16–21, 2009*, San Francisco, CA: International Computer Music Association, pp. 223–6, http://architexte.ircam.fr/textes/Einbond09a/index.pdf (accessed 30 June 2015).

El-Ghadban, Yara (2009) 'Facing the Music: Rituals of Belonging and Recognition in contemporary Western Art Music', *American Ethnologist*, 36/1, pp. 140–60.

Féron, François-Xavier (2011) 'The Emergence of Spectra in Gérard Grisey's Compositional Process: From *Dérives* (1973–74) to *Les espaces acoustiques* (1974–85)', *Contemporary Music Review*, 30/5, pp. 343–75.

Fineberg, Joshua (1994) 'Notes' (preface to the score), *Paradigms*, Paris: Max Eschig.

Kaske, Stephan (1985) 'A Conversation with Clarence Barlow', *Computer Music Journal*, 9/1, pp. 19–28.

Klingbeil, Michael Kateley (2009) 'Spectral Analysis, Editing, and Resynthesis: Methods and Applications', PhD dissertation, Columbia University.

Lavigne, Emma (ed.) (2013) *Pierre Huyghe*, Paris: Centre Pompidou.

Mâche, François-Bernard (1991) 'Itinéraires', *La Revue musicale*, 421–4, pp. 245–9.

Malherbe, Claudy (2008) '*Locus*: rien n'aura eu lieu que le lieu', in *The OM Composer's Book*, vol. 2, ed. Jean Bresson, Carlos Agon and Gérard Assayag, Paris and Vallier: IRCAM and Delatour France, pp. 179–91.

Nouno, Gilbert, Cont, Arshia, Carpentier, Grégoire and Harvey, Jonathan (2009) 'Making an Orchestra Speak', in *Proceedings of the Sound and Music Computing Conference, July 23–25, Porto, Portugal*, pp. 277–82, http://cmr.soc.plymouth.ac.uk/publications/SMC2009.pdf (accessed 30 June 2015).

O'Callaghan, James (2012) 'Mediated Mimesis: Transcription as Processing', in *Proceedings of the Electroacoustic Music Studies Network Conference Meaning and Meaningfulness in Electroacoustic Music, Stockholm, June 2012*, http://www.ems-network.org/IMG/pdf_EMS12_ocallaghan.pdf (accessed 30 June 2015).

Potter, Keith (2013) 'Le Minimalisme', in *Théories de la composition musicale au XXe siècle*, vol. 2, ed. Nicolas Donin and Laurent Feneyrou, Lyon: Symétrie, pp. 777–802.

Rea, John (2008) 'The Sorcerer as Apprentice: His Notes (the Computer in/and Teaching the Craft of Composition)', *Circuit: Musiques contemporaines*, 18/1, pp. 72–91.

Sanio, Sabine and Scheib, Christian (eds) (2004) *Übertragung – Transfer – Metapher. Kulturtechniken, ihre Visionen und Obsessionen*, Bielefeld: Kerber.

Schöllhorn, Johannes (2000) '"Comment savoir de quoi l'ombre est l'ombre?" Remarques analytiques sur la relation entre *...explosante-fixe...* de Pierre Boulez et ma réalisation intitulée *berstend-starr*', in *Arrangements, dérangements: La transcription musicale aujourd'hui*, ed. Peter Szendy, Paris: Ircam and l'Harmattan, pp. 121–30.

Schwarz, Diemo (2004) 'Data-driven Concatenative Sound Synthesis', PhD dissertation, Université Paris 6-Pierre et Marie Curie.

Stanyek, Jason and Piekut, Benjamin (2010) 'Deadness: Technologies of the Intermundane', *The Drama Review*, 54/1, pp. 14–38.

PART VI
Audiovisual Documentation in Ethnomusicological Research

Chapter 19
New Trends in the Use of Audiovisual (and Audio) Technology in Contemporary Ethnomusicology

Giovanni Giuriati

The issue of using audiovisual documentation in ethnomusicological research has a long history. Visual anthropology, or ethnographic film, in fact appeared at the beginning of the twentieth century, almost at the same time as the motion picture itself was invented, as Rouch (1968) reminds us. Among the first examples of the use of film in documenting rituals and dances, one might mention the works dedicated to the Australian aborigines (by Baldwin Spencer, 1901), the Kwakiutl Indians (by Edward Curtis, 1914), and other cultures in various parts of the world (Heider 2006). In European ethnomusicology, this interest can be traced back to the work of a few pioneers, in particular a seminal paper, 'Esquisse d'une méthode de folklore musical', published in 1931, in which the Romanian scholar Constantin Brăiloiu stresses the importance of the use of photographs and images in musical ethnography. I explicitly mention this text among others not only because it is related to audiovisual documentation as such, but because, in stressing the importance of the use of images in ethnomusicological research, it was particularly important for the development of Italian ethnomusicology. I should, however, begin by quoting my own two teachers in this field, both engaged in such endeavours: Diego Carpitella and Mantle Hood.

Carpitella was the first to use film documentation in Italian ethnomusicology, back in 1959, when, with his Beaulieu camera, he shot images of the choreutic-musical therapy of Apulian tarantismo, documenting (along with photographs) the 'two phases' of the *tarantata* dance.[1] Later, Carpitella pursued his interest in visual ethnomusicology, making several documentary films (some for RAI Radiotelevisione Italiana, the Italian public broadcasting company)[2] and becoming President of the Associazione Italiana di Cinematografia Scientifica (AICS), organizing the *Giornate del film etnografico* (1977, 1980) with AICS and the Istituto delle Tradizioni popolari/Etnomusicologia dell'Università di Roma 'La Sapienza',

---

[1] See *Meloterapia del tarantismo*, a documentary film enclosed with the new edition of *La terra del rimorso* (De Martino 2008). For a discussion of the musical and choreutic aspects of tarantismo, see Carpitella (1961).

[2] For Carpitella's filmography, see Tucci (1992).

and later the MAV (Materiali di antropologia visiva) at the Museo Nazionale delle Arti e Tradizioni Popolari. Let me quote Carpitella's idea as to the relationship between sound and image in ethnomusicological research, thus confirming that this topic was highly important to both him and Italian ethnomusicology:

> One could say that it was Edison Phonograph that provoked a separation between sound and image: before it became possible to isolate sound and document it via recording, performance was never imagined through sound, but was contemporaneous, in synchrony. *Ipso facto*, that ethnomusicology at some point also became 'visual' in its documentation is perfectly logical and pertinent: a synaesthesia was produced involving two events that we forcedly used to consider independent. The fact that visual ethnomusicology is a recent, very recent discipline, is due to further technological developments that allowed sound to be synchronized with images.[3] (Carpitella 1989: 17)

Carpitella continues, recalling how the first synchronized filming *in situ*, *Pierres chantées de Hjorou*, was shot by Rouch and Rouget in Niger in 1968:

> Image provides the elements of the performance: body, posture, performing technique, shape and size of the instrument, vocal techniques, the instruments' materials, performance's proxemics, natural and social context, distinction between performers and audience, participants and non participants; definitions of the social level; settlement and geo-anthropic traits, and so on. All features that can obviously be written, photographed, tape-recorded, but that cannot provide the same amount of information, so verisimilarly.[4] (Carpitella 1989: 18)

I also remember, from my days as a doctoral student at the University of Maryland Baltimore County, the emphasis Mantle Hood conferred on audiovisual documentation in his research seminars and in the course he taught on Field and Lab Methods.

---

[3] 'Si può affermare che sia stato proprio il Fonografo Edison a provocare la divaricazione tra suono e immagine, poiché prima che si potesse isolare il suono e documentarlo mediante l'incisione, l'esecuzione non è mai stata immaginata attraverso il suono, ma è stata contemporanea e sincronica. *Ipso facto* che l'etnomusicologia ad un certo punto sia divenuta, nella documentazione, anch'essa "visiva", è quanto mai logico e pertinente: si è avuta la sinestesia di due eventi che "artatamente" ci siamo abituati a considerare separati. Il fatto che poi l'etnomusicologia visiva sia anch'essa una disciplina recente, recentissima, è dovuto ad ulteriori sviluppi tecnologici, affinché si potesse sincronizzare il suono con l'immagine.'

[4] 'L'immagine fornisce gli elementi della performance: corpo, postura, tecnica di esecuzione, forma e misura dello strumento, tecniche vocali, materiali per strumenti, prossemica dell'esecuzione, contesto naturale e sociale, differenziazione tra interpreti e spettatori, partecipanti o no; definizione del livello sociale; insediamento e caratteri geoantropici, ecc. Tutte denotazioni che naturalmente possono essere scritte, fotografate, registrate per il suono, ma che non possono dare la quantità d'informazioni così verosimili.'

His film *Atumpan: The Talking Drums of Ghana* is one of the first works in this field, and is still considered to be exemplary. In his manual for the discipline, *The Ethnomusicologist* (in the chapter on 'Field Methods and the Technical Equation'), Hood devotes space to 'the motion picture':

> The motion picture enables him [the ethnomusicologist] to capture unlimited detail that the best memory or still photography record cannot retain. It offers the possibility of placing music and related art forms in the natural environment of the society with which they are identified and which they, in turn, help to identify .... A piece of film with sound track can never capture a total record; but with sensitive usage of it can come closer, in my opinion, than any other form of documentation. (Hood 1971: 278–9)

He continues with several technical details – about editing, crew, type of camera – in a perspective indebted to the Hollywood motion picture system, which was in fact close to the University of California at Los Angeles, where Hood was based at the time.

The first systematic theoretical contribution within ethnomusicology belongs to Steven Feld, who in 1976 wrote the seminal essay 'Ethnomusicology and Visual Communication' (Feld 1976). He reflects on the history of the use of film in ethnomusicology up to then, mentioning several examples of scholarly approaches that can represent different research models: Gerhard Kubik with his films on African music used as a basis for musical transcription; Hood (already mentioned); Alan Lomax with his Cantometrics, and even more with Choreometrics, in which film materials were clues to detect parameters, especially of social behaviour surrounding music and dance, and the Institute für den Wissenschaftlichen Film in Göttingen, with the *Encyclopedia Cinematographica* aiming to produce an objective catalogue of worldwide musical expressions. Furthermore, one can mention the British National Film and Television School and its long tradition of documentary films, including ethnomusicology; and, of course, the important French school under the influence of Rouch, with a lineage including Gilbert Rouget, Hugo Zemp and others gathered mainly around the Département d'ethnomusicologie at the Musée de l'Homme in Paris – a significant engagement highlighted by the institution of the Prix Bartók awarded to the best documentary film in ethnomusicology at the Bilan du Film Ethnographique held annually in Paris.[5]

Each above-mentioned 'style' adopted its own peculiar way of filming, in terms of image selection, camera movements and editing, and implied different views and aims of audiovisual documentation in ethnomusicology.

---

[5] Twenty years after the creation of the Bartók Prize, in 2015 the Société Française d'Ethnomusicologie released *Around Musics – Ecouter le monde*, a boxed set containing 12 DVDs of 12 of the 20 documentary films awarded the Prix Bartók. The set includes also a booklet with an introduction, 'Filmer la musique', written by Bernard Lortat-Jacob and Hélène Lallemand.

The Pervasiveness of Audiovisual Documentation in Research and Dissemination

It is not my intention to retrace the history of the relationship between ethnomusicology and film. Others, starting with Feld as early as 1976, have discussed this issue much better than I could. However, I feel it is appropriate to mention the forebears of our discipline, presenting various trends, aims and approaches in filming traditional music.

Coming to more recent times, the use of audiovisual materials in ethnomusicological research has changed dramatically. While in the past filming traditional music was a specific aspect of ethnomusicological research that required special skills, aims and technology, nowadays video documentation is arguably the privileged way of documenting an event, and sound is, if necessary, extracted from video. In the past, it was exactly the opposite, with the tape recorder as the ethnomusicologist's main tool and the camera as a possible addition to it. The re-composed unity between sound and images to which Carpitella referred in the 1980s has gone far in the last decades. The main research tool in the field has increasingly become the video camera, rather than the tape recorder; if we go to congresses, seminars or university courses, research papers often feature some audiovisual material, usually within a multimedia *PowerPoint* presentation. It is safe to state that audiovisual material is considered the best way to describe and analyse the process of music making, musical performance, music as interaction, relationships between music and dance, music and theatre, rituals and ceremonies, therefore becoming the primary means of documentation in ethnomusicology. Moreover, audiovisual material has become the main source in classrooms for teaching purposes. Perhaps the most significant and comprehensive example is the *JVC Video Anthology of World Music and Dance*, comprising 30 VHS videotapes and nine books, which – even though full of shortcomings – has become the standard reference in many university courses on 'World Music' and ethnomusicology worldwide.[6]

Many issues about audiovisual documentation in ethnomusicology are discussed: let me briefly mention just a few, in order to suggest a broader perspective.

Our research materials are sometimes taken from the World Wide Web, and especially from YouTube: this pervasive and versatile source for audiovisual images is modifying our use and perception of reproduced images by proposing a constant flow of (mostly) self-referential videos that a sharp critical eye should interpret and understand within their proper context. While YouTube videos can be powerful sources for scholarly research and teaching, with a nearly infinite array of documents available and ready to use,[7] there is an increasing risk that they

---

6 For a description of the project, see 'JVC Anthology of World Music and Dance', *Multicultural Media*, http://www.multiculturalmedia.com/page.php?page=60 (accessed 30 June 2015).

7 It is a specific case of the use of audiovisuals that could be encompassed in the larger issue of 'virtual fieldwork' (Cooley et al. 2008). On the issue of YouTube and

might be consumed without awareness of the context and of their purpose. On the contrary, taking them as fragments of a supposed reality, there is no possibility of applying to those video clips any critical analysis and interpretation. Therefore, we aim to provide analytical tools and references in order to the great number of videos available on the World Wide Web less confused and musically undetermined.

Contrary to what Feld witnessed when he wrote his seminal article in 1976, today we have to measure ourselves in our research within the context of a history of audiovisual documentation and with the different methods and styles of audiovisual representation of traditional music established in recent decades. Different choices in shooting images, editing, narratives and so on, which already imply choices in research and representation, strongly affect our ways of documenting on video. Actually, the old-fashioned conception that images are some kind of objective reality of an event is long gone (even though it still lingers on …).

Another commonplace is that it is sufficient to take a camera and shoot some footage to make correct audiovisual documentation; on the contrary, there are plenty of principles and 'rules' to observe in order to film correctly, guaranteeing all the while absolute freedom of choice in what and how to represent: panning, zooming, long sequences, editing, solo or team work and so on are among the researcher's explicit (and often implicit) choices. Hugo Zemp explicitly wrote of all this in relation to ethnomusicology in his essays published in the late 1980s. Therefore, there is also a grammar that a researcher in visual ethnomusicology (visual anthropology) has to learn and know, both while in the field and while planning his/her fieldwork (Zemp 1988).[8]

Generally speaking, one can state that audiovisual sources are important tools for ethnomusicological research in two different domains, both increasingly relevant: archival materials and contemporary original documentation.

Exploring Archives

Audiovisual archives are fundamental for researchers dealing with music from oral traditions. Sounds are the primary sources. Transcription comes later, and only if necessary, concerning very few studies among the thousands of documents kept at present in ethnomusicological archives. Sound archives can document the process of change that music undergoes in a given area of the world, and enable researchers to compare similar repertoires on a diachronic scale. What were in the

ethnomusicology, see also a forthcoming book, Ignazio Macchiarella (ed.) *Ethnomusicology in the Era of YouTube*, published under the auspices of the Italian Committee of the International Council for Traditional Music.

[8] A revised version of this chapter was published in Italian by Hugo Zemp (1989) in the volume *Ethnomusicologica*, which collects contributions to the International Seminars in ethnomusicology that Carpitella organized during 1977–89 at the Accademia Musicale Chigiana in Siena. Visual ethnomusicology has been a constant theme of those seminars.

past sound archives are shifting increasingly to audiovisual materials, documenting not only sound, but also other significant aspects of musical performance: gestures in instrumental or vocal production, or more generally, performance context, which is an integral part of the meaning transmitted in music production.

In recent times, ethnomusicology is becoming increasingly a historical discipline, able to trace its sources back over a century.[9] Over such a considerable time span, it is possible to infer patterns of change, acculturation processes, contaminations, breaks in the tradition, revivals and so on. Archival material is fundamental in such research as a primary source of documentation. This is why ethnomusicologists are increasingly shifting to archival research. Furthermore, going back to archive documentation, besides shedding new light on unknown (or little-known) documentation, can help us reconsider and revisit previous ethnomusicological research, with new insights coming from our contemporary perspective.

This is the case with research on Italian folk music, particularly research on the Carpitella-Lomax collection which Maurizio Agamennone deals with in Chapter 20 in this volume. If we go back to the seminal recording campaign of the 1950s, when Lomax and Carpitella toured throughout Italy to record thousands of documents of the little-known musical tradition of peasants, shepherds and fishermen, we can reconsider those tapes and find new insights overlooked at the time of the research. We can mention, in this respect, Walter Brunetto's work at the Archivi di Etnomusicologia of the Accademia Nazionale di Santa Cecilia: he compiled a new catalogue of the so-called 'Raccolta 24',[10] finding many new documents not included in the first catalogue of the 1970s (Brunetto 1995; 2013).

Furthermore, while in the past we used to consider only musical examples as sound documentation, overlooking all the other sound materials (verbal interaction between researcher and performers, errors, repetitions, comments), nowadays we may reconsider these documents, whose 'extras' may be precious for a number of reasons: for example, they may enable us to reconstruct the modalities and methods of past research.

The 'authenticity' of folklore is an issue that springs from such reconsideration of old recordings: listening to old tapes, namely to the interaction between researchers and informants, what emerges is the quest for the 'ancient', for the 'authentic' that was very much in the mind of the researchers when approaching the musicians or the singers. Such an approach led them to discard all that was considered hybrid, contaminated by Western tonal harmony or not sufficiently 'archaic'.

---

[9] The first sound archives devoted to oral tradition music can be traced back to the turn of the nineteenth century, when the Phonogrammarchiv was established in Vienna (1899) and the Phonogramm-Archiv was founded in Berlin (1900). For a retrospective on the 100-year existence of the Berliner Phonogramm-Archiv, see Berlin and Simon (2002).

[10] The sound documents of the Carpitella-Lomax collection recorded during the well-known 1954–5 campaign are kept in the Archivi di Etnomusicologia ('Raccolta 24'), divided into regions, labelled with different letters of the alphabet (24a, 24b and so on).

This cultural position led to a selective attitude towards the sound documents to be recorded, and also towards the way of recording. We may say that sound archives contributed to creating a sort of philology of the musical performance in oral traditions. The approach based on recordings as a sort of normative text had significant repercussions on the development of musical processes among the communities where the recordings were made; those processes were set in motion precisely by documentation and ethnomusicological research, thus forcing we researchers to reconsider later on our modalities of documenting musical traditions.

Therefore, accessing archival sources enables us to reconstruct a context of research, providing information not only on the sound document itself, but also on our research methods, theoretical frameworks, priorities, and the interactions between researcher and musicians, thus putting archival sources into a historical perspective.

Furthermore, going back to the archives also enables us to reconstruct the life of those repertoires, finding and retrieving additional information on the context of the performance, the performers and the recordings made in past times. In turn, this may lead us to return to the field of those recordings, interviewing participants in the events (or their relatives), thus enabling us to put into a historical perspective documents often implicitly considered as a sort of immutable text, rather than part of a dynamic cultural interaction.

There is plenty of such research in ethnomusicology. Let me just mention the Berlin example, during the celebrations of the centenary of the first recording kept in the Phonogramm-Archiv: we listened to the first recording kept in the Phonogramm-Archiv made by Stumpf on Siamese music;[11] immediately afterward, some Thai musicians played the very same piece 'live', highlighting the dramatic process of change that oral tradition music also undergoes. This is also a concern in Italian folk music research. Antonello Ricci and Roberta Tucci worked on Carpitella's recordings among the Albanians of Calabria (Ricci and Tucci 2006): they visited the places where the recordings were made in 1954 and interviewed the participants of those days, reconstructing as far as possible the recording context. Let me also mention the important work of local researchers, who are sometimes the best-placed to retrieve information and data from local contexts: for example, Luigi D'Agnese, Curator of the Museo Civico Etnomusicale in Montemarano, has worked on the period Lomax spent in Irpinia in 1955.[12]

There is also the perspective of restitution of archival materials: the communities that were bearers of those documents may have lost memory of those performing practices, and want to retrieve them for various purposes. Again, audiovisual material can be of great interest and assistance in such a process.

---

11 On the circumstances of those first phonograph recordings made by Carl Stumpf in 1900, see Christensen (2002): 21–2.

12 D'Agnese wrote an unpublished text, 'Alan Lomax a Montemarano' (1955), in which he reconstructed the days Lomax spent in that little town in January 1955 by interviewing the local participants in those recording sessions.

More generally, nowadays it is rare for ethnomusicological research on a given musical culture or repertoire not to rely on both video and audio archival material, with the intent of providing a diachronic perspective. This trend must not be overlooked, since archives are becoming among the most important workplaces for ethnomusicologists newly putting to the fore, even more than in the past, the foundational relationship between recorded sound (and image) and our discipline, placing ethnomusicology among the historical branches of musicology.

Reflecting and Creating Change in Contemporary Research

In contemporary ethnomusicology, audiovisual documentation has become more than a specific and separate mode of communicating research; rather, it is now part of an integrated methodology encompassing different kinds of media and conveying results of a given study. Easy access to technology for video reproduction allows one to work with film not as a separate product with respect to other media; furthermore, audiovisual material is often used for manifold purposes.

This brings up new ways of making and communicating research, highlighting issues such as the new relationship between researchers and musicians, new technological issues, collaboration, restitution and the relationship between written and audiovisual documentation.

This is also a consequence of two recent changes in ethnomusicological research: the change in the object of study, and a different relationship between researchers and musicians.

As far as the object of study is concerned, the so-called traditional musics documented by ethnomusicologists are increasingly intertwined in a mediatized and global world of music making: circulation of repertoires and technologies makes the idea of specific music belonging to secluded areas (if this ever was the case), separated from the global flow, untenable and out of date. Rather, we can witness a musical soundscape where the 'authentic', the traditional, yields to the hybrid, the contaminated, the transcultural. The research must proceed accordingly, dealing with the new audio and video technologies used not only by researchers, but by musicians themselves, whether they are part of the record industry or not. Research on local traditional music following the path of oral tradition – fully embedded in the communities' ritual and social life, without much influence from the external world – still exists, but is becoming more and more marginal.

This new configuration of musical processes of production, transmission and reception implies that audiovisual projects during fieldwork are not to be conceived only as projects of documentation for the researcher's own benefit or for archival purposes. Rather, video cameras and tape recorders are becoming increasingly specific tools to view several different projects from a new perspective, thus highlighting a stronger interaction between researchers and musicians. We must bear in mind that musicians, in any part of the world, have access to and control the musical process, including that of self-representation. They produce their own

CDs, have access to the Internet, post their videos on YouTube and master digital technologies. As an example, my Cambodian teacher Meas Saem, master of the *roneat ek* (xylophone) and one of the leading experts of the Palace tradition, knows Western music notation. When I first met him in 1987, he was using music sheets to notate Khmer tunes. At present, we are discussing which version of *Finale* is the most effective to notate Khmer music.

In addition to mastering technologies, so-called 'traditional' musicians are making music that can be hardly defined as traditional and that the ethnomusicologist wishes to document as part of an ever-changing musical landscape, whether in Asia, Africa or rural Italy.

In other words, as one may read in Steven Feld's Chapter 6 and Nicola Scaldaferri's Chapter 21 in this volume, audiovisual technology can be employed today in several ways that obviously include documentation, but also encompass the creation of experimental music, soundscape compositions, and collaborative and creative projects, including researchers participating as musicians and sharing technological competences – a rather unconventional perspective compared to the common perception of ethnomusicological research, even though it had already been imagined by some of our forebears many years ago.

Before concluding, let me refer to technology, given that it has always been, and still is, a main concern for our discipline. It is difficult to keep up with technological developments in this field, and equipment dating from ten years ago is now so obsolete that it almost cannot be used for a professional production. The rapid pace of technological development can represent an opportunity, but also a problem, because of the difficulty in keeping up with changes, increasing costs and the problems of standards.

Another aspect of the status of contemporary audiovisual documentation that has changed dramatically is accessibility. In the field, it is impossible to shoot a video in a context of a musical performance, a ritual or a ceremony without including in the frame others who are, in turn, taking pictures or filming the same event: they can be members of the community itself, tourists, television crews, anthropology (or ethnomusicology) students, fellows researchers, using all kind of equipment, from cellular phones to sophisticated video cameras. The option of not including such figures in our shooting is virtually non-existent. In doing so, we should perhaps consider that we are 'faking' by pretending to reconstruct an image corresponding to our imagery of what a rituals should 'look like'; this image, however, is not pertinent to contemporary contexts.

Therefore, our own filming an event becomes one among many, not the unique documentation of it. Several of those images taken during the event will be posted on the Internet in the following days (or even hours!). I often quote the example of Montemarano, where I was conducting research during the Carnival when I was called on the phone to be informed 'You're on YouTube!', the footage posted soon after I participated as a performer in the Carnival parade.

These new bulimic ways of capturing images of our society force us to reconsider our work and our research methods, charging us with new responsibilities in relation to the event we are documenting and the people who are part of it. Our research has to measure up with a number of audiovisual documentations of one and the same event, emphasizing our role in constructing a 'critical memory': rather than communicating what was unknown before, we should provide critical tools and documentation aimed at comprehending a phenomenon that is already available in many ways.

Finally, one last remark: this wide and 'democratic' access to audio and audiovisual technology, along with the possibility of reproducing documentation in a number of easy ways, has also generated processes of disseminating traditional music, now separated from the original performers. Audio documents can be sampled and reproduced in all sorts of contexts and re-functionalized for global circulation, triggering both conflicts and new forms of musical creation, in a perspective of musical cosmopolitanism and transculturalism.

We are forced, therefore, not least in the light of this new role played by audiovisual technology and documentation, to reconsider our own role as researchers in several ways: first of all in our placement in the field, where collaborative, dialogic, interactive modes of research become more necessary, and most often such modes place centre-stage audiovisual documentation in the form of the various and multifaceted products that this technology allows us to use today. But audiovisual technology also reminds us nowadays that the object of our study can have a mediatized life of which the ethnomusicologist is not the depositary. This implies that we have another 'field' to explore, using a dynamic, interactive and critical approach to this material – the Internet, the World Wide Web, social networks, video clips and audiovisual self-representations of musicians. This new field full of challenges forces us to reconsider our work and research tools.

References

Berlin, Gabriele and Simon, Artur (eds) (2002) *Music Archiving in the World: Papers Presented at the Conference on the Occasion of the 100th Anniversary of the Berlin Phonogramm-Archiv*, Berlin: VWB-Verlag für Wissenschaft und Bildung.

Brăiloiu, Constantin (1931) 'Esquisse d'une méthode de folklore musical', *Revue de Musicologie*, 12/40, pp. 233–67.

Brunetto, Walter (1995) 'La Raccolta 24 degli Archivi di Etnomusicologia dell'Accademia Nazionale di Santa Cecilia', *EM. Annuario degli Archivi di etnomusicologia dell'Accademia Nazionale di Santa Cecilia*, 3, pp. 11–187.

——— (2013) 'Il viaggio in Italia e il viaggio nel tempo. Aspetti, storia e problemi conservativi della raccolta Lomax-Carpitella', *AAA TAC: Acoustical Arts and Artifacts – Technology, Aesthetics, Communication*, 8, pp. 37–50.

Carpitella, Diego (1961) 'L'esorcismo coreutico-musicale del tarantismo', in *La terra del rimorso. Contributo a una storia religiosa del Sud*, ed. Ernesto De Martino, Milan: Il Saggiatore, pp. 335–72.

——— (1981) 'Pratica e teoria nel film etnografico italiano. Prime osservazioni', *La Ricerca Folklorica*, 2/3, pp. 5–22.

——— (1989) 'I seminari di etnomusicologia a Siena', in *Ethnomusicologica*, ed. Diego Carpitella, Siena: Accademia Musicale Chigiana (Quaderni dell'Accademia Musicale Chigiana 43), pp. 7–23

Christensen, Dieter (2002) 'Berlin Phonogramm-Archiv: The First 100 Years', in Berlin et al. (2002), pp. 19–31.

Cooley, Timothy J., Meizel, Katharine and Syed, Nasir (2008) 'Virtual Fieldwork: Three Case Studies', in *Shadows in the Field: New Perspectives for Fieldwork in Ethnomusicology*, ed. Gregory Barz and Timothy J. Cooley, 2nd edn, New York: Oxford University Press, pp. 90–107.

De Martino, Ernesto (2008) *La terra del rimorso* [1961], Milan: Il Saggiatore.

Feld, Steven (1976) 'Ethnomusicology and Visual Communication', *Ethnomusicology*, 20/2, pp. 293–325.

Heider, Karl G. (2006) *Ethnographic Film*, 2nd rev. edn, Austin, TX: University of Texas Press.

Hood, Mantle (1971) *The Ethnomusicologist*, New York: McGraw-Hill.

Ricci, Antonello and Tucci, Roberta (eds) (2006) *Musica arbëreshe in Calabria. Le registrazioni di Diego Carpitella ed Ernesto de Martino (1954)*, Rome: Squilibri.

Rouch, Jean (1968) 'Le film ethnographique', in *Ethnologie Générale*, ed. Jean Poirier, Paris: Gallimard, pp. 429–71.

Tucci, Roberta (1992) 'Diego Carpitella: bibliografia. Con un'appendice nastro-disco-filmografica', *Nuova Rivista Musicale Italiana*, 26/3–4, pp. 523–72.

Zemp, Hugo (1988) 'Filming Music and Looking at Music Films', *Ethnomusicology*, 32/2, pp. 393–427.

——— (1989) 'Filmare la musica', in *Ethnomusicologica*, ed. Diego Carpitella, Siena: Accademia Musicale Chigiana, pp. 269–94.

Chapter 20
Recording Out-takes: What can be Discovered in the 'Historical' Recordings of Traditional Music

Maurizio Agamennone

I have titled this chapter 'Recording Out-takes' because I will examine only those short segments of magnetic tape that concern aspects usually considered marginal in sound documentation. In so doing, I have largely ignored the musical works themselves in order to concentrate on what precedes the musical performance and might actually accompany it, before and afterwards. I will consider what is usually abandoned, destroyed, or simply eliminated, when it passes from the recording in the field to the studio, analysis, publication, and to the critical edition of the sound documentation.

The historical-cultural context of these recordings embraces several remote locations of central Italy in the years 1954–60, and is the work of two celebrated documentarians, Alan Lomax and Diego Carpitella. These are 'historical' recordings not only because they were realized 60 years ago with technology and procedures quite distant from those currently used today, but above all because they document musical practices which have largely died out and are no longer relevant within contemporary society and culture, representing ceremonial customs and rituals typical of pre-industrial society, predominantly rural and agricultural.

The Institutional Landscape

In terms of methodology, Lomax and Carpitella practised a kind of 'urgent anthropology' at a propitious time, before dramatic social processes (massive emigration, depopulation of the countryside, rapid industrialization) modified many of the expressive customs of Italian rural populations. Alan Lomax had already been in Europe for a few years, and arrived in Italy after travelling the Iberian Peninsula to make some records for the Columbia label and for his BBC radio programmes. Diego Carpitella had worked for some years with the Centro nazionale di Studi per la musica popolare (CNSMP) (National Centre for Folk Music Studies) at the Accademia Nazionale di Santa Cecilia in Rome, which operated in close collaboration with RAI Radiotelevisione Italiana (Italian state television). In 1989 the CNSMP assumed the name Archivi di Etnomusicologia

(AEM) (Archives of Ethnomusicology), at the express desire of Carpitella, who became its first curator only a few months before his death. In spring 1954 Carpitella had just returned from some important and innovative experiences in sound documentation, realized together with two great personalities, later key figures in Italian and European ethnology and anthropology: Ernesto de Martino, in 1952, and Alberto Mario Cirese, in spring 1954.

Between summer 1954 and the first months of 1955, during the course of an adventurous and intense journey,[1] Lomax and Carpitella produced the so-called 'Raccolta 24' ('Collection 24') of the CNSMP-AEM, whose impressive documentation depicts traditional music performed in the Italian countryside that was until then largely unknown.[2] Two years later, in 1957, they released two LPs on the Columbia label,[3] which were released in an Italian edition almost twenty 20 years later,[4] and the bulk of this collection was preserved in the archive, albeit silent for a long time because of the ongoing great difficulty of access. Carpitella galvanized vigilant and constant interest with his extensive presence on the radio (see Carpitella 1992) and by mentoring numerous degree theses when teaching in the faculty of Rome University. The activities of the CNSMP experienced a long standstill during the 1970s and 1980s. Recently, a large selection of the materials included in 'Collection 24' has been released in the USA as a series of recordings, *Italian Treasury*.[5] Recently, a legal controversy pitted the heirs of Lomax against the Accademia Nazionale di Santa Cecilia concerning ownership rights of 'Collection 24'.

The Ethnographic Landscape

Today, finally, an Italian edition is being prepared with philological criteria, extended historical-cultural investigation and musicological analysis, within the framework of an ambitious long-term publishing programme.[6] During the preparation of the

---

1 The vicissitudes of Alan Lomax's Italian 'journey' are effectively retraced and chronicled by Goffredo Plastino (2008).

2 On the events that led to putting together and preserving this impressive documentation, and on the differences between what is kept at the AEM in Rome and at the Association for Cultural Equity which holds the impressive archive put together by Lomax in New York, see Brunetto (2013).

3 *Northern and Central Italy and the Albanians of Calabria* and *Southern Italy and the Islands*, edited by Alan Lomax and Diego Carpitella, The Columbia World Library of Folk and Primitive Music, vols XV and XVI, New York, 1957.

4 *Folklore Musicale Italiano*, vols 1–2, curated by Alan Lomax and Diego Carpitella, two LPs, Pull, QLP 107–8, Rome 1973.

5 *Italian Treasury*, curated by Goffredo Plastino, 11 CDs, Rounded Records, 1999–2005.

6 The Italian edition of 'Collection 24' of the AEM is the result of an agreement between the Accademia Nazionale di Santa Cecilia and the publisher Squilibri: it calls for specific volumes with one or more CDs enclosed, relevant to the various regions and areas

first volume (Agamennone 2014) I was able to draw upon the audio documentation preserved at the AEM and to identify the recording out-takes which I intend to discuss here: these concern the recordings made in Puglia, on the promontory of Gargano and in Salento, between the summer of 1954 and the summer of 1960.

Lomax and Carpitella spent a lot of time together – travelling the dusty roads of the Italian peninsula in an old Volkswagen van packed with their equipment (tapes, tripods, microphones and tape recorders) in which they also sometimes slept – often conversing with the informants and taking notes on the events: this contributed greatly to consolidating the friendship between the two great documentarians and to complementing favourably their individual attitudes. Years later, the account of this experience brings certain aspects into better focus, with regard to some unique, but efficient, expressive aspects:

> Lomax spoke 'Itagnolo', if you can put it like that, because he came from Spain and tried to speak Italian, but it was an *Italianized* Spanish. Anyway, sometimes I was the interpreter, which created not just a little difficulty for me; it was problematic to render the sense of some gestural expressions verbally: for example, the well known gesture 'OK' often gave rise to misunderstood and malicious interpretations …. Sometimes, Alan demanded the immediate translation of very unusual vernacular expressions that could not be easily interpreted, out loud, often having to do with subtle nuances or a particular situation. In any case, though, Lomax made himself well understood, the music helped him enormously in this because every so often he would take the guitar and start to play, singing cowboy songs. At heart, it had to do with situations that inspired curiosity and congeniality. People always wanted him to stay. (Diego Carpitella, in Agamennone 1989: 26)

In fact, both of them had wide experience in the field, acquired under very difficult conditions. Before arriving in Italy, Lomax was in Spain during the harshest period of Franco's dictatorship, and he had certainly had the opportunity to test effective dialogue techniques, in order to break through the barrier of suspicion when a foreigner and stranger comes to your home to pose unusual questions. Lomax and Carpitella's 'journey' had a broadly panoramic character and called for very short visits, with recording sessions often limited only to a few hours.

The skills they had acquired allowed them to 'optimize' the interaction, even when contact was ephemeral and occasional:

> At heart, we were a bit like pedlars, we immediately noticed the climate and went straight off to identify the sources; in the end we had a precise sense of which persons could be the ones who knew what we were looking for. The levels of these musical pieces were so/to such an extent defined that as soon

explored by Lomax and Carpitella; numerous releases have been announced, the first of which (*Collection 24/B*) will be dedicated to Salento.

> as they 'tuned in' to that which could have been defined sociologically as the peasant/pastoral or artisan/rustic-country category, immediately the timbre, the way of performing and of singing, the gestures, the movements of the body unequivocally revealed themselves. (Diego Carpitella, in Agamennone 1989: 26)

The expertise of the two documentarians helped to forge a particularly satisfying relationship with the informants encountered in the field, whether intrumentalists or vocalists. The interaction of the time can be understood as a relationship between 'specialists' – which, in fact, the two scholars were, as were many of their informants, recognized and identified as representative performers of the local repertory.

The Guitarist of the Gargano

Thus, the dialogue between fieldworkers and local interpreters seems to be a friendly interaction, albeit of very short duration: the informants know their milieu fully and handle the encounter with the external observer well, thus creating a strongly dialogical 'interplay', on equal terms. It is not clear whether, finding himself together with Carpitella at Monte Sant'Angelo, on the Gargano, on 25 August 1954, Lomax played the guitar in front of his informants to inspire greater 'complicity'. Surely, the result he achieves is extraordinary. On the tape preserved at the AEM one can hear the instructions Lomax addressed to 'Diego' – who acts as his recording assistant[7] – as well as some misunderstandings between them, the announcements of the performance, several signs of interruption of the recording, but above all the 'pivotal' invitation the Texan researcher addresses to his Puglian informant, in perfect 'Itagnolo': 'Show me how it's strummed.' The 'guitarist of the Gargano' answers by proposing, in rapid sequence, a wonderful inventory of the many accompaniments he is able to perform: it is a sort of self-presentation of the performer – a 'specialist', evidently – who shows to the scholar an 'anthology' of what he can do, outside any context or social relationship: in the local tradition, the same guitarist would have hardly had the opportunity to propose the same 'anthological sequence' to the usual recipients (singers and dancers); on the contrary, each singing and dancing act requires its specific accompaniment, related to different customs.[8]

[7] 'Chitarra battente, Diego, let's go right to … Oh Diego, ten seconds. Stop, stop' are some of the instructions that Lomax imparts, starting and interrupting the recording several times; Lomax's 'Itagnolo' looms large over the spoken parts, though with great communicative efficiency.

[8] The original sound document is currently indexed as 'Rhythms of accompaniment of the chitarra battente' (AEM, Collection 24/B, piece 105, Monte San'Angelo [Foggia], 25 August 1954; see Brunetto 1995: 144).

Traces and Memories of the 'Journey to Italy'

Another trait of the method employed by Lomax emerges here: his curiosity and his keen interest in performers, whom he considered as persons with specific skills and knowledge, managed and expressed through individual practices. This was not only about being attentive to the 'traditions' – to the complex social scenarios in which the different musical practices are revealed – but, moreover, to the personal behaviour of the 'informants', with their essential peculiarities and differences. It is then evident that, under the given conditions, a privileged relationship with outstanding interpreters makes the recording process easier, faster and more reliable: particularly in the relationship with the intrumentalists, considered as local 'specialists' in leading the dancing, in accompanying the singing, in several ritual processes. It is also true that in the field, our documentarians encountered singing practices every bit as exuberant, widely representative of local customs that are still very vibrant. Lomax articulated this on various occasions:

a. in a recollection of Carpitella offered in 1991 – 'The people wanted to sing, and when they finished, [Diego] made them feel happy and proud of having done so' (Alan Lomax, in Plastino 2008: 42);
b. celebrating his old family roots – 'Diego and I felt truly at home in Lombardy. The last name of my forebears is Lomazzi, and the family fled from this zone to escape religious persecution during the time of the Albigese. Everything seemed natural: the place, the music, the people. It was as if a profound bond connected me to this environment, and the women who sang were like my distant cousins' (Lomax 2008: 172);
c. recalling and comparing events that occurred in the field in Italy with previous research experiences carried out elsewhere – 'One was skinny, with crazy brown eyes and tousled hair, distracted, had not had anything to eat the whole day long – another with a dark African face, large mouth, many black-stained teeth. And they sang for me the most moving song that I had heard in all of Italy, a song that reminded me of the endless pain of the blacks of Mississippi and Texas who had sung for me many years before' (Lomax 2008: 155).

On the other hand, in those days, large group polyphonic singing fully unfolded during work or other required activity, often with local differentiations of genre:

> In southern Italy, where young women don't have permission to go out with the boys, dance with them, sit with them in the parlor, and not even to talk with them on the street, the girls, all of them, sing during work. All of the songs are about love, and their shrill, high, voices can be heard from afar, across the olive groves, and they say to the boys who pass by: we are here, we are thinking of you. (Lomax 2008: 136)

Similarly: 'In Puglia, in the sheds where they work on tobacco, the young women sing sitting on the ground, with their shirts unbuttoned, quickly and carefully threading the fragrant green and gold leaves of tobacco with a long steel needle' (Lomax 2008: 144).

Analogous research focused on the men's activity:

> The government offers some of these unemployed men a bit of work on the roads. And so, in Puglia, I followed my friends to a road in the countryside: with a hammer they broke some stone boulders, and to pass the time, they sang a song that was bitter, dry like the warm summer wind. (Lomax 2008: 151)

These last observations refer to the polyphonic practices of large groups with broadly inclusive participation:[9] Lomax describes how they are done while they are happening. Moreover, it was precisely during his 'journey' to Spain (1952) and Italy (1954–55) that the American scholar began to develop his ideas on the strong connections between vocal styles and the customs relevant to gender relationships and to sexual morality, which later merged in his *opus maximum* (Lomax 1968). Lomax often indulges in impressionistic descriptions with very strong narrative passages, allowing his own emotional reactions to emerge, underlining a few reasons for affectionate and 'mythic' affinity – Lombardian women are his distant 'cousins', the Salento stone cutters and labourers are his 'friends'. In this sense, his account of the 'journey to Italy' seems much more sensitive than his companion's comments on this adventure. Carpitella's prose is much more reserved, less inclined to simple cultural assimilations, without personal references, and more careful in defining the first analytical and taxonomical hypotheses as to musical expression, which at the time were lacking a critical literature. It might be useful to compare some texts from the same period influenced by the shared 'journey to Italy' (Lomax 1955–56; 1956; Carpitella 1956a; 1956b; 1961). Some historical-cultural hypotheses proposed by Lomax are today unacceptable, even if offered with warm enthusiasm at the time; vice versa, Carpitella's observations – prudent, dry and focused on the analysis of the stylistic music features –still seem persuasive. Perhaps, being closer to the observed customs, Carpitella was much more cautious and discreet, whereas Lomax was outside the same practices, thus indulging in a larger interpretative euphoria, combined with a freer expression of his feelings; in addition, the differences were undeniable between the two formidable documentarians, who were, for this reason, close friends. Moreover, I do not intend in the slightest to praise a 'cold' approach over a 'warm' one, in both ethnographic survey and in critical interpretation.

[9] Everybody present, in a defined space and context, can take part in the performance and place themselves, also migrating, within the different vocal parts of the polyphonic structure.

In the Field in Salento

On 16 August 1954 Lomax is with Diego Carpitella in Salento, in Martano, a village consisting of a linguistic 'island' where Greek-Salentino, a Hellenic dialect, was and is still spoken today: he is standing before a group of young people assembled to sing into the microphone of his Magnecord PT-6. Some of the singers intone, in alternation, a monody that, at the time, was probably still performed during the course of the archaic threshing done with a horse pulling a type of sled.[10] On the tape, which is the witness to this event, at the beginning of the piece, Lomax gives a few directions to Carpitella, expressing himself, again, in 'Itagnolo': 'Ready Diego [yelling]!!! OK! Ten seconds.'

Besides this, he intervenes to support the performance, at a hesitation of the singer, and to ask for a repetition of the strophe: 'Again, Again! Start with this strophe again!'

At the end of the long piece on tape (almost eight minutes), Lomax intervenes to check some procedures of the performance (I've indicated in italics the singers' reactions to the scholar's requests):

> Uh, there's something, something interesting to understand because we don't sing like … this way. I see that today … nervous here?
> [Perhaps Lomax means 'tense', and he probably touches the chest of the vocalist, as the next reference to the lungs shows, offered by the others present.]
> Nervous?
> *No no … nervous? Me? No …*
> And how … sing wi …
> *With the lungs, he sings with the lungs. Don't tremble you say …. Sing with the lungs …*
> Where you sing … Sing a little!
> [Other voices … the informant resumes singing: *Veni veni me disse e ma na massara*]
> I don't hear it from here. [Apparently, Lomax touches the singer's body and notes the muscle tensions that support the vocals; one can assume he continues to touch the chest and the neck of the informant to test for possible tension.]
> Wh … where?
> *I have a headache.*
> … No, Diego.[11]

---

[10] The melodic profile and the vocal action reveal analogies with the wagoners' singing: one hears commands directed to the animals at the end of a phrase. Moreover, they sing some verses typical of the *trainiéri*, as the drivers of trucks used for transporting people and goods were called locally.

[11] The original sound document is currently indexed as 'Canto per la trebbia' (AEM, Collection 24/B, Work 20, Martano [Lecce], 25 August 1954; see Brunetto 1995: 140). This dialogue was not published in the recent American edition of the Lomax collection:

This curious 'recording out-take' suggests a behaviour that is particularly 'invasive'. Lomax questions the singers; he doesn't limit himself to posing questions, but touches them, literally puts 'his hands on them'. He had identified a vocal utterance supported by a rather intense tension, as in most Italian vocal practices, inducing him to verify the conditions with a certain insistence. The tape is interrupted by the singer's voice acknowledging he has a headache: this could confirm this slight discomfort as a consequence of the vocal exertion protracted for several minutes, or – suspecting a certain impatience in the Texan documentarian – as a reaction to his insistent questions. On the other hand, Lomax had already accumulated considerable knowledge of the local singing styles and different vocal techniques, both in Europe and the US; drawing on his broad experience, he could put a sharp comparative perception into play. Probably, thanks to these quick and urgent assessments, he began to develop the taxonomic templates that were improved in the following decade (Lomax 1968).

On the same day, 16 August 1954, still in Martano in Salento, two weepers perform different versions of the *moroloja*[12] and are immersed in a complicated conversation with Carpitella concerning the performance and the symbolic meaning of the Greek-Salentine funeral lamentation. The dialogue is very warm-hearted, at times playful: one perceives a mutual curiosity between the 'informants' and the scholar[13] in the alternation between the Romance dialect (during the dialogue) and the Greek-Salentine dialect (for the performance of the lamentation's fragments). The encounter often elicits laughter and takes on a jovial mood. Carpitella requests information about the handkerchief waved by the extended arm, wielded along a horizontal axis from left to right and vice versa, and determined by a binary metre. The weepers answer that such a movement helps to 'give the beat' and to 'give air' – to stabilize the body movement and the metric-rhythmic flow, as well as to support the singing. The dialogue is held mainly by the weepers, who respond to the questions, translating easily from the Greek-Salentine dialect into the Romance dialect and Italian. Moreover, Carpitella's account of a previous experience recording a funeral lamentation amuses the Salentine weepers – as one can hear in the audio documentation; the scholar himself seems to quite enjoy recounting it. Carpitella refers to a previous experience in Molise – not in Abruzzo, as one hears on the tape[14] – together with Alberto Mario Cirese, with the Albanese

---

Italian Treasury: Puglia: Salento, ed. Goffredo Plastino, Rounded Records 82161-1805-2, 2002.

[12] This is what funeral lamentations are called in the local Hellenic dialects of a small inland area of southern Puglia known as Salentine Greece; on the Greek Salentine *moroloja*, see Corti (1995) and Montinaro (1994; 2009).

[13] The informants address Carpitella with the title *signurìa*, which locally indicates respect and a subordinate position to the interlocutor.

[14] Carpitella's 'geographical blunder' can be explained: in 1954 Molise was part of a single administrative region, composed of Abruzzi and Molise (Constitution of the Italian Republic, Art. 131). With constitutional law no. 3 of 27 December 1963, Molise was separated from Abruzzo, attaining recognition of its cultural identity, whereas

(*arbëreshe*) communities settled in the region. It was in Ururi, South Molise, a small region in central Italy, where, to fulfil an explicit request of the local weepers, who otherwise would not have been able to 'weep', Carpitella lay down on the table motionless, pretending to be dead, while the women finally wept. In contrast to what he tells the Salentine weepers, he wasn't very happy: in fact, the moment he got off the table he was extremely relieved that everything was over and refused to repeat the 'fiction' again.[15] In Molise – a few months before, in May the same year – the urgent request at the beginning of the ritual, as a contrived 'spark', had the intention of documenting the singing expressions and observing the postures and body movements. Even if activated artificially, following a request and an external action (the 'fiction' of the researcher in the field ... and on the table, outstretched and motionless, between the candles!), the 'weeping' was nourished by a psychological and emotional independence of the performative methods inscribed in the ritual setting, and deeply stored in the body's memories.[16] In Salento, however, the same experience changed meaning completely – from the original inconvenience, in Molise, to a more playful intent – and became an effective narrative issue of interaction, highlighting common experiences and facilitating the dialogue: the distance between informants and researcher was reduced, thus avoiding repetition of the previous 'woeful' fiction. The Salentine dialogue continues on tape: times, places and itineraries of weeping in the Greek-Salentine customs emerge more precisely, with some comparative evaluations of the Lucanis' customs suggested by the scholar. The weepers point out that the ritual use of weeping, even if in decline, is still alive at the time and considered extremely demanding and strenuous. The conversation ends with a very affectionate farewell of one of the two informants ('Mó signurìa, l'ha 'ntisu lu lamentu ... pò scrivere tantu' ['Now, sir, you've listened to the lament: you can write a lot about it']); by the way, Lomax – whom Carpitella calls 'the professor' – was absent on the occasion, due to a slight indisposition.[17] In the dialogue, if some of the

its administrative and legislative jurisdiction was ratified only later, in 1970, with the Republic's new regional organization.

[15] The episode has been retrieved thanks to Rosolina Cirese Savino, cousin of the anthropologist Alberto Mario Cirese, recently deceased, who was present at the recording (see Agamennone and Lombardi 2005: 21ff.).

[16] This perception of a partial autonomy of performative methods inscribed in the performers' body and in the scenario of the ritual is central in Diego Carpitella's teaching. This could even happen for the identification and recording of lullabies and other expressions for infancy; rocking a pillow in the absence of and as a substitute for 'real' babies called forth gestures and behaviours inscribed deep in the body memories of mothers, grandmothers and aunts: expressive modules which were difficult to stop or adulterate even before the presence of external researchers or the intrusion of recording equipment.

[17] The original sound document is currently indexed as 'Interview about the funeral lamentation with examples' (AEM, Collection 24/B, piece 13, Martano [Lecce], 16 August 1954; see Brunetto 1995: 139). This long dialogue was not published in the recent American edition of the Lomax collection: cf. *Italian Treasury. Puglia: Salento*, ed. Goffredo Plastino, Rounded Records 82161-1805-2, 2002.

ceremonial expressions are excluded, the interlocutors seem to be on the same level; the weepers are two 'specialists', celebrants of a particularly emotional ritual in local life; they know their reality very well and possess an exclusive know-how: therefore, the dialogue with the external scholar proceeds at a fast pace, on the right track, and is guarded by cautious expressions. Even over such a short time, mutual confidence is activated between the 'discussants' within a safe interaction: the weeping specialists provide the researcher with information which only they hold, allowing the scholar to use and write about them, as is his métier. Namely, the idea of a musical text – within oral tradition – is much more recognizable and stable in the individual action: the text is 'hidden' in the mental and acoustic model that the weeping specialist holds in her memory, and takes an emotional shape only during the performance, according to the intention of whoever acts. It is not subsumed to another individual project, except that of another specialist, with whom she acts in close coherence and co-operation.

The environment in which the dialogue takes place is also important in orienting the interlocution methods. Listening to the original sound document, one senses a domestic venue. Carpitella indicates some photo portraits of the weepers' relatives, defined precisely as to kinship. The only witness alien to the dialogue is a rather young child, as is evident by his crying and by a tender sing-song heard in the background. In this case, too, the relationship between the scholar and his informants seems like an interaction between 'specialists', the dialogue moving forward as a friendly interaction.

The Explosive Euphoria of the Women's Singing (Avetrana, 1960)

Diego Carpitella went through a completely different experience at the end of the decade, again in Salento, but in an area where Romance dialects are spoken, and without Alan Lomax's company and help. On 16 June 1960, in the village of Avetrana (Taranto), our documentarian found himself facing a large group of women involved in the performance of several typical polyphonic pieces conceived for a large group. It concerns a way of performing traditional music throughout Italy, where participation is inclusive (whoever is present can take part in the singing) and the individual action can be extremely mobile, even within the group. Frequently, the following behaviours emerge:

d. individual migration from one part to another in the polyphonic structure;
e. sudden doubling;
f. temporary absence from the group;
g. delayed entrance into the group;
h. possible antagonistic undertaking of the role of voice leader for the intonation of the monodic incipit.

In this performative scenario, the idea of a possible text becomes much more blurred, subordinated to the individual choices converging in the action of the group.

Thus, the musical text consists of the various and subsequent results of many possible options, drawn from a common mental model, made up of an amalgam of performative opportunities: these are chosen and set up by means of variable and unpredictable individual actions. Furthermore, these practices of large group polyphony are often exterior to a strictly formalized ritual scenario: they happen casually or at work, without any eurythmic function nor specific programmes, just for the pleasure and euphoria of singing in a group, and can embrace instances of solidarity as well as antagonistic impulses.

This is exactly what seems to cause difficulties in ethnographic survey. During the 1950s, the documentarians worked under the pressure of many circumstances and demands, including:

a. being in a constant state of 'urgent anthropology';
b. the speed of the ethnographic research, which did not allow long stays or return visits;
c. the aim of collecting materials that could also be used in radio programmes or recordings;
d. economic restrictions that implied the sparing use of magnetic tape and other materials;
e. (creating) a broad panoramic documentation, considering the few sound documents preserved at the time in the archives.

Therefore, the research aims mainly to collect stable and balanced performances, representative of coherent and reliable texts, rather than performative practices, which can be quite flexible and changeable. The predominant goal seems to be the survey of pieces that are defined, closed and coherent in successive strophic iterations, preferably balanced in timbre and dynamics. In Avetrana, however, Carpitella comes across an impetuous and passionate singer tenaciously standing in the way and making the survey difficult. The documentarian, then, is forced to assume the tactics of a stern confrontation with his informants: suggesting, asking or imposing behaviours and precise performative methods that strictly correspond to a model the researcher has in mind, in the form of a closed, coherent and defined text. In the recording out-takes, on tape, one hears:

a. Carpitella's voice repeatedly interrupting the performance and requesting a 'better' repetition;
b. other participants signalling: 'Silence!';
c. others ordering the singing to start 'On command!';
d. besides the scholar, all those giving instructions are men, in front of a group made up almost exclusively of women.[18]

---

[18] The episode described here is indexed as 'Sotto l'orologio' ('Beneath the Clock'), in AEM Collection 53, piece 46, Avetrana (Taranto), 16 June 1960.

In another recording out-take, the voice of the documentarian doesn't conceal a certain irritation faced with unacceptable behaviours: Carpitella repeatedly asks his 'informants' not to talk to each other once the tape has started running, and to decide – again, before the tape has started – who and which verse should start the performance.[19]

For this reason, with regard to the intentions and the expectation of the documentarian, facing the euphoric group of Avetrana:

a. the action must begin in absolute silence;
b. verbal interventions unrelated to the singing are not allowed (suggestions, invitations to start, corrections, disputes about the roles, laughing, expressions of agreement and affection);
c. the decision concerning which piece to sing and who should start the performance must be made before the tape has started;
d. the beginning of the recording, in the complete silence, is marked by the silent gesture of the researcher.

At times, disagreement on the starting procedure is rather animated: in addition to the interruptions required by Carpitella, there are excited interventions from others present, and from the same vocalists, overlapping in the evaluation of the methods of intonation. Moreover, in the following repetition of the same piece and in the alternation of the vocalists, the melodic profile of the starting monodic intonation transforms sensitively: again, this is the consequence of individual choices which apparently prevail on the opinions of the other vocalists and over the researcher's supervision, as well as over the other witnesses, who by now are also responsible for the recording. The mayor of Avetrana was also present at the long and strenuous recording session: his judgement was at times conclusive in guiding some of the vocalists' singing, as Carpitella himself suggests. The scholar seems to almost lose patience:

a. He asks his 'informants' for a performance 'identical' to the previous one.
b. Then he makes a heartfelt complaint ('Well, then, we didn't understand each other!').
c. Finally, he proposes a new performance, appealing to the mayor for a crucial intervention.
d. The mayor, shortly before, had imperatively selected one of the informants as voice leader ('You start!'), assuming the role of conductor of the performance.[20]

---

19 This can be heard in the piece entitled 'Neri so' l'occhi mia' ('Black Are My Eyes') (AEM, Collection 53, piece 47, Avetrana [Taranto], 16 June 1960).

20 This can be heard in the piece entitled 'All'erta di lu sonnu, non cchiù dormite' (AEM, Collection 53, piece 48, Avetrana [Taranto], 16 June 1960).

In front of the performers and the other people attending the recording, Carpitella finds himself in a difficult situation, forced to carry out the following actions:

a. interrupting a performance because, in his opinion, it started wrongly;
b. calling for a new performance, 'identical' to a previous one, considered more suitable or representative;
c. requesting a new performance without any spurious intervention;
d. reproaching the performers in order to avoid any verbal acts, suggestions or agreements.

Under these conditions, his leadership – as a representative of prestigious institutions – also seems to be weakened, progressively flanked by the verbal intervention of the men present but not involved in the singing: they order silence, invoke respect for the unusual practice and impose strict obedience to a start signal external to the group.

Listening to the sound materials, the annoyance and the discord are quite clear. The documentarian, almost as if he were in a radio or recording studio,[21] attempts to obtain 'clean' pieces, without uncertainties or outside interference in the singing, preceded by rehearsals and persuasive agreements, and which represent, as much as possible, coherent and balanced texts: that can be explained by some of the above-mentioned reasons. The group of singers, however, behave as is their habit, and the procedures to start singing are flexible and changeable. In the sound documents, the local expressions 'Ci la zzicca?' ('Who's starting?') and 'Comu la zzicchi?' ('How do you start it?') are frequently heard and adopted by Carpitella himself. Moreover, in further iterations, different vocalists intervene, sometimes with sudden doublings; in this way they can transform the melodic profiles of the first monodic intonation, the variations become numerous and substantial, frustrating the occurrence of 'identical' repetitions wanted by the researcher and the other witnesses. Nevertheless, the expressions of comment, judgement and suggestion during the women's performance, which can appear a spurious insert in the audio recording, are largely legitimate and popular in the polyphony of the large group with inclusive participation: the singers interact freely, in the alternation of roles and the migration among the vocal parts of the polyphonic structure. The uncertainties, the quarrelling relationship among the performers, the comments on intonation, dynamic and timbre imbalances are completely legitimate and are all part of the game: they are part of the model shared by the performative action, in which individual reactions adapt to the needs of being part of a group. These procedures are constitutive and essential parts of polyphonic singing, and are activated in an impromptu manner by the performers.[22]

[21] One of the aims of the research, and one of the conditions of the agreement between the CNSMP and RAI, was to produce sound material that could be used in radio programming.

[22] On the other hand, Carpitella was well aware of the volatility of oral tradition and of the constant variations of performers (this relates to one of the most fertile legacies of his

On the other hand, the reaction can be very different towards the listener 'from afar' – in the archive, on the radio or on a record – without observing the faces and the bodies, without perceiving the space in which the singing flows and the ways in which the singers and other protagonists enliven the space:[23] the researcher, in the field, has to represent this instant of listening, too, inasmuch as the results of his work will be then transferred elsewhere (into the archive, to the radio, to a disc). He therefore definitively fixes in a closed and replicable document a practice that instead is constantly changeable and fluid. The environment of the recording session, in this circumstance also, is determinant in orienting the modes of confrontation: one guesses a rather large space, with many performers, joined to quite a few extraneous participants in the performance (inevitably the children, considering the high presence of women involved), who intervene in quite intransigent terms.

Furthermore, large group polyphony cannot be described as a practice of 'specialists', since, as already noted, it is fully inclusive, thus increasing the possible moments of contact and conflict between researcher and informants. Thus, the contrast between the scholar and the numerous participants in the group singing appears as a possible prescriptive interaction: the difference with respect to the interaction with the 'guitarist of the Gargano' and the 'weepers of Martano' is completely clear.

An Aesthetic Option?

In conclusion, our two formidable documentarians were moved by an aesthetic option, perhaps not fully conscious, but very robust, that induced them – even if as a result of the urgent needs pointed out elsewhere – to search for and to privilege musical expressions characterized by a strong originality that were indeed representative of local choices, of small marginal and peripheral communities. They were marginal, but capable, nevertheless, of preserving and performing emotional and fascinating music, good enough to 'pass' successfully to the radio and to the disc, withstanding comparison with much more prestigious practices and musical texts. It was, thus, a noble and generous aspiration, handing over music of the greatest quality, at times indeed surprising: one can listen to it even now for what it can offer musically, also far from its original context, beyond the dissolution of the local cultures, and even without considering the information and theories that younger scholars have laboriously and tenaciously produced.

Translated by Laurie Schwartz

---

teachings). Nevertheless, on this occasion he appears overcome by circumstances, as if he were contradicting himself: the situation was effectively 'getting out of hand' and almost 'riotous' during the audio recording.

[23] Carpitella was very sensitive to body postures and actions during the musical performance: in fact, he introduced the idea of 'somaticization of sound' in traditional music, leading him to be among the first to experiment with audiovisual recording techniques in documentation and critical interpretation (see Agamennone 1994).

References

Agamennone, Maurizio (1989) 'Etnomusicologia italiana: radici a sud. Intervista a Diego Carpitella sulla storia dell'etnomusicologia in Italia', *Suonosud*, 4, pp. 18–41.

——— (1994) 'Du folklore musical à l'ethnomusicologie. Entretien avec Diego Carpitella', *Cahiers de musiques traditionnelles*, 4, pp. 229–38.

——— (ed.) (2005) *Musiche tradizionali del Salento. Le registrazioni di Diego Carpitella ed Ernesto de Martino (1959–1960)*, Rome: Squilibri (includes two CDs).

——— (ed.) (2014) *Musiche tradizionali nel Salento. Le registrazioni di Alan Lomax e Diego Carpitella (1954)*, Rome: Squilibri (includes three CDs).

——— and Lombardi, Vincenzo (eds) (2005) *Musiche tradizionali del Molise. Le registrazioni di Diego Carpitella e Alberto Mario Cirese (1954)*, Rome: Squilibri (includes one CD).

Brunetto, Walter (1995) 'La raccolta 24 degli Archivi di Etnomusicologia dell'Accademia Nazionale di Santa Cecilia', *EM. Annuario degli Archivi di Etnomusicologia dell'Accademia Nazionale di Santa Cecilia*, 3, pp. 11–187.

——— (2013) 'Il viaggio in Italia e il viaggio nel tempo. Aspetti, storia e problemi conservativi della raccolta Lomax-Carpitella', *AAA TAC: Acoustical Arts and Artifacts – Technology, Aesthetics, Communication*, 8, pp. 37–50.

Carpitella, Diego (1956a) 'Problemi attuali della musica popolare in Italia', *Ricordiana*, 2, pp. 417–21.

——— (1956b) *Ritmi e melodie di danze popolari in Italia*, Rome: Accademia Nazionale di Santa Cecilia.

——— (1961) 'Folk Music (Italian)', in *Grove's Dictionary of Music and Musicians*, supplementary volume to 5th edn, London: Macmillan, pp. 135–54.

——— (1992) *Conversazioni sulla musica. Lezioni, conferenze, trasmissioni radiofoniche (1955–1990)*, Florence: Ponte alla grazie.

Corti, Maria (1995) 'Panta nifta scotinì: sempre notte buia' [1951], in *Otranto allo specchio*, ed. Maria Corti, Milan: All'insegna del pesce d'oro di Vanni Scheiwiller, pp. 33–50.

Lomax, Alan (1955–56) 'Nuova ipotesi sul canto folcloristico italiano', *Nuovi argomenti*, 17–18, pp. 109–35.

——— (1956) 'Ascoltate, le colline cantano', *Santa Cecilia*, 5/4, pp. 81–7.

——— (1968) *Folk Song Style and Culture*, Washington, DC: American Association for the Advancement of Science.

——— (1992) 'L'esperienza etnomusicologica con Diego Carpitella', in *Materiali di antropologica visiva*, 4, *Bollettino dell'AICS*, December, ed. Emilia De Simoni, pp. 19–38.

——— (2008) *L'anno più felice della mia vita. Un viaggio in Italia 1954–1955*, ed. Goffredo Plastino, Milan: Il Saggiatore.

Lomax Wood, Anna (2008) 'Il doppio solitario', in Lomax (2008), pp. 9–15.

Montinaro, Brizio (1994) *Canti di pianto e d'amore dall'antico Salento*, Milan: Bompiani.

——— (2009) *Il tesoro delle parole morte. La poesia greca del Salento*, Lecce: Argo.

Plastino, Goffredo (2008) 'Un sentimento antico', in Lomax (2008), pp. 16–85.

Chapter 21
Audiovisual Ethnography: New Paths for Research and Representation in Ethnomusicology

Nicola Scaldaferri

Introduction

In the work of the ethnomusicologist, the use of audio recordings, photographs and film are a constant presence; thanks to technological developments, there is also a growing use of multimedia attachments for written reports and analyses. Parallel to this, an awareness of how these methods influence the operative process of research is also growing. Methods of ethnographic research have expanded, addressing issues such as the recognition of the limits of the written discourse in research and communication of the experience in the field, the evaluation of the sensorial aspects, or the centrality of the researcher's body. The use of audiovisual methods and their various combinations offers a wealth of sensory experience, connecting the recipient more closely to the idea of real participation in the event and inspiring greater involvement on an emotional level; this also promotes the search for new narrative forms, in which the audiovisual is not simply integrated into a written text.

In recent years, this research and its related theoretical discussions are being carried out at the Laboratorio di Etnomusicologia e Antropologia Visuale/Ethnomusicology and Visual Anthropology Laboratory (LEAV) at the Università di Milano.[1] The basic areas of activity may be summarized in the following points: the intense use of audiovisual media, with an awareness of the implications of their use during ethnographic documentation; a dialogic approach among researchers and with the 'subjects' of the investigation; intense collaborations, both during the fieldwork and the analysis; presentation of the results mainly via audio, video and photography, attempting to go beyond the written text as a form of narration, and highlighting today's more frequent intersections between ethnographic and artistic practices (Marano 2013); the support of some Italian publishers that specialize in multimedia production, particularly NOTA, and Squilibri.[2]

---

1 See http://www.leav.unimi.it (accessed 30 June 2015).

2 See *NOTA Music Web Site*, http://www.nota.it, and *squi[libri]*, http://www.squilibri.it (accessed 30 June 2015). Many of my ideas are indebted to Steven Feld, who has supported this work since the very beginning; I am also indebted to a team of collaborators

The technical equipment of the LEAV, conceived for working in parallel in the field, recording sound as well as filming and photographing, includes several sets of DSM microphones which allow 'recording with the body' (Ferrarini 2009),[3] offering at the same time a kind of aural counterpoint – on the operational and conceptual level – to the eye formed by the photographic lens or the video camera.

The research is mainly focused on specific practices and musical performances, and the results could be defined as 'audiovisual ethnography'. This expression is intended, first and foremost, to integrate completely the components of sound and aural perception into a methodological field often considered pertinent to visual anthropology which nowadays it would often be more appropriate to call 'audiovisual anthropology'. In this regard, as to the intense debate of recent years on the anthropology of the senses, it is still not possible to reproduce tactile and olfactory experiences whose analytic results and interpretations are consigned to written reports; therefore, the audiovisual product remains the most complete in terms of sensory involvement.

At the same time, attention should be addressed to the centrality of the 'ethnographic' experience which considers fieldwork as a favourable context in which strategies of research and negotiations are created, thus defining the premises for the subsequent steps of analysis and reception.

The cases presented here concern two investigations carried out at LEAV. The first, realized with the collaboration of Feld and other researchers, concerns one of the most celebrated festivals of southern Italy, the Maggio of Accettura (Scaldaferri and Feld 2012), where we attempted to approach the complexity of the sonic component. The second, the fruit of a collaboration with the composer and multimedia artist Yuval Avital, deals with an ethnic-religious community for the realization of his opera *Samaritans*, presented at the MiTo festival in 2010.[4] These two experiences provide the starting point for a reflection that goes beyond the single cases and can be extended to the entire discipline.

'Symphony' and 'Ethnophony': Experiencing the Maggio of Accettura through Sound

Accettura, in the province of Matera, is a village of approximately 2,000 inhabitants. The Maggio festival takes place in springtime, and has been an important theme in

(at the beginning, Lorenzo Ferrarini, Elisa Piria and Tommaso Vitali; later also Lorenzo Pisanello and Luigi Scarpa) working at the vanguard of diverse media used as a means of ethnographic investigation and of the related theoretical discourse. Among these, I would like to mention particularly Lorenzo Ferrarini for his research within the context of sub-Saharan Africa (Ferrarini 2011; 2014; Ferrarini and Scaldaferri 2014).

3 For details about DSM Stereo-Surround Microphones, see http://www.sonicstudios.com (accessed 30 June 2015).

4 See *MiTo Settembre Musica*, http://www.mitosettembremusica.it (accessed 30 June 2015).

Italian ethnographic studies ever since the 1960s, when it came to the attention of Giovanni Battista Bronzini (1979).

The Maggio concerns a complex of events centred on the festival of San Giuliano, patron saint of the village, and on the union of two trees cut in the surrounding forest: a large turkey oak (*Quercus cerris*) called the *maggio*, which gives the name to the entire ritual, and a holly (*Ilex aquifolium*) called the *cima*. The events follow one another in an alternation of both profane and religious situations, with strong historical and symbolic inferences, involving the entire community of Accettura for several weeks. The climax is reached in the four days that extend from Saturday to Pentecost Tuesday. During those days, dozens of oxen drag the oak through the village, together with several other trees; the holly is cut and brought to the village, united with the oak to form a new 'being', raised in the town square and climbed with spectacular actions. At the same time, San Giuliano's cult unfolds with intense moments of religious devotion.

The festival is accompanied by an almost uninterrupted torrent of sound. The ritual itself actually flows on the wave of an authentic river of sound. First of all, an 'official' sonorization is programmed, performed by musical groups, fanfares and religious choirs, according to the calendar of the festival. In order to avoid moments of silence, some professional ensembles are invited from the neighbouring region of Puglia: the *bassa musica* groups, formed by winds and percussion, play without interruption, especially when greater physical effort is required, as in the transport and the tree climbing that involves the people of Accettura. At the same time, visitors to the festival bring musical instruments (*organetti* [diatonic accordions], *tamburelli* [frame drums], *zampogne* [bagpipes]), joining the local musicians in long jam sessions. Very often, these sessions involve persons who do not even know one another and who only come together on this occasion to form a temporary community of performers. Similar ways of participation characterize other important events of the same region, especially the 'musical' pilgrimages connected with important Marian cults, such as the black Madonna di Viggiano and the Madonna di Pollino (Scaldaferri 2005a).

I was aware of this form of musical participation at the festival, and of the creation of temporary communities of performers, because I took part as a *zampogna* performer (attracted by the well-known skills of the people of Accettura as singers accompanied by the *zampogna*) and also because of my research on musical practices in the same area (Scaldaferri and Vaja 2006).

It was precisely my direct experience that made me aware of one of the paradoxes of the research on the Maggio festival. The event had been considered, first and foremost, in terms of ritual gesture – also immortalized by renowned photographers and artists – and had occupied scholars in researching the meanings and interpretations (ancient symbols of the trees' marriage, historical traces of profane and religious stratifications and so on) that later found abundant space in the narrative of the festival. However, the sonic component was undervalued. To recall an ironic observation of Roberto Leydi (1991: 119), in this case one could experience, first-hand, the 'deafness' of a certain ethnography, describing accurately worlds where absolute silence seemed to reign – in this case, a 'deafening silence'. Starting from this paradoxical situation, we decided to study the festival of Maggio by focusing primary attention on the musical and sonic components and on the participation forms involved. In doing so, we also bore in mind Steven Feld's theoretical perspective of acoustemology, which considers the auditory experience of sound as a form of knowledge (Feld 2015).

Feld's direct involvement in the Accettura project has its origin in a previous collaboration of ours in 2004, in the same region on the carnival rites with the presence of cowbells, themes that Feld has investigated several times (Feld 2004–7; Blau et al. 2010). The result of the previous work, published in the CD book *Santi, animali e suoni* ('Saints, Animals and Sounds') (Scaldaferri 2005c), illustrates a new way of presenting the research. The core is made up of a soundscape composition accompanied by Stefano Vaja's photographs, with several short essays offering background information, reflections and analyses. Therefore, there was a reversal of perspective: the role usually performed by the written text was entrusted to the narrative sound and to its counterpoint of images, with additional text information.

In the case of Accettura, taking this format for granted, and considering the complex situation, a further step was devised: to examine the festival according to a dialogical and participatory dimension (which in my case meant also being active as a *zampogna* performer), and to offer a representation of this method on the narrative level.

The team consisted of Feld, myself and also two photographers (Stefano Vaja and Lorenzo Ferrarini) and a group of collaborators focused on the typologies of the festival's sounds and musical performances (Fabio Calzia, Cristina Ghirardini, Elisa Piria and Guido Raschieri). In addition, two of the most important *zampogna* performers of the region (Alberico Larato and Quirino Valvano) were with us, involved in the festival both in moments of 'spontaneous' music making, as well as in the official processions. Also important was the involvement of Don Giuseppe Filardi, parish priest of Accettura, in his multiple role of historian, researcher and organizer; but above all, he was the parish priest, thus the actor-director of the delicate equilibrium of a festival mixing San Giuliano's intense popular devotion with ritual and identity practices.

The team was active during the 2005 festival, working in synergy to listen, observe and participate. The final report, completely entrusted to sounds and images, would have to examine both the participative aspect and the multi-form dimension of the festival, allowing it to embrace the numerous stratifications. This was accomplished, first and foremost, in the production of two complementary CDs: one containing Feld's soundscape composition, the other including the 'documentation' I made of the musical practices within the context of the Accettura tradition; in a dialogical essay, several implications of this work are discussed, with reference to previous research experience, particularly that of the Kaluli in Papua New Guinea (Feld 1991; 2012). Alongside these core materials there are two parallel photographic essays by Ferrarini and Vaja, focusing on various perspectives, comprising narrative sequences in colour and black-and-white documentary photos. The audiovisual part was complemented by a collection of short essays focusing on photographic investigations, historical aspects and ethnographic research – the latter discussed by the anthropologist Fernando Mirizzi (Bronzini's disciple).

The final publication, *I suoni dell'albero. Il Maggio di San Giuliano ad Accettura* (Scaldaferri and Feld 2012), may be consulted for the complete contents and for a detailed discussion – especially with reference to the implications and operative modalities. In this chapter, my intention is to develop some details concerning the two CDs: how they were conceived, and the role they assume in the analysis and representation of the event.

The soundscape composition, contained in the first CD, was edited by Feld in the studio from the materials he recorded during the festival with the DSM microphones; these microphones are positioned on the head in correspondence to the ears; the head itself, according to the movements made, is essential for capturing the sound. Therefore, the expression 'to record with the body' is not a metaphor, but reflects a procedure entailing Feld's presence and active participation during the ritual. His participatory 'point of listening', once fixed in the recording, was then reworked in the studio, according to procedures quite similar to those of electroacoustic composition: the memory of the experience and the participation in the event has an important role in the strategies of selecting and editing the materials. Besides the fact that it originates from Feld's personal experience of listening and participating, the soundscape composition somehow reflects the whole team's experience, as evidenced by the musical performances by Larato, Valvano and myself.

The final result is articulated in six tracks, approximately 70 minutes long, corresponding to episodes from the Maggio festival ranging from Saturday afternoon, on the eve of Pentecost, to the conclusion on the evening of the following Tuesday. Some tracks (especially the first three) are mainly descriptive and reflect a chronological survey of the events. Gradually, the tracks are more 'composed', until the sixth (corresponding to Tuesday), consisting of a dense montage in which all the salient moments of the very intense final day are condensed into a few minutes.

The soundscape composition retraces the moments of major sonic interest of the festival, involving real compositional choices. Therefore, it is an actual piece that we can listen to like a real 'symphony': sonic events are placed in relationship with space and time, with points of sonic tension and release, responding to eminently poetic and creative criteria – all things we expect from Feld since his CD *Voices of the Rainforest* (1991), related to his research on the Kaluli.

In the soundscape composition of the Maggio, we can hear the sounds of a small bronze bell mixed with the singing of the birds and sacred choirs, tempering (or balancing) the sonic chaos of the *bassa musica* and the intensity of the songs with the *zampogna*; or a long sequence of sounds of double reeds, recorded in the narrow streets of the village during the procession, which offer us, through changes in sonority, a perception of movement and of the acoustic conditions of the place.

At the same time, listening to – as opposed to observing – the festival proves to be extremely important to analyse the ritual, and reveals situations in part overlooked by the previous research. In fact, moments usually considered secondary by traditional ethnography on the Maggio acquire unexpected relevance if the perspective is that of the ear, not the eye. A sensational example is that of Monday, traditionally considered the day of 'rest' between the two more spectacular days of the trees' transport from the forest to the village (Sunday), and of their rise and climbing (Tuesday), usually singled out by photographers, ethnographers and cinematographers. Feld dedicates the longest sequences – almost half the length of the whole soundscape composition – to this very day. On Monday, in fact, when the people of Accettura are less busy in terms of physical labour, many different actions come together; these are less spectacular, but much more meaningful, especially for their symbolic and religious significance. On this day, the festival's complex and ambiguous stratifications can be better understood, as they are, in some way, reflected precisely in the sonic component.

It is the day, for example, when all the saints' images converge in successive processions, towards the middle of the square, where a large hole to plant and raise the *maggio* is dug out by hand. It is the day when we 'meet again' individually – each with its own time and space – all of the humanly produced sounds (*bassa musica*, fanfares, *zampogne*, bells, sacred and secular songs, chainsaws and work noises), reiterating their massive participation in the event. On that day, the saints' images arrive from the countryside led by a bell in a procession praying for rain; the timing of the religious rites closely intersects that of the secular rites of the workers preparing the trees' rise. The day considered 'weak' by traditional ethnography on Accettura covers great relevance from Feld's point of listening and in his soundscape composition, and leads our attention precisely towards less ostentatious that should probably be read in more depth. In this case it is listening, more than observation, that stimulates a very clear analysis of the ritual, revealing the importance of aspects often considered secondary in ethnographic texts, and becoming a concrete tool of investigation and reflection. This forces us to think about the limits of 'observation', which – almost as a synecdoche – in our language and imagination ends up defining knowledge in itself.

The choice of materials for the second CD was made after the first was completed; I thought of it as a collection of materials to complement the soundscape composition, offering an analytic-systematic cross-section of the Maggio's musical practices, and situating them within the more general framework of Accettura's musical practices.

Whereas in the soundscape composition we retrace Feld's listening and the details of his personal experience (with the double experience of recording with his body and working in the studio), the second CD draws on an enormous amount of sound material, relating to different times and places. It represents a counterbalance to Feld's individual experience, presenting a collective tableau of Accettura's musical practices, in which the Maggio becomes a reference point for the lives of the local people, as well as for the emigrants who return every year expressly for the festival.

For the second CD, recordings were chosen from the following three bodies of materials: (1) the recordings of the 2005 Maggio; (2) my personal sound archive on Accettura from the years 2002–2007 concerning the Maggio festival and other musical practices, including popular music, folkloric ensembles, the activities of the local recording studios and record production; (3) Don Giuseppe Filardi's sound archive, with recordings since 1983 made in Accettura and with the emigrant community in the USA, mostly consisting of vocal materials of religious traditions. In this second CD, the compilation is imbued with a narrative sweep, illustrating the points described in the following section.

First and foremost, the intention was to examine in depth some of the musical repertories related to the 2005 Maggio festival not included in the soundscape composition (or treated by Feld only within the general flow of sounds), and to broaden the selection to recordings of previous celebrations of the Maggio. This begins with the forms of 'organized' music articulating the festival's rhythm (the *bassa musica* pieces, the music for large symphonic band), and with spontaneous forms of musical participation (centred around the *organetto*, the songs with *zampogna*, and instruments such as the *tamburello* [mouth harmonica] and the *bottiglia percossa* [a bottle struck with a key]). At the same time, the presence of musicians from other towns is also documented; they represent a seamless phenomenon of participation, especially on Pentecost Sunday. In the liner notes of the CDs, these connections are pointed out, correlating Feld's 'film for the ears' with in-depth analyses; the two CDs almost represent two components of a closely related diptych.

A second point regards the musical practices related to other festive occasions and rituals, among which the favourite was the eve of San Antonio Abate on 17 January, the opening day of the carnival. The repertory, the instruments and also the performers of Accettura in this occasion almost always coincide with those of the Maggio. However, this winter event has the advantage of being very intimate and attended mainly by local musicians: their virtuosity and performance skills can be appreciated much better than in the Maggio, where they are suffocated by the massive participation.

A third aspect regards forms of musical hybridization created mainly by the youth bands and folkloric ensembles that forge new expressive paths with traditional materials, often using modern instruments (such as synthesizers) and working in the recording studio. Here are pieces that we listen to again, performed by the *bassa musica* during the entire Maggio festival, or which imitate famous songwriters, or re-elaborate the forms of traditional song. Moreover, on these occasions the female voice emerges, whereas it tends to remain in the background during public moments of the festival.

Finally, the voices recorded in Accettura – especially the elderly, most of them passed away – but also from the other side of the Atlantic, with the Accettura community in New Jersey, where we hear singing and the performing of folk stories of San Giuliano and San Antonio, help us to understand the temporal depths of these rites. The intensity with which the emigrants preserve them contributes to creating the sense of belonging to the original community, even if far away.

The CD documentary is articulated in 25 tracks, intertwining all these themes and trying to suggest to the listener the relation between memory and re-elaboration, contemporary practice and historical perspective. Hence, it is not about a deconstruction of the soundscape composition, but of a path in which the sound materials are anthologized and presented in their complexity.

Whereas Feld, with his individual and analytical approach, suggests both aesthetic and cognitive ideas of the event, the second CD is an attempt to create an operation of 'ethnophony' – in place of 'ethnography', here both intended in the strict sense of the term: through listening, it is possible to understand aspects, stratifications and connections, both diachronic and synchronic, of the event.

In both CDs, even if with different slants, we are far from assigning to the recorded sound the function of a supporting 'document', of a documentary 'attachment' to the written narrative. Instead, an attempt was made to assign to the recorded sound an independence from the investigation and its representation, as well as to offer to the listener an aesthetic and cognitive experience.

From Religious Rite to Multimedia Theatre: *Samaritans* by Yuval Avital

The Israeli composer Yuval Avital, one of the most active artists in the area of multimedia projects today, has coined the expression 'opera iconosonora' (icon/sonic opera) to describe some of his works. The definition and its explanation were provided by the artist during an interview about his opera *Samaritans*, premiered at the MiTo festival in Milan in September 2010. To recapitulate Avital's thoughts on the matter:

> In ancient art, sound, word, gesture and image were strongly interconnected; the division between the various arts occurred later in the development of culture. This is one of the key points of this opera: for me, in fact, there is no hierarchy among the various codes, no single music with a predominant role which images and poetry must follow. I understand opera as a 360-degree composition, where all things coexist harmonically and offer cues for creativity. … Multimedia, also as to technology, represents the most challenging and complete manifestation of performing arts. In creative work, we are at times accustomed to think that doing many things means not doing them well: the composer should only compose, the author should only write. In the case of this opera, however, work was carried out on many levels; I wrote the score and poetry at the same time, developing the research in the area of the images too. The use of various media and technologies also follows the logic of different works in parallel. The result is not hierarchical, but rather organic; the opera – defined as 'icon/sonic' – constitutes a sort of directional temporal axis along which ideas and concepts are developed, and languages oriented towards various channels of sensory and intellectual perception are integrated. (Avital 2010)

In many of Avital's works, specific research in multimedia combines with the meeting of non-academic and non-European musical traditions. The different languages of his works, oriented towards diverse perceptual channels, often embrace sound objects and ceremonial situations significant on the cultural, ritual and religious level. Live sounds and action onstage create a counterpoint to their original musical forms that appear on video or in the elaborated recordings; additional information is added through written messages or performed texts. Static and motion images, recorded and live sounds (amplified or also manipulated in real time) are absorbed into the 'icon/sonic' project; this happens with the clear awareness of offering a kind of global fruition in which, in the words of Michel Chion (1990), one form of perception influences also the other, ending up by transforming it in some way.

Samaritans certainly represents one of Avital's most challenging experiments: with media and staging, it touches some of the key expressions of music and identity of one of the most unique and problematic ethnic-religious communities of the Mediterranean. At the same time, it attempts to establish a dialogue between cognitive, religious and artistic aspects, employing the multimedia components during the research and dialogue in the field and during the opera creation on stage.

Strongly present in Western imagination (especially because of their presence in the New Testament, for example the Good Samaritan and Simon Magus), today the Samaritans form a small ethnic-religious community of approximately 800 members, strict observers of the Law of Moses.[5] They live between the village of Kiryat Luza, halfway up the sacred Mount Gerizim (in the West Bank, right above Nablus), and the Israeli city of Holon, near Tel Aviv. They are Israeli citizens, and have also established excellent relationships with the Arab world and the Palestinian Authorities – some are also Palestinian citizens. The religious cult of the Samaritans is principally based on the text of the Pentateuch (which differs from the Hebrew version in over 125 occurrences) and on the centrality of the figure of Moses. The spiritual leader is the high priest, still identified today as the most elderly member of the family of priests, who – according to their genealogy – descend directly from Aaron, brother of Moses. The Samaritans believe that on Mount Gerizim, the biblical mountain of benediction (*Deuteronomy* 2:29), there are their principal worship locations (Isaac's sacrifice rock, the twelve rocks transported by Joshua, Jacob's ladder), while nearby is the well dug by Jacob and Joseph's tomb. For centuries the Samaritans have climbed the mountain, following the priests who carry the Pentateuch for the major holiday events; they don't recognize the sacredness of the mount of the Jerusalem temple, and they still continue today to perform the bloody Passover sacrifice, killing lambs, on the slopes of Gerizim.

Together with their language, religion and ritual ceremonies, musical practice is an important element for the identity of the Samaritan community: its core is mainly the cantillation and the melodic ornamentation of the sacred text. Research and studies carried out on Samaritans' singing (starting with the sound collections of Robert Lachmann, Johanna Spector and Avigdor Herzog

[5] See *The Samaritan Update*, http://www.thesamaritanupdate.com (accessed 30 June 2015).

preserved in the Jerusalem National Sound Archives) show specific traits in the formal organization of the songs, in the ornamentation techniques, and in certain polyphonic procedures connected to complex customs and ceremonial functions. Therefore, a 'documentation' becomes quite problematic in the classical ethnomusicological tradition, because it often consists in the decontextualization of separate performative elements through recording.

All of this clearly emerges in one of their most important anniversaries, Yom Mikrata (Day of Reading), consisting with the complete cantillation of the Pentateuch in a polychoral performance (from which the so-called 'large group' polyphony flows) uninterrupted for 18 hours, during which hundreds of cantors alternate inside the synagogue; actually, they are all the male members of the community. This takes place during the days preceding the holiday of Shavuot, and develops into an impressive pilgrimage to Mount Gerizim.

The opera *Samaritans* was the occasion for my collaboration with Avital, thus converging the requirements of a multimedia creative project and my own personal interest in investigating the performative and devotional forms of such a peculiar religious community. Specifically, my interest is mainly the centrality of Mount Gerizim for Samaritans' rituals; for some time I have been conducting research into forms of devotional and musical participation around sacred mountains, locations of worship and destinations of important pilgrimages. Indeed, it concerns phenomena touching upon several religious spheres of Abrahamic derivation present in the Mediterranean, some of which I had observed in the realm of Christian and Islamic traditions (Scaldaferri 2005a; 2013). Even with the considerable differences within different religious and cultural contexts, such events are characterized by similar performative components, especially concerning ways of participation, defined by an intense musical activity and by the animal killing in a more or less ritualized form.

We carried out the fieldwork in June 2010, with the support of Maga Global Arts and equipment provided by LEAV: specifically, I took care of the technical aspects, making the video films, audio recordings and photos, while Avital managed the logistics, the conversations and relations with the community and the cantors. The research started from the actual needs of the artist – who had already prepared a first draft of the opera – or, to be more precise, we collected audiovisual documentation in the traditional sense (interviews, films, photography and recordings of their ritual practices, with particular attention to the Yom Mikrata and the pilgrimage, also including rituals of circumcision and betrothal): all of this was later used in the multimedia part of the opera.

Moreover, there were specific in-depth analyses, chiefly concerning the life stories of very important personalities. Among these, in particular, the story of Avigdor Herzog, a Hungarian Jew, survivor of the Shoah, pioneer in the study of Samaritans' music, fully accepted by the community to the extent of being considered 'half Samaritan' – which is extremely significant if one considers that proselytizing is not allowed among the Samaritans. Herzog's human story is intertwined with that of the mythic Samaritan cantor Ratson Tsedaka, his main informant. Over 80 years old, resident in a nursing home in the hills of Jerusalem, Herzog was interviewed several times, and also at the National Sound Archives while he re-listened to his old recordings of the great cantor Ratson, and while he illustrated his structural and stylistic analyses of Samaritan singing.

In a community as closed and conservative as the Samaritans', resistant to every form of curiosity and defending themselves from all sorts of morbid attention, every act we undertook was subject to negotiations. These were principally led by Benyamim Tsedaka (Ratson's son), an important cultural catalyst in the community as well as director of the vocal ensemble that later came to Milan for the performance, but also by the highest priest in office, Aahron Ben Ab-Hisda (who passed away in 2013). The high priest had in fact granted his consent for the entire project, somehow submitting it to his control; he also sent a priest, Aabed Cohen, to Milan for the MiTo festival, as a member of the vocal ensemble, appointed to perform certain vocal parts and to guarantee the ritual's correctness.

After all, the final destination of the opera – within an important international festival, with the presence of a group of local cantors onstage – was the indispensable premise to obtain quite a broad accessibility. Indeed, this was not a research project addressed to a few enthusiasts, but aimed to have a greater impact that could be capitalized upon by the same community to promote its own knowledge and visibility. This occasion contributed to carrying out an identity-making role for a small community constantly exposed to the risk of extinction. At the same time, the entire operation was conducted with extreme seriousness and determination – by Avital at the fore – respecting their prerogatives, mores, customs and needs (also considering certain cultural prohibitions). The artistic destination of the research, far from being shaped by functional motivations only in service of the creative whim, really started from absolute respect for their cultural mandates and moved strictly within the frame allowed by the community.

Respect and negotiations also influenced the choice of particular technologies used in the field recordings: for example, the use of less invasive microphones such as the DSM for recording sounds of public ceremonial situations, or the more traditional Shure VP88 microphone for interviews and performances carried out in people's homes. We also had to take into account the specific restrictions imposed by the rigorous respect for the rules of the Sabbath, extended to any element connected to the idea of fire (including the use of lighters and matches and turning on engines); thus, the total prohibition of the use of electricity during the days of Yom Mikrata and the pilgrimage of Shavuot influenced sound and video recording systems. Already during the research in the field, in the dialogue and negotiations, the technological elements unpredictably represented an important bone of contention from the point of view of the ethical implications.

The intensive work of tracking the recorded material, films and interviews, a long series of meetings, dialogues and introductions connected with some of the key events of their tradition, resulted in the production of a consistent body of audiovisual material on the community: this is particularly relevant considering the scarcity of research and extant documents, and the objective difficulty encountered during the research.

Avital's opera *Samaritans* unfolds through the metaphor of the journey, becoming almost a reformulation of the journey undertaken by the artist to know them at their source. On stage, the Samaritan cantors perform their forms of sacred traditional singing and 'interpret' gestures specifically called for by Avital and based on the collection of rituals acquired from the direct contact with their tradition. This takes place in dialogue with the complex multimedia component, interacting with a live instrumental ensemble (strings, flute, guitar, piano, percussion, accordion, *zampogna*), for which Avital composed a score that evokes stylistic elements derived from the Samaritans' singing.

The multimedia installation allowed the realization of cross-references and relationships between the audiovisual statements and the actual presence of the cantors on stage.

While Herzog's story, his relationship with Ratson and the visit to Jerusalem Archives roll by on the screen with music, images, subtitles and narration, onstage there are Ratson's sons, Benyamim and Yefet, also cantors. The images and the singing of the pilgrimage to Gerizim, proposed in a mediatized form, are in counterpoint with the ritual and musical action actually proposed also onstage by the Samaritan cantors. The great cantor Natanel Ben-Avraham Ha Cohen, filmed in his dwelling on Gerizim, towers from the screen and is in a duet with his son Aabed, the priest, present onstage. Therefore, multimedia becomes the means for different narrative typologies to happen at the same time and interact, creating relationships between people, spaces, times and places, and merging into the same narrative path.

Instrumentalists and cantors from different linguistic and cultural backgrounds, figures who fulfil important roles in their original communities, interact and create a dialogue related to the sonic and gestural components, and in which the performative dimension pushes the original meanings towards new forms of fruition. This all takes place without losing sight of respect for certain situations, especially when religious and identity-making elements are significantly endowed. Thus, it is not just a performance, but the re-statement of an actual ritual, respecting the prerogatives of whoever is on stage at that moment. In the specific case of *Samaritans*, the priest onstage reminds us that the sacredness of a text – not depending on its intelligibility – does not vanish by moving it to another place; moreover, a prayer remains always the same for whoever carries it out, even if spectators from other cultures are present, or if it interacts with people who are doing something else at that moment, such as playing a violin or a guitar. In any case, since forms of proselytizing are not allowed among the Samaritans, their prayer is precluded to others.

The collaboration with Avital on this project began with the understanding that what we were undertaking was not a work of traditional 'ethnography'. My competence and experience in mediatizing sounds and rituals – the reasons for which I was initially involved – in harmony with my interests and curiosity, aimed, in the first place, at the production of a work of art. The research was therefore situated along that wake of blurred genres – discussed by Geertz – quite frequent in recent years, between artistic and ethnographic practices. In this specific case, it became even more interconnected because of my involvement as a multi-instrumental performer at the première during the MiTo festival, as well as in the concert leaflet that also included a conversation with the composer. Superimpositions and breaking the boundaries of genre are, by now, far from being a random occurrence (Stella 2009; Schneider & Wright 2010; Marano 2013): they almost represent an established norm, thus being more aware that the points of contact generated by operative procedures are more relevant than theoretical positions and boundaries of the discipline.

Nevertheless, if the *Samaritans* project also resulted in a work that is strongly 'documentary' and 'ethnomusicological', this is due, above all, to how Avital conceived the opera itself. His idea of 'icon/sonic opera' and his passion for rich and intense stories, personalities and materials, placed in a multimedia, organic and non-hierarchical context, has set in motion a cognitive and exploratory mechanism, contributing significantly to the level of knowledge, reflection and dialogue. Avital's multimedia journey in the theatre built a memorable event for the community, thus presenting a powerful, emotional narrative with a remarkable communicative impact. Thanks to the multimedia installation, it transmitted incisively a large body of information and concepts, notwithstanding the artistic appreciation that could arise. At the same time, the in-depth studies of the singing techniques, carried out with Herzog and with the cantors, were necessary for Avital to acquire a mastery of the stylistic traits in writing his opera; moreover, it was probably the most astute stylistic analysis of the Samaritans' singing ever conducted. Finally, creative ideas end up having consequences on the level of knowledge.

Some Conclusions

The cases discussed here can certainly be considered exceptional, elaborated for particular contexts, as much for the specificity of the research objects as for the characteristics of the collaborations. Then again, they are examples of procedures that the 'ethnomusicologist' uses today, and which technological transformations and the blurring of genres can soon steer toward new paths. They certainly force us to reflect upon the present, but also, reconsidering the past, upon the effective connections between field research, use of audiovisual devices, and presentation of the results in cognitive terms.

Ethnomusicology, though having used audio technologies and, later, video recording as perhaps no other discipline, probably did not consider enough that the recorded sound – in the words of Mark Katz (2004) – is, above all, a mediatized sound. A sort of 'documentary prejudice' (Scaldaferri 2014) prevailed, permeating research methods for a long time. The act of recording has indeed often been considered almost as a purely functional step, with the audio data tied to a support such as a neutral and objective document; this was assumed as a starting point for further levels of research (descriptive and analytic levels), and began from transcriptions (Scaldaferri 2005b). Far from being a mechanical and objective process of fixation, the recording of sound and image – the same concerns photography – always involves technical, theoretical and aesthetic choices, and is guided by hypotheses and circumstances of the research that can condition it importantly. This occurs not only in Feld's recent cases (see Chapter 6 in this volume), or in Arom's famous re-recording experiments in Central Africa (Arom 1991; 2013), but a more timely recognition on the research of the past clearly emerges, beginning from Bartók onwards (Scaldaferri 2008; 2014).

In the case of field research, what has an important role is the process of creating a shared dialogue and journey that the researcher, more and more consciously, realizes with the protagonists of his/her investigation. Therefore, the mediatization of an event and of a performance (carried out with audio recordings and film) is not limited to a neutral process of (decon)textualization, aimed at producing a text 'on' and 'about' which one may write and speak, as if perpetrating the renowned narrative strategies of literacy. Rather, it is closer to a kind of transcodification, whose results, also in cognitive terms, require modalities pertinent on the level of language, method and strategies of narrative presentation, as well as the reconsideration of certain boundaries of the discipline.

An intense sound montage provided by a soundscape composition is much more analytical, descriptive and communicative that any photographic sequence, cinematographic or ethnographic report; a good example is Feld's final track for Accettura, for its extreme concision and temporal compression, seizing and giving us, just by listening in a few dense minutes, the crazy concluding day of the Maggio, as no film (or written description) could ever have done, just as an 'icon/sonic' story can hardly be matched in its evocative and communicative power, not least because of the amount of information transmitted, to a written ethnographic report.

Anthropologist Eugenio Imbriani wondered some years ago, with regard to the debate on the issue of writing in anthropology that implied redesigning, in part, the discipline's outlines: 'If it is understood that anthropologists write, the next theme to reflect upon is: what does ethnographic writing resemble? What literary genre can it approximate?' (Imbriani 2002: 19). Perhaps also we could begin by asking ourselves which musical genre our so-called 'field recordings' can approximate.

Translated by Laurie Schwartz

References

Avital, Yuval (2010) 'Samaritani. Viaggio iconosonoro alla scoperta di una cultura millenaria', theatre programme, MiTo Settembre Musica, Milan, 21 September.

Arom, Simha (1991) *African Polyphony and Polyrhythm: Musical Structure and Methodology*, Cambridge: Cambridge University Press.

——— (2013) *Le ragioni della musica. Scritture di musicologia africanista*, Lucca: LIM.
Blau, Dick, Amanatidis, Agapi, Panopoulos, Panayotis and Feld, Steven (2010) *Skyros Carnival*, Culver City, CA: VoxLox.
Bronzini, Giovanni Battista (1979) *Accettura – Il Contadino – L'Alberto – Il Santo*, Galatina: Congedo.
Chion, Michel (1990) *L'audio-vision. Son et images au cinéma*, Paris: Nathan.
Feld, Steven (1991) *Voices of the Rainforest*, Rykodisc, CD 10173.
——— (2004–2007) *The Time of Bells*, CD, Culver City, CA: VoxLox, 4 vols.
——— (2012) *Sound and Sentiment: Birds, Weeping, Poetics, and Song in Kaluli Expression*, 3rd edn, Durham, NC: Duke University Press.
——— (2015) 'Acoustemology', in *Keywords in Sound*, ed. David Novak and Matt Sakakeeny, Durham, NC: Duke University Press, pp. 12–21.
——— and Scaldaferri, Nicola (2012) 'Documentazione e rappresentazione sonora. Un dialogo sulla festa del Maggio', in Scaldaferri and Feld (2012), pp. 74–91.
Ferrarini, Lorenzo (2009) 'Registrare con il corpo: dalla riflessione fenomenologica alle metodologia audio-visuali di Jean Rouch e Steven Feld', in Stella (2009), pp. 125–48. English trans.: http://lorenzoferrarini.com/portfolio/recording-with-the-body/ (accessed 30 June 2015).
——— (ed.) (2011) *L'esperienza del corpo*, Milan: Cuem.
——— (2014) 'Ways of Knowing Donsoya: Environment, Embodiment and Perception among the Hunters of Burkina Faso', PhD Dissertation, University of Manchester.
——— and Scaldaferri, Nicola (2014) 'The Sambla Baan', *Releasr beta*, http://releasr.com/film/thesamblabaan/ (accessed 30 June 2015).
Katz, Mark (2004) *Capturing Sound: How Technology Has Changed Music*, Berkeley, CA: University of California Press.
Katz, Ruth (1974) 'The Reliability of Oral Transmission: The Case of Samaritan Music', *Yuval: Studies of the Jewish Music Research Centre*, 3, pp. 109–35.
Geertz, Clifford (1983) *Local Knowledge: Further Essays in Interpretive Anthropology*, New York: Basic Books.
Imbriani, Eugenio (2002) *La scrittura infinita. Antropologia tra racconto e oblio*, Nardò: Besa.
Leydi, Roberto (1991) *L'altra musica*, Florence: Giunti & Ricordi.
Marano, Francesco (2013) *L'etnografo come artista. Intrecci fra antropologia e arte*, Rome: CISU.
Scaldaferri, Nicola (2005a) 'Devotion, Music, and Rite in Southern Italy: The Madonna del Pollino Festival' (with photos by Stefano Vaja), in *Performing Ecstasies: Music, Dance, and Ritual in the Mediterranean*, ed. Luisa Del Giudice and Nancy van Deusen, Ottawa: Institute of Medieval Music, pp. 169–83.

——— (2005b) 'Perché scrivere le musiche non scritte? tracce per un'antropologia della scrittura musicale', in *Enciclopedia della Musica*, vol. 5: *L'unità della musica*, ed. Jean-Jacques Nattiez, Turin: Einaudi, pp. 499–536.

——— (ed.) (2005c) *Santi animali e suoni. Feste dei campanacci a Tricarico e S. Mauro Forte* (CD by Steven Feld, photos by Stefano Vaja), Udine: Nota DCBook.

——— (2008) 'La ricerca sul campo e la registrazione del suono: interazioni teoriche e tecnologiche', *Musica/Tecnologia*, 2, pp. 73–82.

——— (2013) 'Baba Tomor: l'Albania dei Bektashi', in *Con i Dervisci. Otto incontri sul campo*, ed. Giovanni De Zorzi, Milan: Mimesis, pp. 49–68.

——— (2014) 'Voice, Body, Technologies: Tales from an Arbëresh Village', *TRANS Revista Transcultural de Música*, 18, pp. 1–21.

——— and Feld, Steven (eds) (2012) *I Suoni dell'albero. Il Maggio di S. Giuliano ad Accettura*, Udine: Nota CD Book.

——— and Vaja, Stefano (2006) *Nel paese dei cupa cupa. Suoni e immagini della tradizione lucana*, Rome: Squilibri.

Schneider, Arald and Wright, Christopher (eds) (2010) *Between Art and Anthropology: Contemporary Ethnographic Practice*, London: Bloomsbury.

Shelemay, Kay Kaufman (1996) 'The Ethnomusicologist and the Transmission of Tradition', *Journal of Musicology*, 14/1, pp. 3–51

——— (2006) 'Music, Memory and History', *Ethnomusicology Forum*, 15/1, pp. 17–37.

Spector, Johanna (1964) 'Samaritan Chant', *Journal of the International Folk Music Council*, 16, pp. 66–9.

Stella, Maria Carmela (ed.) (2009) *Pratiche artistiche e pratiche etnografiche*, Milan: Cuem.

Figure 21.1 Arrival of the *cima*, transported to the village by hand
Photo: L. Ferrarini.

Figure 21.2 The *bassa musica* performs during the transport of the *cima*
Photo: L. Ferrarini.

Figure 21.3 Steven Feld using DSM microphones to record Nicola Scaldaferri playing the *zampogna* to accompany a competition between singers during the transport of the *maggio*
Photo: L. Ferrarini.

Figure 21.4 The rise of the *maggio*, united to the *cima* in the town square
Photo: S. Vaja.

Figure 21.5 Avigdor Herzog and Yefet Tsedaka, filmed while listening to recordings of the cantor Ratson Tsedaka, Yefet's father, at the National Sound Archives, Jerusalem, June 2010
Photo: N. Scaldaferri.

Figure 21.6 The cantor Natanel Ben-Avraham Ha Cohen at home in Kiryat Luza (West Bank), June 2010
Photo: N. Scaldaferri.

Figure 21.7 *Samaritans*, Milan, MiTo Settembre Musica, 21 September 2010. Images of the cantor Natanel Ben-Avraham Ha Cohen projected onscreen interact with cantors live onstage

Photo: S. Vaja.

Figure 21.8 *Samaritans*, Milan, MiTo Settembre Musica, 21 September 2010. The priest Aabed Cohen, Natanel's son, in duet with his father's video recordings

Photo: S. Vaja.

Index

Page numbers in **bold** refer to figures, tables and music examples.